THE
KINGDOM
OF
KENT

K.P.Witney

CW00553068

PHILLIMORE

1982

Published by
PHILLIMORE & CO. LTD.
London and Chichester

Head Office: Shopwyke Hall,
Chichester, Sussex, England

ISBN 0 85033 443 8

Text set by Fidelity Processes
Printed and bound in Great Britain by
THE BOWERING PRESS LTD.,
Plymouth, Devon

CONTENTS

LIST OF ILLUSTRATIONS

ACKNOWLEDGEMENTS

I wish to express my thanks to the following for permission to reproduce illustrations:
The Master and Fellows of Trinity Hall, Cambridge, for the ancient map of Thanet
(Plate I); The Merseyside County Museums, Liverpool, for the Kingston Brooch (Plate II);
The Royal Museum, Canterbury, for the Kentish round and square headed brooches
(Plates III and IV). The Schleswig-Holsteinische Landesmuseum, for the Nydam ship
(Plate 1); The British Museum, for the coins of Egbert II and Eadberht Pren (Plate 3);
The Kent County Library, Springfield, Maidstone, for the illustrations of St Augustine's
Cross (Plate 2), St Mary-in-Castro, Dover (Plate 4), St Pancras and St Martin's churches,
Canterbury (Plates 5 and 6) (photographs by Francis Frith & Co., Andover, Hants.), and
the demolition of Reculver church (Plate 7). Aerofilms Ltd., Boreham Wood, for the
aerial view of Reculver (Plate 8).

FOREWORD

In a sense the history of England begins in Kent: it is here, almost certainly, that some of the earliest barbarian tribes to enter the country settled in the fifth century. They left their traces on and in the soil where the landscape historian and the archaeologist can detect them. Being closer to the continent than is the rest of Britain, Kent was naturally influenced more rapidly and more thoroughly by newcomers from across the Channel than was Mercia, East Anglia, Wessex or Northumbria. Men like Augustine and Theodore came to Canterbury and instituted revolutions in religion and religious organization. Above all they brought writing. There is probably as much written evidence for the south-east of England in the pre-Viking as there is for any other part of the country, if not more, which is as it should be. The charter was most likely introduced first into Kent and Kentish royalty provided the Old English church with saints as well as land. All this means that although Æthelbehrt was the last high king to come out of the south-east in the Dark Ages, his kingdom continued to be an important centre. The documents, like the soil, have been looked at many times, in the publications of local archaeological societies, in national periodicals and in ambitious works of inter-pretation like Jolliffe's much-debated account of the Jutes in 'Pre-feudal England', but perhaps because Kent had no Bede, what has been lacking up to now is an attempt to put all the pieces together. Inevitably any attempt to reconstruct a Dark Age kingdom must recognize that there are gaps, and at times hypothesis must take the place of evidence. Indeed, in this period, there can be no historical reconstruction without hypothesis, and this means that there is always a danger of being led into the creation of a fairy-tale world. Nevertheless, because Kent has such a wealth of diverse source material the problem is rather to master as many of the sources as possible, to see if they all cohere in a single reconstruction. Kenneth Witney has pored over the written evidence and the discoveries of archaeologists, and he has set his findings in a landscape of which he has unrivalled knowledge, as any reader of *The Jutish Forest* must be aware. Here is a reconstruction of early Kentish history from the soil up.

IAN WOOD

ACKNOWLEDGEMENTS

A good deal of the work on this book I have had necessarily to do on my own, but I owe a special debt of thanks to Ian Wood for encouragement, information and advice, all the more valuable as coming from such an eminent centre of Anglo-Saxon studies as the School of History of Leeds University. Also, as ever, I am greatly indebted to my wife and family for their comments and support, and for putting up with all the tiresomeness inevitably associated with a work of this kind.

I could not have begun to make headway on the work without the use of the really splendid facilities provided by the Institute of Historical Research in London, and the ever willing help received from the Kent Library Service. Although I hope that this book may have a wider interest it is to a Kentish public that it is chiefly addressed, and to Kentish audiences that it owes its genesis. When speaking about my previous work on the Weald it was impossible for me not to become aware of the deep interest felt by people throughout the county in an historical heritage that is still so plainly imprinted on its landscape. It is to this—and to much shrewd questioning—that I have tried to respond, leaving the correction to those who may follow, as I have followed so many others.

INTRODUCTION

THE ANGLO-SAXON CHRONICLE says that in A.D. 455 the German chieftains Hengest
and Horsa, who had been invited into the country by the British ruler Vortigern to help
defend it from its enemies, fought against him at Aylesford (on the River Medway), that
Horsa was killed in this battle, and that after it Hengest 'succeeded to the kingdom and
Aesc his son'. The kingdom established by this victory was that of the Cantware, or men
of Kent, which was ruled for three hundred years by the dynasty of the Eskings, or
descendants of Aesc. In the middle of the 8th century the dynasty was extinguished in
the male line and the kingdom fell under the domination of Mercia, against which the
Cantware twice rebelled, but with only fleeting success. During one of these interludes
the crown was offered, in default of direct heirs, to a certain Ealhmund, who came from
a cadet branch of the Wessex royal family which may have intermarried with the Eskings;
and his son Egbert, at first driven into exile, returned to win the throne of Wessex, to
destroy the power of Mercia at the battle of Ellendun, fought in 825, and to claim Kent
as his patrimony. In this way the kingdom of the Cantware became wedded to Wessex,
by which it was carried into the realm of England.

The history of the Kingdom of Kent (which lasted for as long as Roman rule in Britain
had done) has too often been treated as incidental to other themes. Kent has been seen as
a persistent thorn in the side of the larger powers of Wessex and Mercia; as the vehicle
by which Roman Christianity was brought into the country; and as an extreme, and
puzzling, example of the diversity of customs and institutions among the English people.
Yet a kingdom which contributed so much to the formation of England deserves to be
studied in its own right. The Jutish people whom Hengest led, and who composed the
bulk of the Cantware, were neither a large federation like the continental Saxons, nor
the descendants of a powerful folk like the Angles; they were one of the smallest and
most obscure of the German tribes, whose very homeland is disputable, and the foothold
which they established in Britain was itself a small one. But it was they who first opened
the way to the English conquests, and throughout the entire period of the heptarchy, in
the clash of nations grown much larger than themselves, they remained a force to be
reckoned with, having in the end the casting vote in the contest for supremacy.

The destiny of the people was conditioned by the position they occupied, in a corner
of England commanding the narrow seas. This brought them into early trading relationships with the continent and made them the first to reach out to the remnants of the
Imperial tradition, and to the Roman Church which had tended and inherited it; while
at the same time depriving them of that movable front against the British upon which
the powers of Wessex, Northumbria and Mercia waxed until they eclipsed their south-
eastern neighbours. It would be possible, by balancing these factors, to form an almost
determinist view of the history of the kingdom; in which, even, it could be made to
appear predictable that its fortunes should reach their zenith at the close of the 6th

century, when the advantages of the continental connections were being reaped and the frontier nations were only starting to emerge from their formative stages. But this lays too much emphasis upon the setting, and allows too little to the character of the country, and of its society.

Although there are areas of great fertility in Kent, much of the land is poor or indifferent. Its chief asset in Jutish times was its variety. The tracts of rich arable soil, mostly in the north-east and along the Thames foreshore, were ample for a small nation of a few thousand. They were complemented by the woodland and rough grazing of the Downs, the coastal marshes and saltings, and the great oak forests of the Weald; while everywhere the country was in easy reach of the sea, which penetrated it in deep tidal estuaries. It was, therefore, well provided with fuel and fisheries, and ideal for raising stock: swine, oxen and especially sheep, upon which much of the rural economy depended. The loosely knit organization of Kentish society was well adapted to exploit these advantages, and the Kentish ceorl, or freeman, enjoyed exceptional privileges in the use and disposal of his land. A wealthy farming community, nourished by trade, is less tempted than others to military adventures, and after they had won their land the Cantware ceased to be a belligerent people; even the great Æthelberht, who made himself the most powerful ruler in England, relied more upon statecraft than force to achieve his ends. But the people had much to lose, were proud of their independence, and showed great spirit in defending it. They were also deeply attached to a royal house which, whatever the failings of individual rulers, understood the needs of the nation and enjoyed because of this a rare immunity from dynastic upheavals. This partnership became for three hundred years the bedrock of Kentish security.

The history of the kingdom falls into two distinct phases, with the long reign of Æthelberht (560-616) marking the transition between them. During the first, heathen, phase the conquests of Hengest were consolidated by his son Aesc (correctly Oisc), who was remembered as the true founder of the dynasty, and the continental connections were fostered by Eormenric, his grandson and Æthelberht's father. Kent then was richer and more advanced than any of the English nations, with a growing overseas trade and well established crafts, of which that of the jewellers was supreme. It was on this foundation of wealth that Æthelberht won, and held for 20 years, an ascendancy over all the peoples south of the Humber and east of the Severn. The second, Christian, phase developed naturally – though far from smoothly – out of the contacts with the Rhineland and Merovingian France, opening up still wider vistas and bringing with it all the benefits of literacy and learning. It coincided, however, with a decline in Kentish power which had started a little before Æthelberht's death. If a single date can be put to the watershed it is 604, when the rebuff administered to St Augustine by the Welsh Church was also a public humiliation to his patron, undermining his authority among the English kings, a setback from which he had grown too old to recover.

The alliance with the Roman Church was the accomplishment of the royal house, whom the Cantware followed at first dubiously and never with any excess of fervour. Yet it did much to arrest, or at least mask, the decline of the kingdom, through the influence emanating from Canterbury and the special favour reserved by the church for those who had befriended it. On Æthelberht's death Kent was the only English kingdom in which Christianity managed to survive, and then barely; it was spread from there into Northumbria; and the Church's debt to the Eskings was compounded by their unswerving championship of the Roman cause at a time when it seemed that Celtic forms of observance, which had also found their way into Northumbria and won favour there, might come to supplant it over most of England. The protection and support which the church had received it repaid in the days of its own triumph. At a time of almost incessant warfare among the English kingdoms, caused by the growth of the predatory power of Mercia, Kent enjoyed an extraordinary immunity. Between the landing of St Augustine in 597 and the death in 762 of the last direct descendants of the royal line there was only a single spell of twenty years (from 674 to 694) during which the peace of the kingdom was interrupted, and that at a time of dynastic uncertainty when the premature death of Egbert I had left his sons Eadric and Wihtred still children, so offering a pretext for intervention to both Wessex and Mercia. This crisis was eventually overcome by the resolution of the people, the fighting qualities of Egbert's brother Hlothere, and, after his death in battle and a further period of anarchy, the sagacity of the young Wihtred, who restored the ruling line and strengthened the compact with Canterbury. There followed another seventy years of tranquillity, the last that the nation was to enjoy.

In 762 the security of the kingdom vanished with the foundering of the royal line. In the absence of direct heirs the throne became open to a variety of contenders, and this once more exposed it to the intervention of Mercia, now at the height of its power under Offa. The resistance of the Cantware, greatly outmatched in strength, was forlorn but heroic; they were impelled by pride in nationhood and a consuming hatred of the Mercians, upon whom they inflicted wounds for which they were never forgiven. In the end they were both outmanoeuvred and overwhelmed. The support which they had at first enjoyed from the church was struck away from them by the influence that Offa was able to exert in Rome, the creation of a new metropolitan see at Lichfield which halved the authority of Canterbury, and the appointment of a Mercian archbishop. The last Kentish revolt, an act of pure desperation, began with the expulsion of the arch-bishop and was led by an apostate priest, Eadberht Praen, who was probably of the royal blood and may have been unwillingly inducted into holy orders to pre-empt his claims to the throne. The church had now been fatally estranged and the country left completely alone and friendless. In 798 it was ravaged from end to end, and Praen was led away into Mercia where he was mutilated and enslaved.

But this was not quite the end. Control over the south-east had become crucial to the mastery of England, and the detestation felt by the Cantware made the Mercians incapable of holding it. The dynastic marriage which had led the Wessex prince Ealhmund to make common cause with the Cantware in the days of their resistance, and his own brief rule among them, had left his son Egbert, who was now in control of his own country, the last legitimate claimant to the Kentish throne. The breach with the church was healed with the appointment to Canterbury (restored to its full metro-politan authority) of a Kentish archbishop, Wulfred, who came to act as the custodian of the interests not only of the church but of his own people. By 825 the Mercian royal house was in dissolution, leaving Wulfred in command of the situation; and in that year the Mercian army was defeated by. Egbert at Ellendun, near Swindon. Egbert's first concern after this victory was to occupy Kent, where he came as a liberator claiming his inheritance. The union was an honourable one, which was to be tempered in the Danish wars; and it left the customs of the nation intact, the enduring mark of its individuality.

This is the outline of the story we have to tell, of which, however, many of the details are obscure or disputable. Our understanding of Dark Age England has been greatly increased in recent years through advances made in a whole variety of specialist studies — in land tenures, archaeology, chronology, toponymy, numismatics and genealogy, to name only the chief — but large areas of ignorance remain, and a stage has been reached when the accumulation of knowledge has begun to outstrip synthesis. To examine the history of a single kingdom must itself be a work of synthesis, and it is at the same time a novel undertaking which may help, if only in a small way, to shift the general perspective. The choice of Kent has been a matter mostly of personal interest and familiarity, and it is open to the objection that this kingdom, in its origins and customs, the influences to which it was exposed, and the policies it pursued, was thoroughly untypical; but that, one suspects, was true of all, and it is part of the value to demonstrate the departures from any supposed type. The choice has two clear advantages. The first is that from the beginning of the period of the so-called heptarchy until its very end Kent, though one of the smallest and most peripheral of the kingdoms, nevertheless occupied a central place in the affairs of England, so that it is impossible to recount its history without also traversing that of the whole country. The second is simply that more can be discovered of Kent, and especially perhaps of its society, than of any of the other kingdoms; a product of material advancement in heathen times, expressed in the profuse richness of the grave goods, and a reward for being the first to adopt Christianity, and with it the use of letters. Almost all the specialist studies made of this period of English history have been bound constantly to recur to Kent; and the light they shed upon the development of the kingdom is blended and reflected back upon themselves.

Especially for Kent, there is more written evidence than is commonly realized. It consists, first, of the early sagas, condensed in such works as the Anglo-Saxon Chronicle from records or notes which may have begun to be made in Kent even before the Christian conversion. There is a long succession of monastic writings, starting in the middle of the 6th century with the work of the British scribe Gildas, continuing with the splendid history of Bede, who drew much of his material from Kentish sources, and ending with the Norman and medieval chroniclers — William of Malmesbury, Simeon of Durham, Florence of Worcester and others — who set down scraps of tradition that had survived from a past era. There are no fewer than three codes of Kentish law dating from the 7th century, the earliest and most comprehensive of which was produced by Æthelberht in or around A.D. 603; and these, together with the Penitentials of Theodore of Tarsus, tell us a great deal about the contemporary society. Towards the close of the 7th century there came to be introduced — again first in Kent — formal diplomas of land grants, a mass of which have survived, some in the original but most in copies (which include, however, a number of evident fabrications). And there is also a volume of correspondence, starting with letters sent by Gregory the Great at the time of the Augustinian mission, and increasing in quantity up to the close of the 8th century with those exchanged among eminent churchmen and rulers. It is these letters, together with the diplomas and scraps from the Anglo-Saxon Chronicle, that do most (though still far from enough) to close the gap left by the conclusion in 731 of Bede's *History of the English Church and People*.

The evidence of archaeology, coinage, place-names and so on needs to be interpreted and dove-tailed; a work of detection, but with a large subjective element in it. The written sources pose problems of a different kind. While much of the material is contemporary, or clearly authentic, the greater part of it is not; for the heathen period we are dealing with the stuff of legend, and for the Christian too often with hagiography or religious propaganda — criticisms from which Bede himself is not entirely exempt. The laws are often opaque, and the diplomas need to be carefully sifted, remembering always, however, that even those which textual criticism has dismissed as spurious may not be outright deceptions but represent what was believed to be true. It is only in the occasional correspondence, or very rarely in the preamble to a diploma, that we can get a glimpse of motives unglossed by the monastic chroniclers for their own, edifying, purposes.

This, then, is an era of myth and propaganda, religious or dynastic, shot through with certain clear shafts of light. The difficulty is to steer a middle course between the extremes of scepticism and credulity; to avoid the temptation to make too much of what little evidence there is, or to be too timid in using it. Every student of the period is bound, at times, to err on one side or the other, on which side depending mostly upon temperament. The sceptical approach is the safer, and there is still a great deal of critical demolition to be done; but, for all the risks, speculation — if reasonably based — remains the growing point for the future.

PART I:
THE PAGAN ERA

Chapter One

THE JUTES

THE ORIGIN of the Jutes is one of the major conundrums of early English history, upon which probably more scholarly effort has been expended than upon the entire chronicle of the kingdom which they founded. It is an important problem because in it there lie the clues to the distinctive character of Kentish society not only during the period we are considering but throughout the Middle Ages. Closely bound up with it is the question how far the Romano–British population of Kent survived the conquest, not as mere slaves but as free, or semi-free, communities capable of influencing the customs of the nation. There are probably few people who now hold the view, popular forty years ago, that the Jutes were a small ruling caste who did little more than add a veneer to a native British culture; but there are still many who believe that Kentish society was a synthesis in which a significant Celtic element was included. Before we turn to the vexed subject of origins, however, we must say something about the background to the appearance of the Jutes in Kent, and about the characteristics of the country at that time.

Almost from the beginning of the Roman occupation of Britain the chief threat to it had come from the northern Picts, against whom the defences of the Hadrian and Antonine Walls were built.[1] By the end of the 3rd century, however, it had become necessary to construct another system of defences in the south-east against the increasingly destructive raids of German pirates, known indifferently as Saxons, although they must have been drawn also from a number of other peoples bordering the North Sea, including the Frisians and the Franks of the lower Rhine. The defences consisted of a succession of coastal fortresses on an arc from the Wash to Southampton Water, with others across the Straits; the hub of the system being Richborough in Kent, which was also the headquarters of a fleet; and the whole being put under the command of the Count of the Saxon Shore.[2] The system has been criticized as being too brittle and inflexible, but it seems to have served its purpose well enough. The first half of the 4th century was a period of prosperity for Britain, during which the continuing decline of the cities, whether caused by the taxation policy of the Empire or by the mere inability to sustain plans which had been over-ambitious from the beginning, was offset by the increasing number and wealth of the villas. Throughout this period, however, the external pressures were mounting, and were accompanied by a progressive barbarization of the army as more and more auxiliaries, Germans and others, were taken into service.

In 367 the treachery and desertion of auxiliaries stationed on the Wall led to a disastrous incursion by the Picts, who were joined by roving bands of Saxon and Scots pirates in widespread plundering. Although the walled cities could withstand this onslaught large numbers of the villas appear to have been sacked or destroyed; and although the situation was restored by the prompt action of Theodosius the Younger the economy of the country never properly recovered. It seems that the reinforcements brought over by Theodosius included numbers of German *laeti,* or mercenaries, who were used mainly to strengthen the defences of the Saxon Shore forts and of the towns in their hinterland, where there have been found a number of the distinctive buckles worn by such forces on the continent;[3] and that at a later stage, towards the very end of Roman rule, bodies of German federates were stationed under their own leaders at the approaches to the major Roman walled towns along the east coast from York to East Anglia. Most of the great Anglo-Saxon cremation cemeteries of this area, and of the east Midlands, start with pottery which can be dated to this time.[4]

In 378 the Imperial army was routed at Adrianople by the Visigoths, who had been settled within the Danube frontier as fugitives from the advancing Huns. The effect of this defeat reverberated throughout the Empire and prompted in Britain the rebellion of Magnus Maximus, then *Dux Brittaniarum,* or commander of the frontier forces, who made a bid for Imperial power by crossing to the continent with an army which, after his eventual defeat and death, appears never to have returned. Some believe that Magnus Maximus had prepared against his departure by carrying out a punitive expedition north of the Wall and by reorganizing the defence of the west coast against the Scots by entrusting responsibility to native chieftains, who became the founders of a number of the later British dynasties.[5] Perhaps because of this, and despite the serious weakening of the Roman garrisons, it was not until 396 that it became necessary for a further expedition to be sent to Britain, this time under Stilicho, a Vandal in the Imperial service, who had become the power behind the throne in the western Empire. Yet in 401 Stilicho was compelled to withdraw more troops from Britain to bolster up the situation elsewhere; and in Christmas of 406 there occurred the ultimate disaster when bands of Vandals, Alans and Suevi crossed the frozen Rhine and broke into Gaul, an event which hastened Stilicho's disgrace and execution. The isolated garrisons in Britain, feeling the recovery of Gaul essential to their own safety, elected no fewer than three would-be Emperors in quick succession, the last of whom, Constantine III, transported to the continent, and lost there, the entire field force and most of the remaining auxiliaries. Neither then, nor ever again in the future, could troops be spared to replace them; appeals for help to the Emperor Honorius met with the response that the cities should defend themselves. It seems that they had already expelled the civil administration and were preparing to do so.

The abandonment of Britain was not a deliberate act of policy, nor at the time was it intended to be permanent. The British still regarded themselves as subject of the Empire, and for fifty more years, as they struggled to make headway against the enemies besetting them, they continued to hope that aid would be sent to them. The age was one of increasing anarchy and barbarism. The evidence of the cemeteries suggests that the German federates who had been settled along the east coast as far south as Norfolk were joined by numbers of new immigrants from the continent and had already virtually usurped the lands they occupied;[6] it is doubtful whether they paid even the remotest regard to whatever authority might linger in the towns they had once been supposed to protect. South of the Thames, however, and further to the west, the situation was different. There are traces here of the continuing presence of German *laeti,* but not as independent forces; instead they seem to have been integrated with the Romano–British community, adopting from them the practice of inhumation and wearing a standard form of military

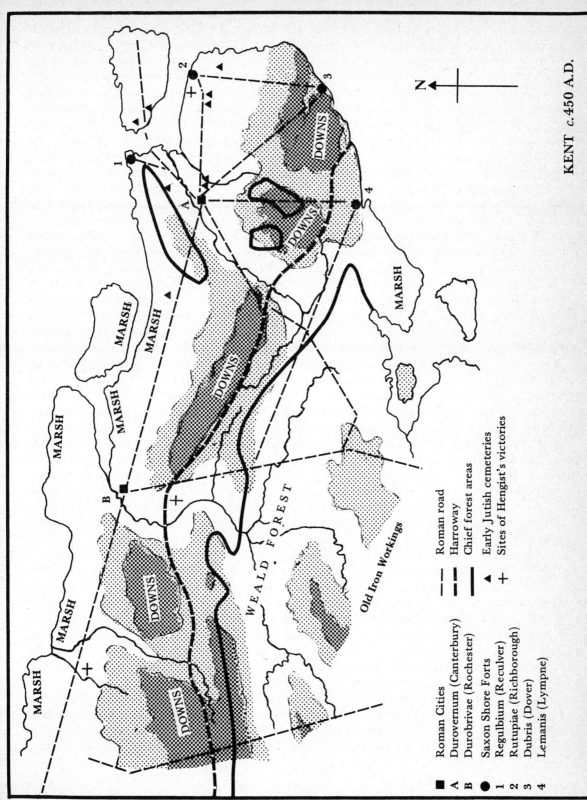

KENT *c.* 450 A.D.

N

Roman Cities
A Durovernum (Canterbury)
B Durobrivae (Rochester)

Saxon Shore Forts
1 Regulbium (Reculver)
2 Rutupiae (Richborough)
3 Dubris (Dover)
4 Lemanis (Lympne)

Roman road
Harroway
Chief forest areas
Early Jutish cemeteries
Sites of Hengist's victories

Scale: Approx 10 miles = 1 inch

MARSH

WEALD FOREST

DOWNS

Old Iron Workings

equipment with buckles and strap-ends representing a purely insular development from the earlier continental designs.[7] It seems that in the south the towns had retained the ability to defend themselves with the aid of these mercenaries, though the Romano-British community itself was reft with disputes as power passed progressively into the hands of the more primitive of the tribal chieftains, whose influence was resented and resisted by the heirs to the old Imperial tradition. But contact with the continent was not entirely lost; and the period witnessed a remarkable growth of Christianity — to the extent, indeed, that Britain became a refuge for the major heresy of Pelagianism.

As the external pressure from the Picts, Scots and marauding Saxon pirates mounted, the presence of the German communities settled in the eastern parts of the country became more menacing, and internal dissensions multiplied, a final, desperate, appeal for help was made in 447 to the Roman commander in Gaul, Aëtius, himself faced with imminent threat of Attila and the Huns and the remorseless westward movements of the Franks. The appeal went unanswered. It was against this background, at some time during the period when Marcian and Valentinian were emperors (450-457),[8] that the British ruler Vortigern took into his service, and settled in north-east Kent, the German leader Hengest, who was said to have come to Britain as an exile from his own people. It seems that even before this time small bodies of German mercenaries had been established in the area, and especially on the approaches to Canterbury, to support the Romano-British forces and *laeti* who appear still to have been occupying the great fortress of Richborough.[9] Whatever Vortigern's motives may have been in this, the establishment of unreliable federates in such a vital strategic area, hitherto free of them, was an act of folly, compounded by the invitation to Hengest, one of the ablest and most unscrupulous warriors of the age. It was to exploit the advantage he had been given that Hengest sought the help of the Jutes, with whom it seems he had previously had dealings (though of no friendly kind), and who were eager to snatch at just such an opportunity.

Even more in the 5th century than now Kent had the character of a promontory thrust out from London towards the continent, with the Isle of Thanet at its tip.[10] At this time Romney Marsh was a delta of mud and shingle banks with relatively little consolidated land, and the Weald was still a primeval forest; so that open and cultivated land was restricted to the north of the province, on a length of some sixty miles from London to the North Foreland, and to a depth varying from fifteen to twenty-five miles from the Thames shore-line to the fringes of the forest or marsh. The grain of the land ran west to east, and it had as a spine the long line of the Downs, a wooded and unproductive country of chalk overlaid with flinty clay and scored with dry valleys. The Downs declined gently northward to a littoral of rich alluvial soils fringing the Thames estuary from London as far as Faversham, beyond which it was interrupted by a spur of clay hills clad by Blean Forest. To the east of this, between Canterbury and the coast at Deal, there extended a broad expanse of chalk wolds covered by deep loam, then as now the granary of Kent. On their southern face the Downs formed a steep escarpment dominating the valley of Holmesdale, which stretched the entire way from the Surrey border to the sea at Folkestone; this consisting in part of calcerous loams with some hill wash, and in part of heavy gault clay, difficult but rewarding to work. Flowing northward from Holmesdale to breach the Downs were three rivers, the Darent, Medway and Stour, with good land in the valley bottoms. These issued from the hills at Dartford, Rochester and Canterbury respectively, and emptied into the Thames or the sea in large marsh-fringed estuaries, severing the Isles of Sheppey and Thanet from the mainland. The estuaries and the rich agricultural lands backing or surrounding them were an invitation to sea raiders; and the off-shore islands provided convenient bases from which larger enterprises might be launched.

In Roman times north-east Kent had been the front of the defence against the Saxon pirates.[11] Here, where the Stour estuary divided to either side of Thanet, were the fortresses of Reculver and Richborough, the base of the Channel fleet, and further to the south another fortress was established at Dover. From each of these places roads converged upon Canterbury — *Durovernum Cantiacorum* — the tribal capital, a walled city guarding the crossing of the Stour just above the limit of navigation, and here the separate threads were drawn together into the single strand of Watling Street, which ran due west along the Thames shore-side to the Medway at Rochester — *Durobrivae*, 'the bridges of the stronghold'[12] — and so by way of Dartford to London. This road system, strategically conceived, also knit together the richest agricultural lands of the province. Yet, by the close of the 3rd century, the north-eastern plains had already become a threatened frontier area; so that, while some villas and other signs of rural settlement have been (and continue to be) found here their number is relatively small. Collingwood has suggested that part of the land was cultivated by the citizens of Canterbury,[13] and much of it may also have been used for the provisioning of the fleet and the troops stationed at the Saxon Shore forts, especially Richborough. Behind Canterbury, along Watling Street, villas and settlements began to appear more frequently and had become plentiful by the time that Rochester was reached.

To the south of the Downs the entry to Holmesdale and the delta of Romney Marsh, into which the Rother emptied from the depths of the Wealden forest, were protected by a fortress at Lympne, near Hythe. This was connected by road across the Downs to Canterbury, and another road ran west to Maidstone, from which it struck north to Rochester, collecting over the first part of its course two metalled ways and a number of unmade tracks which emerged from the Wealden forest and served the iron workings there. Although no road ran the length of Holmesdale the prehistorical Harroway footed the Down escarpment the whole distance from the coast to Surrey and beyond, crossing the Stour at Wye, the Medway near Aylesford, and the Darent at Otford. There was a scattering of villas in the eastern section of the vale, but it was not until the Medway was approached that they became at all frequent. Here there was a marked change. The lower Medway valley, especially around Maidstone, and the Darent valley beyond it, were as thickly planted with villas as anywhere in Britain. Propinquity to London may have had a good deal to do with this, but most of all it indicates that when the villa system was at its most flourishing west Kent was considered secure, as east Kent was not, and that this was well outside the area of military garrisons and provisioning.

In the middle of the 5th century, when Hengest and the Jutes came to Thanet, the Saxon Shore defences appear to have been abandoned, excepting Richborough,[14] and that also is likely to have been ill-garrisoned and in a rundown state. Those of the villas that had not been destroyed in the constant warfare and anarchy following the first great irruption of 367 seem to have fallen into dereliction; there are no signs of occupation by the newcomers other than of a purely chance or casual kind. An impoverished form of city life appears to have continued at Canterbury, and probably at Rochester, behind the shelter of their walls, but over large areas of the countryside the population must have been left to shift for themselves as best they could. A determined body of men, holding the key positions of Thanet and north-east Kent, where they could readily reinforce themselves from the continent, would be able to over-run the greater part of the province before any sizeable forces could be assembled against them from London or further afield. This is what happened; and it was on the Medway at Aylesford that the encounter took place which brought the Jutish Kingdom of Kent into being.

That the Kentish people were Jutes rests upon the authority of Bede, writing more than 250 years after the event.[15] From the time that they first began to refer to themselves in written records the name they took was Cantware, the inhabitants of the old Roman province of the *Cantiaci*; a usage which has been held to demonstrate the strength of the British connection, or at least to have been an acknowledgement of the heterogeneous character of the people,[16] but which cannot be traced any further back than the reign of Hlothere towards the close of the 7th century.[17] Bede went on to say that the inhabitants of the Isle of Wight and of the mainland opposite it were also Jutes and were so called in his own day, and we learn from another source that the New Forest was, in fact, known as *Ytene*, that is the country of the *Yte*, or Jutes, as late as the 12th century.[18] There is strong institutional and archaeological evidence to connect these areas with Kent, from which they appear to have been settled in the 6th century, when the Anglo-Saxon Chronicle records their conquest.[19] It must follow that at this time the Kentish people (or a major part of them) still called themselves Jutes and were so known to others. The term Cantware appears to have been adopted later when the conception of nationhood had replaced that of the tribe, and its choice may well have been influenced by the Christian conversion and the wish to emphasize the old Roman associations.

It may seem surprising that so much doubt should surround the origin of the Jutes since Bede states plainly enough that their homeland lay to the one side of that of the Angles (on the neck of the Danish peninsula) as the homeland of the Saxons lay to the other;[20] and this would allow — without positively requiring — it to be placed in Jutland which might be assumed to perpetuate the tribal name. But the matter is not so simple. The name Jutland derives from the Scandinavian Jötar, and while linguistically this could — just — have been a Danish adaptation of the old term for the Jutes the connection is not an easy one to make.[21] It would, moreover, imply the adoption by a supplanting race of the name of the people it had displaced. Stenton, for one, found it difficult to imagine such a process;[22] although, in fact, the Jutes themselves, when they came to take the name Cantware, seem to have done very much what he found unimagineable in the Danes.

The real obstacle in the way to accepting Bede's statement at its face value is that so many of the clues to the continental provenance of the Jutes point not to Jutland but to elsewhere, in particular to Frisia or the Rhineland. These, admittedly, were areas with which the Kentish people had established close trading and other relationships within a hundred years of the conquest, so that a good deal might be ascribed to later influences, but certain similarities, for instance of the land system, appear too deeply ingrained to be dismissed in this way. Bede is a reliable witness, but even if we accept that he was basing himself on more than a specious resemblance of name, and relying — as clearly he did elsewhere — on traditions handed down among the Cantware, two further questions remain; first, whether the traditions related to the Kentish royal house alone or also to the body of the people and, second, just how far back they reached. Each is pertinent because there are other sources which imply that, while Hengest came originally from Denmark, he was not himself a Jute, and indeed that his early dealings with the tribe which he was later to lead in Kent had been hostile; and because we have also to take account of the confused movements that took place in Germany during the two centuries or so preceding the conquest. There was, during this period, a drift of the tribes south and west towards the troubled frontiers of the Rhine,[23] and certain snatches of written evidence suggest that the Jutes may have been caught up in this.

Tacitus in his account of the tribes in the *Germania* mentions as neighbours of the Langobardi, or Lombards, of the Elbe valley a group of seven tribes which were united in the common cult of the Earth Goddess, Nerthus, naming among them the Angles, the Warni (or Varini) and the Eudoses.[24] Assuming that the Eudoses were the Jutes, as seems probable, this would again be consistent with the belief that in the 1st century they were settled on or near the Danish peninsula, perhaps in Jutland; and there is other evidence, of a round-about kind, which at least hints at an identification with a people whom Ptolemy, writing in the 2nd century, called the Phoundeusiei and definitely located on the west coast of Jutland.[25] A passage from the Byzantine historian Procopius[26] shows, however, that by the beginning of the 6th century the south-westward drift of the tribes had brought the Warni, or a part of them, onto the banks of the Rhine in what is now the Netherlands, in close touch with the Franks across the river and occupying lands which they had previously vacated. By this time the Jutes had already appeared in Kent; but there is some indication that a substantial number of them had also, and probably previously, shifted to Frisia or the lower Rhine. This seems to be the inference from a letter sent by the Merovingian king Theudebert (534-548) to the Emperor Justinian[27] in which he records the conquest of Pannonia — the term applied to that region[28] — 'cum Saxonibus Euciis'. Most scholars are agreed that the Euciis are the Jutes: and the invasion of Kent would more readily have been undertaken from Frisia or the mouth of the Rhine than direct from Jutland. Nevertheless there are ambiguities about the passage, which make it possible to divorce the reference to the Saxonibus Euciis from that to Pannonia and to translate the first rather in the sense of 'the English Jutes' * — which it is all the more tempting to do because we know from Procopius that Theudebert claimed a somewhat indeterminate suzerainty over the peoples of Britain, English and other.[29]

Even if we accept that a body of Jutes was at this time settled in the Netherlands it does not follow that they had long been so, or that the whole of the tribe had moved from its original homeland; the Warni, in their migrations, had left a remnant in their old tribal lands on the Baltic, where Procopius also mentions them,[30] and some elements of the Jutes may have remained in Denmark (if that, in fact, is where they originally came from). In support of this view there has sometimes been cited a passage in a poem by Venentius Fortunatus which mentions the *Euthiones* among the peoples subject to the Frankish king Chilperic (*c.* 580), treating them together with, and between, the Saxons and the Danes;[31] but the order in which the names appear seems to have been dictated by the exigencies of the hexameter form used in the poem rather than by the situation of the Jutes, or any body of them, at this time.[32] The passage, indeed,

* In its wider context the passage refers to the submission of 'Wisigotis, qui incolebant Franciae septentrionalem plagam, Pannoniam, cum Saxonibus Euciis, qui se nobis voluntate propria tradiderunt'.

immediately goes on to refer to the British, which again raises the question whether the
Jutes mentioned in it may not have been those of Kent, then ruled by Æthelberht, who
had married a Merovingian princess and in doing so made some sort of acknowledgement
of Frankish suzerainty, little though it meant in practice.

There is another piece of literary evidence bearing upon this subject. The great English
epic *Beowulf* recounts a tale, sung at the court of the Scyldings or 'Half-Danes', in which
both Hengest and the Jutes feature in a continental setting prior to their appearance in
Kent, that is shortly before 450.[33] The passage is highly allusive, being obviously
intended for an audience to whom the main outline of the story was already familiar, and
for that reason it is difficult to construe. It tells of a visit paid by a Danish prince, Hnaef,
to his sister, who had married the Frisian king Finn; of a treacherous attack made upon
Hnaef and his followers and of his death in the fighting that followed; of the agreement
then patched up between the survivors on both sides; and of how, after a period of
apparent reconciliation, the leader of the remaining Danes, Hengest, took his revenge by
provoking a further quarrel in which Finn was killed and his palace sacked. The Jutes
feature prominently in these events. The obscurity of the account makes it possible to
regard them as allies, or followers, of Hengest, as they were later in Kent, but the
meaning has to be wrenched in order to achieve this. On a straightforward construction
they appear as Hengest's enemies and, indeed, a people so closely associated with the
Frisians as to be almost indistinguishable from them — the reading adopted by such
scholars as Michael Alexander. Although the story came to be embedded in *Beowulf*,
an epic which seems to have taken shape either in the Northumbria of Bede's time or in
the Mercia of Offa [34] a fragment of it, dealing with the fight at Finnsburh in which
Hnaef was killed, has survived independently.[35] It must be supposed to have been a well-
known tale deriving from early Kentish tradition, and embroidered over the years.
However much the detail is discounted, it lends support to the view that the Kentish
royal house, at least, came from Denmark; while at the same time giving colour to a statement made by Procopius that Britain was inhabited by three races, the Britons, the
Angles and the Frisians.[36] Procopius' knowledge of the English seems to have been
derived from Frankish envoys at the court of Justinian, whose own vision must have been
mostly confined to the south-east, that is to Kent and East Anglia, the only kingdoms
of any consequence at this time; which strengthens the supposition that in naming the
Frisians it was to the Jutes that he was really referring. There is another small, but
tantalising, piece of literary evidence which hints at a Rhenish provenance. This is in
Widsith, the most ancient poem in the English language, first written down in the 7th
century but evidently composed much earlier, some believe in Kent.[37] The poem is a
catalogue of German tribes, of which some seventy are named, with their most illustrious
rulers, and in it the Jutes (called *Eats*) appear in close association with the Franks, the
Warni and the Frisians, of whom Finn is described as king.

Linguistic evidence points to the same connection. Old English more nearly resembled
Frisian than any other of the continental dialects. Nowhere were these affinities more
pronounced than in Kent,[38] and indeed they were still strongly marked in the 14th and
15th centuries when the peculiarities of the local idiom began to be noted as a matter
of interest and amusement.[39] There has been much argument among philologists over
whether these Frisian elements were already present in the speech of the first Jutish
immigrants or were developed through trading contacts from the 6th century onwards.

In the nature of things this is not an argument which seems capable of being conclusively decided. Common sense suggests that the commercial dealings, important economically as they were, amounted to no more than a top dressing upon a predominantly agricultural society; but it is probably safest — and sufficient for our purpose — to settle for the verdict reached (in somewhat guarded terms) by R. Derolez in a recent review of the subject that they contributed to a dialectal strain that was already there.[40]

One of the most remarkable features of the English language as a whole is how little its vocabulary owes to the Celtic; it has been calculated that only fourteen common words were taken into the Anglo-Saxon, and of those four are doubtful.[41] Slaves would have had to adopt the speech of their masters, but if any sizeable British communities had survived in Kent in a position to deal on anything like equal terms with their conquerors one would expect this to have been reflected in the idiom, and it is not; no more than elsewhere in England do Celtic influences appear. It is surely contradictory to believe that the Jutes could have adapted themselves to an indigenous land system, and the customs going with it, while absorbing almost nothing of the speech except the names of a few natural features. Proper names, of rivers and so on, might be passed on by individuals, slaves or others, and would be the more readily accepted because the newcomers had no equivalents of their own for them, but it seems that hardly a synonym was borrowed. There were marked differences within England in the extent to which even old river names survived. Professor Jackson has demonstrated how in the eastern areas it was only those of the larger rivers which were taken over, the names of the smaller rivers and streams appearing more and more frequently on the approach towards the Celtic lands to the west.[42] Kent falls into its natural place in this progression. Only the names of the Darent and Rother (originally *Limen*) were indisputably derived from the British, more questionably those of the Stour, Medway and Eden (originally *Averne*, or *Avon*)[43] may also have been; but there the matter ends.

Throughout the period of the migrations the Frisians occupied a pivotal position between the Saxons, Angles and other tribes to the east and north of them, and the Franks and the smaller Rhenish tribes to the west and south; and while their language firmly associated them with the former, their system of land use was more closely in keeping with that of the latter. Early Kentish society showed the same polarity. The forms of land settlement in Kent differed radically from those of Saxon Wessex or Anglian Mercia, but can be closely paralleled on the Rhine. Jolliffe in his masterly study *Pre-Feudal England: the Jutes* (1933) is prepared to narrow the comparison down even further than this, claiming that those features which particularly distinguished Kent from the neighbouring kingdoms were reflected, as nowhere else, in that triangle of country, of which Düsseldorf, Frankfurt and Trier were the apices, occupied during the latter part of the 5th century by the Ripuarian Franks.[44] He concludes from this that the Jutes were, in actuality, a branch of the Frankish people, who only came to adopt 'the common language of England' after they had settled in this country.

Jolliffe sees, as the touchstone of all else, the practice in Kent, as in the Frankish lands, of defining agricultural units in terms of ploughing capacity, with the *dieta*, or day-work of the plough, building up to the ploughland or *sulung*, conceived as the amount of land that could be worked in one year by a full plough-team of eight oxen. In contrast to this, land units in Wessex and most of Mercia, as in the north German lands, were constructed upon the basis of the *virga*, or yard-width of furrow, building up from this to tenements defined in terms of yardlands or *virgates*. The significance of the distinction is that the first system is appropriate to, and associated with, settlement in dispersed, self-contained, farmsteads or hamlets and the second in compact villages surrounded by open fields under strip cultivation. Nor was it only in the dispersed character of settlement that the Kentish and Frankish systems resembled each other; common to both was partibility of inheritance, that is the practice of dividing land on the owner's death into equal shares between his surviving sons, and the attachment to each arable tenement (often at a considerable distance from it) of its own woodland, meadow and other appurtenances, so as to compose, as nearly as possible, a self-sufficient agricultural unit. The institutional framework was also similar. The lathes, or provinces, into which the Kentish Kingdom was divided were replicated, though on a larger scale, in the Frankish *gau*, and the very term can be traced in the names of certain of the Kentish lathes, such as Sturry (Sturige, 675)[45] and Lyminge (Limingae, 697).[46] Finally both in Kent and on the Frankish Rhine forest land was allotted between the provinces in the form of large commons; a distinctive practice which is clearly demonstrated in the Weald.

In addition to all this, there were a number of affinities between the two codes of law. This is especially significant because the prime object of the law, in early times, was to fix the rates of compensation to be paid, in lieu of vendetta, for death or injury inflicted upon different classes of a society which was almost exclusively rural; so that in defining the classes the laws reveal the underlying agricultural economy. Kentish society differed from that of the Anglo-Saxon kingdoms in a number of ways, but chiefly in that the *wer-geld*, or blood-price, of the free ceorl was fixed at one-third, instead of merely one sixth, of that of a noble, and in the existence between the ceorls and the slaves of a class of people (three classes, in fact) known as *laets*.[47] Both these features are to be found in the Frankish laws, though the *laets* are also met in a number of other continental codes, including those of the Frisians. The similarities go further than this. In the earliest of the Kentish laws — those of Æthelberht — blood-price is expressed in the Frankish term, *leod*,[48] instead of the English, *wer-geld*; the compensation payable for such secondary wrongs as rape or the loss of a hand or an eye equates with the Frankish, but not with Wessex, custom; and the same is true of the penalties for theft. Yet it is noteworthy that the laws of the Angli and Varini (the Warni again, in a new association) had just as close an affinity with the Frankish, and in the opinion of Chadwick, who was the first to make a detailed study of these matters, were closest of all the continental codes to the Kentish.[49]

Despite the evidence assembled by Jolliffe historians in general have been reluctant to adopt his conclusion that the Kentish people were Ripuarian Franks. As Hodgkin has pointed out, it is remarkable, if this were so, that no hint should have survived in the traditions of the Cantware of their descent from so illustrious a people;[50] and it is also remarkable that no elements of Frankish speech — except such terms of art as *gau* and *leod* — should have remained in the strongly Frisian dialect of Kent. There is, moreover, a good deal of difficulty, even allowing for all the turmoil and confusion of the folk migrations, in deriving the inhabitants of Kent from so distant an area as the middle Rhine; and some incongruity in doing so on the basis of established custom and law when the Frankish kingdom of Cologne was not founded until 462,[51] by which time the Jutes had already appeared in Kent. The original homeland of the Franks was on the Yssel and the lower Rhine,[52] and it seems that it is in this neighbourhood, if anywhere, that we should look for the source of Frankish influence upon the Jutes, as on the Warni.

The chief defect in Jolliffe's argument is that, without going so far as absolutely to dismiss the possibility that the Jutes may have been neighbours of the Frisians or the Warni, he gives it only the most grudging acknowledgement. His actual words, obviously most carefully chosen, are: [53]

> 'Jutish custom in Britain seems to be intact from king to peasant and the one close parallel to it is the Frankish. Compromise, then, seems to be difficult, and short of some revolutionary discovery within the sphere of the Frisians or Warni, a discovery which the thoroughness of the work already done by Hest makes unlikely, it is to the middle rather than to the lower Rhine that we must look for the eventual impetus towards the first settlement of Britain. Whatever our judgement on this may be, the north is beyond consideration. Our settlers came within the Frankish influence, if not from within the Frankish homeland.'

This is unfortunate, because more recent scholarship has shown the existence in Frisia of a land system and laws which have close parallels with the Kentish, though even more, it seems, with the East Anglian.

These affinities have been studied by G. C. Homans in an article in the *Economic History Review*. [54] His argument is that, contrary to previous belief, the land system prevailing in East Anglia at the time of Domesday Book pre-dated the arrival of the Danes and reached back to the days of the heptarchy. Among the principal features of the system were partible inheritance, with the entitlement of daughters to succeed in default of sons, holdings that had originally consisted of large compact blocks of land surrounding homesteads or small hamlets; the absence (as in Kent) of any uniform rotation of crops, each occupier being free to put his own land to what use he pleased; and the right freely to alienate land, with a consequent prevalence of *soc-men*, or free-holders. As in Kent, the ploughland was adopted as the unit of land computation, although the East Anglian *caracute* and the Frisian *ploeg* were each reckoned at a lower acreage than the Kentish *sulung* (about two-thirds). East Anglia could show no equivalent to the lathe, but embedded in the institutional structure of Frisia was a unit known as the *gau*, which occupied, however, a less prominent position than did the lathe in Kent and appears to have been smaller — a district, one might say, rather than a province.

Allowing for certain differences of scale and relativity, in the institutional framework and the terminology, the system as a whole was one that would have been familiar in Kent. No record survives of the early classes of East Anglian society. In Frisia they consisted (again as in Kent) of noble, free land-holder, *laten* and slave, but the relativities were different; in particular, the blood-price of the noble was only twice that of the free land-holder, and the status of the *laten* was lower than that of the Kentish *laet*. The Frisian laws are especially instructive in revealing the nature of the *laten*, who appears as a tenant farmer as opposed to the free land-holder, and this distinction was clearly carried through into the East Anglian system, where the *lancetti* of medieval times was a villein, bound to the soil, in contrast to the numerous *soc-men*. In general, it seems that if the Frisian land system was brother to the East Anglian it was at least cousin to the Kentish. We are reminded here of the ambiguous relationship in which the Jutes stood to the Frisians in *Beowulf*; a people closely associated with, yet distinct from, them. We must also allow for the Frankish influence apparent, for instance, in the three-to-one relationship between the blood-price of noble and the freeman, instead of the two-to-one relationship prevailing in Frisia. This brings us to a point of contact with the two peoples, somewhere in Frisia, the Netherlands or the lower Rhine, and neighbouring the Warni, whose own laws so closely reflected those of Kent.

It seems that Jolliffe was guilty of too single-minded a concentration upon the Franks; but the chief criticism made of his work when it first appeared was that it had failed altogether to take account of the possibility that the peculiarities of Kentish society owed nothing to German models but were adopted directly from the Romano–British inhabitants of Kent.[55] The arguments for a large British survival in Kent owe nothing to tradition on either side. The British scribe Gildas, writing about a hundred years after the conquest, speaks of wholesale slaughter, eviction and enslavement,[56] and the English sagas collected many years later in the Anglo-Saxon Chronicle dwell upon the thousands of Britons killed in battle and how the remainder fled from Hengest and his son Oisc 'like fire'.[57] But it is possible to dismiss these accounts as hysterical exaggeration or boastfulness, as the case may be. The argument for survival rests upon the belief that not only were the early Jutish settlements confined to areas worked in Roman times, but that the very holdings survived the conquest unchanged; upon similarities between Kentish customary law and that prevalent among Welsh clans in the middle ages; upon a supposed continuity of civic life, particularly in Canterbury and Rochester; and upon the gradations of Kentish society, with particular interest focused upon the three classes of *laets*, inferior to the ordinary freemen though superior to the slaves, and representing (so it has been claimed) the residue of a defeated people.[58] The arguments are to some extent confused by the fact that the customs of the German tribes along the Rhine had themselves been deeply penetrated by Roman and Celtic influences well before the migrations.[59] In sum they appear formidable, but tested individually they are found to be fallible at almost every point.

The general coincidence of the Romano–British settlement areas with those occupied in the early days of the Kentish Kingdom is not, in itself, significant. The invading English showed themselves adept, as time went on, in the clearance and cultivation of lowland forest country; but at the start they seem, almost everywhere, to have taken over the richer and more easily workable soils, most of which had already been cleared, and they would have been singularly foolish had they not done so. Even so, archaeological evidence in Kent reveals a marked shift in the emphasis of settlement, with a heavy concentration upon what had been the threatened frontier lands of the north-east and of the Thames shoreside eastwards of Rochester, to the general neglect of west Kent where the villa system had been most flourishing. It can, of course, be argued that it was the more primitive, and not the more Romanized, of the British communities whom the invaders absorbed, and that it was these, who left few material traces of themselves, that had inhabited the dangerous garrison lands. But the argument is thin. The appearance is that that Jutes were filling a countryside which had, during the later phases of Roman rule, become increasingly depopulated, or which had been worked from behind the safety of the forts or city walls.

Attempts have been made to derive the Kentish land system from a whole variety of Roman or Celtic models, but most of these are unconvincing. They are examined in Appendix A, which also deals with the analogies between Kentish and Welsh customary laws, in which the prevailing land systems were reflected. There were in medieval times a number of quite striking similarities between the Gavelkind customs of Kent and those of the free clan units, or *gwelyau*, of Wales, in which the principle of partible inheritance was accompanied by particular procedures, for instance for the division of a man's land on his death, which were virtually identical to those in Kent.[60] But this parallel, so tempting at first sight, has now turned out to be irrelevant; since Glanville Jones has shown that the *gwelyau* were a late development from the servile, or bond, communities which typified Welsh rural society prior to 1100, or thereabouts, and that it was only then that the custom of partible inheritance, which had earlier applied to the lordship of minor kingdoms in Wales, was extended more widely to land ownership.[61] As a guide to early Celtic practices encountered by the Jutes the *gwelyau* are therefore useless. It is true that Glanville Jones has gone on to suggest that the bond communities themselves provided the model of settlement for the German invaders over much of south-eastern England, and to draw certain specific parallels with Kent.[62] These too are considered in the Appendix. There are a number of difficulties in the argument and the whole basis of it has been attacked by Leslie Alcock, who holds that there is no reason whatsoever to believe that bond communities of the type described existed in lowland England in the 5th century but that the typical pattern of settlement then was in individual farmsteads at different stages of Romanization, from round timber houses to luxurious villas, and with no evidence that the more primitive of these were grouped in subordination to the wealthier.[63]

Since the Kentish settlements were themselves dispersed, and not gathered into villages, the possibility that the Jutes absorbed into their own system a number of the Romano-British steadings, with their occupants, cannot be entirely dismissed; but nor can it be demonstrated. There is no evidence to show that old land boundaries and divisions were retained, and where the settlements were known by the names of individual occupiers, families or kin, these were exclusively Germanic in stock, a verdict which applies to that sizeable group of place-names ending in *-ham* which lie at the earliest levels of Kentish society (pages 84–86 below). The term *wealh*, or Welshman, does very occasionally occur in place-names, such as Walmer, but the term had also become generalized to mean a slave and in the example quoted was attached to a mere, or pool, and so carried no connotation of land ownership.[64] The most notable surviving example from within the Kentish dominions is Wallington in Surrey, which, as the last element in the name shows, was definitely a settlement, or habitation.[65] This was closely associated with a royal court forming the centre of a lathe, and the probability is that the settlement was one of slaves tending the court or working upon its estate (*see* map, page 59). Curiously, if there is one place-name of this type which does seem to suggest the survival of a British family among the free land-holders of Kent it comes from the Weald. In a small area on the boundaries of Cranbrook and Frittenden parishes there occur the names Angley (Anglingele, 1278), Sissinghurst (Saxingeherste, 1206) and Wellinghurst (Walingherst, 1278) which appear to refer respectively to Angle, Saxon and Welsh folk and to have been adopted in deliberate contradistinction to each other.[66] These were forest pastures in a common used by free ceorls from the lathe which centred upon Sturry and later Canterbury (map, page 59). The names of Angley and Sissinghurst are both of 6th or 7th century form, and while that of Wellinghurst looks to be somewhat later the difference in construction is small and may be accounted for by later corruption, the likelihood being that all three of the names were, in fact, coeval.*

Included among place-names ending in -ham is a small group, the Wickhams, which seem to derive from the Latin vicus, meaning a village;[67] and there are a handful of other Latin loan words which appear in Kentish place-names, the most notable example, perhaps, being Faversham, the first element of which comes from faber, a smith.[68] The significance of names of this kind has been studied by Margaret Gelling,[69] and we examine them, in a specifically Kentish context, in Appendix B. The conclusion reached there is that they are unlikely to have represented surviving British communities. Some may have been adopted before the conquest of Kent, by German federates set by the British to guard the approaches to Canterbury; we shall show later than such forces had been stationed at Faversham and near Wickhambreux, and the distribution of the other Wickham names suggests a similar origin. Most of the remaining names derive simply from features of the landscape, being the sort of descriptions that might easily have been picked up from British slaves.

Place-names evidence also bears upon the question of the survival of the cities and civic life. There is nothing to show that the Roman towns in Kent were expunged by the invaders; all of them — with the notable exception of Canterbury — retained at least some shadow of their original names; and certainly both Canterbury and Rochester became important trading places in the 7th century. But even if the towns were not destroyed that is not to say that they may not have been left for a long period deserted; the forts of Richborough and Lympne became permanently so, and the lack of conformity between the Roman and medieval street pattern of Canterbury suggests that it too had been left abandoned for a time.[70] By itself the perpetuation of the Roman names means almost nothing. They would have been familiar to the federate forces stationed by the British in their neighbourhood, and those of the Saxon Shore forts, Reculver, Richborough, Dover and Lympne, must have been known by German raiders for many years before that. The extraordinary garbling of the name of Rochester — from Durabrivae, through the Welsh D'robriw to the Anglo-Saxon Hrofri, and so to Hrofcaester — scarcely implies a continuous civic consciousness.[71] The complete change in the name of Canterbury is more significant than the survival, in more or less garbled form, of all the other names, put together.

But most significant of all is the fact that (as we shall come to describe in Chapter 3) not one of the Roman towns became the site of a Kentish royal court; indeed, the courts seem to have been placed so as deliberately to shun them. Thus Lyminge was some five miles distant from Lympne, and Eastry three from Richborough; Aylesford was well separated from Rochester; and — most remarkable of all — Sturry was sited outside the walls of Canterbury. The choice of these positions, and those of other courts such as Faversham, Milton Regis (or its alternate Rainham)[72] and Sutton-at-Hone, seems partly to have been determined by previous mercenary occupation, but was also clearly influenced by the wish to make use both of the waterways, particularly the tidal estuaries, and of the Roman roads while avoiding the cities or old Roman settlement

* Wellinghurst is now lost, but it seems to have been by Little Bubhurst in Frittenden (Witney, 1976, p. 255), two miles from Sissinghurst and four from Angley. The difference in the form of its name from that of the others is the appearance of -ing- instead of the earlier -inge- in the middle syllable.

sites, even where those were better positioned for the purpose. It seems that in the early days the Jutes had little taste for, or knowledge of, urban life, and that there was no such society left as might have accustomed them to it.

It was only with the growth of trade, the strengthening of Frankish influences, and more especially the coming of Christianity and the renewal of the Roman connection, that Canterbury and Rochester were reoccupied. It was in this period, at the beginning of the 7th century, that Canterbury — *Cantwaraburh*, or the city of the Kentish people — must have acquired its name. In Roman times the cities had been the centres of literacy and the Christian faith. The complete disappearance of both in the wake of the conquest — as remarkable a phenomenon as the almost total loss of the old language — is a further sign of the dereliction of the cities, with the educated classes slaughtered or scattered. Attempts have been made to suggest some continuity of Christian worship, if only in a debased form, and among the slaves; but evidence of anything approaching an organized Christian life is notably lacking. It was to a profoundly heathen country that St Augustine came. Admittedly, derelict churches survived here and there, as at St Martin's just outside Canterbury, and were recognized for what they had been. We know that St Martin's was refurbished for the use of Æthelberht's Christian wife Bertha,[73] and may suspect that the same was done at Eccles near Aylesford (the name comes from the Latin *ecclesia*),[74] at Stone near Faversham, where Roman work has been found in the chancel of a later church,[75] and probably also at Lyminge, where traces of Roman work have been found in the churchyard.[76] But the significant thing about these sites is that each was within a mile or two of a royal court; there is no reason to believe that after the conquest any of them had retained a congregation.

Finally, we must return to the *laets*. In favour of the view that they represented a large surviving British element in Kentish society there may be cited an analogy from the laws of Ine of Wessex (*c.* 694) which deals specifically with the status of the free Welsh who had been incorporated into the kingdom in its westward expansion into Somerset and Devon: these being allotted *wer-gelds*, varying according to the quantity of land they held or if they were landless, to the amounts of 60, 40 or 30 per cent of that of the ceorl.[77] There were, similarly, three classes of Kentish *laet*, although their *wer-gelds* were on a higher plane, amounting to 80, 60 or 40 per cent of that of the ceorl.[78] In absolute terms the discrepancy may have been much greater than this, depending upon whether we can still accept Chadwick's calculation that the life of the Kentish ceorl was valued at twice that of his counterpart in Wessex;[79] in which event the status of the first two classes of *laet* would have been superior to that of the West Saxon freeman and of the third only a little inferior, and their position would have borne no comparison at all with that of the Welsh subjects of Ine.

However that may be, it is clear that the standing of the *laet* in Kent was higher than in any of the continental tribes which recognized this class in their societies. Among the Frisians, for instance, the life of the *laet* was valued at 50 per cent of that of the *frieling*, and among the Warni at 40 per cent; while among the Franks, who had two classes of *laet*, the superior was assessed at 50 per cent , but the inferior at something less than 20 per cent.[80] The first point which this comparison brings out is that whoever the *laets* in Kent may have been the institution itself was a thoroughly Germanic one; and the second that it covered a variety of different types of person intermediate between the free land-holder and the slave, the Kentish *laet* being accounted much nearer to the first than the second. Moreover, the common supposition that among the English kingdoms Kent was unique in adopting this institution is mistaken. Although no early code of law has survived from East Anglia, it is clear from Homan's work that the institution must also have existed there, in derivation from Frisia. Those who wish to argue that this class of society was composed of surviving Britons must be prepared to apply the argument to East Anglia as well as Kent.

In face of the Frisian model, which was so clearly adopted in East Anglia, we do not see how this can be done. On the contrary, it seems evident that the distinction between *laet* and ceorl was simply that between tenant and free landholder; or, translated into Kentish terms, between the occupiers of what later became known as the *inlands*, who were tenants of the royal estate, and those of the *outlands*, whose title to their holdings was indefeasible (*see* pages 61–67 below). So fundamental was this distinction in Kentish land law that, even if there were no analogies to be cited from East Anglia and Frisia, we should have been bound to look for its reflection among the classes of society displayed in Æthelberht's laws; and it is in the *laets* that we find it. Other evidence failing, it is impossible to say exactly what determined the differences between the grades of *laet*. Most likely they were based upon the amounts of land held; but possibly the inferior grades consisted of tenants of the nobility and of the ceorls rather than the king. The price paid for killing a slave was graduated in this way — according to the status of his owner.[81] It may be that some, especially among the lower classes of *laet*, were manumitted slaves, who would certainly include a number of Britons. But the division was essentially an agrarian one, implicit in the Kentish system of land use, and there seems no warrant for the belief that it had a racial foundation. We should assume, rather, that the ceorls were the descendants of the warriors who accompanied Hengest and Oisc, and were rewarded with their own land for doing so, and that the bulk of the *laets* of those who followed later and were settled on lands within the king's gift.

In the end, therefore, almost nothing is left of the argument that Kent, uniquely among the English kingdoms, was based upon a substantial Romano–British foundation, or that any significant number of Britons survived there, except as slaves. Admittedly, this was a large exception. Kent, like all the English kingdoms, and probably more than most, was a slave-owning society; but whatever the British slaves may eventually have contributed to the racial stock of the nation they can have contributed little to its way of life, except through their labour.

Archaeological evidence bears this out. It was to be expected that some Romano-British material would find its way into the early Kentish burials, whether it was acquired during mercenary service, as loot, or through British wives; and we do in fact find occasional coins,[82] a little glassware, a few Celtic hanging bowls or their escutcheons,[83] and a handful of 'quoit' brooches, which are possibly of British origin although that is disputable. The great mass of the material, however, is of continental derivation. This does not mean that it is easy to interpret. The practice of burial with grave goods, which began in Kent with the appearance of the first German federates at some time during the first half of the 5th century, persisted well into the supposedly Christian era, some of the finest examples of jewellery being deposited as late as 620 or 630. There is a span of around 250 years, over the whole of which the study is beset with problems of attribution and dating.

In the absence of contemporary written records or of a native coinage in common use it is extremely difficult to assign precise dates to the discoveries; the occasional, late, association of Merovingian coins with certain of the finds[84] does no more than establish a *terminus post quem*. Comparison with continental finds, with which coins are more often associated and where the historical context is often clearer, can be of help here; but in the end reliance has mostly to be placed on typology, that is the study of developments in styles of ornamentation, with whatever other clues can be found to anchor stages of the progression and allow some judgement to be formed of its pace. A tolerance must usually be allowed, perhaps of twenty or thirty years, and that can be crucial. Moreover the study of typology always has a subjective element in it; different features of a design will impress different observers. And, finally, the significance of the finds must still depend upon the view taken of their origins; whether they were local products, expressive of a native culture, or the work of a single master craftsman developing a foreign theme, or were imported through trade or marriage, or were simply tribute or loot.[85] It is the richest articles, such as jewellery, which present the most serious problems of this kind, precisely because they were treasured; and for much the same reasons the attention of archaeologists has been attracted to them away from more mundane material like pottery, which often has a clearer tale to tell. It is only through the work recently compiled by Myres that this bias has been corrected, with revealing results.[86]

It is not only the grave goods that are significant but also, and primarily, the method of burial. As Tacitus records,[87] cremation was the ancient German practice, but by the time of the migrations inhumation was beginning to be adopted among those tribes, or groups, who had been brought into the closest contact with the Romans or subjected to the influence of the Franks, at different times the allies and enemies of Rome. The major archaeological division in Kent lies between the Medway and the Darent valleys, with Gravesend on its boundary. East of this only the merest traces of cremation have been discovered; but west of it, and extending well into Surrey, we find mixed cremation and inhumation burials, with crude hand-made pottery, and associated with such ornaments as saucer brooches, which are typically Saxon.[88] It is clear that in the second phase of the conquest, after the victory at Aylesford, the Jutes were acting in concert with Saxon allies, who settled in the newly conquered territory. But while this sheds an interesting light on the early campaigns it had little lasting significance. In the total composition of the kingdom the Saxon element was small and uninfluential; it left no traces on the customs and institutions, which were Jutish in inspiration and came to be applied throughout, even in the Surrey lands.

It is in east and mid Kent that our problem lies. Here there are a few scattered signs of cremation, but there is only one cemetery, at Westbere, where these are at all pronounced.[89] Inhumation was, or rapidly became, the prevailing practice; and this appears to bring us back to the Rhineland and the Frankish connection. So, too, at a first glance, does the undifferentiated mass of grave goods, with its garnet and cloisonné jewellery, its filigree work, bird and radiate brooches, biconical wheel-turned pottery, glass beakers and tumblers, and the appearance of such weapons as the continental javelin and the *francisca* or throwing axe, all of which·are notably Frankish in origin or inspiration.[90] Yet there is also present a small quantity of material of a different kind, with Frisian, north German or Scandinavian affinities. It was this combination that first led E. T. Leeds, writing in 1913, to conclude that the bulk of the Cantware were Franks, but with some intermixture of Frisians and with a Danish royal house[91] — a verdict cited by Jolliffe in support of his own.[92]

Subsequent research, new discoveries, further comparative studies and refinements of dating, have put a very different complexion on the matter. It has now been shown that the very earliest of the finds are those that point, not to the Franks, but to Frisia, Schleswig or Jutland; though some late Roman articles appear with them as well, chiefly glassware.[93] These finds tend also to be associated with those sites, such as Westbere, where the existence of cremation has been established, or where, as at Bifrons and Sarre, it can be tentatively deduced from certain of the pottery fragments.[94] Contained in the material are a handful of cruciform brooches the significance of which was noted by the continental scholar Äberg some fifty years ago.[95] This was an essentially Anglian form of ornament, examples of which also occur in Jutland and Frisia; and the Kentish finds, no more than a dozen in all, belong exclusively to the two earliest stages in its development, which dates them to the middle or latter half of the 5th century.[96] More recently Myres has identified, on very much the same sites, a small quantity of distinctive hand-made pottery, with round shoulders and bases and decorated with simple linear patterns, of which Frisia again provides examples but which is most closely paralleled on the west coast of Jutland.[97]. Pottery of this kind has been discovered in several parts of eastern England, but mostly in Kent, though it is scarce enough even there. Some of the Kentish finds, as at Deal and Lympne, have been of a purely isolated and chance kind;[98] at Hollingbourne, where the pots appear to have been used as cinerary urns, they were incongruously inserted into a late bronze age barrow,[99] perhaps by transients; and nowhere do they appear to have been used for more than a short space of time, according to Myres a generation or less.[100] Nevertheless, he sees in this pottery a definite link with Hengest and the Jutes, commenting that:[101]

> 'If one had been asked to guess the style of pottery which a Jutish chieftain with Frisian contacts would have used towards the middle of the fifth century this is very much the answer that one would have given'.*

It is important that this scanty early material should be seen in its proper perspective. Its distribution suggests, as clearly as may be, that it is the relic of federate bands stationed to protect east Kent, and especially Canterbury, from coastal invaders. Some of the pottery has been found in Canterbury itself;[102] but, taking the material as a whole, pots, brooches, late Roman glassware and other articles, together with the traces of cremation, five cemeteries stand out from the others, those at Westbere, Bifrons, Howletts, Sarre (with Monkton)[103] and Faversham — to which there should be added a cluster of small sites around Eastry.[104] Of these places, the first three lie on an arc some four miles to the east of Canterbury covering the approach to the City of the Roman roads converging on it from the Saxon Shore forts; Faversham similarly covers the approach along Watling Street from the western side; Sarre is at the Roman crossing from Thanet to mainland Kent; and the Eastry burials occupy a forward position along the Roman road from Richborough. The inference could scarcely be clearer, and it is supported by Myres' conclusion that the pottery types belong more to the first than to the second half of the 5th century, and that some, indeed, would be best assigned to the first quarter.[105] Most of this material, therefore, appears actually to pre-date the

* The assumption that Hengest was a Jute, because he came from Jutland, and not a Dane, or 'Half-Dane' as *Beowulf* describes him, makes something of a jump in the argument here.

arrival of Hengest, assuming Bede is right in dating that to around 450.[106] The fact that all of the cemeteries contained later material which shows that they continued in use well down into the 6th century, and often beyond, argues that the federates abandoned their British paymasters to join Hengest, a supposition supported by his rapid and apparently unopposed seizure of east Kent. Nevertheless, it seems that we are dealing here only with the harbingers of the forces with which he conquered the province, the bulk of which (according to British sources) he himself recruited from the continent. It is the identity of these newcomers that concerns us, since it is among them that the Jutes must be sought. This is not to belittle the significance of the early material. There may well have been a kinship between the federates and the reinforcements whom Hengest brought over to join them; in fact, one would expect it; but the archaeological evidence cannot be taken as conclusive on the point.

The limitations of this evidence are especially apparent during the second phase of pagan burials, shortly following the conquest. This phase can be dated, very approximately, between 480 and 525, because the various articles which typify it are to be found not only in Kent and east Surrey (then part of the Kentish Kingdom) but also, in some quantity, in Sussex, conquered around 480–490,[107] and on the Isle of Wight, which was settled from Kent around 525.[108] There are only a very few, casual, finds elsewhere. The articles vary greatly in type, and apparently also in origin, but the chief influences detectable are Scandinavian and Frankish, the balance between the two being hotly disputed. Undoubtedly Scandinavian in inspiration, though developed in Kent, was a type of square-headed brooch, the distinguishing features of which were the appearance of highly stylized rampant animals at the top of the brooch foot, with crouching animals at the toe; and a quantity of gold bracteates, or pendants, all of which appear to have been imported.[109] The material of Frankish origin consists mainly, it seems, of such military objects as swords, buckles, and belt fittings together with the earliest type of Dark Age glassware and certain other miscellanea, such as bronze-bound wooden vessels.[110] The ornaments over which dispute has raged most fiercely are a small number of 'quoit' brooches, of fine workmanship, which feature animals treated in a naturalistic style within a double contour, with fur patterns formed by pointed dots, incised lines or chased ovals. E. T. Leeds considered these to be Romano–British survivals;[111] Miss Sonia Hawkes, in an elegant study published in 1958, has argued that they were the product of a Scandinavian master craftsman working at the Kentish court;[112] and Miss Evison in her book *The Fifth-century Invasions South of the Thames*, published in 1965, has contended with equal conviction that they were Frankish.[113] This is a supreme example of those differences in stylistic interpretation which leave the enquirer groping.

It is particularly unfortunate that this should be so when the burials are so clearly those of the first generation of the established conquerors. In his review of Miss Evison's book Myres discounted the significance of the Frankish material, arguing that these objects — swords, buckles, glassware and the rest — were all of a kind eagerly sought and carefully treasured by the German people, and that they might have been acquired, through trade or gift, by migrants of any tribe, for instance in passage through the Low Countries.[114] He is inclined, again, to repose far more confidence in the evidence of the pottery, believing that the complete absence, during this phase, of any wheel-turned pottery is conclusive against the settlers having been Franks, who would never have reverted to the coarser hand-made pots which occur (very occasionally)[115] in association with the other grave material. These are powerful arguments; but while they tell against a Frankish origin for the Cantware they tend, if anything, to strengthen the case for an origin in the Netherlands or on the lower Rhine. The military and other articles would have been acquired more readily, and in greater quantities, by a folk who had been settled there for some time than by mere passers by.

The distribution of burials in this second phase is again highly instructive. While all the earlier cemeteries remained in use, a number of new ones appear, and to a marked extent these are grouped around, if they are not actually at, places which are later known to have been the royal courts of the Kentish lathes,[116] a fact immediately noted by Myres when Jolliffe's account of the lathes was first published in 1933.[117] The earlier cemeteries themselves adapt to this pattern. Faversham, Eastry and also, it appears, Sarre (*see* Appendix C) became royal courts; and the cemeteries at Westbere, Bifrons and Howletts, because they were sited on the eastern approaches to Canterbury, were conveniently accessible to the court at Sturry, placed just to the north-east of the City. Equally signifi-cant is the way in which the more prolific of the new cemeteries pick out the royal vills of Lyminge, Milton Regis[118] and Croydon or Wallington (in Surrey); indeed, there is only a small group neighbouring Rochester — notably at Chatham Lines and Higham — which cannot be associated with any of the courts known to us. The inference is that, during this phase, the practice of burial with grave goods was largely confined to the royal entourage. The mixture of Scandinavian and Frankish material chimes very well with the notion that the Kentish royal line came from Denmark, but the bulk of the people, and their nobility, from somewhere 'within the Frankish influence'.

The third phase of concern to us appears to have begun around 525, and is marked by the appearance, in large quantities and at a wide variety of sites, old and new, of the entire range of Frankish articles, weapons, jewellery, glass and wheel-turned pottery. Although E. T. Leeds had by 1935 come to recognize the significance of the earlier sub-strata of Anglo-Frisian and Scandinavian material he was so impressed by the com-pleteness and 'amazing suddenness' of this later transformation that he refused to accept that it could have been caused by trading connections alone, as others were inclined to believe.[119] The view which he put forward in *Early Anglo-Saxon Art and Archaeology*, published in that year, was that there must have been an actual and massive influx of Franks, amounting virtually to a reconquest, in the course of which (he suggested) the land system was changed to the model described by Jolliffe. It is true that trade alone seems an insufficient explanation for the transformation; the contacts must have gone wider and deeper than that; but it is difficult to believe in a reconquest which passed entirely unnoticed by tradition and caused no break in the continuity of the Kentish royal line. Yet to alter a land system established for 50 years would have caused such a major dislocation that it seems that nothing short of outright conquest, accompanied by wide-scale dispossession, could have achieved it.

A solution to this problem, which at the same time reconciles the archaeological and institutional evidence, was suggested by C. F. C. Hawkes in his article *The Jutes of Kent* published in 1956.[120] The feature to which he drew attention was that the Salian Franks, in their movement across Belgium into northern Gaul, appear for two generations to have abandoned almost entirely the practice of burial with grave goods, and to have reverted to it only in more settled circumstances when the migration was over. He argued that the main body of Jutes were, in fact, Franks though following a Danish leader; that they, too, discontinued inhumation with grave goods until settled conditions had returned; and that when it was revived it indicated no new associations but those which had always been latent among the body of the people. It was (he suggested) this revival, during the second quarter of the 6th century, which accounted for the volume of the Frankish material, the 'amazing suddenness' of its appearance, and the abrupt multiplication of the burial sites; and it expressed a whole range of relationships, through inter-marriage and the exchange of gifts, ideas and techniques, as well as trade. The judgement reached by Leeds in 1913 had therefore been right after all. The conquest of Kent was merely one manifestation, a peripheral one, of the Frankish migration; but the source from which the movement into Kent began was not, as Jolliffe supposed, the middle Rhine, which was occupied at very much the same time, but Toxandria on the left bank of the lower Rhine, the crucible of the Frankish nation.

But masterly as this reconciliation is it is as likely that the range of associations described originated in a different way, through the known return to the continent (though not necessarily to their starting places) of large numbers of the English at the beginning of the 6th century, a development upon which Procopius remarked.[121] Moreover the synthesis is incomplete; the conclusion still wars with the linguistic evidence, and with much that can be gleaned from the written sources and tradition. It seems that to bring all the considerations into harmony, or as near to harmony as it is possible to get, we must adopt a different solution, towards which each new body of evidence disclosed by the experts appears persistently to have been leading us. We may start by accepting (though not on any philological grounds) that the early homeland of the Jutes was, in fact, the west coast of Jutland, where the bulk of the tribe were still situated in the 1st and 2nd centuries when Tacitus and Ptolemy wrote. This agrees with the tradition recorded by Bede (although that may owe more to Hengest's personal antecedents than to the history of the folk). It seems, however, that at some quite early time there must have begun a southward migration, not by the land route which was barred by the powerful Anglian people in Schleswig, but along the chain of islands which lead into Frisia. We should think of this less as a mass movement than a steady infiltration; but it must have started early enough, and by the middle of the 5th century have progressed sufficiently far, for the Jutes to have become by that time the power in Frisian affairs that *Beowulf* shows them to have been. Like the Warni, the tribe would then have been divided into two septs; those who still remained in Jutland being brought within the hegemony of the Danes, now entering the peninsula from the Baltic islands to the east;[122] and those (probably the bulk) who had moved to Frisia adapting themselves to the customs, and taking on the dialect, of that area, where they were also subject to the neighbouring influences of Franks and the Warni. It was, therefore, in Frisia that Jutish institutions acquired those features which Jolliffe believed to be specifically Frankish although in fact they were of a stock common to the Low Countries as a whole. Contact with their kinsmen in Jutland was, however, maintained and is attested in the early pottery styles.

It was also during the first half of the 5th century that the Jutish connection with Kent began. It is improbable that the first federates employed by the British were recruited from so far afield as Jutland; they are more likely to have been new arrivals from there to the Leeuwarden area of Frisia (where 'Jutish'-style pottery is abundant). It was this group, holding the key positions around Canterbury, who opened the path of conquest to their kinsmen, the main body of the tribe previously established in Frisia, with Hengest acting as leader and go-between in the conspiracy. The ambivalent character of his relationships with the Frisian Jutes is a matter which belongs to the next Chapter rather than this. It would, however, become more intelligible if we could assume that he was not, in truth, a Dane but belonged to that remnant of the Jutes which had stayed in its original homeland and so been brought under Danish domination.

Although this seems the best account that can be given on the matter, it would be foolish to claim that all the different strands of evidence have been drawn together and the problem of Jutish origins, which has vexed historians for so long, has been finally resolved. It is still tempting to rest upon the verdict of Hodgkin that:[123]

> 'The Jutish nation with its peculiar customs was made like the "English", and so many other hybrid nations, out of different elements, and after the conquest. It was to all intents made in Kent'.

This seemed as good a verdict as any at the time he wrote, but in the light of more recent knowledge it needs to be modified. It is true that the Cantware as a whole were composed of disparate elements, with their royal house from Denmark, the infusion of Saxons in west Kent, large numbers of British slaves, and perhaps some Angles and native Frisians included in the earlier federate bands. But the further one's enquiries go the more does one become impressed by the uniformity and cohesion of Kentish custom. This was not a polymorphous culture, but a specifically Jutish one, adapted no doubt to the environment of Kent but formed in the Low Countries. In the history of the kingdom the origin of the folk in Jutland is of less importance than their later metamorphosis, and the way in which they were brought by their long sojourn in Frisia, and then by the close association between Kent and the Rhineland, within the orbit of Frankish influence.

Chapter Two

THE CONQUEST, *c.* 450–500

Hengest and Oisc

THE FIRST EPOCH of the Germanic conquest of southern England begins sometime in the middle of the 5th century with the events leading to the foundation of the kingdoms of Kent and Sussex, and ends shortly before or after the close of the century with the great British victory of Mount Badon, fought far to the west, which arrested the advance of the English for more than seventy years. Although the general outline of the events, and the approximate period they spanned, are well enough known, there is great uncertainty about details. This, pre-eminently, is the age of legend, in which the story of Hengest and Horsa is capped by that of Arthur; the problem throughout being to distinguish true tradition from mere myth. Most of the information that has come down to us rests upon oral traditions recorded later, just how late being a prime question; and much of it is seriously contradictory. Since the chronology is vital to the understanding of events we turn to this subject first, before going on to consider what the early sources have to say, and how much of it to believe. We have to examine the time systems both of the heathen and illiterate English and of the contemporary Christian world, and to attempt in the light of this to judge, and where possible to reconcile, traditions preserved on each side of a conflict out of which the English nation began to emerge.

The calendar used by the German tribes at the time of the migrations has been the particular study of Kenneth Harrison.[1] An account of it was given by Bede in his *De Temporum Ratione*. To a primitive agricultural society the regular phases of the moon provided the most reliable clock. The problem was to establish a relationship between the lunar months and the solar year, which governed the seasons, and for this purpose use was made of a system which had first been evolved in Greece and Babylonia. The method, in its simplest form, was to reckon years in cycles of eight, in which three years of thirteen months were interspersed between five of twelve; the relationship achieved at the end of the cycle being close, but not exact, since eight solar years contain two fewer days than do 99 lunar months. A more refined system, worked out by the Greek astronomer Meton *c.* 430 B.C. was to adopt a cycle of nineteen years in which seven were of thirteen months and the remainder of twelve; so arriving at an almost exact correspondence of 6,940 days. It is not entirely clear which of these cycles was used by the Anglo-Saxon (and Jutish) invaders; but, either way, the year was averaged at 365 days and was reckoned to begin at mid-winter, that is on 25th December, within a week of the date adopted in the Christian calendar, circumstances which later made for an easy conversion. Kenneth Harrison believes that notable events, such as battles, could be assigned to particular years within a given cycle by a simple form of record, such as notches made on wood accompanied by appropriate symbols.[2]

31

There was another method that could be employed to set events in a proper temporal relationship to each other. It was the practice in each of the kingdoms to take count of the regnal years of its rulers. The use of this method is seen, for instance, in the statement made in the Anglo-Saxon Chronicle that in 488 Oisc succeeded to the Kingdom of Kent and reigned for 24 years; the date of his accession having apparently been calculated back from the death of Æthelberht, which was recorded by the church to the very day (24 February 616) when it occurred.[3] Obviously there was room for error in this method; and certain discrepancies in the Wessex regnal list, which appears as a preface to the Parker manuscript of the Chronicle, have been used by Leslie Alcock to suggest that very little trust can be put upon it in general.[4] There is, however, little cause to question the date calculated for Oisc's accession, since the years of Æthelberht's reign, 56 according to Bede,[5] must have been accurately known and noted at the time of his death, and this takes us safely back to 560, within some fifty years of the reputed end of Oisc's reign and seventy-five of its beginning. In this case, therefore, the latitude for error would have been small. The entry for 488 provides us with at least one reliable and valuable point of reference, which can be used to take bearings on the surrounding events. In Kent the calculation of regnal years may have gone no further back than Oisc, since the fact that the Kentish royal line named themselves after him suggests that it was he who was regarded as the true founder of the kingdom, a culmination to the victories won by his father (or reputed father) Hengest; but Kenneth Harrison considers it likely that tradition would also have recounted the number of years, or the approximate number, by which Hengest's arrival in Kent preceded Oisc's accession.[6] There was certainly a tradition that 40 years separated Hengest's appearance from the departure of the Romans (*see* later).

In literate Christian communities, such as the British, who in the middle of the 5th century still regarded themselves as part of the Roman world and had maintained exiguous contacts with the continent, it had been customary to date events by reference to the Roman consuls of the time. In 455 a change in the method of calculating Easter introduced by Pope Leo prepared the way for a major innovation. Whereas previously the dates of Easter had been notified in Paschal epistles, in 457 a certain Victorius of Aquitaine produced a table giving the dates for every year from the Passion until his own time and calculating them into the future to complete what came to be known as a Great Cycle of 532 years, at the end of which Easter was found always to fall on the same day of the same month and at the same phase of the moon as at the beginning.[7] Not only did these tables provide an accurate temporal framework reaching back to the start of the Christian era (indeed beyond) and capable of being indefinitely projected into the future, but they could also be used in other ways. The complicated astronomical calculations by which Easter was fixed, together with the entries for the years, required tables of eight columns, against the first of which leap years were sometimes entered. The margin that was often left on the right hand side of the tables, and also (it has been suggested) the spaces on the left hand side between the entries for leap years, could be used to note important events which occurred during the year or interval of years as the case might be. Moreover Victorius' table also contained a list of consuls down to the year of its issue,[8] with the aid of which the dates of earlier events could be converted. Easter tables prepared in different monastic *scriptoria*, spanning different periods of years and recording different events, might later be brought together and the whole of the information combined in the forms of annals. How far, and when, advantage was taken of this system by the British is disputable, but it seems that early use was certainly made of it by the Christian Irish.

The Victorian tables were later supplanted by others prepared by a certain Dionysius Exiguus c. 530, which became standard in England after 660-670. These had two features of some significance to this part of our enquiry. First, they were originally constructed on the basis of Metonic cycles of nineteen years; five such cycles, from 532-626 inclusive, being calculated by Dionysius himself, and another five from 627-721 being added later, by which time the Great Cycle of 532 years originally reckoned by Victorius of Aquitaine had come to be adopted for the new system as well. Second, Dionysius took as his starting point for the Christian era not the Passion but the Incarnation, which meant that when earlier entries from a Victorian table were being collated into a later Dionysiac one there was a danger that the dates would be misplaced by 28 years.[9]

This framework of chronology provides us with a means to test and correct the accounts of the conquest given by the various historical sources. We can start with a few scraps of information by continental writers which throw some light on the events immediately preceding the arrival of Hengest. The *Life of St Germanus of Auxerre* written c. 480 by Constantius of Lyon, within only a short time of the Saint's death,[10] records two visits which he paid to Britain to combat the Pelagian heresy, in 427-8 and 445-6, during the first of which he led the Britons to victory with shouts of 'Allelulia', against a startled band of marauding Picts and Saxons, and during the second of which he was able to come and go unmolested, which suggests a tolerably settled state of affairs. In addition to this there is a brief entry in the *Chronica Gallica*, which was maintained in southern Gaul from about 380-452, recording that in 440-1 Britain 'passed into the power of' or 'was subject to the domination of' the Saxons.[11] This entry has puzzled historians because, on the face of the matter, it was manifestly untrue, and even if interpreted in a less sweeping sense than the words imply is difficult to reconcile, in point of date, with any of the other sources dealing with the conquest, or with the record of St Germanus' second visit to a country over which the Christian British still maintained control, however precariously.[12] Nevertheless it would be wrong to disregard the entry entirely; it seems that it must refer to some event which appeared of crucial importance at the time, at least to the chronicler, whose knowledge of Britain must have been confined mostly to the trade routes across the narrows of the Channel. This might have been a more than ordinarily destructive raid by the Saxon pirates, a rebellion by the German federates settled in the eastern parts of the country, or simply (as Kenneth Harrison has suggested)[13] a complete closure of the Straits to peaceful shipping, in which case St Germanus must have crossed the Channel farther to the west on his second visit. Unless all the other authorities are seriously mistaken it could not have referred to the coming of Hengest or to any systematic occupation of territory.

Of the native sources the nearest to the events is the *De excidio et conquestu Britanniae* written, at some time during the middle of the 6th century, by Gildas, a British monk, who says that he was himself born in the year of Mount Badon, so that much of what he was describing was recent.[14] He might, therefore, have been expected to make a good witness; but unfortunately the work is less a history than a prolonged diatribe directed against the misdoings of the British rulers of his own time, in which the English conquests are used as a terrible example of divine retribution. The language is contorted, and the narrative highly-coloured but hopelessly unspecific. The earlier part, which purports to deal with the end of Roman rule in the island, is so wildly mistaken as to be quite valueless,[15] and it is only as the writer draws near to his own time that information begins to appear on which it seems that some reliance can be placed. The story told is of how, after the departure of the Romans, the British were beset by a variety of enemies, chiefly Picts and Scots; of an unavailing plea for help made to the Roman commander in Gaul, Aëtius, during the period of his third consulship (446–54); of how, after this had failed, a leader of the Britons described simply as *superbus tyrannus*, or the 'pre-eminent ruler', called the 'Saxons' to his aid and settled them in the eastern part of the country; of how, having served successfully against the Picts for a time, these federates revolted and laid waste the land in a series of devastating raids which reached as far as the western ocean, in the course of which towns were sacked and large numbers of Britons slaughtered or enslaved; of how British resistance then stiffened under a certain *vir honestus*, Ambrosius Aurelianus: and of how eventually, after a period of alternating success and failure, the British victory of Mount Badon put an end to the Saxon advance and ushered in a period of peace which had endured until the time the account was written. This has been calculated, on internal evidence, to have been somewhere around 545, since reference is made in the work to a certain Maelgwn of Gwynedd, elsewhere recorded as having died of the plague in 549. The date of Mount Badon (and of the author's birth) is said, in an obscure passage, to have been 44 years either before, or after, some ill-defined event, which is best identified from the texts that have come down to us as that when the history was written. This would put the battle at around 500.[16]

Not only is this account almost devoid of detail but it is deficient in more serious ways. The chronology is left vague or inferential; no attempt is made to say who were the 'Saxon' mercenaries called in by the British to aid them, or where in the eastern part of the country they were settled; only one British leader, Ambrosius Aurelianus, is specifically named, and the English are left entirely anonymous; and we are not even told who were the protagonists at Mount Badon. These deficiencies Bede set himself to correct with information that was evidently derived mostly from English sources.[17] His great work *The History of the English Church and People* was completed in 731, and so some 250 years after the events described, but the traditions he drew upon appear to have been those extant in Kent at a much earlier time. He identifies the British ruler who enlisted mercenary help as Vortigern, and the leaders of the mercenaries as Hengest and Horsa who, he says, came to Britain at some time during the five year period beginning in 449 (correctly 450) when Marcian and Valentinian were joint Emperors, or perhaps during the seven years of Marcian's rule after he had joined Valentinian (who pre-deceased him). As to the date of Mount Badon, his interpretation of Gildas, it may be from an earlier text than has survived, is that it occurred 44 years after the arrival of Hengest and Horsa; but this dating would still place the battle around 500, though with a slightly earlier bias.

The Anglo-Saxon Chronicle, which, as we now have it, was compiled at the court of King Alfred at the close of the 9th century, and has survived in six variant texts, dates the coming of Hengest and Horsa in 449, goes on to describe four victories won by Hengest against the British, the last three in association with Oisc (called Aesc), and later records Oisc's accession to the throne in 488. Three other entries, dated between 477 and 491, recount the conquest of Sussex by the Saxon Aelle. Nothing whatever is said of Mount Badon. These and other of the earlier sections of the Chronicle are thought on internal evidence, such as the archaic case-endings and the pre-Alfredian forms of proper names which are sometimes used, to have been originally put together in Wessex during the latter half of the 7th century, following the introduction of the Dionysiac Easter tables.[18] While adopting the same starting point as Bede — the appearance of Hengest and Horsa — they continue differently to provide a more detailed account of what followed. Neither Bede nor the Wessex chronicler appears to have doubted that the advent of Hengest marked the first, and crucial, stage of the English conquest of Britain; they have nothing to say about the earlier German federates whom archaeological evidence shows to have been settled in parts of eastern England as much as fifty years previously.

We have to consider what trust can be placed, first, in the Chronicle's general account of events and, second, in its dating. The material must originally have come from sagas sung at the courts of the early English kings, and traces of this poetic level survive in the descriptions given of how the Welsh fled from the English 'in great terror' or 'like fire'. The crucial issue is when these oral traditions first came to be committed to writing. Obviously this might have happened in Kent at any time after the Christian conversion c. 600; but Kenneth Harrison has drawn attention to the possibility, hitherto curiously neglected, that it could have started as much as forty years earlier, on the marriage of the young Æthelberht, shortly before his accession in 560, to the Frankish princess Bertha, who was a Christian.[19] We know that Bertha was literate from a letter sent to her by Gregory the Great in 601 in which he refers to her as 'instructed in letters',[20] and she came to England accompanied by a bishop, Liuthard, with perhaps one or two deacons to assist him.[21] Some of the names handed down by tradition survive in forms which suggest very early written recording; this is true, for instance, of those of the British kings Conmail, Condidan and Farinmail, said in the Chronicle to have been killed in 577, and notably so of the version of Vortigern's name, *Uertigernus*, which appears in Bede's *Chronica Maiora*[22] — to which one might add that it seems doubtful whether the Chronicle would have preserved the memory of the two Kentish nobles Oslaf and Cnebba who fell in a defeat inflicted on Æthelberht by a Wessex army c. 568, unless these had been written down at the time, or shortly after, and in Kent. But whether the first records were made before or after the conversion, the accounts given in the Chronicle of Hengest's victories have a great deal of verisimilitude. As Stenton has pointed out, the archaism of the names of the various battles is itself an indication that tradition had been faithfully followed, without later attempts at improvement;[23] and, as we hope to demonstrate, the course of the campaign, as it can be traced in the Chronicle, is not only strategically plausible, but matches the archaeological evidence.

Since the two central figures around whom the early sagas revolve are those of Hengest and Vortigern it is particularly necessary to justify a belief in the authenticity of both, which not everyone would be prepared to accept without reservation. Although neither is named by Gildas, the form in which Vortigern's name has been handed down by Bede has helped to persuade even so sceptical a critic as David Dumville that he was, in fact, the *superbus tyrannus* of Gildas' account.[24] The evidence for Hengest's existence is still stronger. Even if we were to set aside the Anglo-Saxon Chronicle and the other early traditions preserved, for instance, in *Beowulf*, which have a cumulative force that it is very difficult to ignore, we are left with the genealogy of the Kentish kings, in which he appears as Oisc's father. This is given by Bede,[25] and there is reason to believe that the record from which he took it appeared as an accompaniment to the code of custom drawn up by Æthelberht c. 603, which was modelled on various continental codes that were prefaced by king lists.[26] Whatever legends may have accumulated around Hengest during the 150 years between the conquest and the preparation of this document, it is scarcely credible that a purely fictitious character could have been invented in that time. The most questionable point is, perhaps, whether Oisc was really Hengest's son rather than his younger collaborator and heir. The fact that the Kentish royal line called themselves Oiscingas is bound to raise this doubt. Bede's genealogy in fact speaks of 'Oeric, surnamed Oisc';[27] it was the surname that was perpetuated; and it may not have originated with Oeric but with some earlier ancestor, who appears nowhere among those assigned to Hengest, whose descent (in the tradition recorded by Bede)[28] was traced back three generations to Woden. The alliteration of names is a valuable clue to ancestry. That of the Kentish royal house shows a well marked regression as far back as Oeric or Oisc,* but not beyond him to Hengest. The doubt therefore persists. But even if Hengest was an adoptive ancestor of the Kentish kings they were in a true sense his heirs. The fame of the man would have been enough for them to wish to claim descent from him.

AETHELBERHT'S DESCENT (BEDE)

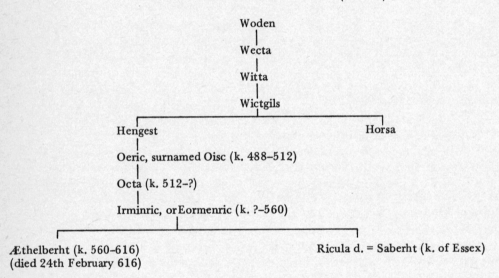

The dating is a more dubious matter. Here there are two major criticisms to be met. The first is that, assuming Gildas to have been right in saying that the appeal by the Britons to Aëtius was made during his third consulship, i.e. no earlier than 446 (and this statement seems to have rested upon direct documentary evidence),[29] then the dates given by Bede and the Chronicle for Hengest's arrival allow very little time for all the events which Gildas says occurred during the interval. It may, of course, be that Gildas got his account of events out of sequence, or that the various occurrences which he mentioned were not consecutive but over-lapped, some taking place in one part of Britain

---

* Oeric, or Oisc, was followed by Octa, and he by Eormenric. The later progression is shown in the use of diphthongs which in the Kentish dialect converted to *E*, e.g. Æthelbert, otherwise *E*thelbert.

and some in another;[30] but, even so, it seems that the Chronicle's date of 449 for Hengest's arrival must be too early, and that Bede's statement that it occurred during the joint *imperium* of Marcian and Valentinian is acceptable only if it is placed towards the end of that period, say in 455. It remains to be considered how the dates could have been calculated at all. On this, Kenneth Harrison has shown that it would have been a simple matter for anyone armed with the Easter table prepared by Victorius, with enough elementary knowledge of Roman affairs to distinguish which of the consuls listed in the early part of that table were also Emperors, and who was also conversant with the traditions preserved in Kent of the regnal years of its kings, extended back to include some estimate of the time which elapsed between Hengest's landing and Oisc's accession, to match this information and conclude that the landing must have taken place when Marcian and Valentinian were ruling.[31] This would allow a margin of five to seven years, and was unlikely to be wrong. Furthermore, since Liuthard must surely have brought an Easter table with him when accompanying the Christian bride Bertha into a heathen land, the reckoning could have been made within a few years of 560;[32] and it would still have been reliable even if it was not made until after the conversion, the factors being the same. But if this was one source it seems that there was also another; which was the tradition preserved among the English (and also mentioned by Bede) that the landing occured 40 years after the departure of the Romans.[33] It looks as though it was this that was drawn upon by the Chronicle in arriving at its date of 449, and it may also account for Bede's uncharacteristic error in citing that, instead of 450, as the date when the joint rule of Marcian and Valentinian began. Obviously, a round figure of 40 years applied retrospectively to an event of somewhat uncertain definition was unlikely to produce a completely correct answer; and that reached by the Chronicle appears to have been some five or six years astray.

The Chronicle also goes on, however, to ascribe exact dates to each of the subsequent battles. It seems curious, to say the least, that four out of five of the entries dealing with the conquest of Kent are spaced at intervals of eight years. It used to be thought that the cause of this apparent artificiality was that in converting the early traditions into Anno Domini dates and entering them into an Easter table use was made of the spaces on the left hand side of the table between the quadrennial indications of leap years.[34] Kenneth Harrison, however, disputes this theory.[35] While it is possible that the use of a rubricated B (for Bissextilis) to mark off leap years against the left hand column would have occupied sufficient space to create quite a large margin on this side, it is not clear why it should have been decided to resort to this rather than to a margin on the right, in which the entries could be fitted more exactly. Moreover, taking all the entries for the pagan period, the coincidence of the various events with leap years is no greater than might have been expected on a purely random basis. It seems more likely, on the face of it, that the spacing of the events was influenced by the practice of the English during the migration period of reckoning years in cycles of eight. But Kenneth Harrison questions this view also. It is not certain whether it was the eight or nineteen year cycle that was used at the time.[36] He suggests that the fascination of playing with figures is all too liable to lead people astray; that allowance must be made for historical coincidence; and that, once again taking all the entries for the pagan period together, the dates could be grouped in a variety of other ways so as to provide different, but equally plausible sequences.[37] Nevertheless, for the early part of that period, which is what now concerns us, the eight year sequence is pronounced. This is very much a matter for experts, but it does seem difficult to dismiss the matter as purely coincidental; and others, whose opinions are to be respected, have not thought it possible do do so.[38]

In recounting the victories of Hengest, and later of Aelle, the Chronicle was drawing upon sagas, and even if the events could have been remembered as occurring at exact intervals of years after the landing this is hardly a context in which one would expect to find such precision. Given the circumstances and the audience, it would surely have been enough to recount the battles in their order and to indicate the approximate span of time — say, four cycles of eight years — which they covered. When, much later, it came to assigning Anno Domini dates to these events, and entering them in Easter tables, the calculated date of Hengest's landing could be taken as the starting point and the subsequent events then tailored to the four cycles of years by some such expedient as assigning one battle to each, the first being put in the same cycle as the landing and the others at the very beginning of theirs, so producing the sequence of 449 (the landing), 455 (the first battle), 457, 465 and 473. This, or something like it, would serve well enough as a means of conversion. It follows, however, that not only would the spacing between the battles be unreliable but that if the chronicler had fixed on too early a date for the landing — by some six years, as it seems — then this error would work its way right through, and would be liable indeed to become exaggerated as a result of bringing the battles forward to the start of the cycles to which they had been assigned. This would explain the fact that the last reference to Hengest in the Chronicle, reckoned forward from the assumed date of his landing, is separated by what seems an unnaturally long gap of 15 years from the entry recording the accession of his heir Oisc, reckoned back from the death of Æthelberht on the more reliable basis of regnal years. But from beginning to end we are left with a sound enough framework of around forty years, within which the schematic dating of the Chronicle is not really a matter of great moment, and cannot detract from its value in recounting and ordering the battles.

We come now to the *Historia Brittonum*, a work which is supposed to have been compiled at some time at the beginning of the 9th century by the Welshman Nennius from a miscellany of earlier material. Among the elements that go to the composition of this work is what is sometimes known as the *Kentish Chronicle*, an elaborate account of the English conquest of that kingdom. If this could be trusted there would be little need for further enquiry; but not only is the story so lurid, and so romanticized, that it strains credulity, but the whole tenor of it is to blame the misfortunes of the British not upon any lack of valour on their part — far from it — but on the infatuation of Vortigern for Hengest's daughter and the foolish indulgence he showed to Hengest in order to win her hand, a weakness repaid with consummate treachery. It is the sort of tale that would create a very poor impression if presented by a defendant in a court of law; and most historians have treated it with the greatest scepticism, amounting with some to outright incredulity.[39] In recent years a determined attempt at rehabilitation has been made by John Morris.[40] It appears, however, that the raw material used in the *Kentish Chronicle* came from English sources, but was then worked over and elaborated — it would be fair to say doctored — to provide a version of events as favourable as possible to the British. The verdict on the matter must be that of David Dumville, who has declared that he, for once, is 'not prepared to write fifth-century British history on the basis of legends re-told from Anglo-Saxon sources by a Welshman in the ninth century'.[41]

Nevertheless, it would be wrong to dismiss the work entirely. It does seem, here and there, to have used scraps of material neglected in the much terser account of the Anglo-Saxon Chronicle; and there are certain facts woven into the narrative — the names of battles and of individuals — which, put in their proper place, acquire some significance.

Also appearing in the *Historia Brittonum*, but distinct in origin from the Kentish material, is an account of events leading up to Mount Badon, in which the legendary Arthur makes his *debut* as the victor in that battle and in eleven others preceding it;[42] and bound up with the whole is a set of Easter annals — the *Annales Cambriae* — prefaced by a number of chronological calculations. It seems that the annals were first collated at St David's towards the close of the 8th century,[43] but they reach back to the middle of the 5th. Leslie Alcock believes that the first of the constituent tables began to be constructed then, from which time the entries were contemporary with the events described, and that the chronological calculations, which deal with still earlier happenings, were a true and original introductory. The *Annales* make two references to Arthur, first as the victor of Mount Badon, dated by the order of years to 518, and then 21 years later as perishing with his enemy Mordred in the fateful battle of Camlann; but, unfortunately, textual criticism has shown that while most of the entries may well have been contemporary there were a number of later interpolations, including both of these.[44] We are still left, therefore, with an unverified legend, all the more questionable because Gildas, who was born in the year of Badon, made no mention of Arthur in connection with it, or at all, although he did name an earlier British champion, Ambrosius Aurelianus. A date of 518 for Mount Badon is in any case too late to square with Gildas' testimony, whichever way that is interpreted. Given that this entry is an insertion made from tradition, there remains the intriguing possibility (admitted by Leslie Alcock)[45] that when incorporating the record in a Dionysiac Easter table an error of 19 years may have been introduced by putting it in the wrong Metonic cycle; a form of confusion that is known to have occurred in certain of the early West Saxon annals.[46] The date could then be corrected to 499, which would conform with what Gildas says; and on Bede's reading of this, that the battle was fought 44 years after Hengest's coming, would anchor that firmly to 455. Taking all the evidence together, no more likely dates than these could be suggested for the two events.

The prefatory calculations have some interesting features, but are almost equally fallible. The most striking of them is one dealing with the coming of the English, which is calculated to have occurred in the 400th year after the Incarnation, in the fourth year of Vortigern's reign, and during the consulship of Felix and Taurus. The calculation is obviously mistaken in referring to the Incarnation rather than to the Passion, and the date should accordingly be corrected to 428, when Felix and Taurus were, in fact, consuls.[47] If the coming of the English is to be taken as meaning Hengest's arrival then the date is more than twenty years earlier than that adduced by Gildas, Bede and the Anglo-Saxon Chronicle, and impossible to reconcile with the record of regnal years of the Kentish kings, since it would ascribe an incredible longevity both to Hengest and to his successor Oisc. It now seems, however, that the calculation was not made in the 5th century but later, and was based upon a fundamental error which has been traced by David Dumville through the *Kentish Chronicle*, where it also appears.[48] We find here the statement that 40 years of terror supervened between the death of the Roman commander Magnus Maximus (a great figure in Celtic legend) and the arrival of Hengest, which would indeed date the latter to 428; the whole, however, being no more than a misrendering of the English tradition, used by the Anglo-Saxon Chronicle to fix its own date for Hengest's landing, that this occurred 40 years after the departure of the Romans — a very different matter. This error does not necessarily invalidate the next entry in the calculations which records that eight years after the coming of the English there was a 'dissension', or battle, between Ambrosius (? Aurelianus) and a certain Vitolinus, apparently at Wallop in Hampshire. We do not know from where this derives, but it would confirm that there was discord among the British at the very time that Hengest launched upon his conquests, and would square chronologically with Gildas's account of Ambrosius Aurelianus as the leader of the British in their rally against the invaders during that period of fluctuating fortunes which preceded Mount Badon.

It seems, therefore, that all we can take from the Welsh sources (Gildas apart) are a few garnishings to add to the straight-forward, if laconic, account in the Chronicle. The work done by Kenneth Harrison makes it possible to treat the story it tells as substantially true, if unreliable in the dating; and, as we have said, it accords with the archaeological evidence and is inherently convincing. Nevertheless, in tracing the course of the conquest we shall be entering an academic minefield. In taking Kent as our subject we have been left with no excuse for avoiding it.

We must start by going behind the written sources to those small groups of German mercenaries who are shown by archaeological discoveries to have been settled in the surroundings of Canterbury, probably during the second quarter of the 5th century. We have suggested in the previous chapter that these people were Jutes recruited in Frisia, but that most of them had only recently arrived there from their ancestral home-lands in Jutland to join earlier migrants who were already well established in the Low Countries. We must also return to the passage in *Beowulf* which deals, however ambiguously, with the first encounter between Hengest the 'Half-Dane' and the Jutes of Frisia. This looks like a prologue to the invasion of Kent, and it may well have been retailed in that way at the Kentish court. We have suggested, hesitantly, that in fact Hengest may not have been a Dane but one of that remnant of the Jutes who had stayed in their old lands and so come under Danish hegemony. If this were so a great deal that is otherwise puzzling in the story would fall into place. It is easy to understand the hostility nurtured by the Frisian Jutes towards their Danish supplanters, and so the treacherous attack upon the young prince Hnaef and his followers; but it is the ambivalent relationship between Hengest and the Jutes, first their enemy and later their leader in Kent, that is the heart of the problem, and this would be more easily explained if we could regard him as connected with them yet following a Danish lord, to whom he was bound by obligations of honour. Whether or not honour decreed that he should have died in company with Hnaef, it left no other excuse for surviving him than to avenge the killing,[49] and when, after a dark winter of brooding, that vengeance was taken it was in circumstances which themselves amounted to a treachery. After this we can well believe that it was as an exile, attended only by his war band, that Hengest first arrived in Kent; information which comes from a passage in Gildas that is clearly based on Kentish tradition, since it quotes the English word 'keels' in describing the three ships from which the party landed.[50] As an exile seeking mercenary service it was to Kent that Hengest would naturally have looked, Frisia having been the recruiting ground for the federates already established there; and they (we have suggested) were Jutes nearer to his own branch of the tribe than those who had recently been his antagonists.

Hengest was no ordinary mercenary, but a war leader of exceptional ability and boldness, and it is hard to believe that his continental reputation had not preceded him. It is not surprising that Vortigern should have been eager to employ him. C. F. C. Hawkes has suggested[51] that this was prompted not only by external threats but by rifts among the Britons themselves, in which the inheritors of the old Imperial tradition, like Ambrosius Aurelianus, were opposed by those rulers, like Vortigern, with a more primitive tribal background; that the plea to Aëtius had been made by the Roman faction in opposition to Vortigern's policy of relying upon the help of barbarous and undisciplined federates; and that the settlement of Hengest and his war band in Thanet was a counter move by Vortigern designed to guard against the possibility that Roman reinforcements might actually be sent to the aid of his rivals. The antagonism between Vortigern and Ambrosius Aurelianus is emphasized in the *Historia Brittonum.*[52] This is not a reliable source, and it had every reason for trying to disassociate Ambrosius Aurelianus, the patriotic hero of Welsh tradition, from Vortigern, the dupe and villain; but (as we have seen) some colour is given to the story of internal feuds by the entry in the chronological computations annexed to the *Annales Cambriae* which recounts the 'dissension' between Ambrosius and Vitolinus — whoever he may have been. If, however, 455 was the date of Hengest's landing there could then have been no danger of intervention by Aëtius, who had been murdered in the previous year. Gildas says that the Picts were the enemy against whom the federates were recruited; but, while this may have been true in general, it is very doubtful whether it was so of those whom Hengest joined in east Kent, which, pre-eminently, was an outpost against continental foes.[53] It seems that the threat to be warded off must have been from German pirates, which means that nowhere was there a greater danger of treachery and collusion.

The Anglo-Saxon Chronicle says that it was at Ebbsfleet that Hengest landed.[54] The tradition that he and his companions came in three 'keels' need not be regarded as exact, but merely as conveying that the party was a small one. It is, however, instructive to consider what the tradition implied. We can form some idea of the size of the vessels at this time from the remains of one, dating approximately from the close of the 4th century, that has been recovered from a peat bog at Nydam, near the Flensburg fjord in Schleswig.[55] This was a long, low, narrow vessel, propelled entirely by oars and capable of carrying 50 people at the very most. It has been persuasively argued that the Nydam ship was built for use on the shallow and protected waters of the Baltic, and that the vessels which carried the German raiders across the North Sea must have mounted sails, as the Sutton Hoo burial ship may have done.[56] That was an altogether larger vessel, but it was constructed nearly 200 years after Hengest's time. Moreover Procopius, writing *c.* 550 of a war expedition from Britain to the mouth of the Rhine, goes out of his way to mention that the vessels has no sails.[57] Those Hengest used may have been stronger and more capacious than the Nydam ship, but even so it seems doubtful whether three of them could have accommodated more than 100 people, not all of whom would necessarily have been warriors since some wives and children may also have been included — and indeed probably were if this was a band of exiles. The difficulties of the sea passage in such small vessels emphasizes the need, before any large enterprise could be launched, of establishing a secure base where reinforcements could be assembled over a period; and it was just such a base that Hengest had been given, commanding the shortest crossing from the continent. Once such forces had been mustered it needed only that Canterbury should be secured to open up the route along Watling Street or (less directly) the Harroway, so putting the whole of Kent at mercy; and with Kent occupied London could either be taken or neutralized. It could not have taken long for a person of Hengest's opportunism to size up this situation.

According to the Chronicle, Hengest was accompanied by his brother Horsa, a far more dubious figure, who makes no appearance in continental legend and only a fleeting appearance in Kent, since he is said to have been killed in the first engagement there.[58] Kentish tradition preserved his name, which may also be commemorated in that of Horsted near Rochester (*Horsum Stydae*, 860-62),[59] and Bede says that a monument to him existed in east Kent.[60] The doubts arise partly because of the implausible association of the name Hengest, meaning a stallion, with that of Horsa, meaning a gelding, and partly from the very reference to a monument, which implies a literacy otherwise unknown in this company. Myres has suggested that a Roman monument in which all the letters had disappeared except *Hors* (from some such word as *Cohors*) might have been mistaken for such a memorial and used to give substance to a purely mythical figure.[61]

At this point there is one scrap of information from the *Historia Brittonum* to which some weight can perhaps be attached, since it has the appearance of having been based upon an English tradition omitted in the abbreviated account of the Chronicle. It says that among those whom Hengest summoned to him in Thanet were his son Octa [*sic*] and his nephew Ebissa.[62] In fact, Octa was not Hengest's son but his grandson, as appears from the Kentish king list cited by Bede[63] (he was also Æthelberht's grandfather, which is something that tradition would certainly not have got wrong). He cannot even have been born at this time. The point scarcely needs to be laboured, however, because it is clear that the *Historia* had confused him with Oisc, as it continued to do. At first sight the name Ebissa suggests a connection with Ebbsfleet, but this is illusory. The rendering of Ebbsfleet in the Anglo-Saxon Chronicle is *Ypwinesfleot*,[64] it next appears in a charter of 1038 as *Hyppelsfleote*,[65] and it was still known as *Heopwines fleot* in the 12th century;[66] so that it was several hundred years after the writing of the *Historia* before it assumed its present form (probably through a mistaken identification with Aebba, the first abbess of Minster in Thanet, to which in later years Ebbsfleet belonged). There is, however, another apparent echo of the name — given the frequency with which the consonants *b* and *p* were confused in early records. The battle of Aylesford, in which the Anglo-Saxon Chronicle says that Horsa was killed, is described in the *Historia* as '*Rithergabail* in British, or *Episford* in English'.[67] The British version of the name means 'Horseford'. Lieberman has suggested that this was a foregoing translation from the English with the substitution of *o* for *p* in the first syllable of *Episford* to produce *eoh*, which was the Anglo-Saxon for a horse;[68] but a simpler, and perhaps more likely, explanation is that the translation took the names *Ep(b)issa* and Horsa to be synonymous. It is not at all impossible that Ebissa (or something like it) was the true name of Horse, that being a nick-name acquired through connection with his brother Hengest, so that we are dealing with a real, and not a purely mythical, figure. As for the monument, a number of plausible explanations can be advanced; one being that the imposing prehistoric megalith at Kits Coty, overlooking Aylesford, came in Kentish folklore to be mistaken for a memorial erected to Horsa after the battle.[69]

There may also be a grain of substance behind the *Historia*'s tale that Hengest brought with him a daughter whom Vortigern married, giving Hengest lands around Canterbury in return for her.[70] Stripped of the accumulations of legend, there would have been nothing intrinsically implausible about such a marriage, since this was a common method of sealing alliances (and by German custom a bride-price would be expected); it is the use made of it in the account to blame almost all British misfortunes upon Vortigern's infatuation that strains credulity. The inference, however, is that Hengest had been put in control of those earlier federate groups stationed around Canterbury. The fact that the sites they occupied were either at, or close to, what later became the royal courts of Sarre, Faversham, Eastry and Sturry indicates that these were the bases from which the campaign of conquest was mounted. All the key points in north-east Kent had been made over to Hengest, except (it seems) the fortress of Richborough, where there are no traces of occupation by federates, but some by Romano-British forces. If Canterbury itself was not actually in his hands it was to be had for the plucking.

All that Hengest now needed to achieve the mastery of the richest lands in Kent, and a purchase for further conquest, was to reach an understanding with the forces under his command, to reinforce them regardless of British objections or misgivings, and then to seek a convenient excuse for a rupture. Gildas says that soon after the 'Saxon' mercenaries had been established they sent back word to the continent that Britain was a fertile country and the people cowardly, whereupon they were joined by a larger fleet and a great body of warriors.[71] What may seem remarkable (but is apparent from the evidence given in the previous chapter) is that the reinforcements who came over were the Frisian Jutes. How Hengest's quarrel with them was made up we do not know, but their kinship with the Kentish federates was, no doubt, a factor he was able to exploit. Frisia was well placed for the passage of forces to Thanet, and the bait held out to the Jutes sufficiently tempting to over-ride old enmities at a time when their own position in the Low Countries must have become increasingly uncertain. With the westward movement of the tribes the pressure along the Imperial frontier was constantly growing, but the way across it was blocked off by the Franks, menacing not only what remained of the Roman forces in Gaul, weakened by the death of Aëtius, but also the smaller German tribes driven by movements behind them towards the Rhine. There could be little future for the Jutes where they were, but exciting prospects in Kent, for whose richness and vulnerability they would not need to rely upon the testimony of Hengest alone, since they would have heard of it from their kinsmen already there, who had now joined with him in opening the door to them. It seems that, for all their past treacheries to each other, Hengest and the Jutes were fated, in the end, to come together in a common complicity.

Any account of the conquest of England must start with the realization that we are not dealing here with the sudden onsurge of whole tribes but with pioneering bands breaking an entry into new lands, reinforcing themselves and moving forward, with the steady influx behind them of the communities for whom they had prepared the way. It was, therefore, a slow process extending over a long period. Collingwood has estimated that the population of lowland Britain during the Roman occupation was in the neighbourhood of one million;[72] and, even if we allow for a decline in the years of anarchy preceding the conquest, at no time up to the defeat at Mount Badon could the English have been in any way comparable in number. A comparison of this kind nevertheless gives a misleading impression of a relative military strength. Not only, it seems, were the Britons disunited, but the mass of peasantry was not trained to arms,[73] as were the English ceorls. There was a limit to the number of men who could be effectively deployed in the warfare of the time. If at the outset Hengest had been able to muster one thousand experienced warriors, his own war band, the original federate groups and the newcomers, that would have been ample. The British forces met in the various battles are unlikely to have been much larger; we can dismiss as poetic hyperbole the Chronicle's accounts of the thousands who were killed.

The weapons used by the English are known to us from the early burial sites.[74] The ordinary warrior was equipped simply with a thrusting spear and a wooden shield with a heavy iron boss, useful for offensive as well as defensive purposes; and he might also have a stabbing knife, or *scramasax*. Nobles, or leaders, carried (as treasured possessions), long double-edged swords, sharply pointed at the tip and with little in the way of hasp or hand-guard, though the pommels were sometimes quite elaborately decorated. The Jutes, in particular, also made use of the continental javelin and the *francisca*, or throwing axe,[75] a typically Frankish weapon and one employed by them with often devastating effect. The only traces of bows and arrows also come from Jutish graves, at Chatham Lines, Eastry and Bifrons in Kent and at Chessel Down on the Isle of Wight.[76] Body armour and helmets make no appearance at this time, or later except in one or two royal burials, notably Sutton Hoo. Whereas the earlier Saxon raiders had been baulked by the fortifications of the Roman towns, Gildas tells us that these newcomers had learned the use of battering rams,[77] and the Saxon forces who conquered Sussex under the leadership of Aelle must certainly have had them in order to achieve their greatest feat of arms, the storming of the Roman fortress of Anderida (Pevensey).[78] The arms and equipment of the British appear to have been similar, saving such weapons as the *francisca* but there was one difference in the style of fighting. The English were adept seamen, but on land they fought almost entirely on foot; Procopius goes so far as to say that horses were unknown to them.[79] By contrast, there is sufficient evidence from the early British sagas, like *Y-Gododin*,[80] that the Britons, or certain of them, were accustomed to fighting with the sword from horse-back, and this is likely also to have given them some advantage in mobility.

It took time for Hengest's plans to mature. The Anglo-Saxon Chronicle, though astray in its dates, may not be far wrong in allowing six years between his arrival and the eventual outbreak. The occasion for this, Gildas tell us, was a dispute over provisions.[81] The British had not contracted to maintain the mass of fighting men whom Hengest had brought over for his own purposes. It is an indication of their weakness that they had been prepared, for so long, to support an ever growing force which they must have realized had become a menace to their own security; but they had only to demur for Hengest to seize upon the pretext. When the outbreak did occur it seems that the greater part of Kent, including all the richest agricultural lands, fell to the Jutes virtually without a blow being struck; there is no indication that Canterbury was taken by storm, and nor would it have needed to be. With its loss the Britons had no hope of defending the line of the Stour, even if forces could have been mustered in time. For Hengest the advance to the west lay along the route either of Watling Street, to the north of the Downs, or of the prehistoric Harroway to the south of them, and by whichever way the river barriers of the Medway and Darent had to be surmounted before London was reached.

It seems that the southern route was the one first chosen and that resistance was met, exactly where it might have been expected, at the Medway crossing near Aylesford, where the Chronicle tells us that the first battle was fought and Horsa was killed. It does not say in so many words that this was a victory, but that is clearly implied in the statement that afterwards Hengest succeeded to the kingdom with his son Oisc — who is not mentioned as having fought in the battle but was associated with Hengest in all those that followed. According to Kentish tradition, relayed by Bede, Oisc had been with Hengest from the very beginning,[82] but if so he must still have been a child at the time of the landing and had only now come to fighting age. On the alternative view that he was not Hengest's son but his adopted heir he must be seen as a young leader of the Frisian Jutes. Certainly the settlement of the kingdom, the task which he inherited, was on pronouncedly Frisian lines.

The battle of Aylesford confirmed the conquest of those lands, including the Medway valley but extending no farther west, that are archaeologically recognizable as Jutish Kent (page 25 above). When the advance was resumed it was with the aid of new allies, and after a pause which may have been considerably longer than the two years appearing from the artificial chronology of the Chronicle. It tells us that the next battle was fought at a place called *Crecganford*. Although there has been some reluctance among place-name scholars to accept that this was Crayford the site is named in the *Historia* as *Derquentid*, that is the Darent, and so supports the common-sense identification, considering the close proximity at Crayford of the two major crossings of the Darent and Cray used by Watling Street.[83] This was the best defensive position left to the British along the northern line of Hengest's advance. Nevertheless, they suffered an overwhelming defeat, from which, the Chronicle says, they fled to the shelter of London. The significance of the battle was not only that it completed the conquest of Kent — it did far more than that — but that it was fought in an area later marked by Saxon burials of a kind also encountered well to the west in Surrey. It therefore shows, for the first time, the enlistment of help from the Saxons, with whom Hengest and the Jutes were to work in close co-operation for many years after. It seems that this particular branch of the people were those who later became known as the Middle Saxons. While it is to Middlesex that they have left their name, the greater number of their settlements lay south of the river, partly in Kent but mostly in Surrey, which means simply 'the south region', a description that establishes the early connection with Middlesex.[84] The Surrey lands remained part of the Kingdom of Kent for more than two hundred years, and although by the middle of the 6th century Middlesex (with London) had come under the rule of the East Saxon kings this seems to have been on the sufferance of Æthelberht, who treated London very much as his own fief (page 116 below). The Middle Saxons, although recognized as a distinct people, appear never to have established a kingdom of their own, but to have remained for many years clients, or subjects, of the Eskings, uniting with the predominant Jutes to form the nation of the Cantware.

Even when we discount the Chronicle's story of the 4,000 British killed at *Crecganford*, it is clear that the battle was a major catastrophe for them, which left the remnant impotently cooped up in London. It is improbable that the City was ever taken by storm, or we should have expected some account of it to have come down to us; most likely it was left to rot away, isolated and impoverished, until the revival of continental trade, and the coming of Christianity, led to its reoccupation by new masters. There was little in the surrounding lands to tempt settlement but the river seems to have been crossed, and lands occupied without molestation, quite soon after the battle. Pottery of an early type has been found along the Middlesex bank of the river, including, at Hanwell, some of specifically Kentish (or Jutish) design.[85] The effects of the victory, however, went much wider than this. With London masked the whole of the Thames was opened up to new bands of Saxon adventurers, upstream as well as down. There is no reliable information by which to date the foundation of the Kingdom of Essex; we first learn of it towards the close of the 6th century when it was existing, as it had probably always done, in the shadow of Kent; but whatever, and whenever, the origins of the kingdom itself there is archaeological evidence of 5th century settlement (admittedly sparse) both in Essex and Hertfordshire.[86] Far more important for the future, a considerable number of Saxon settlements, which can be dated to the last half of the 5th century, were founded on the upper Thames around Dorchester. Whether this area was approached by the Thames or from the Wash along the Icknield Way (as E. T. Leeds believed) has been the subject of much debate. There is archaeological evidence for both, and it seems likely that the routes converged.[87] The example of triumphant land taking by Hengest and his followers was contagious, and the victory at *Crecganford* appears to have inflicted such crushing losses on the British as to have undermined the whole of their defences in the south-east, so precipitating a massive eruption from the English settlements which had been building up around the Wash.

It is impossible to know how many years separated the engagement at *Crecganford* from the next, which the Chronicle calls *Wippedsfleot*; it says eight, but that is purely schematic. This battle is the most difficult of all to place, first in its site and then in the sequence of events following *Crecganford*. A *fleot* was an estuary, and *Wippedsfleot* has a suspicious similarity to *Ypwinesfleot*, which is the Chronicle's rendering of Ebbsfleet. It is true that the Chronicle speaks of the two as though they were separate places and derives the name of the battle from a certain Wipped, who is said to have been killed in it; but that was the sort of expedient to which it was inclined to resort to account for place-names which it found otherwise unintelligible (later connecting Portsmouth, for instance, with an individual called Port and the Isle of Wight with a certain Wihtgar, although the names of both clearly derived from the Roman, *Portus* in the first case and *Insula Vectis* in the second).[88] It looks as though tradition had handed down two references to Ebbsfleet, both garbled, and the Chronicle had failed to put them together.

The identification is strongly supported by the description given in the *Historia*, which is 'the inscribed stone by the Gallic sea', the whole context suggesting that it was near Thanet, and probably at Richborough. The *Historia*, indeed, claims the battle as a great British victory, the culmination of a triumphant counter-attack, as a result of which Hengest and the Jutes were driven out of the country entirely. It is then left with the difficulty of explaining how, after all, this achievement was undone and Kent and the surrounding lands passed permanently into the hands of the invaders. This it contrives, first, by reviving the story of Vortigern's infatuation for his wife and consequent insane indulgence towards Hengest, and second by recounting an elaborate tale of a conference between the two sides, to which the Jutes came with daggers concealed beneath their cloaks, and at which they massacred all the British chieftains except Vortigern, whom they took hostage, extracting from him the surrender not only of Kent but of

Sussex, Essex and Middlesex as well. This is pure myth-making, and worse. The judgement must be that of the eminent French historian Ferdinand Lot, who says, roundly:[89]

> 'That there is no historical basis for these assertions is evident. We are not even in the presence of popular legend. The author pursues his romance.'

Nevertheless there are again certain grains of fact that can perhaps be sifted from the account. The lurid tale of treachery and massacre may contain echoes of the earlier seizure of Canterbury by the federates who had been expected to guard it. The story of Vortigern's enforced surrender of territory is at least significant in suggesting that Essex and Middlesex were lost to the British at very much the same time as Sussex, which appears to be true.

The English, so far from regarding *Wippedsfleot* as a defeat, commemorated it in their sagas and boasted of the number of British chieftains killed in it. It may nevertheless seem puzzling in the order of events (and a gift to the myth-makers) that the battle should have been fought so far to the rear, close indeed to the site of the original landing in Thanet. The likely explanation is that the westward advance of the Jutes had left certain pockets of British survival, notably around the massive stronghold of Richborough, surrounded by tidal waters and marsh, and that just as 25 years later the Saxon conquest of Sussex culminated in the storming of the old Roman fortress of Anderida, so in Kent the destruction of the British remnant who had taken refuge in Richborough constituted the final, mopping-up, operation of the campaign. The late presence of British forces in Richborough is indicated by the discovery there of the distinctive belt buckles used by those forces during the period of isolation and self-defence; a number of which found their way, presumably as spoils of war, into early Jutish cemeteries surrounding Richborough at Sarre, Bifrons, Ash and Dover.

This engagement, although it put the seal upon the conquest of Kent, was an interruption in the main course of events. The Chronicle records that, following it, 'Hengist and Aesc fought against the Welsh and captured innumerable spoils, and the Welsh fled from the English like fire'. No battle is named, and it looks as though we are concerned here not so much with a single encounter as with a whole series of devastating raids, such as Gildas describes, which were carried out from one end of the country to the other, as far as the western ocean, accompanied by massive slaughter and destruction.[90] The Cantware cannot have been the only ones concerned in this; the evidence is of a general breakout of the English from their bases along the east coast. While the Cantware may have co-operated from time to time with other roving bands, there appears, at this stage, to have been no concerted plan of campaign. Hengest is not credited by Bede with the *bretwaldaship*, or supreme command, of the English forces, such as was later assumed by Aelle of Sussex,[91] but seems merely to have been fighting his own hand. It does not follow that there were no set-backs; if there were we should not expect the Chronicle to have mentioned them. Indeed, it is presumably in this period that we should place that first, notable, British victory said by Gildas to have been won by Ambrosius Aurelianus. If, as the chronological computations associated with the *Annales Cambriae* say, his early activities as a military leader had been centred upon Hampshire this would help to account for the persistent British occupation of this seemingly exposed area for another 40 years, until well after Mount Badon. It seems, however, that whatever land seizures may have been made by others, the Cantware themselves were now bent not so much on occupation as on plunder. What loot they picked up from the raids it is difficult to say, though some pieces have been found here and there, such as a bronze box of purely classical design unearthed with Roman coins from a warrior's burial at Strood.[92] We may guess that the object of the raids was, as much as anything else, to lift stock and to furnish the farms in Kent and Surrey. For Hengest they were a fitting culmination to a long career of warfare and adventure; for Oisc a prelude to the more serious work of fashioning an ordered settlement out of the confusion of land taking. In 488, we are told, Oisc succeeded to the kingdom. We know nothing of the last few years of Hengest's life, but more than thirty years had elapsed since he first came to Thanet. If — as it appears — he arrived in the country an already seasoned fighter he must have been over sixty when he died; and Oisc himself would have been entering upon middle age.

Shortly before Hengest's death and Oisc's accession there began the second major episode in the conquest of southern England, the foundation of the Kingdom of Sussex by the Saxon Aelle and his three sons. The Chronicle says that they first came to Britain in 477 in three ships, landing at Cymensora, which has been identified as The Owers off Selsey Bill, where they defeated the Britons and drove them into the Wealden forest. Eight years later a further battle was fought, and five years after that, in 491, the Roman fort of Anderida was taken with the slaughter of all its occupants. This suggests a campaign which cleared Sussex from west to east and extended over a period of 14 years, during which, no doubt, reinforcements were steadily being built up. That it should have taken the course it did, instead of turning westward from Selsey into Hampshire, is again suggestive of the firm British defence that appears to have been established there, perhaps under the leadership of Ambrosius Aurelianus. The dates given to the events are open to all the usual reservations, but there is some reason to believe that they may not be far off the mark. While cremation burial is not altogether unknown in Sussex,[93] inhumation was the usual practice there, which suggests that this body of Saxons had not come directly from Germany but had been in contact with Frankish influences; and the same is suggested by the presence of material of Frankish origin in early inhumation burials at the two large cemeteries of Alfriston and High Down.[94] There is a reference by Gregory of Tours to the presence of Saxons near Angers c. 463, and place-name evidence indicates that during the early period of the migrations some bands had established themselves along the northern coast-line of Gaul.[95] During the latter half of the 5th century these Saxon enclaves would have been exposed to the pressure of the advancing Franks. It looks as though Aelle and his followers may have been constrained by this to transfer their activities across the Channel.

With the conquest of Sussex the stage was set for the final campaign, culminating in the battle of Mount Badon. The position in south-eastern England on the eve of that campaign was that two kingdoms, Kent and Sussex, had been firmly established; that settlements had been made around London and on the north bank of the lower Thames that were later to form the nucleus of the Kingdom of Essex; that others had been thrust out into the upper basin of the Thames around Dorchester, but had not yet been forged into a kingdom; that the largely Anglian settlements around the Wash had been extended along the waterways, and in particular the Ouse, so as to link with the Dorchester area; and that pockets of British resistance had been left, not only in Hampshire, but probably also in less accessible and attractive areas, such as the Chilterns and north Essex. The period of uncoordinated pillaging and destruction was drawing to a close; the English forces were about to be drawn together under a single acknowledged leader.

On the British side the story hitherto had been one of almost unmitigated disaster, relieved only by one or two victories achieved under the leadership of Ambrosius Aurelianus. But out of this constant adversity a more resolute generation had emerged, led, so tradition says, by Arthur. As we have said, the section of the *Historia* which recounts Arthur's exploits appears to be based upon different sources than those dealing with Hengest, Vortigern and the conquest of Kent, but there is nothing to show how early they are.[96] Once the entries in the *Annales Cambriae* have been set aside as late interpolations there remains no other reference to Arthur which can be regarded as at all contemporary except a passing comment in the late 6th century saga *Y-Gododin* in which he is used as the standard of comparison for a warrior; and it has been suggested that even this may have been written in later.[97] Perhaps the best argument for his authenticity is that such a mass of legend could hardly have accumulated around nothing; but whether, after stripping all the encrustations away, we should be left with the victor of Badon is another issue. Happily, it is one on which we can afford to remain neutral. From the standpoint of Kentish history it is the fact of the battle that matters, not the identity of the British leader.

Gildas describes Badon as a siege, evidently of a hill-top, and very likely (or so some believe) one that was defended by old entrenchments. It has been suggested that the English rendering of the name, including a reference to an encampment, would have been *Baddanbyrig* or *Baddanburg*, and so Badbury. No fewer than five Badburys are known, ranging from Dorset to Lincolnshire, but two of these lie close together in the area of the upper Thames, near Faringdon and on the downs overlooking Swindon, of which the second, or rather the encampment dominating it at Liddington, is the site favoured by Hodgkin.[98] As against this it has been argued that in British parlance the *d* in Badon would have been pronounced *th*, rendered in Anglo-Saxon by the symbol *đ*, and that the site was near Bath, which the Anglo-Saxon Chronicle names as *Bađancaester* in an entry under 577.[99] Either way, the battle can be seen as the parrying of an English advance south-westward from their settlements on the upper Thames with the object of gaining the Severn valley; and since it was the British who were strategically on the defensive, and in command of the ground, the assumption must be that it was they who were besieged, and broke the containment.

Who exactly were the English leaders in this battle is debatable. John Morris says that Oisc is the only English king directly stated to have fought in it;[100] but this comes from no better source than a 12th–13th century Welsh romance.[101] The *Historia*, for what it is worth, implies that the chief opponent of the British was Octa, whom it persists in confusing with Oisc. The relevant passage is one which first records Hengest's death and the succession of Octa [*sic*], and then begins the next sentence with the words, 'Then Arthur fought against them in those days . . .'.[102] Leslie Alcock believes that there is a disjunction in the text here, marking the end of the *Kentish Chronicle* and the start of the section recounting Arthur's exploits (which he credits); that 'them' in the second sentence of the passage was not intended to refer to the Kentish royal house, but to the English in general; and that the south-eastern kingdoms were unlikely to have been involved at all in a battle fought so far from their own homelands.[103] Other considerations apart, his final conclusion ignores the *bretwaldaship* of Aelle (attested by Bede), a position which implied an over-all military command over the English and could not have been achieved merely in the conquest of his own kingdom. It also ignores another consideration to which Myers has drawn attention; that is, the apparent coincidence of Badon with the abrupt decline of Sussex from a position of supremacy to one of such complete obscurity that over the next 200 years we do not know even the names of the kings who succeeded Aelle.[104] While Kent suffered no such absolute decline it was not until seventy years after Badon that it again made any showing as a military power; the battle appears to have coincided with a marked shift in the policy of its kings away from further adventures in Britain to a fostering of its continental connections, the attitude being one of defence and consolidation.

It is difficult to believe that the groups of Saxon settlements on the upper Thames, which had not yet been welded into a kingdom, could have launched on their own such a major military expedition as was crushed at Mount Badon, or that the battle should have inflicted such a check on the whole course of the English conquest, and have had such reverberations, if these had been the only contestants. Everything suggests that this was a combined enterprise undertaken under the leadership of Aelle at a time when archaeological evidence shows a particularly close association between the kingdoms of Kent and Sussex.[105] In such circumstances it is very likely that Kentish forces would have taken part, but much less likely that they would have been led by Oisc, who must have been around fifty at the time and lived to reign for at least another twelve years after the battle. They might have been led by the young prince Octa, or perhaps — since Bede's genealogy traces only the direct ancestry of Æthelberht, disregarding any cognate branches of the royal line — by another of Oisc's sons, who did not survive the event. But there is little to be gained by speculations of this kind. Whether or not the Cantware were present at Badon (as they probably were), and although they had less at stake in the battle than others (their own homes now being far removed from the theatre of operations) the outcome was bound to affect the policies of a kingdom uncertainly poised between military adventure and a more settled mode of life.

Of the battle itself we know only what the British sources tell us, which is that for three days and nights Arthur carried the cross of Christ upon his shoulders (the *Annales Cambriae*) and that 960 men fell in a single day at his hands alone (the *Historia Brittonum*). Although these statements are capable of being rationalized,[106] and need not of themselves destroy belief in the historicity of Arthur, they certainly do nothing to promote it. All that can safely be said is that the battle was a disaster for the English, and that the slaughter must have been very great. That Aelle was killed in it is highly probable; he drops completely from sight, with the eclipse both of his dynasty and of his kingdom. But, overwhelming though the British victory may have been, it was still not enough to cancel out the previous defeats, or to recover more than a relatively small part of the lost ground. It won the British a long period of peace, or at least immunity from major onslaught, which lasted until the offensive against them was resumed by Ceawlin of Wessex during the last quarter of the 6th century, when Bath was at last taken and the line of the Fosse Way over-run (*see* pages 90–91 below). Archaeology shows a disruption of the pottery sequences in the Saxon cemeteries along the upper Thames,[107] which suggests a period of acute peril and disturbance. But the settlements there do not appear to have been entirely eliminated; they remained to be forged, some thirty years later, into the Kingdom of Wessex, which henceforward became the front of the English advance towards the south-west. There are also signs of a recession by the English towards their bases around the Wash with some recovery by the British of the middle ground between there and the Thames; and the expansion of the settlements in Middlesex and Essex appears to have been checked.[108] The unity of the English was shattered and the *bretwaldaship* lay in abeyance for 70 years, until Ceawlin revived it. But if English power was disrupted by defeat, victory brought no lasting concord to the British; Gildas' account is eloquent of continuing trouble and dissension.

Whatever blood-letting the Cantware may have suffered at Badon, their own kingdom was put under no serious threat. The prestige of the dynasty had not been invested in a battle in which the chief part had been taken by others; Oisc's rule had become firmly established; and the people were left in the enjoyment of the rich prize which Hengest had won for them. It is true that his appearance in Kent was no more than a continuation of a long period of mercenary employment, settlement and infiltration, but this does not in any way diminish his achievement. The conquest of Kent was different from everything that had gone before; a systematic occupation of territory, from which there emerged the first of the English kingdoms, a society knit by common obligations of loyalty and observing a common custom. The triumph of the Jutes was bound to act as an example to others, and the effect of their victories in destroying the defences of the British around London exposed the whole of the south to the gathering strength of the invaders. When every allowance has been made for Bede's partiality towards the Kentish royal line, which introduced Christianity to the English, for the dynastic propaganda that flourished on this, and the reward it earned in the written preservation of old traditions that may have been lost elsewhere, it still remains difficult to deny that Hengest's coming marks the one sure beginning of the history of the English nation.

Chapter Three

THE SETTLEMENT: *c.* 488–512

Oisc

THE INSTITUTIONS AND CUSTOMS that distinguished Kent developed organically from the first settlement of the country, when some order had to be imposed upon the confused land-taking that must have accompanied its conquest. This was the task which fell to Oisc, who was remembered as the true founder of the kingdom; and he brought to it conceptions familiar in Frisia and the Rhineland, from which the bulk of the folk came — a continuity of Jutish custom, but adapted to a new environment. The warriors whom Hengest led were the harbingers of a much larger migration which cannot have been completed until Oisc's time; and Hengest himself was an adventurer, whereas Oisc stands out as the first of a long line of Kentish kings more noted for their statecraft. It is fitting that they should have called themselves by his name. This was an uncommon, not to say outlandish, one; and although it was correctly rendered by Bede it had, by the time that the early traditions came to be written down in the Anglo-Saxon Chronicle, been changed into the more familiar Aesc, which fitted into the alliterative sequence adopted by the later Kentish kings. It was a peculiarity of the dialect to convert such diphthongs as Æ into E (as happened with Æ (E)thelberht),[1] so that in this roundabout way the royal line of the Oiscingas, so named by Bede, was transmuted into the more euphonious form of the Eskings,[2] which has been used in this work.

We are dealing with an evolutionary process. The system we shall describe took perhaps two hundred years to achieve its full definition, and was then already beginning to change into something different. But precisely because this was an evolution, with continental antecedents, the germs of the system must have been present in the first settlement, and there is indeed good evidence to show that they were. The institution which provided the framework for all else was the lathe, a province of the kingdom formed around one or another of the primary settlement areas — a river valley, say, or a littoral — typically containing within its boundaries tracts of downland pasture and of marsh, and having its own allotment of Wealden forest. Each of the lathes centred upon a royal court, which was also a small vill or township, but otherwise the settlements were loosely grouped on the better soils and consisted of individual farmsteads, or at most hamlets, surrounded by their own arable fields. There was a tripartite division of land. First, there was the king's own demesne, kept and worked on his behalf; second, there was the *inland*, which was part of the royal estate let out to tenants, whom we have identified as the *laets* of Æthelberht's laws; and, third, there was the *outland*, occupied by the free ceorls in their own right. With the arable holdings there went the use of meadows, pastures, marshes and woods, the *inland* tenants being accommodated in those belonging to the king, and the occupants of the *outlands* having their own provision. Both groups owed certain rents and services to the king (and to him alone) but these were far from onerous, even for the *laets*.

The bulk of the evidence on which we have to depend in order to reconstruct this society is not contemporary with it. It has been necessary to retrace the evolutionary process, working back from Domesday Book. The picture that emerges is clear enough, and the developments shown are consistent; but to say that the essential features of the system already existed at the beginning of the 6th century requires justification, when written records did not begin until a hundred years later, and the various diplomas and land grants, which provide the most direct evidence of all, cannot be relied upon until about seventy years after that. The diplomas ascribed to Æthelberht and to his successor Eadbald are plainly spurious,[3] although they may (indeed probably do) rest upon true tradition.[4] There is, however, at least something to be gleaned from one of them, which purports to record the grant by Æthelberht to St Augustine's Abbey in 605 of the 'vill' of Sturigao or Cistelet.[5] Although the document itself is a later concoction the names are authentic enough and survive in those of the present day villages of Sturry and Chislet, both of which were early possessions of St Augustine's. In their original forms they appear to represent alternative names for a lathe — the Stour *ge* or province — of which it seems that Sturry was the eponym and must once have been the royal court; and the fact that the name of this lathe came later to be changed so as to refer not to Sturry, or to the Stour, but to Canterbury (*Burh-ware-let*) emphasizes the antiquity of the earlier description because it implies that it originated before the revival of Canterbury, which was itself a direct consequence of St Augustine's mission. The surrender of Sturry by the king at the time when Canterbury was reoccupied would certainly have precipitated the change. The probability is that it did, in fact, occur in Æthelberht's reign, even if the charter we have is a fabrication made to authenticate a claim known to be just but incapable otherwise of being documented.

This reasoning would carry the lathe back into the 6th century. It is not decisive, but it is indicative. So, too, is the structure of the lathes, as they can first be traced (Map 2), which shows every sign of antiquity; and this is even more true of the structure of the Wealden commons associated with them, which were merely extensible corridors of advance into a no-man's-land of forest aligned upon the Roman roads and prehistoric tracks that traversed it, and with Roman roads also used to mark off the woods belonging to the king from those devoted to the free ceorls of the *outlands*.[6] These, however, are the least of the indications. The archaeological evidence is both clearer and takes us further back. We have described how the very earliest of the heathen cemeteries, dating from the reign of Oisc, were either at, or clustered closely round, what are later known to have been royal courts forming the nuclei of lathes (page 28 above). Faversham, Eastry, Milton Regis, Sarre, Lyminge, Wallington (in Surrey) and Sturry itself are all clearly marked out in this way, and the later spread of the cemeteries points up other courts, such as Wye. Jolliffe has demonstrated how the essential characteristics of the Kentish lathes, each with its allotment of forest land, was transplanted to the Jutish areas of south Hampshire, occupied from Kent in the immediate aftermath of Oisc's reign, and how in the Meon area in particular other features of the Kentish land system — scattered hamlet settlement, comparable obligations in rents and services, and comparable rights, for instance of wardship — survived side by side with the very different Saxon system introduced with later Wessex rule.[7]

Finally, there is the intriguing analogy with Sussex, where the *rapes* constituted the nearest approximation to lathes to be found outside Kent, and where other Kentish features appear, if only intermittently and in a somewhat rudimentary form.[8] The Hastings area is a special case, because there is good reason to believe that this remote and forested country was actually pioneered from Kent at some time in the middle of the 7th century (Chapter 7, page 138 below); but although the Kentish characteristics are especially marked in this part of Sussex they are by no means confined to it. Exactly how this came about is a mystery. There is no reason to doubt that — as Bede says[9] and the name demonstrates — Sussex in general was an area of Saxon settlement, so it seems that the Jutish features in its land system must somehow have been acquired after its conquest through contact with Kent. But Sussex became the most isolated and backward of all the English kingdoms, screened from Kent by the great wilderness of the Weald, and there was only one period in the whole of its early history when its relationship with Kent is known to have been at all close. This was at the very beginning, in the period preceding the battle of Mount Badon, when Aelle and Oisc were reigning and archaeology shows an intimate connection between the two courts (page 27 above).* While it is impossible to be dogmatic, it does look as though the initial settlement of Sussex was modelled to some degree upon that of Kent, the earlier established of the two kingdoms, and that traces of this persisted through the long period of isolation that followed — another indication, added to that from Hampshire, that the model already existed in Oisc's time. Jolliffe may have gone too far in speaking of the 'Jutish South-East',[10] but the intermingling of Jutish with Saxon features in Sussex does suggest a strong Kentish influence during the first, formative period.

It would be foolish to suggest that during Oisc's reign there was already a precise demarcation of the lathes and commons; that the distribution of land between the king, his tenants, and the ceorls had been neatly accomplished; or that rents and services had been consistently standardized. That would imply an intimate knowledge of the remoter areas of the country, and a degree of administrative competence, which cannot have existed then. It seems, for instance, that the Wealden commons started as little more than frontages from which the forest could be penetrated,[11] and it is improbable that exact boundaries had yet been drawn between the lathes across the Downs, marshes and woodlands which separated the main settlement areas from each other. It is a prototype with which we are dealing, and in order to uncover that we must start from the five lathes which existed in the middle ages. At the Norman Conquest there had been seven — Sutton-at-Hone (near Dartford), Aylesford (near Maidstone), Milton Regis (near Sittingbourne), Wye (near Ashford), Canterbury (called *Borowart*, i.e. *Burh-ware-let*), Lyminge (near Folkstone) and Eastry (near Sandwich) — not only smaller in size but more closely adapted to the topography of the country. There is clear documentary evidence for at least two previous combinations. Although Domesday Book included Faversham in the lathe of Wye it remained a royal manor, and a charter of 850 shows that, at that time, it had its own wood in the Weald.[12] Hollingbourne although it had now been combined with Aylesford, was described as a lathe in a document *c.* 975

---

* Æthelberht, as high king, must have been paramount over Sussex, but we know of no dealings which he had with it, and it was not until 70 years after his time that it became Christian — a signal mark of its isolation.

apportioning responsibilities for the upkeep of Rochester bridge.[13] This, however, takes us only part of the way. It seems that when Kent was still independent the number of lathes had been greater still and that topography was then paramount.

The progressive amalgamation of the lathes had been accompanied by a change in their character from agrarian into judicial and administrative units. The further we reach back into the Jutish era the more the administrative paraphernalia is shed until the lathes emerge each as a single vast agricultural estate centring upon a royal vill and with the king as the sole lord.[14] The change from the primitive system began with the Christian conversion, that is early in the 7th century, when the need to endow the Church led Æthelberht and his successors to make grants of land to the various religious foundations, the rents and services of the occupants being transferred at the same time; and this was followed, especially during the period of Mercian supremacy in the 8th century, and later when Kent had lost its independence, by similar grants to lay magnates. As the ecclesiastical and lay estates grew in number and size benefactions were sometimes made to the Church by nobles as well as the king, or lands were acquired by exchange or purchase. Within each of the lathes, therefore (except, as it happens, Milton Regis where few grants were made and the old order persisted almost intact) there came to be built up a multiplicity of lordships encroaching upon that of the king. Already by the beginning of the 9th century this process had been taken a stage further through grants made by the great lords to their own followers, or through parts of their estates being entrusted to the management of different stewards. From this there emerged the manors surveyed in Domesday Book: and as the lands which remained in the king's own lordship were whittled away they, too, took on the appearance merely of royal manors. The original unitary estates had been completely fractured; but the very complexity of the manorial system, coupled with the growth of public business, left a place for the lathes as judicial or administrative entities.

Nevertheless, certain features of the old system remained fossilized in the new. In particular, the distinction between *inland* and *outland* holdings persisted; the occupants' obligations were still fundamentally the same, although now mostly owed to the manorial lords and not to the king; and the same methods were employed for assessing them. These methods were certainly in use at the beginning of the 8th century, when they were well known to Bede,[15] and they had clearly been devised — or formalized — while the old order was still largely intact, we believe during the latter half of the 7th century. The principle was not confined to Kent, but the expression it took there was unique. It rested upon the notional entities of the *sulung* and the ploughlands.[16] We call these 'notional' because while each, theoretically, was supposed to denote the amount of land that could be worked in a year by a full plough-team of eight oxen, the values given to them — 200 acres in north-east Kent and from 160 to 180 acres elsewhere[17] — were far in excess of what a plough-team could actually accomplish, which seems to have been around 100 acres;[18] and because the individual units departed widely from the norm, so that four *sulungs* at Chislet, for instance, had actual acreages of 200, 185, 75 and 27[19] — although this seems to have been an extreme example and others can be set against it, such as the eight *sulungs* at Reculver, which had acreages varying only between 201 and 213.[20] But, most of all the reckoning was artificial because it bore almost no relationship to the actual land holdings, but constituted a purely fiscal mesh spread across them.[21] From each of the *sulungs* or ploughlands certain defined rents and services were due, and the occupiers, few or many, shared these obligations between them. Because, despite their description, these were units not of measurement but of account, they could be adapted to the fertility of the soil, or to other local factors, to produce the variations we have described. It is probable, nevertheless, that, within a lathe, the conventional figure represented a near average of the individual units. In Thanet, for instance, there appear to have been about 120 ploughlands, nominally of 200 acres each (Appendix C), and Hasted, writing at the end of the 18th century, says that the island then contained something under 27,000 acres,[22] a close enough approximation considering the amount of land that had been gained from the shrunken estuary of the Wantsum.

The terms ploughland and *sulung* are synonymous (or nearly so) since *sulh* is the Anglo-Saxon for a plough; a grant of land on Romney Marsh made in 774 by Offa of Mercia, during his period of paramountcy in Kent, refers specifically to 'three ploughlands which the Kentish people call three *sulungs*'.[23] Nevertheless they were, or came to be, differently applied. Ploughland was the generic term used for agricultural land as a whole, without distinction of tenure, but *sulung* came to be used selectively for the *outlands* only, that is for the free holdings of the ceorls.[24] Both standards are used in Domesday Book, though there are certain gaps in the record of ploughlands. Allowing for these it appears that in Kent there were, at the time of Edward the Confessor, around 3,000 ploughlands, of which 1,225 were also *sulungs*, i.e. about two out of five. The reason for the double computation was that purely public obligations, as distinct from the ordinary run of rents and services, were imposed exclusively on the *outlands*.[25] They included, for instance, the payment of *geld*, a national levy, and the upkeep of bridges, duties which had originally been substituted for, or connected with, military service; and this had been the traditional responsibility of the otherwise privileged ceorls, who as freeholders had a direct landed stake in the fortunes of the country.

All else apart, these assessments throw a revealing light upon the early structure of the lathes. The significant feature that impressed Jolliffe was that the number of *sulungs* scattered between manors in each of the Domesday Book lathes were found, when added up, to come to a round figure, or within a fraction of one;[26] a clear indication that the distribution predated the manors and was made at a time when the lathes had still been largely intact in royal possession. The system, it seems, had been to assess each of the lathes in a round number of *sulungs* and then to distribute these among the *outland* holdings, or groups of them, with due regard to size, productivity and other factors, leaving the occupiers of each *sulung* to bear the obligations corporately. The totals for the various Domesday Book lathes appeared to Jolliffe to be made up in multiples of 80, which could be separated out so as to produce a pattern of eleven earlier lathes each with an assessment of either 80 or 160. To achieve this result he had to assume that the most western of the lathes had lost land to Surrey (implying that the original apportionment was made when Surrey was still part of the Kentish Kingdom) and to engage in some difficult juggling with the figures, particularly in north-east Kent and the Medway area. Although his division conforms to such early documentary evidence as we have — for instance of the original independent status of Faversham and Hollingbourne — and to our knowledge of the royal vills, there are some dubious elements in it which suggest that his insistence that the original assessments were made always in multiples of 80 is too inflexible. He appears, for instance, to have been misled by the assessment of 80 *sulungs* given in Domesday Book to the royal manor of Milton into believing that the manor was identical with the lathe, the whole of which he assumed to have remained intact in the king's possession; whereas a closer study shows that not only were there four additional *sulungs* held from Milton manor itself but that some parts of the lathe had been granted away — at Newington, for instance, and at Tunstall — and if these are taken into the calculation the total for the lathe is found to be increased to almost exactly 100. This is a difficult method of approach and Jolliffe's arithmetic can be faulted at a number of points;[27] but it certainly seems that the *sulungs* were distributed in round figures, and it is probable that this also applied to the generality of ploughlands (as instanced by the example of Thanet: see Appendix C), although the gaps in the record leave only a hint of this.

It looks as though the assessments on which Jolliffe relied, and which remained embalmed in Domesday Book, date from the 7th century. A comparable system, based upon a unit known as a *hide*, was used in the other English kingdoms, and Bede in describing the conquest of Anglesey and the Isle of Man by the Northumbrian king Edwin (616–632) was able to cite the hidage of both, according, he says, to the English reckoning.[28] It does not follow (*pace* Finberg)[29] that the system already existed in Edwin's time, since Bede was speaking for his own, a hundred years later. More to the point is that the first written records of land grants in which reasonable confidence can be placed, and which date from 674–5, already deal in terms of *hides* for land under Mercian control and of ploughlands in Kent;[30] and by the close of the century this had become common form. The distribution of *sulungs* in Kent, as Domesday Book shows it, not only reflects a period before there had been any significant development of the lordships but, as Jolliffe noted, it seems also to have been made at a time when Surrey — or east Surrey at least — was still a part of the Kingdom of Kent, which it ceased to be on the death of Hlothere in 685, or very shortly after (*see* pages 160 and 164 below). In keeping with this, the Weald is left almost entirely outside the calculations, as virgin common land; except, significantly, that some *sulungs* and ploughlands appear where the Medway emerged from the forest south of Maidstone, and others are to be found along the Chart hills on its northern fringe, for instance around Sutton Valence. There are also a few on Romney Marsh, showing that a start had been made in consolidating it and putting it down to the plough. If this spread of settlement is compared with the distribution of the early forms of place-name, especially those ending in *-ham* (pages 84–86 below) and *-ingas* (pages 136–138 below) it again suggests a 7th century date, and one rather nearer to the end of the century than to its beginning. This takes us a long way back, but still 150 years short of Oisc's time; and it cannot therefore be assumed, without further evidence, that the pattern of lathes revealed by the assessment had gone unchanged since then.

A different approach can be used to test, or correct, Jolliffe's conclusions, and this has been attempted in my own work, *The Jutish Forest*. The method here is the indirect one of first identifying the Wealden commons, and then seeing what light they can throw upon the structure of the lathes to which they originally belonged. The commons are specifically mentioned only in a few of the early documents, mostly of the 8th century, which provide clues to the general position of only four or five of them. It can, however, be demonstrated that the developments in north Kent by which the lathes were progressively broken up into lordships, and those into manors, were mirrored in the Weald by the division of the commons first into large 'sub-commons' serving the various lordships and ultimately into a host of manorial dens, or swine pastures. By identifying these dens and the manors to which they belonged — for which there is ample evidence — it is possible not merely to reconstruct the commons but to define, with a good deal of precision, the areas of north Kent to which they were attached; leaving uncertain only the position in the far east and north-east where the lathes were too distant from the Weald to have had commons there.[31] There are certain scraps of Wealden evidence which help to fill even this gap in our knowledge. For instance the juxtaposition of Tenterden, deriving from the *Tenet-ware* or Thanet folk,[32] with the den of *Burwarsile*, deriving from the Canterbury folk — a deliberate expression of anti-thesis[33] — strongly suggests that Thanet was once a lathe separate from Canterbury, to which Domesday Book unites it: and other evidence can be found to support this (Appendix C).

Nine distinct commons emerge from this study, including one which appears originally to have served a lathe straddling the border between Kent and Surrey, a striking con-firmation of Jolliffe's conjecture. In the simplicity of their design, and the governing influence upon it of the Roman roads and iron tracks, the commons show unmistakable signs of age; they appear to take us back to the very foundation of the kingdom. The lathes to which they belonged are also well delineated, and account between them for the whole of upland Kent except for the north-eastern corner. But this area, between Canter-bury and the coast, was the cradle of the kingdom, where other clues to the identity of the lathes abound; and these help us to complete the picture by adding three more lathes, those of Eastry, Thanet and — a little more dubiously — Barham (or Kingston), which was based upon the valley of the Little Stour (Appendix C). The pattern, as the Map shows it, differs from Jolliffe's in a number of ways but can be reconciled with this method of calculation subject to one significant modification; which is to substitute for his assessments of 80 or 160 *sulungs* to a lathe a wider range (though still in round figures) of from 60 to 220. As can be seen, the lathes varied considerably in size, some being at least three times as large as others. Throughout, topography was the governing factor. Each of the lathes formed naturally around an area of primary settlement with the royal court at its centre; and all were then gathered together into the unity of the kingdom. In this they bear as clear a stamp of antiquity as the Wealden commons which were coeval with them.

Those commons were valuable partly for fuel, but chiefly for the pannaging of swine, which were sent there in the autumn to fatten on acorns and beech-mast. Equally important to the economy of the lathes was marshland for keeping sheep, which were the source, not only of wool and mutton, but of milk for cheese-making.[34] The lathes abutting upon the Thames had ample marsh within their own boundaries; but some, such as Wye, were land-locked, and it seems that the Wantsum marshes between Thanet and mainland Kent were insufficient for the populous lathes surrounding them. These were catered for on Romney Marsh and along the Rother levels, on a system which appears to have been very similar to that adopted in the Weald. Romney Marsh proper, that is to say the land lying to the north of the old sea defences of the Rhee Wall (which follows the general line of the road from Appledore to New Romney)[35] appears to have been partly reclaimed in Roman times, though still subject to frequent flooding; the bulk of Walland Marsh to the south of the Wall was not recovered until the 13th and 14th centuries; but, further to the east, tracts of marsh had built up behind the protective

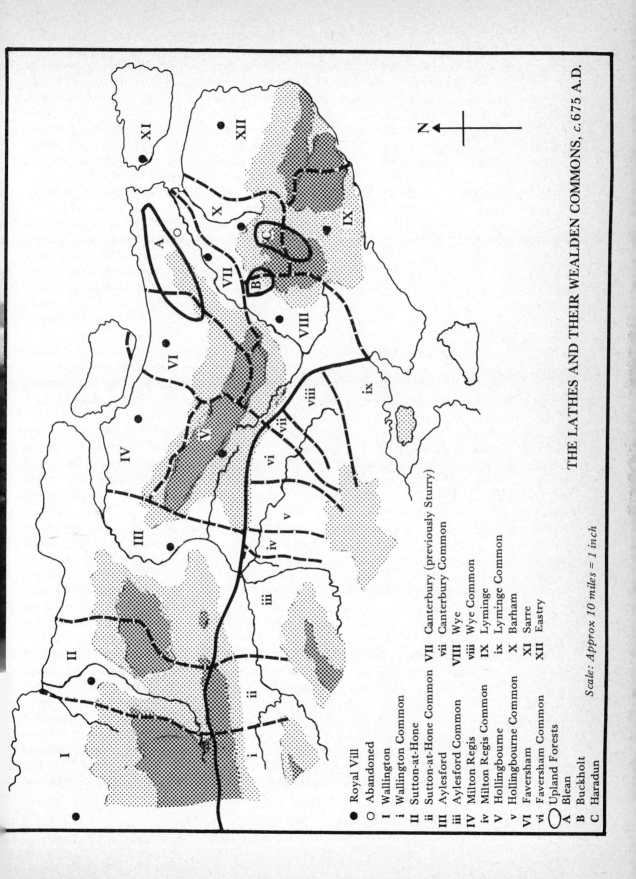

Royal Vill
Abandoned
I   Wallington
i   Wallington Common
II Sutton-at-Hone
ii Sutton-at-Hone Common
III Aylesford
iii Aylesford Common
IV Milton Regis
iv Milton Regis Common
V   Hollingbourne
v   Hollingbourne Common
VI Faversham
vi Faversham Common
    Upland Forests
A   Blean
B   Buckholt
C   Haradun

VII Canterbury (previously Sturry)
vii Canterbury Common
VIII Wye
viii Wye Common
IX   Lyminge
ix   Lyminge Common
X   Barham
XI   Sarre
XII Eastry

THE LATHES AND THEIR WEALDEN COMMONS, *c.* 675 A.D.

Scale: Approx 10 miles = 1 inch

shingle banks of Dungeness. Because of the inundations and shifting channels of the
Rother, it is more difficult here than in the Weald to trace the boundaries of the old
lathe commons; nor is there the same plenitude of written evidence. No detailed study
of the subject has yet been undertaken, and any conclusions must be tentative. It does
seem, however, that Romney Marsh was segmented in much the same manner as the
Weald; Lyminge lathe having the use of the lands on the east, lying to either side of where
the Dymchurch Wall now stands[36] (the sea has encroached here);[37] the Canterbury folk,
or *burh-ware*, occupying the middle segment, including Burmarsh, which takes its name
from them;[38] and the inhabitants of the Little Stour valley the westernmost segment on
an arc netween Ruckinge (which had very early connections with Ickham)[39] and
Appledore (which appears as an appendage of Adisham in 1006).[40] The Rother Levels,
surrounding the Isle of Oxney, seem to have been allotted to Eastry lathe, judging from
the amount of land later held here by the great manors of Eastry and Wingham.[41]
Finally, there is a charter of 858 which mentiones the *wi-ware-wics*, or dairy farms of
the men of Wye, in an area which has been identified between Ivychurch and New
Romney;[42] and the royal manor of Wye was paramount over Denge Marsh.[43]

The original character of the lathes as unitary estates stands out clearly from the Map.
Each of them was, in effect, a self-sufficient agricultural entity. This can be illustrated
from four examples taken from different parts of the country. The lathe of Aylesford
was formed upon the lower Medway valley; its arable lands and meadows lay mostly
along the course of the river and on the peninsula of Hoo at its mouth; it had downland
pastures and woods to either side of the valley, marshes along the Thames, and its own
forest common in the Weald directly to the south. The lathe of Faversham lay behind
the estuary of the Swale; its arable lands were concentrated on the rich brick-earth soils
threaded by Watling Street; it had ample marshes on the estuary and a deep hinterland of
down; and although it was separated from the Wealden forest it was nevertheless given
its own common there, in the area of Headcorn.[44] The lathe of Wye was situated, and had
the bulk of its arable and meadow lands, on the gathering grounds of the Stour; it, too,
had its share of down pasture above the Stour, and a Wealden common at its threshold;
but it had no coastal marshes, a deficiency remedied by giving it the use of sheep pastures
at the south-eastern tip of Romney and behind Dungeness. The small lathe of Barham
on the Little Stour was also land-locked, and although well provided with arable, meadow
and downland pasture, barely touched upon the northern marshes and was too far distant
from the Weald to have a forest common there; but it, like Wye, was given sheep-runs
along the Rother, and in default of a Wealden common made use of the local forests
of Blean and of *Haradun* (now Hardres), which it bordered.[45] We have here four varieties
of what was still essentially the same model. Each of the lathes was, to all intents, self-
supporting, and it was only in times of disturbance or war, when the concerns of the
kingdom transcended all others, that its inhabitants would have cause to look beyond it.
Although it would be too loose a description to say that the Kingdom of Kent was a
federation, it had a good deal of that character. It was an association of distinct groups of
folk — the Wi-ware, Tenet-ware, Limen-ware and the rest — acknowledging a common
custom and authority.

At the hub of each of the lathes was a royal township. In the early days the kingdom
had no single capital; public business — such as it was — was transacted when 'the king
called his people to him' (Æthelberht's words)[46] at whichever of the lathe courts he was

visiting or which happened to be most convenient for the purpose. Although the kings might have their own favourite residences — such as Faversham appears to have been for much of the 6th century[47] — the royal entourage was constantly on the move from one court to another. Apart from the need of the king to show himself to the people, the necessities of the royal household could be best met by visiting each of the estates in turn and living off its produce — that is, off the yield of the demesne lands, which the tenants of the lathe had some share in working, and off their rents, which, to begin with, must have been paid entirely in kind, since it is not until the end of the 6th century that we find the first signs of a money economy. Even in the early days the king's entourage must have been considerable, consisting of his family, servants and personal slaves; certain indispensable craftsman, such as smiths;[48] and well-born companions, including the band of young warriors with whom all the leaders of the time were expected to surround themselves and to entertain generously, and most of whom, no doubt, came from the class of hereditary nobility, the *eorlcund* men of Æthelberht's laws.[49] Because of this constant movement the courts had to be sited at places which were not only nodal to their own lathes but provided good communications between each other. All were therefore close to Roman roads or to the prehistoric Harroway, which followed the southern scarp of the Downs, and, since any bulk movement of goods was more easily carried out by water than by land, most were also upon estuaries or navigable rivers.

While the structure of the lathes was simple, their internal anatomy was not. We have said that the fundamental distinction was between the *inland*, which was the king's own estate, part of it being kept as demesne and part let to tenants, and the *outland*, which consisted of freeholds occupied by the ceorls in their own right. Only in the Weald was the division neat and clear-cut. Here it can be shown that the royal woods — the *snoad* of early charters, a term surviving in such place-names as Kingsnorth — formed a broad band along the northern perimeter of the forest, the freehold farmers making use of the commons deeper in.[50] In north Kent the king's estate lay widely scattered throughout each of the lathes. One reason for this was that the king required for himself and his tenants not only arable land but also meadows, marshes, woods and down pastures, which were often to be found only at a distance from the vill — hence the numerous Kingsdowns, Kingswoods and Kingsnorths surviving in Kent, with complementary references in early charters to *mons regis, silva regis* and the synonymous *cyninges-snade* or *fihrde*.[51] But the arable fields were also mingled, demesne, *inland* tenancies and *outland* holdings inter-locking in a complicated mosaic; and this is best explained in terms of an initial, largely uncoordinated land taking in the wake of the conquest upon which a form of order was later imposed. Despite the apparent confusion there are features of the distribution which give us at least some inkling of what happened.

There were, in the first place, notable concentrations of *inland* around the royal vills, a phenomenon clearly revealed in the Domesday Book assessments of those manors that incorporated the vills and remained at the core of their respective lathes, and of which some still belonged to the king although others, such as Wye and Lyminge, had over the course of time been granted away to the church. The test cannot be applied in any discriminating way to Milton Regis because here the manor survived, not as the kernel of its lathe, but as virtually the whole of it; nor to Sarre, which never emerged as a separate manor; nor to Eastry, where the assessment is incomplete, the number of ploughlands being unrecorded. In every other case we find that the proportion of *sulungs* to ploughlands was low, and in most very markedly so; in other words that these manors were unusually deficient in freeholds. The extreme example is Dartford (with Sutton-at-Hone) which contained 40 ploughlands but only one and a half *sulungs*, and so must have consisted almost entirely of demesne and *inland*. The same appears, on a smaller scale, at Aylesford, with 15 ploughlands and one *sulung*. At Faversham and Hollingbourne the feature is less pronounced, but in both the proportion of *sulungs* was below the average. It stands out strongly at Lyminge and Wye which each had only seven *sulungs*, compared to 60 ploughlands in the first case and 52 in the second. And one among a number of reasons for believing that Kingston near Canterbury was once the royal vill of a lathe — as its name implies — is the great preponderance of *inland* at Barham to the one side of it (32 ploughlands to six *sulungs*) and Bishopsbourne to the other (50 ploughlands to six *sulungs*).

A detailed comparison between the ploughlands and *sulungs* brings out another feature with great clarity; that is, the extent to which, beyond the immediate vicinity of the royal vills, the *sulungs* were concentrated in the richest agricultural areas of the country, cleared and cultivated in Roman times (*see* map, page 83). Whereas, over Kent as a whole, about two-fifths of the ploughlands constituted *sulungs*, in Thanet and on the north-eastern wolds* the average was around two-thirds; the same was true of the Medway valley from Rochester as far south as Malling and round almost to Wrotham; along the Thames shore-side from Faversham westward to Plumstead the average was well over a half†; and the peninsula of Hoo seems to have consisted of *sulung-land* entire. The Stour valley conformed to the normal proportion of two-fifths, but the Downs (including the Elham valley) fell well below it. The clearest contrast, however, is provided by Holmesdale to the south of the Downs. In the Folkestone area only one ploughland in three was a *sulung*; this proportion diminished steadily westward until the Medway was approached; beyond which it dropped to as low as one in five around Otford and on the Surrey border. To a quite remarkable extent the incidence of the *sulungs* reflects the relative fertility and tractability of the land.

Although we have suggested that the distribution of the *sulungs* did not become crystallized until the 7th century, by which time some adjustments had no doubt been made, the bias remained very much as one would expect it to have been in the immediate aftermath of the conquest. During this period, it seems, the royal courts were set up at particularly favoured sites, and the lands immediately surrounding them taken by the king; leaving the kindred groups of fighting men, under their *eorls* or other leaders, to take their pick of the rest, which then constituted the *outlands*. This initial, haphazard, phase of claim-staking would still leave a large residue of workable land, which would include a few pockets on the better soils, but would lie mostly beyond them, on secondary soils or in less accessible areas, where only a few, sporadic, freeholds had been established. This residue could be used by the king to settle as his own tenants those later arrivals from the continent for whom the fighting men had cleared the way, or strangers (including perhaps a few Britons) who in one way or another had attached themselves to his cause; while some of the choicer remnants might be converted into

---

* In Eastry lathe there are serious gaps in the record of ploughlands; but the incidence of *sulungs* was certainly very high and the figures we have show only a little less than a two-thirds proportion.

† There is no record of the number of ploughlands in Milton lathe, but the number of *sulungs* — 100 in all — is considerable for the size of the lathe, which contained in Sheppey large areas of tidal saltings.

demesne to supplement the king's own resources or to serve as appanages for the royal *athelings* — brothers or grown sons of the king — who would have their own households and need the means to support them. (Finglesham near Eastry, which means 'the prince's settlement'[52] and is the site of an early and rich cemetery,[53] seems to have originated as an appanage of this kind). This large residuum, consisting mostly of tenancies but with some demesne embedded in it, would then constitute the bulk of the *inlands*.

Within each of the lathes some early apportionment, however rough and ill-defined, would have to be made between the woodlands, marshes and pastures to be used, in the one part, by the king and his tenants and, in the other, by the freeholders; a division which (as we have said) can be seen at its simplest and most primitive on the northern fringes of the Weald, where the scarp of the Chart Hills and certain stretches of Roman road lent themselves as convenient boundaries.[54] As, later, the plough began to encroach upon these marginal lands — a process well in train by the 7th century — the new, scattered, clearing or innings would inherit the status of *inland* or *outland* as the case might be. And, finally, towards the close of the 7th century the introduction of the fiscal assessments of ploughlands and *sulungs* would not only formalize the rents and services due from the different classes of occupier, but in doing so would require precise boundaries to be set between the lathes. Of course, there is a great deal of supposition in all this, but it fits such evidence as we have and seems true to the circumstances of the time.

It is difficult to gauge the extent of the demesnes in the 6th century. We know a good deal about those of medieval Kent from such studies as have been carried out by Du Boulay of the archbishop's lands[55] (an excellent sample since nearly a quarter of Kent was then within the lordship of Canterbury, which had lands in every part of the county); from the examination of particular manors, such as Wye;[56] and from royal inquisitions undertaken into others, such as Folkestone, in the reigns of Henry III or Edward I.[57] A valuable indication is also given by Domesday Book, which records for each manor the number of ploughs kept on demesne as compared to those in the hands of the peasant occupiers. Allowing for considerable variations from place to place, it seems that at the time of the Norman Conquest something like 22½ per cent of the arable land was in demesne. The evolutionary process by which the lordships and manors emerged from the earlier unitary lathes makes it tempting to suggest that most of the demesne lands existing then had been inherited, in direct line, from the Eskings; but it is clear that a great deal of it had, in fact, been created later. The margin between demesne and tenant land could quite easily be shifted, in one direction by increased lettings and in the other through the forfeiture of holdings in default of rents and services, or by taking in those that fell vacant, as many must have done in the devastation wreaked upon Kent during the Mercian wars at the close of the 8th century and in the Danish raids that followed. New arable demesnes could also be created out of the superfluity of royal woods and pastures, or the purchase by a lord of *outland* holdings, which were freely saleable, to form the nuclei of the numerous small manors which had come into being by the time of Domesday Book.

Particularly revealing here is the contrast shown in Domesday Book between the position in Milton lathe, which had kept its original boundaries, and the hundred of Eyhorne, neighbouring it to the south, which had once composed the lathe of Hollingbourne. It seems that in the first little more than five per cent of the arable was in demesne, but in the second nearly 35 per cent. Milton was old settled land and almost the whole of the lathe was still contained in a single royal manor, centring upon the vill; here, more than anywhere in Kent, the ancient order had persisted. Hollingbourne lathe had been formed upon the valley of the Len, a narrow strip of open country dominated by the high Downs on the one side, and on the other bounded by the broad expanse of the Chart woods, merging into the Weald; it had been broken up into a medley of manors, many of them very small and based upon footholds won upon the Downs, or more especially in the Chart, which was royal forest; and it was in these, rather than in the larger manors of the vale, that the highest proportions of demesne lands were to be found. Obviously a great deal of new demesne had been created in this area, most of it on small patches of land cleared from the royal woods, and so disposable in such a way. There may have been an actual shrinkage of demesne in Milton, but nevertheless the proportion of just over five per cent of total cultivated land is probably as good a representative figure as we can hope to get for the early days of the kingdom. It follows that the great bulk of arable *inland* was then held by tenants, who in most parts (though by no means all) must have outnumbered the select body of freeholders.

In seeking the character of these ancient demesnes we have no inventories that are the least contemporary to help us; but at the core of certain of the larger and more venerable of the medieval manors we find what appears to have been a common pattern, which can be exemplified from the once royal manor of Wye, where we should expect to see a continuity. The arable demesnes here lay close to the vill in a number of compact open fields, frequently adjoining each other, and of anything up to 100 or 150 acres each; solid blocks of land that might have been the rump of yet larger fields but could not easily have been put together by piece-meal acquisition (though some later accretions may perhaps be detected in the smaller fields, and crofts of a few acres apiece associated with them).[58] We may take this as the prototype; though much of the same model is to be found elsewhere, for instance in a number of the archbishop's manors, and at Folkestone,[59] of which we first learn *c.* 635–640 when King Eadbald founded a monastery there for his unmarried daughter Eanswith — a somewhat unusual royal appanage (*see* page 128 below). The lay-out of the arable in a few large, or very large, fields was the most efficient that could be devised to give ample room for the working of the plough-teams while at the same time allowing for the rotation of the staple crops, cereals and pulses, with periodic fallowing.

The rents and services owed to the manorial lords in medieval times had been inherited with the *inland* and *outland* holdings incorporated in the manors, and were still governed by the fiscal assessments devised centuries earlier when only a few grants had been made to the church and the great mass of the people were answerable to no other lord than the king. One modification was made shortly after Domesday Book when the growth of population, and the consequent fragmentation and multiplication of the holdings, suggested that a finer fiscal mesh was required than that of the ploughlands and *sulungs*. This was supplied (except in north-east Kent, where the old régime persisted) by dividing the original units into quarters, which were thus notionally of 40–50 acres each,[60] although the actual acreages again departed very widely from the norm. In the case of the *sulungs* these fractions were known as *yokes*, a term which had already made some appearance in the early charters[61] and seems to have been adopted by analogy with the single yoke or two oxen which formed a quarter of a full plough-team. For other ploughlands, occupied by those who had now come to be called *inmen*,[62] a variety of descriptions was used, such as *logi* at Gillingham,* but sometimes the term *yoke* was employed as well, with the distinction that these *yokes* were said to be 'servile',[63] that is, were in the nature of copyholds rather than freeholds. This is as convenient a distinction as any to employ, and we propose to do so.

The rents and services exacted in medieval times from the yokes, free and servile, were rooted in immemorial custom; so deeply rooted, in fact, that although they varied in detail from place to place they still remained essentially the same in substance and scale from one end of the county to the other. As the old rentals show, the customs prevailing at Sundridge near the Surrey border[64] were plainly of the same stock as those at Gillingham in mid-Kent,[65] at Wye further to the east,[66] at Northbourne on the Straits of Dover,[67] and on the manors of the archbishop and of St Augustine's Abbey, wherever situated.[68] This is in keeping with Jolliffe's belief that the customs derived directly from the ancient Jutish society of Kent; in support of which he assembled a mass of evidence from the early charters and laws and continental analogues.[69] Of course there had been some evolution, though less than might have been expected. It is when one comes to identify and examine the changes that the outline of the original system stands out in all its simplicity.

The free yokes (or outland holdings) of manorial times were so termed because the occupiers could sell or devise their lands without leave, what remained on a man's death being equally divided between his surviving sons (or daughters in default of them). The lands were held by independent title. It was strictly in keeping with this principle that a man's holding descended to his heirs even when he had been executed for felony, and that the wardship of heirs vested not in the lord (as was the general practice) but in the nearest relative who did not directly benefit from the inheritance.[70] Moreover an outland tenant could be distrained for failure to fulfil his ancient customary obligations only through the complicated process known as *gavelate*, by which the lord had to proclaim the default in three successive sittings of his court before making complaint to the sheriff, and even then might not take possession of the property until it had lain waste for a year and a day and the tenant had been given every opportunity to recover it by the payment of restitution and a fine.[71] These exceptional privileges attached to lands which had been defined in the early days of the Kentish kingdom, and they point, behind that, to a state of partnership between the Eskings and the fighting men whose ancestors had first shared with them the spoils of conquest.

Discarding certain later accretions, the occupiers of the free yokes were liable to a money rent, or *gafol*, charged at the rate of 1d. or 1½d. an acre, although sometimes rents in kind, mostly of staple produce such as corn, were paid instead. In addition to this there were certain traditional renders which amounted to little more than a token, mostly hens and eggs, or a lamb or two, but sometimes more unusual items like cummin, pepper or male hawks (at Newington).[72] The occupier also made a return for his pasture or fishing rights, a tithe of all the swine he sent to pannage in the Weald,[73] cheese from sheep kept on the marshes,[74] and in coastal areas herrings,[75] or even oysters[76] or salmon.[77] Labour services were remarkably light. Each yoke owed the ploughing and

---

* Baker, 1964, pp. 1–23. Whatever the derivation of the term *logi* may have been, at Gillingham the obligations imposed upon the *logi* and *yokes* were distinct, and more onerous in the case of the former.

sowing of one, or at the most two, acres of demesne, and the reaping of perhaps half as much again, with certain carefully defined tasks of carting, carriage or fencing.[78] In sum these can have made little demand on a man's time; they did not begin to approach the regular, unpaid, week-work on the lord's demesne that was the common lot of the villein over much of medieval England.

The outland holder was thus essentially a rent payer, which is why the customs applying to him came to be known generically as *gavelkind*. Before coins came into common use, which was not until the 7th century, all rents must have been in kind; commutation would later become a mutual convenience, although it had not been completed everywhere even in medieval times, and certain of the choicer items had understandably been reserved. These holdings were the ancient warrior lands of the kingdom, and (rent apart) the one fundamental obligation attaching to them was service in war: it is doubtful whether, in the early days, any other was required, except in the delivery of the food rents at the royal court. There is nothing to show how the later services originated, but it is a reasonable guess that as the lordships multiplied and rents came to be paid in money the task of delivery was diverted to the movement of the lord's own surpluses from one of his establishments to another. At the same time the development of the manors, with the creation of new demesnes and their dissemination everywhere, must have increased the demand for labour while making it more feasible for the outland tenant to give some assistance as an off-set to rent, although this amounted to very little. The uniformity of the arrangements suggests that in this matter, as in others, the ecclesiastical lords had been in the lead and had been pursuing a common policy throughout their widespread lands. The surprising thing is not that changes occurred but that they were so superficial.

The inland tenants of medieval times were also discernibly the successors of the *laets* of an earlier age. The inman had no independent claim to his land, and while custom came to ensure that it passed to his children in accordance with the normal processes of partition he could not alienate it without leave and might be dispossessed of it, without hindrance or preamble, if he defaulted upon any of his obligations. The nature of those obligations was also very different. The inman, too, paid rents in money or kind, but these were altogether less uniform and appear to have represented not so much a charge on his holding as miscellaneous payments for the privilege of using woodlands, pastures and so on which had originally belonged to the king and had now mostly passed to the manorial lords.[79] Essentially, the inman held his land by services of a special kind. He had no military obligations, except to assist in the defence of his own neighbourhood if it was attacked, and his ploughing and reaping services were little more onerous than those of an outland holder. Instead, he undertook a multitude of odd tasks, such as, at Sundridge, picking and storing the lord's apples and clearing the corners of his meadows after haysel,[80] and, at Westbere, cutting wooden props for the lord's vines and picking the ripened grapes.[81] Above all he was employed as a herdsman and drover, and on a whole variety of carrying duries known as *average*, which were largely — but by no means exclusively — concerned with stocking the lord's hall on notice of his arrival with his usual retinue of companions and servants.[82] So large did duties of this kind bulk that at Wye, for instance, the servile yokes were sometimes known as *iuga averagia*,[83] and elsewhere, as at Westbere, the inlands were called *averlands*.[84] Clearly, the origin of these services went very far back, to the time indeed when the Kentish kings were constantly on the move from one court to another, and they explain why each of the courts was ringed by inlands. The routine work on the arable demesnes, including the great bulk of the ploughing, harrowing, sowing, threshing and grinding must have been done by slaves, with the inmen — or *laets* — lending a hand at particularly busy times like harvest; but the slaves could not be trusted with tasks like droving, carting stores or relaying messages which would take them out of supervision, and these fell to the *laets*, who were freemen, and tenanted.

It was, however, the warrior class of the ceorls who were the mainstay of the early kingdom. While it would be unrealistic to conceive an orderly apportionment of land in the turmoil of the conquest, it is reasonable to assume that there was some general standard against which the fighting men could stake out their claims. If any hint of this is to be found we must return to the original standard of the sulungs. Acknowledging that these came to be used as fiscal counters which bore little precise relationship to land ownership, the question nevertheless remains whether the choice of term did not reflect some earlier underlying reality. This question acquires all the more point when usage in Kent is contrasted to that in the Anglo-Saxon kingdoms, which had their own unit of account, the *hide*, employed in very much the same way. This was supposed, in theory, to represent the amount of land needed to sustain a family,[85] was also superimposed upon the actual holdings, and was given a nominal acreage, varying in different areas and still only approximating to the facts. An early example of the working of this system is the Tribal Hidage, prepared for the Mercian kings during their period of supremacy in the middle of the 8th century as a means of assessing the dues owed by their own people and by the client kingdoms — including Kent and Sussex which were assessed, over-all, at 15,000 and 7,000 *hides* respectively.[86] The contrast between the Kentish unit, expressed in terms of ploughing capacity, and the Anglo-Saxon unit, expressed in terms of family sustenance, seems (behind all the artificialities) to have been based upon different conceptions of land entitlement; and with this there also went a significant difference of scale.

The nominal value of the *hide* ranged from 40 acres, prevalent over much of Wessex, to 120 acres in East Anglia,[87] where it seems that the indigenous unit of the *caracute* — akin in origin to the sulung — had been taken over and converted.[88] In an agreement reached in 812 between Archbishop Wulfred and the Mercian king Cenwulf about the exchange of certain lands around Canterbury and Faversham it was explicitly stated that the sulung was equivalent to two *hides*.[89] Most writers since Vinogradoff[90] have assumed that this was a stable and long-established relationship; but, in fact, it seems to have been a novel formula reached at a time when Kent was only just beginning to recover from the campaign of destruction waged against it by Cenwulf in 798 and land values (reflecting the yield of rents and services) were lower than they had ever been (pages 219–220 below). The earliest comparison appears, a hundred years previously, in a statement by Bede that the Isle of Thanet comprised 600 *hides*.[91] This is revealing not only because the use of the round figure supports other evidence which goes to show that Thanet was originally a lathe on its own, but because the only way in which the figure can be related to Kentish assessments is by assuming that Bede was translating 120 ploughlands in Thanet, each conventionally of 200 acres, into five times as many *hides*, each conventionally of 40 acres (*see* Appendix C). And if we are right in thinking that there were some 3,000 ploughlands in Kent then its assessment in the Tribal Hidage expresses exactly the same ratio.

It must, surely, be wrong to believe that because by the 8th century the sulungs and *hides* had become fiscal artefacts they had never been anything else. Behind the use of these contrasting standards we can glimpse earlier conceptions of what, ideally, the ceorl's portion should be; the inference being that in the first land seizures the Kentish ceorl was entitled to as much as could be worked by a full plough team, but the Anglo-Saxon ceorl to a sufficiency only, and that in each case there was an understanding of the return to be made in rents and services. The lavish entitlement in Kent need not surprise us. Often, no doubt, it was more than a man could work on his own or with the aid of his family, but if so other labour was readily available; the laws of Æthelberht show that the household of an ordinary ceorl might contain any of three classes of female slave as well as unpaid labourers or 'loaf-eaters'.[92] This was opulence; but the province conquered by the Jutes was one of the richest in Roman Britain, with large expanses of fertile land which had long been cleared and cultivated. We can do no more than guess at the number of fighting men who took part in the conquest; but such information as we have of the size of the war bands in the days of the heptarchy shows that they were often surprisingly small.[93] It seems that 2,000 would be a generous estimate for those engaged under Hengest in one stage or another of his campaigns. There was, therefore, ample land for the seizing. No doubt the amounts actually taken varied according to locality, soil and personal circumstance, and sometimes fell below the full entitlement. Moreover, within a generation or two the original tenements would have begun to be broken up, erratically, depending upon the number of surviving children, whether they chose to take their own shares or to continue to work the land in partnership, or whether any of them decided to sell out and seek their fortunes elsewhere; while, conversely, there would be opportunities for holdings to be extended or accumulated by gift, purchase or the bride prices paid for daughters. As this fragmentation proceeded, and the disparities grew, it must have become more and more difficult to relate the obligations to individual land holdings. It was, no doubt, in order to remedy this situation that the new fiscal system was devised, in which the earlier conceptions of sulungs and plough-lands were taken over, re-ordered and conventionalized; so providing a permanent framework within which the obligations both of the outland and of the inland tenants could be set and would remain stable for every unit, irrespective of changes among the land holdings within it or the number of occupiers between whom the obligations were shared. What mattered was that the king, and later the lords who followed him, could rely upon receiving a known total of rents and services, and that in time of war a known number of fighting men could be mustered by sulungs from each of the lathes. It is to be assumed that elsewhere the *hide* became institutionalized in very much the same way.

It seems that at the foundation of the kingdom the ceorl received not only a lavish entitlement of arable land but all the other easements needed to support a farming economy in which stock raising was almost as important as tillage. To begin with common use may have been made not only of the Wealden forest, but of the ample pastures that existed in the hinterland of Down, river and coast; but in time the strong Kentish bias towards individual property came to assert itself in the appropriation of these rights, so that even in the Weald the outland tenants contrived, by persistent occupation, to establish claims to their own *den-baera* or swine pastures,[94] and in north Kent only a few patches of common were left, to be perpetuated in place-names ending in *-minnis* (a charter of 839 describes them in the vernacular as lend held *in gemenisse*,[95] in distinction presumably to the *mons regis*, or Kingsdown). The principle of several ownership appears everywhere in the early charters. The very first of which the original survives records the grant by King Hlothere to the Abbot of Reculver in 678 of certain land in Thanet 'with everything belonging to it, fields, pastures, marshes, copses, fens, fisheries, with everything, as has been said, belonging to that land'.[96] In later years this became almost common form, so that, for instance, the grant to the archbishop in 812 of a sulung of land at Graveney near Faversham was said to include 'all fields, salt-pans, pastures, woods meadows, marshes, shorelands, fisheries' etc. rightly pertaining to it;[97] and, similarly, the grant in 822 of five ploughlands at Milton near Otford included all associated 'fields, woods, meadows, pastures, waters, mills, fisheries, fowling grounds and hunting grounds'.[98]

It would be inappropriate to speak of any 'entitlement' for the inland tenant, or *laet*, who held his land at the king's gift. The existence of three classes of *laet* suggests that there were, in fact, considerable variations in size among the early inland holdings, although the blood-price of the superior class, which was four-fifths that of the ceorl, also suggests that (if the difference of status is taken into account) many in this group must have held as much land as the ceorls, with the implication that those in the lowest group would usually have held — or be conceived as holding — about half as much. It is an intriguing thought that the three rates of 80, 60 and 40 shillings[99] may have been based upon a conception by which 10 shillings stood for each of the draught animals in a plough team and the totals were supposed to represent quantities of land proportionate to what could be worked by a full team. In practice, no doubt, the standard would be a mere approximation; but the notion would have been exactly of a kind to which this society was accustomed.

The inland tenants, like the ceorls, had the use of meadow, pasture and woodland, although in their case this was a privilege rather than a right, and one which often had to be paid for. The early records are particularly revealing about the use made by them of the royal wood or *snade*; the general practice being for the king to confer privileges which were carefully regulated either by amount or by season. Thus the medieval records show that at Wye the tenants of each of the servile yokes were allowed to husband and cut ten acres of the King's Wood, paying in return a due known as *husbote*;[100] there are a number of charters which stipulate how many swine may be pannaged in the *snade* by different groups of tenants, such as those at Ickham who are shown by a charter of 791 to have enjoyed the privilege of taking 50 into the royal woods in Blean Forest;[101] and particularly illuminating is a charter of 863 which accompanies the grant of certain salt-pans, apparently near Faversham, with the right to take four waggons into the king's wood during the six weeks following Whit Sunday 'when the other men are cutting wood that is in the King's commonage'.[102] It seems that the *laet*, though lacking the independent status and security of tenure of the ceorl, and far more burdened with labour services, was almost as well found.

There were, finally, two classes of society with whom we have barely dealt, the hereditary nobility of the *eorls*, and the slaves. The term *eorl* is again unique to Kent, and it is a misleading one. These people had little in common with the great earls of later times, who took their title from the Scandinavian *järl*,[103] nor were they lords in the sense of commanding the rents and services of a subordinate peasantry (unless, by purely private arrangement, they had chosen to let out some of their land, as may have happened). Æthelberht's laws make it clear that the king himself was the lord of every free man, and they mention no other.[104] The *eorl*, it seems, was an occupier of the outlands, like the ceorls, but one who had hereditary duties of attendance upon the king and leadership in war, a descendant, in fact, of one of Hengest's captains, or the head of a kin group of warriors, who had been rewarded with an especially large entitlement of land — perhaps three times as much as the ceorl, judging by relative blood-prices.[105] Mostly, no doubt, this would be worked by slaves, who were the foundation upon which the wealth and freedom of all the other classes rested. It was not only the *eorls*, but the ceorls also, who benefited from their labour, which made it possible for the large holdings to be handled; and if the services given to the king by the inland tenants were of a select kind this was because they were needed merely to supplement the work done by the king's slaves on the demesne land. Du Boulay has shown how, in medieval times, the tenant services met only a fraction of the lords' needs,[106] by far the greater part of which had to be left to hired hands, who were the true successors of the slaves. The services would certainly not have diminished over the years (on the contrary, it had been the constant, if often unavailing, endeavour of the lords to increase them)[107] and even if the quantity of demesne had increased three-fold, or more, it is clear that, from the very beginning, they can have amounted only to a supplementary aid. While slavery was prevalent in all the early English kingdoms the very expansiveness of Kentish society suggests a peculiarly strong reliance upon it — and this must qualify every verdict.

We shall have later to consider how blood-prices in Kent compared with those in the other kingdoms, this being the best test of the relative standing of the different classes of freemen. Certainly the life of a Kentish ceorl was valued at more than that of his counterpart in Wessex or Mercia, but whether by much or little is a vexed question. The gradations of Kentish society, with its three classes of *laets* and different categories of slaves, have prompted the belief among certain writers that this was a stratified community, autocratically ruled.[108] It is true that because of the ability (and longevity) of the early Eskings the dynasty became firmly implanted and suffered much less disturbance than most; but to describe the society as either dominated or hierarchical is to miss the point. Excepting the slaves (admittedly a large exception) the distinction in status did not imply the subordination of any one class to another, but merely defined the relationship in which each stood to the king. Royal authority was exercised in accordance with established custom, and in Kent, perhaps more than anywhere else, in partnership with the free land-holders, who were not only better endowed, but more privileged and independent in their rights, than the peasants of Wessex or Mercia. The true verdict is, surely, that of Jolliffe, who saw in the institutional structure of the lathes a means by which 'life in that primitive age could be lived without servitude, without debasing inequality, and yet preserve a fabric of order, adequately protected justice, and continuity'.[109] It was the compact between a secure ruling line and an exceptionally robust body of freemen which gave Kent the ability to withstand for so long the challenge of kingdoms of much greater size and military power than itself.

Chapter Four

THE SWARMING, *c.* 512-560

Octa and Eormenric

IN THE TWENTY YEARS or so following Mount Badon, as Sussex was plunged into darkness with the failure of Aelle and the eclipse, if not the extinction, of his dynasty, Kent was left as the only established English kingdom; itself unthreatened, but deprived of the capacity (even if it had the wish) to assume the leadership over the disjointed Anglo-Saxon communities. The unity of the English had been rent by the defeat, and by the British recovery following it, which had separated the mainly Saxon settlements of the south from the groups of folk in the eastern midlands and East Anglia, who were themselves divided by the marshes of the Humber from those around York and Holderness and yet further to the north.[1]

It seemed that the threat had been lifted from the British, but this was an illusion. Scarcely ever can the sea lanes have been more busy. On the one hand, there is evidence of a return migration to the continent from southern England, mainly it seems by the more restless spirits, who could see little scope for their warlike ambitions in Britain — although a way was found by a body of adventurers from Kent who in 514, or thereabouts, made a descent upon the British enclave around Southampton Water, an expedition which was to have momentous consequences, since out of it there grew the Kingdom of Wessex. On the other hand, there appears to have been a continuing reinforcement from Germany of the settlements along the east coast, the leading part in this being taken by the Angles — whose ancestral lands in Schleswig, Bede says, had been left deserted until his own day[2] — though with a considerable admixture of Frisians and others. This was accompanied, as the numbers built up, by a rounding off of the occupied territories, a constant forward probing, and the coalescence of the settlements unto the nuclei of kingdoms. These events, with all their cross-currents, may have gone unnoticed by Gildas and others in the security of the west, or have reached them only as the echoes of far-off skirmishing. Yet, as the 6th century wore on, the stage was being prepared for a further major onslaught against the British and a struggle for supremacy among the nascent English kingdoms themselves.

Far to the north, the foundation of the kingdoms of Bernicia and Deira, the constituents of Northumbria, can be traced back to the middle of the century. The Anglo-Saxon Chronicle says that it was in 547 that Ida, the first known king of Bernicia, began to reign at Bamburgh, and this accords with tradition on the British side.[3] It seems that Bernicia must have originated as an off-shoot by sea of settlements in the East Riding and the plain of York, the heart-land of Deira,[4] where the Chronicle tells us that Aelle succeeded to the throne in 560. South of the Humber the small kingdom of Lindsey appears to have been formed as early as this, or earlier.[5] The lands around

71

the Wash were occupied by a congeries of people, later known as the Middle Angles, although they never produced a dynasty of their own, and it seems that it was from here, rather than from the Humber, that the first settlers came to establish in the valley of the Trent the Kingdom of Mercia — 'the people of the mark', or border[6] — of which nothing is recorded until the 7th century, although the founder of its ruling line, Icel, appears from the genealogies to have been reigning at the beginning of the 6th.[7]

All these emergent kingdoms remained for the time hemmed in by the British. The exception was East Anglia. Its dynasty took its name from Wuffa,[8] the grandfather of Raedwald, a younger contemporary of Æthelberht. This would take the kingdom back at least to 550; but according to the genealogical tables accompanying the *Historia Brittonum*, which were derived from 8th-century Mercian records, it was Wuffa's father, Wehha, who was the founder of the nation.[9] It comprised not only Norfolk and Suffolk but the Isle of Ely and some part of Cambridge as well; a rich country considerably larger than Kent, and so, Stenton believes, the most powerful of all the English kingdoms by the middle of the 6th century.[10] Although East Anglia was isolated from the rest of England by the fens to the west and a broad belt of forest land along the border with Essex, it was open by sea to the continent. Probably it and Kent were the only two kingdoms which impinged in any way upon contemporary European consciousness. It is significant that Procopius, writing at this time, specified as inhabitants of Britain the Angles and Frisians (no doubt comprehending the Jutes in that description)[11] but entirely disregarded the Saxons, whose fortunes, after the defeat at Mount Badon, were now at their lowest ebb; and it is of more lasting significance that it was during the 6th century that the name Anglia, and so later England, came to be adopted abroad as that of the country. But although the dynasty of the Wuffingas was clearly of Anglian stock Frisian influences were especially pronounced in their kingdom, the customs of which closely resembled those of Kent, despite the absence of direct contact between the two nations.

The battle of Mount Badon fell in the middle of the reign of Oisc. Whatever casualties the Cantware may have suffered in that engagement it seems to have done little to disturb the peaceful ordering and settlement of Kent, under the influence of which there grew up at some time in the middle of the 6th century — it is impossible to say exactly when — the Kingdom of Essex, for many years a dependency of its larger neighbour.* Kent was the paradigm of the English kingdoms and its dynasty the first and most securely founded. In general, the institution of kingship was a new and tender growth among the invaders.[12] Tacitus, writing of the German tribes of the 1st century, says that their kings were chosen for their noble birth but had only limited powers.[13] It was the migrations themselves, with the incessant fighting accompanying them, that brought the great continental dynasties, such as the Merovingians, into prominence. Once these had established themselves they laid claim to ancient royal ancestry, usually of divine origin, just as in England all the kingly lines, except that of Essex, traced their descent back to Woden, and it claimed to be sprung from another deity, Seaxneat.[14] Nowhere, however, was there any really settled rule of succession. Thus when Clovis, the founder of the Frankish

* The first that is known of Essex is from Bede's account (II, 3) of the marriage of Æthelberht's sister Ricula to a king of that nation called Sledda. It is to be assumed that this marriage (itself an indication of dependency by Essex) was arranged by the bride's father, Eormenric, at some time before 560.

empire in Gaul, died in 511 his inheritance was divided between his four sons, more (it seems) for reasons of expediency than anything else, and the subsequent history of the Merovingians is marked by recurrent divisions of land between royal heirs, accompanied by much brawling and intrigue, with reunification wholly or partially achieved from time to time under the stronger or more unscrupulous of them.[15] Among the English kingdoms there was often great dynastic instability, of which Wessex provides the extreme example.[16] The conception here appears to have been that any prince of the royal blood, descended in the male line from Cerdic, the founder of the kingdom, had a right to contend for the throne. There were, therefore, frequent palace revolutions, interspersed with periods of joint rule, or the division of the realm among sub-kings owing an unreliable allegiance to some senior figure, who might at any time be ousted and whose authority amounted to as much or as little as he had the ability to make it. The same tendencies were observable elsewhere, for instance in Mercia.

Kent was the exception to this. For nearly two hundred years, from the accession of Oisc, c. 488 until the death of Egbert I in 673, the kingdom was kept as a unity, without any sharing or delegation of royal authority, and the throne passed in orderly succession from father to son, with remarkably little sign of dynastic disturbance. This does not mean that there was any settled rule of primogeniture. Of those who followed Oisc, we have no means of knowing whether Octa, Eormenric or Æthelberht were elder sons, or indeed whether they had any brothers,[17] though some or all of them are likely to have done; and there was at least one occasion later when an elder son is known to have been passed over.[18] The heir seems usually to have been marked out in advance by the current ruler in consultation with the notables of the kingdom, and it was common practice later to obtain his endorsement to land grants or major acts that might be thought to diminish the royal patrimony or prerogatives.[19] That by the end of the 7th century a presumption had developed in favour of the eldest son is suggested by the example of the two pairs of brothers, Egbert and Hlothere, and Eadric and Wihtred, in each of which it was the elder whose name conformed to the alliteration of the royal line and who, in fact, came to the throne first, although unexpected circumstances led to the younger succeeding later. But evidently there was nothing binding in this; the choice was a considered one, in which judgement of character and ability played a part. The remarkable thing is how smoothly the system worked. There were very few pretenders to the throne, and those there were received almost no sympathy or support from the people. It was only on Egbert's death in 673 that the system began to break down, and then because his sons were children, incapable for the time of reigning (*see* pages 145–147 below). Until then it had been one of the chief strengths of the kingdom. It was, for instance, the assured authority which Æthelberht enjoyed among his own people that was the decisive factor in his rivalry with his great contemporary Ceawlin of Wessex, who had no such advantage (pages 91–92 below).

To speak, as John Morris does, of the 'autocratic monarchy of Kent, cast in a European mould',[20] is to misunderstand the situation. Dynastic stability and autocratic rule are quite different things, if anything antithetic to each other, as the later history of Mercia shows; and in this matter Kent owed nothing to the example of the Merovingians or of the other continental houses. The achievement was its own, and was based upon a close understanding and community of aim between the Eskings and their people, confirmed in Æthelberht's reign but founded in those of his precedessors. Much was no doubt due to the ability of Oisc, but a great deal also to Octa and more especially (one suspects) to Eormenric. We should not fall into the trap of believing that because so little has been recorded of these two — to the extent, indeed, that we do not know when the one succeeded the other — they were meagre and insubstantial figures. The wealth of the Kentish grave-goods of the time is the surest corrective to that view. It is simply that the Anglo-Saxon Chronicle, exclusively in the passages dealing with this period, and predominantly throughout, concentrates upon accounts of warfare and conquest, and has therefore little or nothing to say of rulers whose concerns were of a different kind. In doing so it gives a misleading impression of the temper of early English, or at any rate Kentish, society. It is true that it was a society much taken with tales of heroic exploits and informed by a strong sense of obligation and personal honour, but it would be wrong to think of it as persistently bellicose. The great mass of the people were farmers, preoccupied with their land, and what they chiefly sought from their rulers was effective protection. The nobility might have wider ambitions, but mostly they expected from the king, in return for their loyalty, a certain munificence [21] — and there were often more politic ways of satisfying that need that by incessant warfare. During the reigns of Octa and Eormenric the kingdom remained secure, and it luxuriated. The strong bond of trust built up between the Cantware and their dynasty during this period was enduring. The people wanted an orderly succession, free from feuding, and were impatient of anyone who attempted to disturb it; an attitude exemplified more than a hundred years later when the murder by Egbert I of two young kinsmen whose intentions he distrusted caused grave offence to the church but seems to have raised hardly a ripple in the nation (pages 142–144 below).

A long period of peace was needed to nourish this tradition of dynastic stability, and for this the conditions of the time were uniquely favourable. Kent, from its position, was peculiarly exposed to the impact of the great folk migrations, but by 500 the first wave of these was spent, or was dying away in minor swirls and eddies; and it was not for another 300 years that the Viking menace began to gather. In Britain itself the effect of Badon had been to produce an uneasy equilibrium, which no-one yet (and certainly none of Kent's neighbours) had the power to disturb. Sooner or later the struggle for mastery was bound to be renewed and Kent to be drawn into the conflict, but that was still in the future; in the meantime the sea-lanes to the continent were once again open and unmolested, and no country was better placed to reap the benefit of it. The resources of the land, with its great wealth of wood and pasture, were only now beginning to be properly exploited, and if the population was growing there was still an ample surplus capacity. Kent could afford to turn its back upon the rest of Britain and to cultivate its links with the continent, where it had both means and opportunity to obtain those luxuries that added a savour to an otherwise primitive existence.

Yet it would be wrong to believe that this metamorphosis from a warrior society could be achieved without friction, or that the old, atavistic, impulses could be easily stifled. On Oisc's death there were evidently still elements among the Cantware who hankered after the heroic style of life, with its restlessness and adventure, and it was this that accounted for the great swarming from Kent that occurred during Octa's reign and may have spilled over into the earlier part of Eormentic's. Land shortage cannot have been the reason for this,[22] except in the very qualified sense that there may have been some among the emigrants who had found their patrimony reduced by the workings of partible inheritance and were looking for a less laborious means of restoring their position than the pioneering work of breaking in new land, of which there was still plenty to be had in the surrounding amplitude of estuary and down. The community was purging itself of those in whom the sense of folk wandering was still strong and who found the prospect of a settled life distasteful. In general, this seems to have been a voluntary movement. Mercenary employment had been traditional among the Germans and, as Tacitus records, it had been the accepted practice for warriors whose own tribes were at peace to adventure elsewhere.[23] Those of the Cantware who wished to return to the continent and to seek service under the powerful and munificent Merovingian kings were at liberty to do so; nor do we have to rely upon Procopius' account for the size of this exodus,[24] since there is plenty of other evidence for it (to which we shall return). But not all of the movement was to the continent. There were also those who were unwilling to accept that Badon had closed the door to further conquest and plunder at the expense of the British, and who, if the king was not prepared to lead them in this, were determined to strike out on their own. This was the company that, in 514 or thereabouts, made a descent from the sea upon the lands around Southampton Water. That the expedition should have been mounted within two years of Oisc's death is unlikely to have been a coincidence. There is a hint that Octa's accession had been disputed by a number of turbulent *eorls* and their followers, who had been defeated and driven out; a cleavage in Kentish society in which, for good or ill, but decisively for the whole future of the nation, the stable elements had triumphed.

The leaders of the dissidents were capable men who, in choosing the point of assault upon the British, knew exactly what they were about. The country around Southampton Water, which may once have been defended by Ambrosius Aurelianus, lay at the furthest reach of British power, masking a hinterland of down and well-watered valleys that invited seizure. In the normal course it might have been expected to fall a prey to Sussex; and it is indicative of the confusion and impotence into which that kingdom had been plunged by the defeat at Badon that the prize had been left to others to snatch. Since it was from this expedition that there stemmed the foundation of the Kingdom of Wessex (as well as of the Isle of Wight) the Anglo-Saxon Chronicle, with its strong West Saxon bias, pays particular attention to it, while at the same time taking pains to conceal its origin in Kent, which is betrayed by other evidence. The record of events is in other ways confused, repetitive and sometimes contradictory because, as Kenneth Harrison has demonstrated, it is based upon two different accounts with discrepancies of 19 years in their dating, caused by mistaking the Metonic cycle when entering one of the accounts into a Dionysiac Easter table.[25] If allowance is made for this, and the two versions united, a clear and consistent story emerges; and if the succession of the West Saxon kings is traced back from the close of the 6th century to the foundation of the dynasty by Cerdic it becomes evident that of the two series of dates the later must be the correct one.

The story is that in 514 Cerdic, his son Cynric, and his kinsmen Stuf and Wihtgar landed and defeated the British at a place called Cerdicsora, which has been identified from the fictitious name, Natanleod, given to the local ruler as Netley, just to the south-east of Southanpton.[26] In 519 Cerdic and Cynric won another victory at Cerdicesford, which is perhaps Charford on the River Avon some seven miles south of Salisbury,[27] following which the Kingdom of Wessex was established. The Isle of Wight was seized in 530 and then, according to the Chronicle, 'given' to Stuf and Wihtgar. Cerdic himself is said to have died four years later, but the northward progress of the conquest was marked by further victories won by Cynric at Salisbury in 552 and at Barbury Castle just south of Swindon in 556; here bringing the forces into the Vale of the White Horse and into contact with the Saxon settlements on the upper Thames, which became welded into the kingdom. The statement that the Isle of Wight was 'given' to Stuf and Wihtgar is highly suspect; it helped to validate the claims of Wessex to the Isle after its seizure at the end of the 7th century; but what is more likely to have happened at the time is an agreed division of interest, by which after coastal Hampshire had been won Cerdic and Cynric turned to the north in search of further conquests and their kinsmen to the south.

The kingdom which was founded on the borders of Hampshire and Wiltshire cannot at the time have been known as Wessex, a name acquired with the settlements on the upper Thames, which were in alignment with Middlesex and Essex. Bede says that the nation was first known as that of the *Gewissae*,[28] and a certain Giwis features in Cerdic's ancestry, as supplied by the Anglo-Saxon Chronicle.[29] Most of this however, has been shown to be a fabrication, with the names lifted from the pedigree of Ida of Bernicia.[30] The interesting thing about Cerdic is that his name seems to have been, not English, but a variant of the British Ceretic, which implies that he had a British mother*.[31] As his son Cynric was of fighting age at the time of the landing at Southampton Water it seems that he himself must have been born *c.* 480, or earlier, during the period of wide-spread plundering throughout southern England and when Hengest was still alive; mixed unions cannot have been uncommon at that time. The Chronicle goes out of its way to say that his kinsmen Stuf and Wihtgar were West Saxons, but this seems to have been not so much an error as a deliberate untruth, since Asser in his *Life of King Alfred* says definitely that they were Jutes,[32] and he had every reason to know because Alfred's mother came of this stock. In fact, while there is no reason to doubt the authenticity of Stuf, it is questionable whether Wihtgar ever existed; his name seems to have been concocted from that of the Isle of Wight, itself derived from the Roman *Insula Vectis*. Myres may well be right in thinking that the true reference was not to an individual but to the Wihtware, or inhabitants of the Isle of Wight[33] (a characteristically Kentish usage). A passage mentioning 'Stuf and the Wihtware', i.e. his people, could easily have been misconstrued in this way.

But whatever the obfuscations of the Chronicle it is clear that this expedition came from Kent. For this we have not only the testimony of Bede,[34] corroborated by Asser, that the people of the Isle of Wight and south Hampshire were Jutes; we also have the evidence assembled by Jolliffe of the persistence of Kentish customs and institutions among the inhabitants of the Meon valley[35] — the Meonware — and the unmistakably Kentish character of the grave-goods found in the main burial sites, notably Chessel Down on the Isle of Wight.[36] There is etymological evidence to the same effect. Stenton has drawn attention to an unusual form of place-name which appears to be peculiarly Jutish, and which consists of a common noun, an adjective, or a personal name, followed by the participle -*ing*; a form which resembles, but is wholly distinct in derivation from, the plural -*ingas* names which we examine later.[37] This type of place-name is common in

---

* A later example of the same thing is provided by Ceadwalla of Wessex, who also bore a British name, although descended in the male line from the royal house of Wessex (A-SC sub. A.D. 685).

Kent. It occurs once in West Sussex (by Pagham), once on the Isle of Wight, and at least six times in southern Hampshire. The only other area where it is to be found is between the Berkshire Downs and the upper Thames, where there is a series of examples, testifying to the Jutish composition of the forces which Cerdic and Cynric led northward to the foundation of the Kingdom of Wessex. There is one point at which the Chronicle itself appears momentarily to drop its guard. This is where it refers to Cerdic and Cynric as 'aldormen', i.e. ealdormen,[38] a term which did not exist at the time. This is more than an anachronism; it is inappropriate in every way, since an ealdorman in later usage was generally an official and always a subordinate.[39] The description does however echo, and has every appearance of being derived from, the contemporary (and unique) Kentish term for a noble, i.e., *eorl*: and it is significant that the Chronicle also calls ealdormen the two Kentish nobles, Oslaf and Cnebba, killed at the battle of *Wibbandun c.* 568.

Although this expedition was a major accomplishment of the Jutes it brought nothing but disadvantage to Kent itself. The small kingdom of the Isle of Wight lingered on until the end of the 7th century, when its dynasty was finally extinguished by Caedwalla of Wessex.[40] It made virtually no impact upon English affairs and appears to have retained little or no contact with Kent; the markedly Kentish character of the early grave-goods at such cemeteries as Chessel Down is absent from the later, and this seems to have been the very last of the English communities to adopt Christianity, as Kent was the first.[41] From its inception the Kingdom of Wessex acknowledged no ties with Kent. It stood as a barrier to Kentish expansion, and one that grew ever more formidable with time. When Æthelberht came to the throne in 560 Kent may still have been the more populous of the two kingdoms, as it was certainly the richer; but the balance tilted inexorably against it as Wessex continued to expand, against weak British resistance, first into Somerset and Dorset, then into Devon and eventually into Cornwall, until by the middle of the 8th century, when the Tribal Hidage was compiled, its assessment stood at 100,000 hides compared with 15,000 in Kent[42] (by then bereft of Surrey). Although Æthelberht was able, in the end, to establish a supremacy over Wessex, as over all the other kingdoms south of the Humber, he could find no firm basis on which to perpetuate it, and none of his successors had the resources to repeat his achievement.

But however ominous for Kent this development may have been, the migration to the continent brought the kingdom nothing but good. If we had to rely solely upon Procopius' account of the exodus which took place from Britain during the first half of the 6th century[43] we should be unaware of the major contribution which Kent made to it; the evidence for which is to be found in the quantity and distribution of the distinctive square-headed Kentish brooches (dating from this period) in the Low Countries and along the length of the Rhine, but especially in the area around Cologne and Coblenz (where one specimen discovered at Engers is an almost exact replica of a brooch from the cemetery at Milton Regis).[44] It was this wealth of evidence which at first led archaeologists like Leeds to believe that the Jutes originated from the middle Rhine; a judgement which more recent scholarship has reversed by showing that it was in Kent that this style of ornament was evolved, out of Scandinavian models.[45] Nor is it only in Flanders and the Rhineland that the ornaments appear. A remarkable cemetery at Herpes in Aquitaine has yielded grave-goods so purely Jutish in type that they can be fully matched only in Kent — or at Chessel Down on the Isle of Wight.[46] This is in an area seized by the Franks after their overthrow of the Visigoths in 507.[47] The finds corroborate Procopius' statement that the Merovingian kings — he names Theudebert specifically — settled the immigrants on unoccupied, or newly occupied, lands; to which he adds the significant remark that they made this the basis to a claim to paramountcy over England, lending colour to it by including English envoys in the missions sent to the Emperor Justinian in Byzantium. For a Jute born somewhere in Kent this certainly would have been a widening of horizons.

Procopius supplies this information by way of introduction to an account of a war expedition sent from somewhere in England, at some time during Theudebert's reign (533–548), against the Warni of the lower Rhine. The story he tells is that the king of the Warni took as his second wife a sister of Theudebert, at the same time betrothing his son Radiger to the sister of an English king; but he then fell mortally ill and on his death-bed advised his son to marry his step-mother, renouncing the English princess, because the Frankish alliance was the more expedient. Upon hearing of this slur upon his family the English king sent against the Warni an immense expedition of 400 ships, led by his brother, who soundly defeated Radiger, enforced the original marriage contract, and then returned home with family honour vindicated. The account is no doubt greatly exaggerated, but should nevertheless be accepted as substantially true, since Procopius records it so shortly after the event. It seems that the only two English king-doms which were situated, and at that time would have had the capacity, to organize a maritime expedition on anything like this scale were Kent and East Anglia. Considering the close associations which had existed between the continental Jutes and the Warni, reflected in the similarity of their customs (page 18 above), and the contacts which had been re-established between the Cantware and the Rhineland, it is tempting to suggest that this expedition came from Kent, where a new generation had come to fighting age since the defeat at Mount Badon. An insult of this kind could not possibly be passed over, however pacific the general inclinations of the king might be. The conjecture is strengthened by the marriage later contracted between Æthelberht and the Frankish princess Bertha as one feature of the policy of dynastic alliances followed by Eormenric, of which another was the betrothal of his daughter Ricula to Sledda of Essex. But East Anglia had also had close connections with the Low Countries and was a vigorous and newly united nation. That Procopius refers to the English king as *rex Angliae* is not conclusive of the point, since this had become a generic description, and Pope Gregory was later to address Æthelberht by the same style.[48] The probability is that this expedition was launched by Wuffa, from whom the East Anglian dynasty was named, and who must have been ruling at about this time; but we certainly cannot discount the possibility that the king was Eormenric, in which case the enforced marriage would have been of an aunt of Æthelberht and the leader of the expedition his uncle. It is an attractive supposition.

However that may be, it is clear that Kent, of all the English kingdoms, had the closest connections with the Rhineland and benefited most from them, because the Jutish emigrants to the continent, unlike Cerdic and his companions, maintained their links with their native country. This is manifest from the sudden appearance in Kentish burials of a whole range of Frankish weapons, ornaments and other articles, superceding, and in their sheer quantity tending to submerge, all that had gone before (pages 25 and 28 above). Professor Hawkes has suggested that a complex of relationships was involved, including inter-marriage, the exchange of gifts, and the transmission of new ideas and techniques;[49] and Professor Grierson has stressed the importance of factors of this kind in a society which set a high value on qualities of munificence.[50] So long as the bonds of kinship held between the Jutish communities on the continent and the native Cantware the jewellery and artefacts of the Rhineland were bound to find their way into Kent, to be copied, and eventually improved upon, there. Booty would have been brought back from such an expedition as was launched against the Warni, as well as, in this case, a royal bride-price. According to the custom of the age, and the practice of the Merovingians in particular, Theudebert's claim to supremacy over the English kingdoms (especially, it is to be supposed, Kent) would have been marked by gifts, and the English envoys whom he included in his missions to Byzantium would certainly not have returned empty-handed. Contacts were being established at the highest level and were widening out so as to touch, if only at second-hand, upon the fringes of the Mediterranean world. The swarming that occurred in Octa's reign was bearing rich fruits in that of Eormenric. And at whatever level gifts were exchanged or received much of the benefit would have been passed on through the open-handed practices of the time, and so come to pervade the whole of the society.

Yet the increase in prosperity during Eormenric's reign, so evident in the grave-goods, cannot be completely accounted for in this way, nor can the advantages have been so one-sided as this would make them appear. We are at the point of development where the exchange of gifts merged into barter, and that into more general trade. In the absence of written records we can do little more than guess at the nature of this traffic, its medium and agents. Coins had ceased to reach Britain in any number before the end of Roman rule, and their circulation persisted for only a short time after;[51] but it seems that at some stage during the 6th century there began to appear in the country a few of the Byzantine gold coins known as *tremisses*, followed by more minted by the Merovingian kings (Theudebert being the first), a number of which were found in the Sutton Hoo burial c. 625, and which before that are supposed to have been adopted as the standard for the shillings of Æthelberht's laws.[52] It is unlikely that these coins served in any proper sense as a currency in Æthelberht's time, or indeed for many years after; most of them were probably used as ornaments or kept as a form of kingly treasure; and only exceptionally can they have become a medium of overseas trade. For that purpose we should look rather at the small silver coins, known as *sceattas*, to which frequent references also occur in Æthelberht's laws, although tangible evidence of their use in England does not appear until later. When it does appear the distribution of the coins shows that they were produced primarily to serve the carrying trade in north-western Europe, then in the hands of the Frisians, whose chief entrepot was at Duursted near the mouth of the Rhine, and that it was in Frisia that they were first minted, although by the 7th century they were also being struck in London and probably at one or two other sites in the south-east.[53] The absence of early finds has led certain numismatists to conclude that they did not become current in England until well after Æthelberht's time, and that the *sceattas* mentioned in his laws were merely units of account, that is to say notional entities providing a common standard against which goods could be valued.[54] It is, however, difficult to sustain this argument in the face of the plain statement in the laws that blood-price should be paid by the slayer in his own money or property, *sceatta* being the term used for money here.[55] It would be stretching matters too far to suggest that the coins were already current in Kent in Eormenric's time, 50 years earlier, but it is reasonable to infer that the Frisians were then already acting as the middle-men in trade between Kent and the Rhineland, even if this was still being conducted through a form of barter. They were old associates of the Jutes and ideally situated to handle a traffic which the exodus from Kent and the contacts which it had established with the Frankish lands had nurtured.

As to the nature of this traffic, there is evidence enough of what Kent received. These were luxury articles including, besides the weapons and jewellery, glass-ware,[56] wine contained in the typical Frankish wheel-turned beakers, gold which might have travelled from the Mediterranean, garnets which came originally from the Far East, and no doubt other more perishable goods such as spices. Of what was given in exchange all we can positively say is that slaves must have been a major item. We have already remarked upon the prevalence of slaves in early Kentish society, and Britain as a whole was a notorious source of this traffic, which was fed by the internecine wars, although penal slavery, which features later in the laws of Wihtred of Kent,[57] was absent from those of Æthelberht. Most of the information we have on the commerce in slaves from Britain comes from the first half of the 7th century, when their redemption was considered an act of Christian charity in Merovingian France; for instance, at some time before 641, Eligius, the future Bishop of Noyon, redeemed a shipload of up to a hundred slaves, chiefly 'Saxons'.[58] The trade was certainly flourishing well before that time, however. As testimony of this we have Bede's story of Gregory's encounter with the youthful English slaves in the market at Rome,[59] and the instructions he gave for the purchase in France of English boys to be trained up in preparation for St Augustine's mission.[60] It seems that in later years this traffic also was in the hands of the Frisians, who used as their centre London, a city which revived under Kentish influence and in which the Eskings still retained certain rights as late as the reign of Hlothere (673–685).[61] There can be little doubt that Kent, as the bridge to the continent, was already deriving considerable profits from this trade in Eormenric's time.

The rest is speculation. Two of the more important primary products of the time were iron and salt, the latter for preserving fish and cheese and curing the carcases of animals slaughtered in the autumn for want of winter feed. It seems that the Roman iron workings in the Weald had extended into Kent, but the Jutes made little or no use of these deposits; perhaps because the industry had foundered well before the conquest, and the workings, at a depth in the forest, had been mostly forgotten.[62] Prior to the Norman Conquest there is only a single reference, in a charter of 689, to an iron mine in Kent, and that was not in the Weald but near Lyminge,[63] where there were evidently poor deposits of iron stone which ceased to be worth working when the richer fields of the Weald were rediscovered. (Similar early workings have recently been found near Harrietsham.) Salt was a different matter. Kent with its long coast-line, and plenitude of woods to supply fuel, was well equipped to produce it. Salt-pans are mentioned at a number of places in 8th century charters, for instance at Faversham, Lydd and Sampton near Hythe (to which wagon-loads of firewood were brought from the Wealden forest).[64] Some of it may have found its way abroad, but at this time its chief value for trade was probably as a preservative of such exportable products as cheese and fish, in which Kent was rich.

The earliest indication of the bulk movement of goods, coast-wise if not across the Channel, is provided by the siting of the royal vills. As we have said, all of these were on, or else close to, Roman roads or the prehistoric Harroway, so that the king and his entourage could move easily between them; but seven of the twelve were also on tidal estuaries or navigable rivers, and an eighth, Lyminge, within easy reach of the Rother, or Limen, from which it took its name. In Anglo-Saxon times, and indeed throughout the Middle Ages, goods were much more easily transportable by water than by land; and while, in the early days of the kingdom, access to the sea may have served a military purpose in mounting maritime raids against the British or receiving reinforcements from the continent, the sites were also well chosen for the movement of agricultural surpluses from one royal estate to another, a movement that could easily be diverted to overseas trade. There is evidence of specialization among the vills, for instance at Faversham, the great craft centre of the kingdom, and at Wye, which means a sacred place[65] and must, it appears, have been the centre of religious observances by the early kings.* We should expect some specialization to have applied in agricultural as well as other matters. Thus the vills of Aylesford, Hollingbourne, Wye and Lyminge, which bordered the great royal forests on the perimeter of the Weald and had a disproportionate share of them,[66] must have produced surpluses of pork and faggots for fuel, and the vills of Eastry and Sarre, in the corn growing lands of the north-east, of all kinds of cereal. But from a trading standpoint we should be inclined to look more at the vills abutting on the Thames, and especially at Milton Regis with the wide expanses of marsh at its threshold and across the Swale estuary in Sheppey, which means 'the isle of sheep' and was so known from the earliest times (*Scepeig*, 700).[67] Wool had been one of the major exports from Roman Britain,[68] and woollen cloaks are known to have been the chief items of English merchandise in the 8th century (page 211 below). Whatever primary products were exported from Kent in Eormenric's reign in exchange for the luxury goods that were then entering the country we should expect fleeces to have been the chief among them, with perhaps some salted cheese and fish in addition. The circumstances of Faversham were very similar to those of Milton Regis, which may well account for its prominence among the royal vills in the 6th century.

The amount of trade at this time should not be exaggerated. It must, to begin with, have been an intermittent traffic; even when it developed in a more regular way it can have comprised only a small part of the total economic activity of the kingdom; and most of it must have been channelled through the royal vills, with the king reaping the immediate advantage. But through the generosity expected of a king, his companions and those in authority, the benefits would soon begin to percolate throughout the community, adding to the lives of the people just those touches of ostentation and luxury that were particularly prized in a generally harsh and unaccommodating age. Whereas the exodus from Kent at the start of Octa's reign may have been prompted by a sense of frustration, and of narrowing horizons, induced by the defeat at Mount Badon, it had by the end of Eormenric's itself produced the cure for that malady. The

---

* Margaret Gelling has suggested that a number of heathen place-names originated after the coming of Christianity and represented places where, exceptionally, the pagan religion lingered on (*Signposts to the Past*, 1978, pp. 158-59). This cannot be so of a royal vill like Wye; nor does it fit other Kentish sites like Woodnesborough, which was closely associated with the royal vill of Eastry, being in fact only a mile outside it.

impulse behind the original migrations owed nothing to him; but fortune had run his way and he had learned how to cultivate it.

It is almost impossible to judge the scale of this movement or the effect that it had, if not in reducing, at least of helping to halt the growth of, the population of the kingdom. One would expect that the peace which Kent enjoyed throughout this period, together with the increasing prosperity, would within a generation or so have made up any losses; but the difficulty is to find some body of evidence which can be applied with such discrimination that it will allow us to monitor the spread of settlement over a period as short as 50 years, or, failing that, at least to compare the situation at the close of Eormenric's reign to that which had existed two or three generations back, when the first land seizures had been accomplished. We are concerned here with habitation, which followed the plough. The process should not be seen as the penetration of entirely virgin country — the whole of Kent except the deeper recesses of the Weald had been put to some use from very early on — but as the conversion to arable land of some of the superfluity of wood, rough grazing and pasture.

The evidence of the burial sites is valuable, but it can be misleading and is almost certainly incomplete. The deposition of grave goods did not entirely cease until the end of the 7th century, so that we are dealing with a span of around 250 years, and although the dating of the finds has now become so much more assured than it was other difficulties remain. On the face of it, what this evidence suggests is a steady expansion from certain areas of primary settlement — in north-east Kent, along the Thames shoreside and on the shelf of land above Romney Marsh — up the river valleys and throughout much of Holmesdale, with almost no encroachment on the Downs until the pagan era was well past. But the trouble is that we do not have a finished picture, since new discoveries are constantly being made, such for instance as the cemetery recently excavated at Orpington which yielded the first tangible evidence of 5th century occupation of the Cray valley.[69] Moreover the dating, and very identification, of burials depends upon the graves having been furnished, as even in the richer cemeteries most of them were not. We have described how in Oisc's reign the practice of burial with grave goods appears to have been confined largely to the royal entourage (page 28 above). It revived more generally only after his death and seems then to have spread rapidly in the richer areas of east Kent and the Thameside which had been brought into close association with the continent, but more tardily elsewhere. There is, therefore, a danger of mistaking for the march of settlement what was merely the spread of the new practice among already established communities.

The point is well illustrated from the Medway valley upstream of Rochester. If we were to judge solely from the discovered burial sites we should conclude that this area was sparsely inhabited before the 8th century; the finds at Aylesford, Maidstone and Wrotham amount to very little,[70] and the larger cemeteries at Holborough[71] and Eccles[72] appear from the general east–west orientation of the graves and from the nature of the few articles that have been found in them, to date from the early Christian era, c. 650. Yet for the first immigrants to have neglected the Medway valley, which was so thickly planted with villas in Roman times, and where the land was so open and accessible, would have been an extraordinary thing; and the high proportion of sulungs to plough-lands — matching that in Thanet and the north-east — suggests that, in fact, they did not do so (page 62 above). It may be that there is some major site awaiting discovery

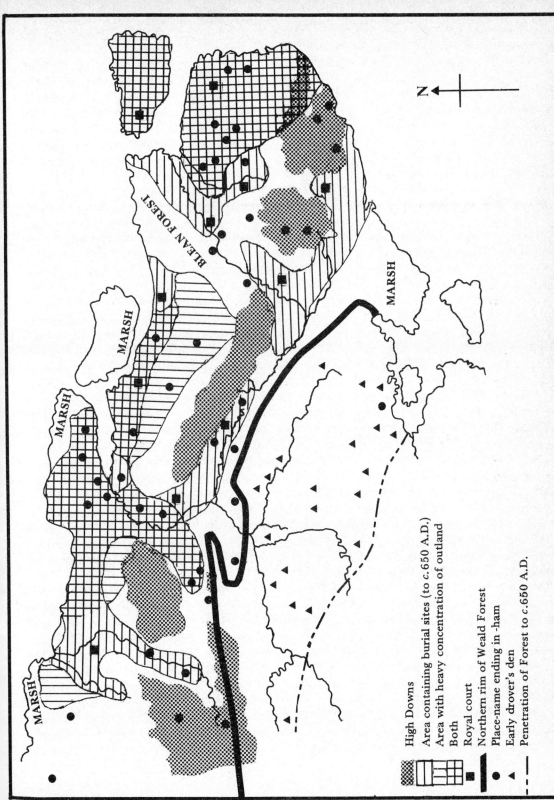

PROGRESS OF SETTLEMENT, 6th AND 7th CENTURIES

BLEAN FOREST

MARSH

MARSH

MARSH

MARSH

MARSH

N

High Downs
Area containing burial sites (to c.650 A.D.)
Area with heavy concentration of outland
Both
Royal court
Northern rim of Weald Forest
Place-name ending in -ham
Early drover's den
Penetration of Forest to c.650 A.D.

Scale: Approx 10 miles = 1 inch

here which will transform the whole picture; but the probability is that this area, divorced from continental associations and far from the centres of influence in east Kent, responded late to the new trends. And even more should we expect this to be true of small and isolated settlements on the Downs. In judging the distribution of population during the early years of the kingdom we should not, therefore, allow ourselves to become mesmerized by archaeological evidence which, even if it were complete, could still supply only a part of the answer, but also pay attention to the incidence of the sulungs. Unfortunately, there are ambiguities here too, because it seems that the pattern presented to us is that of the 7th century; and while it is easy enough to discern from it which were the prime areas of early settlement, since these remain clearly imprinted on the design, it is not safe to attempt anything more. We still know too little of what happened at the next stage.

It is this gap that place-name scholars have been attempting to fill, but study of this subject is now in a state of flux. Moreover, as Margaret Gelling has demonstrated else-where,[73] and is manifestly true of Kent, many of the early settlements were named simply from the local topography — it might be a bourne, a hill or a valley — so that their character was concealed, not revealed, in the description. We have, therefore, to concentrate upon those classes of name which definitely proclaim habitation, and of which the samples are sufficiently large to be significant. Of these, the names ending in -*ton* did not begin to be formed until the 7th century, and those ending in -*ingas* (now commonly shortened to -*ing*), which used to be thought among the earliest of all, have been shown by the work of John McNeil Dodgson not to have appeared before the end of the 6th, and seem mostly to have been later than that.[74] They are, therefore, irrelevant to our present enquiries, although we shall have something to say about them in due course. For the present all we are left with is the sizeable group of names ending in -*ham*. These seem particularly promising because a number of scholars believe that they ceased to be formed towards the end of the 6th century, and if we could accept that we should have a really valuable indication of the progress of settlement during the period we are now studying.

The antiquity of the -*ham* names has long been recognized by scholars. It is shown by their archaic construction, the terms with which they are compounded (which include some Latin loan words, as in Faversham and the Wickhams: *see* Appendix B) and their concentration in the eastern parts of England. There is little doubt that many of them date from the migration period. The precise meaning of the word is not easy to define. The common rendering of 'village' will not do for Kent.[75] Its first written appearance is in Æthelberht's laws, where it seems to be used in very much the modern sense of 'home'; a man who has purchased a bride and finds that there has been dishonesty (presumably because she is not a virgin) is to return her to her *ham* and reclaim his money.[76] But what is meant, more precisely, is that the girl is to be sent back to her kindred. In Kent place-names with this ending appear hardly ever to have been attached to individual holdings or farmsteads; those of which we have knowledge came almost always, in later days, to be assumed by manors and are now usually preserved in the names of parishes. This helps to set the scale. It seems that, in Kent at least, a *ham* was a group, or constellation, of settlements, which might exceptionally constitute a small township (as in the case of Faversham) but commonly extended over quite a sizeable trace of country, and was generally defined through its occupation by a kin or the followers of some particular individual, an *eorl* or other notability.

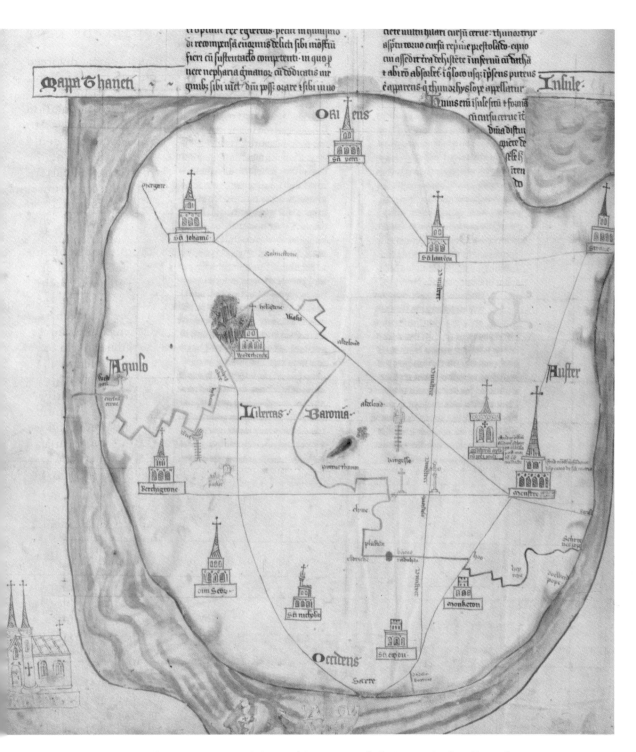

I. Early 15th-century map of Thanet (disorientated) depicting the Stag Legend.

The first problem about -ham names is to distinguish them from another group which originally ended in -hamm but have now, through shortening, become reduced to the same form, although their meaning — broadly a water meadow — is quite different,* and they do not have the same connotations of age. Margaret Gelling has gone so far as to declare that, because of this, no certainty will ever be possible about the origin of a number of names with this common suffix.[77] There are, however, certain tests that can be applied (see Appendix D), and those who have studied the matter with particular reference to Kent — Wallenberg,[78] Reaney[79] and Dodgson[80] — have reached a fair amount of agreement, subject to only a few disputable cases (also dealt with in Appendix D). The true -ham names that they have sifted out amount to around 50, which is a useful sample.

There is, however, a more serious stumbling block. It is very difficult to know just how long a temporal span names of this kind had, and there is a temptation to abbreviate it so as to emphasize the antiquity of the form in general. A notable example of this appears in the study carried out in 1973 by Barry Cox of the incidence of the names in East Anglia and in the midland shires which once constituted the Kingdom of Mercia.[81] The argument in this article is that the association of the names with Roman roads is so close that they must have originated in the immediate aftermath of Roman rule, and that some may have been bequeathed by the early federate groups established in these parts of the country at the beginning of the 5th century. This may be so; but the question is how long they continued to be formed. On this, their proximity to the Roman roads is a very fallible guide, since it is arguable that the influence exerted by the roads would have been less strong in the period of early settlement than during the later stages of expansion and consolidation, with the growth of trade and the development of the kingdoms of East Anglia and Mercia. On that basis, while some of the names might well have dated from the 5th century, and more from the 6th, as many are likely to have been of 7th century origin. And this view is supported by the distribution of the pagan burial sites which, in the midlands, has only a casual relationship to the Roman roads (as Barry Cox's own maps show), and suggests that the early settlements were influenced less by those than by terrain, in particular, the river valleys,[82] the -ham names having a wider pattern in which the attraction of the roads becomes more apparent.

Another study, and one which brings us much nearer home, is that carried out by Dodgson of the distribution of the names in the south-eastern counties,[83] from which he concluded that they continued to be formed down to the close of the 6th century, but no later. The consideration that weighed most with him was the absence of the names from the body of the Weald. This undoubtedly sets a term to them, but a later one than he appears to believe; since such evidence as there is suggests that in Kent the settlement of the forest had barely begun before the 8th century, except at the sally ports of the Medway and Rother (where a few -ham names are to be found, as at Peckham south of Maidstone and Freezingham in Rolvenden parish). We deal with this later in Chapter 10, pages 187–190; but it should be noted now that the fiscal assessments dating (we believe) from the late 7th century treat the Weald as virtually void. There is, in fact, nothing to

---

* Among the meanings suggested at different times are land in a river bend, a promontory amid marshes, and a valley bottom; but meadow was the sense which the term had in medieval Kent, cf. the reference to a ham of meadow in a survey of Yalding manor in 1263 (Inquisitiones Post Mortem, AC 4 (1868), pp. 312–13).

show that -*ham* names were not still being formed down to the close of the 7th century, overlapping with the -*ton* names that were then beginning to supplant them; and it is significant that in Æthelberht's laws, promulgated *c.* 603, *ham* was still being used to denote a settlement, a meaning which *ton* had not yet acquired.[84] A good touchstone is the name of Westerham[85] — 'the western *ham*' — which could not have originated until Surrey had been lost to Kent. We know that this did not occur until after the death of Egbert I in 673, and it seems not to have become final until Hlothere's death 12 years later (pages 146, 153–54 and 164 below). We are thus left with a time span for the -*ham* names of around 250 years, say from 450–700, a modest duration compared to that of the -*ton* names, which continued to be formed at least as late as the 13th century.

It follows that the -*ham* names can provide no guidance to the progress of settlement in any specific period of the 6th or 7th centuries unless some means can be found of distinguishing in date among different groups of them. Some attempts at refinement have been made, and are considered in Appendix D, but the conclusions reached are often questionable, and the studies have not yet been carried sufficiently far to be of real use. They are certainly of less use at present than the evidence of the burial sites, ambiguous though that is. When, therefore, we suggest that by the end of Eormenric's reign the effects of the earlier swarming had been made good (but probably little more) we are dealing in nothing better than informed guess-work. It is clear, nevertheless, that the relief to the pressure of population brought about by the exodus must have been beneficial in itself. In practical terms, it would have moderated the division of holdings among heirs and put land upon the market as those who left sold or otherwise disposed of their shares. The ceorl's portions may have become more scattered, but are unlikely, in sum, to have been much diminished. Kent remained a country of substantial yeomen farmers, and was still so in Æthelberht's time, as his laws show; and to this agricultural wealth new graces were being added. It is no wonder that the Kentish royal house should have taken pride in Eormenric's memory, as is apparent from the frequency with which, in later years, their names — Eormenred, Eormenhilda, Eormenburga and Eormengyth — harked back to his. This was not otherwise a common form of name in England, and it is a sign of how closely wedded the Kentish people still were to their Germanic past that it should have been taken from that of the great Gothic king and war-leader of the 4th century, whose home was in the Crimea.

It was a robust, prosperous and self-confident society confirmed in its loyalty to the dynasty and purged of its more anarchic elements, that Eormenric bequeathed to his successors. The marriage of Æthelberht into the Merovingian royal house was both the crown and recognition of this achievement. That the marriage took place while Æthelberht was still a prince, and so on the initiative of Eormenric, rests on the contemporary testimony of Gregory of Tours, who in recounting the death in 589 of Bertha's mother, Ingoburga, says explicitly that she left behind an only daughter 'whom the *son* of a certain king in Kent had taken in marriage'.[86] It follows from this that the union occurred before 560, when Æthelberht succeeded, and so also before Bertha's father became king of Paris, which was not until 561.[87] It was not, therefore, the daughter of a reigning monarch whom Æthelberht married but of an heir presumptive to some part of the Frankish dominions. The match was a trophy for the Eskings none the less. As we have said, it had become the practice among the Merovingians for a king's territories to be divided between his sons on his death. Charibert's father (and Bertha's grandfather) Clotaire had inherited as his share of the Frankish lands Soissons, with the Meuse valley and much of what is now Belgium and north-east France, which explains the association between Eormenric and this branch of the family; but Clotaire outlived his brothers and for a prief period at the end of his life united the whole of the Frankish dominions under his rule.[88] For the Eskings this was a most prestigious connection; and while the Merovingians no doubt regarded it as a demonstration of their claim to paramountcy over Kent (itself a matter of prestige rather than substance) they would scarcely have entrusted a Frankish princess to a kingdom which they considered to be barbarous. With this marriage Kent was accepted into the orbit of civilization of the post-Imperial world. That it was still a heathen country does not seem to have troubled the Merovingians. They were concerned that Bertha should be fortified in her Christian faith by the presence, as her personal chaplain, of Liuthard, who Kentish tradition says was Bishop of Senlis,[89] but beyond this they showed no proselytizing zeal. Whatever spiritual influence Bertha and Liuthard may have exercised upon Æthelberht was reinforced by his consciousness of the Roman world to which the church had become heir, and was unlikely to have outweighed policy in that considering and capacious mind. It was not the consequences of the marriage, but all the circumstances surrounding it, that put Kent in the path of Christianity.

Eormenric was the last of the Eskings to die a heathen and so to be buried according to the old rites. His grave is unknown; but when in 1858 the London, Chatham and Dover railway was extended past Faversham the construction cut across an area called from time immemorial the King's Field and in so doing uncovered a wealth of jewellery, weapons and grave goods of all kinds, dating from the 5th to the 7th centuries, most of which were sold off privately by the navvies, and so dispersed, though much has now been retrieved and placed in museums.[90] This was the largest, and richest, accumulation of Jutish relics ever to have been found in Kent, and it was also unusually eclectic. It included much Frankish material, bird and animal brooches or the like, Merovingian gold coins, Saxon saucer brooches, a girdle hanger of Anglian type, and escutcheons from Celtic hanging bowls[91] — just such a miscellany as might have been expected to have been gathered up, through gifts or by other means, into a royal household. It is an intriguing thought that among the graves disturbed by this excavation may have been that of Eormenric, and perhaps also those of his predecessors Octa and Oisc.

Chapter Five

THE ASCENDANCY

Æthelberht, 560–616

IN POPULAR HISTORY the part played by Æthelberht in the Christian conversion has obscured his other achievements; yet well before the mission of St Augustine he had made himself the dominant power throughout the whole of England south of the Humber, and during the 56 years of his reign he brought his own kingdom to a state of prosperity and material magnificence which surpassed all others. The testimony of his greatness is to be found not only in the works of the Christian chroniclers, but in the profuse richness of the pagan cemeteries of his time, and in the new meaning he gave to kingly rule, the search for which was perhaps the most powerful of all the impulses which led him to Rome. It is with the first period of his reign, in which he won his ascendancy in face of formidable opposition and despite initial set-backs, that we shall chiefly deal in this chapter, describing in doing so what recorded custom and archaeological finds reveal of contemporary Kentish society. We leave until the next chapter the account of the conversion.

Bede tells us the exact date of Æthelberht's death, 24 February 616, and it can be deduced from this, and the known years of his reign, that he came to the throne in 560.[1] There is, however, no reliable record of when he was born. It is true that 552 is given as the date in the Canterbury Epitome of the Anglo-Saxon Chronicle, a bi-lingual text, part English and part Latin, which was written at St Augustine's Abbey *c.* 1100 and adds to the common stock of information certain purely Kentish material;[2] but while, no doubt, the date derived from ancient tradition preserved at Canterbury it is clearly erroneous. A boy of eight could not have succeeded to the kingdom, and we know that Æthelberht was already married when he did so. It is possible that we are confronted here with yet another error of 19 years caused by mistaking the Metonic cycle when entering an early tradition into a Dionysiac Easter table; in which case the true year of his birth would have been 533, and he would have been 27 years old at his accession, and 83 at his death. There is nothing impossible about this. It was an age in which those who survived the perils of infancy often showed a remarkable constitutional strength and longevity. If the Anglo-Saxon Chronicle is to be believed, Penda of Mercia was around eighty when he fell in battle against the Northumbrians.[3] Theodore of Tarsus was already 68 when he came to the country as archbishop in 669 and nearly 90 when he died,[4] still in charge of affairs and active to the last. Æthelberht was less fortunate. There are signs of a marked failing in his powers during the last 10 years or so of his life, a tragic decline into dotage.

If in the final years of his reign Æthelberht had outlived his authority, during the first he was overshadowed by his great contemporary Ceawlin of Wessex, whom he eventually worsted. The character and aims of the two men were as dissimilar as the kingdoms they ruled. Ceawlin was the warrior king of a frontier state still in its formative stage, and his over-riding preoccupation was conquest over the British; judging by events he was a considerable strategist as well as a fighter, but success, and the single-minded pursuit of his objects, made him neglectful of dangers at home. Whatever adventurous impulses Æthelberht may have felt as a young man, he matured into a statesman with a patient and contriving mind, to whom conquests against the British were an irrelevancy from which his own kingdom had nothing to gain, and whose interests were drawn in the opposite direction, reaching out across the Channel to Merovingian France and beyond it to the Mediterranean world and the remnants of the Imperial civilization. He had come to a stable inheritance in which, through the ability of his predecessors, the royal authority had been firmly implanted, a security which Ceawlin lacked. Both men succeeded to the throne in the same year.[5] They were uneasy neighbours, rivals in ability, neither of whom could accomplish his own ends without fear of the other. Conflict between them was inevitable; and the course it took was perhaps predictable, with Ceawlin triumphing at the outset but the final victory going to Æthelberht.

The Chronicle tells us that in 568 'Ceawlin and Cutha' (his brother) 'fought against Æthelberht and drove him into Kent: and they slew two *aldormen*, Oslaf and Cnebba, at *Wibbandun*'. There is a great deal of ambiguity surrounding this passage; in particular it is difficult to decide whether Ceawlin or Æthelberht had been the aggressor. At first sight the entry reads as though Æthelberht had launched an attack upon Wessex and been repulsed; but the matter takes on a different appearance if, as was once confidently assumed, the site of the battle was at Wimbledon, since this would imply the invasion and annexation by Ceawlin of those Surrey lands which had belonged to Kent almost from the foundation of the kingdom. Place-name scholars are now inclined to reject this identification,[6] but they have suggested no other. Wherever the battle may have been fought, the question of initiative turns upon the precise meaning attaching to the term 'Kent' in the Chronicle's account, and that upon when the account first came to be written. We have suggested elsewhere that the naming of the two *eorls* Oslaf and Cnebba who fell in this battle implies that a Kentish source had been drawn upon, and an early one at that (pages 34–36 above); it supports Kenneth Harrison's conjecture that some contemporary record might have been kept by Liuthard, installed as chaplain at Æthelberht's court.[7] In any event, the account of Ceawlin's exploits appears to have formed part of the proto-Chronicle supposed to have been kept in Wessex as early as the middle of the 7th century,[8] or only a little later. The significance is that at that time Surrey can have consisted merely of one or more lathes in the Kingdom of Kent; it was only through its loss to Kent in the last quarter of the century that it became distinguished from the others. To a chronicler writing around 660–70 (or to Liuthard 100 years earlier) the statement that Æthelberht had been driven into Kent would have meant that he had been driven into Surrey, not out of it.

If this reasoning is correct, then the site of the battle of *Wibbandun* should be sought farther to the west, somewhere on the boundary between Hampshire and Berkshire. And this is what one might otherwise expect. The conquests which had led to the foundation of the Kingdom of Wessex had taken a course from Southampton Water through Wiltshire to the upper Thames, and on Ceawlin's accession had only just been completed (pages 75–76 above). Between Wessex and Kent there would remain an area of disputable territory —

broadly within the triangle of Newbury, Andover and Basingstoke — and we suggest that it was this that passed to Ceawlin as the result of a battle in which either side might have been the aggressor. It is possible to think of a number of reasons why Æthelberht might have forced the issue; for instance, the eagerness of a young man to win military renown, or concern at the rapidly growing strength of Wessex, fencing Kent in on its western boundaries, and the desire to scotch this danger before it became too late. Nevertheless, what we know of the characters of the two men, and the course of later events, both suggest that it was Ceawlin who launched the attack, to round off his dominions and as a preliminary to the campaigns which he contemplated against the British. Before committing himself to those it was prudent to clear his rear from any possible interference by Æthelberht, and an exemplary defeat inflicted upon the Cantware would hold out the still brighter prospect of reviving the *bretwaldaship*, which had lapsed since the days of Aelle, and so bringing the combined strength of the southern English to bear against the traditional enemy. This, in fact, is how matters turned out.

That the battle went as it did need not surprise us. It was fought far from the centre of Kentish power, but close to that of Wessex, from which an assault could have been mounted with little warning. During the long years of peace under Eormenric the Cantware must have become inexperienced in warfare; whereas Ceawlin was not only a consummate warrior but a veteran who some twelve years previously had fought at the side of his father Cynric at Barbury Castle,[9] and his forces would have been battle hardened in constant skirmishing against the British. The inference is not that any part of the old established Kingdom of Kent was annexed but simply that Æthelberht had been thrust back within its confines. Given the uncertainties of demarcation it is possible that west Surrey may have formed part of the disputed territories which were now lost; Kentish custom left none of the deep imprint here that it did in east Surrey, or the imprint was erased;[10] but, however that may be, it was Æthelberht who was to have the final say in the days of his own supremacy, and we know that in 670 or thereabouts Egbert of Kent was exercising authority as far to the west as Chertsey.[11]

The Chronicle tells us that three years after *Wibbandun*, in 671, a certain Cuthwulf (it seems, another brother of Ceawlin)[12] defeated the British at *Bedcanford* and captured Limbury (above Luton), Aylesbury, Benson and Eynsham. Contrary to appearance, the site of the battle was not Bedford;[13] we do not know where it was; but the list of places captured suggests that the Wessex royal house was now consolidating its hold upon the upper Thames and clearing the British from the line of the Icknield Way, which they had reoccupied after Mount Badon. A direct link was being established with East Anglia and the English settlements radiating from the Wash, which could thus be brought within Wessex influence. It may be from this time that the *bretwaldaship* of Ceawlin dates. This was more than an honorific. The term means, literally, 'Britain ruler',[14] and the institution expressed the underlying unity of the English people. In origin, however, it had a decidedly military bias; its creator, Aelle of Sussex, had led the combined strength of the southern English against the British; and it seems that this is how Ceawlin conceived his own mission. His object was to reverse the decision of Badon and carry through to success the strategies which had foundered in Aelle's defeat nearly eighty years previously.

The plan of campaign was identical to that adopted by Aelle; a thrust south-westward from the upper Thames towards the Bristol Channel. The blow was delivered in 577 and resulted in an overwhelming victory. In that year, the Chronicle says, Ceawlin and Cuth-wine defeated the British at *Deorham* (Dyrham, six miles north of Bath),[15] killed three of their kings, and captured the cities of Gloucester, Cirencester and Bath. At long last the line of the Fosse Way and the lower Cotswolds had been over-run and the English had broken into the Severn valley, so sundering the British kingdoms of the south-west from those of Wales and the borders. The scale of the operation suggests that Ceawlin had invoked his right, as *bretwalda*, to call upon the support of the other English kingdoms, and the very early form in which the names of the British kings appear in the Chronicle's account argues, or so D. P. Kirby believes,[16] that the events were recorded in writing either in the late 6th or the early 7th century, which could only have been in Kent. It is probable that the Cantware took part in this campaign, though they had nothing themselves to gain from it except plunder (and battle experience), and it must have been irksome to a man of Æthelberht's ambitions to be compelled in this way to assist in the aggrandizement of Wessex. Seven years later, in order to round off his success, Ceawlin struck northwards towards the Warwickshire Avon, winning another victory at *Fepanleag* (near Stoke Lyne in north Oxfordshire)[17] and going on from that to capture 'many villages and countless booty'. Out of these campaigns there came into being the territory of the Hwicce, at first subordinate to Wessex, but 40 years later wrested from it by the emergent power of Mercia; an event which the Chronicle records, in a supreme meoisis, by saying that, after a battle fought at Cirencester in 628, the result of which it omits to mention, Cynegils of Wessex and Penda of Mercia came to an unspecified agreement. The West Saxon bias illustrated by this entry is matched by the prevarication shown in the account of Ceawlin's downfall.

Successful as the start of the campaign of 584 may have been, it ended on an ominous note. Cutha was killed in the fighting and we are told that Ceawlin returned home 'in anger', the cause of which is unexplained. The Chronicle follows this with three enigmatic entries, which record that in 591 Ceol (Cutha's son) succeeded to the throne, that in the following year a great slaughter took place at Adam's Grave (Alton Priors in Wiltshire)[18] and Ceawlin was expelled, and that in 593 he perished with two others, Cwichelm and Crida, of whom the first appears to have been another brother of his[19] and the second, from the name, also of the royal kin. On the next occasion that we hear of the *bretwaldaship* it had passed to Æthelberht, and although Bede, who is the informant,[20] does not tell us when he acquired it there are two pieces of indirect evidence which, taken together, suggest that it was during the course of these events. The Wessex regnal list prefaced to the Parker edition of the Chronicle credits Ceawlin with a reign of only 17 years, which cannot be reconciled with the entries in the text and has been used to cast doubt upon the reliability of the list in general.[21] A different complexion is put upon the matter, however, if we assume that a confusion has occurred here with the period of Ceawlin's *bretwaldaship*, beginning *c.* 571 and ending during the obscure period between his return from the campaign of 584 and his expulsion. The assumption is strengthened when we find in the Canterbury Epitome of the Chronicle the remarkable statement that Æthelberht was baptised in the tenth year of his reign.[22] This again can make sense only if the true reference is to his *bretwaldaship*, which would then date from *c.* 588. It seems that something happened while Ceawlin was away waging his last campaign against the British, the nature of which the Chronicle was reluctant to reveal, but which first threatened, and then shortly destroyed, his supremacy; and that whatever part Æthelberht may have played in this it was to his benefit that it redounded.

It is possible to interpret the events purely in terms of a palace revolution led by Ceawlin's nephew Ceol, prompted by a military set-back suffered by Ceawlin and perhaps associated with Cutha's death, and causing such disruption in Wessex that its power was eclipsed, so that the *bretwaldaship* passed to Æthelberht almost by default. It is not easy, however, to believe that Ceol, or any other of the Wessex princes, would have been bold enough to challenge Ceawlin without some assurance of outside support; and still more difficult to conceive that Æthelberht, for all his ability and force of personality, would have been accepted as *bretwalda* not only by Wessex, but by East Anglia and kingdoms as far afield as Lindsey and Mercia, with a military record marked only by the defeat at *Wibbandun.* If this occurred it would have been a remarkable achievement in itself; the whole history of the institution shows nothing similar. The reticence of the Chronicle is highly suspicious. We are told nothing of the circumstances in which Ceol came to the throne, nor who exactly was the victor in the battle of Adam's Grave, nor at whose hands Ceawlin and his companions perished. The Chronicle is not usually as evasive as this in dealing with internal dissensions between rival branches of the Wessex royal house, but only when attempting to obscure unpalatable triumphs by outsiders. Everything appears to point to Æthelberht as the moving spirit in these events and to the involvement of the no longer inexperienced Kentish forces. It is very likely that he conspired with dissident elements among Ceawlin's own kin, so exploiting what was to become the abiding weakness of Wessex that authority tended to be divided among princes of the royal house — Cutha, Cuthwulf, Cuthwine, Ceol, Cwichelm and Crida have all featured in this account — and that any prince who could show his descent from Cerdic might contest the kingship.[23] The timing of the action, following a check inflicted upon Ceawlin while he was away campaigning to the north, so destroying his reputation for invincibility, must also have been carefully chosen. It seems that for long years Æthelberht had been patiently waiting for just such an opportunity to avenge the defeat at *Wibbandun.* When the intervention came its effect was decisive. Although the strategic disadvantages of Kent could never be permanently removed it was another 100 years before Wessex again presented any serious threat to the kingdom.[24]

Whether Æthelberht had to fight in order to enforce his supremacy on other kingdoms we do not know; it is not something that the Chronicle would have gone out of its way to tell us; but probably the overthrow of Ceawlin would have been enough. The degree of his influence over the different kingdoms must, however, have varied considerably. At one extreme, Essex was virtually a dependency of Kent; Æthelberht's sister Ricula had been married to a king of Essex, and it was by Æthelberht that her son, his nephew, Saberht, had been put on the throne.[25] At the other, although Bede tells us that his authority extended as far as the Humber,[26] his influence over the more remote kingdoms, like Lindsey and the still small and obscure Mercia, must have been attenuated. At this time neither Sussex nor the Isle of Wight was of much account. The dealings that mattered were those with Wessex, and perhaps most of all with East Anglia, shortly to reach the peak of its power under Raedwald. North of the Humber, in the kingdoms of Deira and Bernicia, Æthelberht's writ did not run.

If Æthelberht won the *bretwaldaship* by force of arms it was in other ways that he maintained it. Evidently, he had no interest in prolonging the onslaught upon the British.

Campaigns on the Severn had nothing to offer the Cantware; and the frontier states could be left to make what headway they might without the whole force of the English being mustered to help them in activities that could only tip the balance of strength in their favour to the detriment of the eastern kingdoms. The *bretwalda* was a king writ large, and as was bound to happen the institution was now re-interpreted in Kentish terms, in which the ruler was seen not as a conqueror and plunderer but as the protector of his people, the composer of differences, and magnificent gift-giver. The prosperity of Kent was the foundation of Æthelberht's power. This was, in an almost literal sense, the kingdom's age of gold, and no other ruler of the time could have lived in such state or cut so imposing a figure (though Raedwald of East Anglia was later able to do so). But munificence and display were not in themselves enough; if the *bretwalda*'s role was to be no longer that of a war leader but of an arbiter among kings a strong moral authority was needed to back it. Whatever other influences may already have been working upon Æthelberht before he won his supremacy, the achievement of that must have been the decisive factor which turned him towards the Christian Church, which understood just as well as he did the value of ostentation and had behind it all the majestic tradition of Rome.

It is typical of Æthelberht's cast of mind that the first use to which he put the gift of literacy brought with Christianity was in codifying the customs of the Kentish people. This, the earliest authentic document in the English language of which a record has survived, was probably produced *c.* 602–3,[27] but the picture it presents is as true of the earlier part of Æthelberht's reign as of the later. Bede says that the code was 'inspired by the example of the Romans',[28] but this is so only in the sense that law-giving as a function of royalty was a conception inherited from Rome through the medium of the Church.[29] The substance of Æthelberht's laws owed nothing to Roman examples but was mostly a recapitulation of existing customs, Germanic in stock, many of which the Jutes must have brought with them from the continent; the format being modelled, it seems, on earlier Frankish, Gothic and Burgundian laws, although the detailed provisions and scales of value were specifically Kentish, representing native variations upon certain common themes. That the church was the intermediary by which these other codes were made available to Æthelberht is highly probable; almost certainly the work was approved and encouraged by St Augustine; and the document must have been prepared by Christian scribes. But, as Bede tells us, the contents were based upon the advice of the *sapientes*, or wise men, of the kingdom[30] and consisted of a judicious distillation of traditional lore, with some adaptations or interpretive innovations, and with a good deal omitted as common knowledge.

The clearest innovation is in the first clause, which adapts the customary rules dealing with thefts to those from the church; but the remaining 89 clauses make no mention of the church at all, even in matters of marriage, and appear indeed to be quite untinged by Christian thought. The standards expressed are still those of a pagan society in a violent age, governed by obligations of honour tempered with pragmatism. In this society the protection of the individual devolved primarily upon his kin, and the feud was an accepted institution; but since resort to feuding involved the innocent with the guilty, brought the wronged no material satisfaction, and must often have created acute conflicts of loyalty among those with connections on both sides, some honourable alternative was both wanted and needed if the community was not constantly to be torn apart.[31] This was provided in a scale of compensation, proportionate to the offence and sanctioned by long-standing custom, which would discharge the guilt and so 'buy off the spear'. There were also other safeguards which custom had evolved; notably, certain special protective rights given to all freemen, from the king downwards, over their own homes and households, and the recognition that the protection of the individual was the responsibility not only of his kin but of his lord, which in Kent at this time meant the king, and no other. These customs could be developed, in the first case to produce a rudimentary notion of the king's peace, and in the second as a counter-poise to the purely private remedy of the feud; a matter in which the king and church shared a common interest, since both were concerned to increase the area of public authority and order. As Professor Wallace-Hadrill has emphasized,[32] the chief significance of Æthelberht's code – apart from the light it throws on contemporary practice – is that in causing the law to be written down (with whatever *lacunae*) the king was making it his own. In that there lay the germ of future development, irrespective of any adaptations or adjustments contained in the code itself.

One feature of the code which must have been novel in England at the time is that all values are expressed in monetary terms, and not only those of the gold shilling, based upon the Byzantine and Merovingian *tremiss*, but of the silver *sceatta*, derived it seems from the Frisians, of which 20 were reckoned to the shilling.[33] This gave the code a greater precision and concentration than would have been possible if the payments had had to be rendered in terms of goods or livestock; but the principal values must have been converted from earlier payments of that kind, which still continued, and it is important as a matter of perspective to establish what the relationship was. Chadwick, writing in 1905, made use for the purpose of the values set on a variety of domestic animals in the laws of Athelstan of Wessex (who reigned between 924 and 940).[34] In these the price of an ox is given as a gold *mancus*, which had the same weight as the old Roman *solidus*, believed by Chadwick to have been adopted for the Kentish shilling, and the price of a sheep is given as a shilling, reckoned however in the Wessex fashion of that time as containing five pennies (it had been only four pennies previously), which had about twice the silver content of the *sceatta* of Æthelberht's code. Now that it is believed that the Kentish shilling was based, not upon the *solidus*, but the *tremiss*, which had one third of its value,[35] it follows that three would have been required for the purchase of an ox. Æthelberht's shilling was, however, twice the value of Athelstan's, reckoning by the number and weight of the silver coins composing it, so that two sheep could have been bought with it. An ox was thus six times as valuable as a sheep; a relationship confirmed in Athelstan's laws, which show that some 30 pennies, or six of the contemporary Wessex shillings, went to the *mancus*. On these calculations the blood-price, or *leodgelde*, of the Kentish eorl, which was 300 shillings, equated to 100 oxen, and that of the ordinary freeman, which was 100 shillings, to 200 sheep; correspondingly, the values set on the lives of the three classes of *laet* were 160, 120 and 80 sheep.[36]

These were substantial payments which must usually have been far beyond the capacity of the slayer and his close relatives to provide unaided. It is all the more curious, therefore, that a clause in the code says that they are to be made in the slayer's own money or goods, which in the latter case are to be undamaged or unblemished;[37] a provision which certainly did not accord with later custom and cannot easily be reconciles with others in Æthelberht's code itself. The later established practice was for the

obligation to be shared among the slayer's kin. It is probable that the import of the
provision was merely that he should be responsible for organizing these contributions
and for the condition of the goods and livestock that were handed over. The general
custom, it seems, was for the obligation to be assumed, in diminishing proportions,
among kin to three, four or more degrees of consanguinity; exactly how far, and in
what proportions, we do not know because this was one of the matters which all the
English laws treat as common knowledge, and although details of the Scandinavian
customs are available they are liable to be misleading. The compensation was shared
correspondingly among the relatives and kin of the slain.[38]

The clearest description we have of the practice comes from an early 11th-century
document preserved in the Textus Roffensis, which may reflect a development from
Wessex rather than Kentish custom, or an amalgam of customs from the different
kingdoms which had by then become forged into England.[39] There were, however, two
features which were almost certainly present in Kent in Æthelberht's time. The first was
the greater responsibility carried, and compensation received, by kin on the paternal
than on the maternal side; it seems twice as much in each degree of relationship. The
second was the payment of compensation in instalments, of which the first, known as
the *healsfang*, had in the 11th century to be paid within 21 days of the slaying, amounted
to one-tenth of the total, and represented the contribution made by the close relatives
on the one side to those on the other, this inner circle consisting of a man's children
and brothers and a paternal uncle. Further instalments were to follow at 21 day intervals.
Æthelberht's code requires 20 shillings to be paid 'at the open grave' and the whole sum
within 40 days;[40] but the figure of 20 shillings probably relates to the blood-price of the
ceorl, adopted here (as elsewhere) as a standard to be scaled up or down in its application
to an eorl or a *laet*, the proportion remaining constant at one-fifth in each case. This
shows much the same system in operation, although the initial instalment is higher, the
commitments of the inner group correspondingly greater, its composition perhaps somewhat different, and the time-scale more compressed; all of which suggests that the
Kentish freeman of the 6th century was wealthier than his English counterpart of the
11th, a conclusion that need not surprise us. The *healsfang*, besides discharging the
responsibilities of the immediate family, served as an earnest of intent; it represented as
much as the family could be expected to get together in a short time, pending contributions from the wider kin. Æthelberht's code provides that where the killer has fled
'the land', i.e. presumably the kingdom, so putting himself beyond the reach of
vengeance, the kin may buy off their own liability at half the blood-price.[41]

The code also deals with the payments to be made for a whole variety of physical
injuries not resulting in death; no fewer than 40 of the 90 clauses are devoted to this.
Once again, it seems, the figures cited are for injuries inflicted on a ceorl, and would be
scaled up or down for an eorl or a *laet* in proportion to the full *leodgelde*, or blood-
price. Apparently, the destruction of a man's genital organs was regarded as a peculiarly
atrocious action, for which the compensation fixed was three times the full *leogelde*;[42]
a sum which must usually have placed the deed beyond any hope of composition, as a
dishonour which could only be avenged in blood. The injuries ranked next in seriousness
were the destruction of an eye or the lopping off of a foot, for each of which 50 shillings
was payable,[43] so that total blinding or mutilation was treated as equivalent to taking
a man's life. To destroy the hearing in an ear or to disable a shoulder were considered

somewhat less injurious, since these were to be paid for with 30 shillings.[44] But the code deals with far more trivial harms than these, and in the most meticulous detail. Thus stab wounds in the thigh are assessed according to the depth of penetration;[45] the thumb and each of the fingers is separately priced;[46] so, too, are the teeth, working from the front round to the back molars;[47] and even toe-nails, that of the big toe being rated at 30 *sceattas* and those of the other toes at 10 apiece.[48] Compensation is also prescribed for assaults causing no more than temporary injury or disfigurement, such as striking a man on the nose (3 shillings),[49] pulling his hair (50 *sceattas*)[50] or bruising him (one shilling, with an additional 30 *sceattas* for a black bruise showing outside the clothing).[51] If much of this now seems rather ludicrous, it illustrates how sensitive this society was to considerations of mere dignity, and how easily a trivial brawl could flare up into a feud unless damped down at once by some satisfaction which, small as it might be — perhaps a single sheep or less — could be given and accepted with honour.

In addition to his *leodgelde*, every freeman had certain protective rights, known as his *mund*, for breach of which he was entitled to compensation. The king's *mund* was set at 50 shillings, that of the eorl (by inference) at 12 shillings, and that of the ceorl at six.[52] It was an infraction of a man's *mund* for anyone to be killed on his *tun*, or premises (including in the king's case the royal hall or court),[53] or for anyone to force his way into them or to break through the surrounding enclosure, even if no other offence was committed; and those who accompanied the offender were also liable, though at a lower rate.[54] The same principle applied to the supply of a weapon used against a man in a quarrel or in a highway robbery; and if he was killed as a result the liability of the weapon-giver was increased from six to 20 shillings.[55] As we shall describe later, the *mund* also extended to the protection of a man's slaves, who had no blood-price of their own. The conception was not peculiar to Kent; it is found in the laws of other kingdoms, such as Wessex;[56] but in Kent the ceorl's *mund* was exceptionally high, since if the blood-price of the Kentish ceorl was twice that of his counterpart in Wessex (as Chadwick believed)[57] then his *mund* was four times as much, and even otherwise it was at least double. Evidently, a quite unusual importance attached in Kent to the sanctity of a man's household; but this might have been expected in a society of homestead rather than village dwellers, and one in which the ceorl occupied his land by individual and indefeasible right. The *mund* was at the same time a fence to privacy and an acknowledgement of independence.

The king's *mund* of 50 shillings had a wider application than this. In particular, it was used to protect the *leude* of the realm when assembled at his summons.[58] As we have seen, this term was derived from the Frankish *leudes*, who were the king's armed followers,[59] and in Kentish usage probably connoted the eorls and ceorls (but not the *laets*) who shared with the king responsibilities for defence and the transaction of public business, when all private quarrels were to be laid aside. To molest anyone at such an assembly was not only treated as a breach of the royal *mund*, but entitled the person who was harmed to a double rate of compensation;[60] and even at other places and times, for instance when the king was a guest at a man's house, his presence shed the same special protection (which was also invoked for meetings and services of the church).[61] We have here the germ of the king's peace, a conception developing out of a common right to privacy and respect into a guarantor of public order, by which the king was seen as having throughout the realm something on the same privileges and standing as the head of a household enjoyed in his own home.

An extension of the same principle was the royal *wite*, or fine, of which two examples occur in Æthelberht's laws. The first was concerned with thefts.[62] The primary emphasis here was on resttitution, by which theft from a freeman was to be compensated three-fold, from the king or a priest nine-fold, and from a bishop eleven-fold – a remarkable generous provision, no doubt intended to manifest to a still largely heathen and sceptical people the great veneration in which Æthelberht himself held the church. To this the *wite* was an added ingredient. Commonly, at this time, thefts must have consisted of the lifting of stock, just the sort of activity calculated to provoke a maximum of disturbance and violence; and the same was true of the other offence for which the *wite* was invoked, the abduction and dishonouring of a maiden.[63] These were not matters that could be left entirely to private settlement; the infraction of the peace required, and justified, some royal intervention, being tantamount to a breach of the king's *mund*. On the amount of the *wite* Æthelberht's laws are uninformative, and it may well have had a wider incidence than they show; but it seems from the laws of Hlothere and Eadric that the maximum rate, imposed for the more serious offences, was 50 shillings, but that for lesser infractions this was scaled down, normally to 12 shillings.[64] As Chadwick observed, this example, supported by an even clearer analogy from Wessex, makes the connection with *mund* apparent.[65]

But there was an even more powerful reinforcement of royal authority; the conception of lordship, which was very deeply rooted in early Germanic society, and embraced the whole ethos of the bond between a war leader – which was the original role of the king – and the fighting men who followed him in battle and were his companions in peace, and which took on a territorial emphasis as the leader came to reward his followers out of conquered lands. In Æthelberht's laws the king appears as the sole lord of every free-man, for the killing of any one of whom 50 shillings had to be paid to him in *drihtinbeage*[66] – literally 'lord-ring', an archaic term which must hark back to a time when, in the absence of currency, compensation was paid in rings.[67] A number of writers, from Liebermann on,[68] have been reluctant to accept this provision at its face value, finding it difficult to believe that the king could have stood in so direct a personal relationship to every one of his subjects (slaves only excluded), and have therefore suggested that the term *frigne mannan* should be given a restricted meaning. There is nothing elsewhere in Æthelberht's code to support this; indeed, rather to the contrary; but there is a clause in the later laws of Hlothere and Eadric which appears to confine the expression to those with a blood-price of 100 shillings, i.e. to the ceorls (and obviously the eorls also) but to the exclusion of the *laets*.[69] This is considered further in Appendix E. There is an argument for excluding the *laets* from the definition because they were not descended from the original warrior company, as the ceorls were, and had not inherited the same military obligations; as against which, all or most of them were the king's own tenants and in that sense would have had the king as their lord. But even if the term 'freeman' is to be construed as meaning, in effect, a freeholder it must have embraced all the ceorls, who were precisely that. It is difficult to see what narrower construction could possibly be put on it, or to understand on what grounds Finberg could have concluded that there was a class of freemen distinct from the ceorls 'but perhaps including some of them'.[70] There is nothing in any of the Kentish laws which seems to warrant such a differentiation.

If we accept Æthelberht's code at its face value as meaning that every man who was personally free owed the king an unsubtracted loyalty as sole lord we may find the idea a startling one, but it nevertheless accords with the Kentish system of land tenure described in the previous chapter, by which in the early days all dues and services were owed to the king without intermediary. This means that the hereditary nobility of the eorls had none of the attributes of lordship, though they excelled all other freemen in wealth and dignity. It also meant that the king had an obligation of honour to avenge the killing of any one of his subjects, failing proper restitution; a protective interest which, where the victim was a ceorl, was valued at half that of the kindred themselves, and in two special cases — those of the king's own smith(s) and messenger(s) — was placed on a par with theirs, the normal rate of *drihtinbeage* being doubled to 100 shillings.[71] The smith was, pre-eminently, the royal sword-maker and the term may also have included that other master craftsman, the jeweller, whose work appeared on sword pommels as well as in brooches. The term used for messenger, *laadrincmannan*, is unique, but he was clearly a particularly trusted official of the royal household, not merely a bearer but fulfilling more of the functions of a herald.* There is no mention yet of any other royal officers, such as the reeves who make their appearance 70 years later in the laws of Hlothere and Eadric.[72] It seems that all public business was still conducted by the king himself, perhaps with the advice of his intimates, but without delegation. This was still a small community, and there had not yet been a depersonalization of rule.

Æthelberht's code tells us a great deal about the position both of women and of slaves. Although this was a patriarchal society, in which brides were bought, women were well protected both physically and financially. A free-born woman — distinguished, it seems, by wearing her hair long (*locbor*) — had while unmarried the same blood-price as her father and brothers[73] and maintained this status after marriage, irrespective of that of her husband, which however determined that of the children. The price paid for a bride was a matter for bargain with her family, in the course of which, it appears, agreement would also be reached about the sum to be settled on her as the 'morning gift' on the day after the wedding.[74] If any fraud was discovered, for example that the girl was not a virgin, she was to be returned to her family and the bride price recovered.[75] If a girl was forcibly abducted not only was 50 shillings payable to her kin in compensation (with an additional 20 shillings if she had been pledged elsewhere) but the union had to be regularised through the agreement of a bride price; or, if the girl was returned in default of this, the compensation was increased by 35 shillings and a further 15 shillings went to the king as *wite*.[76] An abduction which left a girl dishonoured and husbandless was thus treated almost as seriously as a killing. So, too, was adultery. For this offence the man had to pay the full blood-price (whether of himself or of the woman is left ambiguous) and also purchase another wife for the husband — who presumably had some choice in the matter, although the clause does not say so — this being a fair recompense for the bride price paid for the woman he had lost.[77] In addition a free-born woman

---

* That these servants of the king were freemen, and not slaves whose value to him had been rated at the equivalent of a ceorl's blood-price, as has sometimes been suggested, is clear from the context of the provision, which is unmistakably that of *drihtinbeage*.

was responsible for her own misconduct, 30 shillings being the prescribed rate of compensation.[78] In all these matters the kin on either side would, no doubt, be expected to play their accustomed parts, in contribution to the payments or in sharing what was received. The family and kindred were therefore as much concerned to restrain their members from immorality as from violence.

It appears that a wife was free to leave her husband if she wished, but that the choice then lay with him whether the children, if there were any, should go with her or not. Either way, the wife had the same claim on her husband's money and goods as if she had been left a widow; a half share if the children went with her, and a lesser, but unspecified, proportion if not[79] — this being in addition to the 'morning gift' settled on her after the wedding. A husbandless woman was not, however, expected to fend for herself; the responsibility for her protection reverted to her paternal kin, one of whom acted as her guardian.[80] This was a privilege as much as a burden because it appears that the guardian took over the property in return for maintaining the woman and her children, so long as those remained dependent. The value of the asset can be gauged from the special *mund* set up to protect guardianship rights; for breach of which compensation was as high as 50 shillings if the widow was of noble birth (eorl*cundre*), 20 shillings if she was of the 'second class', presumably of ceorl stock, and 12 or six shillings if she was of the third or fourth classes, which apparently represented higher and lower grades of *laet*.[81] These rates of compensation were doubled if the guardianship was usurped by someone who had no right to it.[82] The provision confirms that a woman's status depended upon her own birth and remained unaffected by her marriage, and that it was her own kin, and not her husband's, who continued to be responsible for her; in particular, it shows that the nobility was a hereditary one, embracing women as well as men, though incapable of descending in the female line.

Slaves feature extensively in the code, but under a variety of descriptions. The precise term for slave was *theow*, but quite often *esne*, meaning a servant, is used instead, and sometimes other terms descriptive of the individual's function or circumstances, such as *birele*, a serving maid, or *hlafaetan*, which means literally a 'loaf-eater', that is a dependent.[83] A slave had no blood-price of his own and was treated as having no kin; his protection devolved upon his owner, and harm done to him (or her) was dealt with as a breach of the owner's *mund*. It follows that the value set upon the life, or chastity, of a slave varied considerably according to whether the owner was the king, an eorl, or simply a ceorl. It also varied according to the slave's function. Broadly speaking, there were three classes of female slave, the serving maid, the 'grinding woman', and the ordinary field woman; but only a single class of male slave, the all-purpose labourer.

The serving maid, sometimes called *birele* which means a cup-bearer, was clearly a valued member of the household, whose chastity was protected by the full weight of the *mund*, that is 50 shillings if she served the king, 12 shillings if she served an eorl, and six shillings if her master was a ceorl.[84'] The two lower grades of female slave were also reasonably well protected if they belonged to the king; the compensation exacted for misconduct with a royal 'grinding woman' was 25 shillings and with a field woman 12 shillings.[85] In a ceorl's household it was proportionate, which meant, however, that it absolute terms it was low, a mere matter of 50 *sceattas* in the first case and 30 in the second,[86] or (to set the matter in perspective) the sort of sums that would be payable for knocking off her master's thumbnail or the nail of his big toe. Clearly, misconduct with a man's female slaves (excepting his serving maid) was lightly regarded, although if the woman was married to another slave the offence was considered more serious and the compensation doubled.

Among the male slaves, the life of the king's *fedesl* was valued at 20 shillings and that of the ceorl's *hlafaetan* at six shillings.[87] These are curiously archaic terms, but their meanings, a 'fatted animal' and a 'loaf-eater', are similar in implying a servant who was not hired but only fed and maintained. In the normal course each would be a farm labourer. The difference in the relative status of the two is far less than might be expected from the ownership. Thus the life of the king's *fedesl* was valued at less than the chastity of one of his grinding women, whereas that of the ceorl's *hlafaetan* was set on a par with the chastity of his serving maid, that is at the full rate of the *mund*, equivalent to the price of two oxen. The contrast is less surprising when one considers not merely the ownership but the circumstances of employment; the *fedesl* in large numbers scattered throughout the royal demesnes, the *hlafaetan* in ones or twos on small farms where they would have become almost as much members of the ceorls' households as the serving maids themselves.

A slave was protected not only in life or chastity but in certain other ways as well. The destruction of an eye and foot had to be compensated at the full value set on his or her life (that is, presumably, at half the value in either case alone; the same proportion as applied with a freeman).[88] If a slave was robbed on the highway three shillings had to be paid in compensation.[89] However hard, the conditions of life were not entirely brutish. As we have seen there could be marriages between slaves, and the chastity of the wife was then doubly protected.[90] Evidently, too, a slave could own some money and goods, since if he killed another without cause he himself was responsible for meeting the price, and if he stole he had to make a two-fold restitution.[91] More light is thrown on this matter by the Penitentials of Archbishop Theodore (668–690), which show that a slave might be provided with his own dwelling and means of support and was entitled to keep any money or livestock earned by his own labour — presumably through work done independently of that required by his master.[92] It has been suggested that it was this form of settlement which distinguished the *esne* from the *theow*, who was maintained in his master's household,[93] but it seems that the *theow* also could have goods,[94] and the distinction credits the early codes with a greater precision of draftsmanship than they are likely to have possessed. Whereas later laws, both in Kent and in Wessex, laid down certain offences for which a slave could be flogged,[95] nothing of this appears in Æthelberht's code. No doubt the slave's lot depended, as ever, on the character of his master. The king's serving maid was a person of some consequence, and perhaps influence; and on many of the small farms both maids and 'loaf-eaters' must have been on a footing of real confidence and friendship with the families they served.

The poise of Kentish society differed from that of the Anglo-Saxon kingdoms; a comparison most clearly brought out in the laws of Ine of Wessex, promulgated *c.* 694 and so closely contemporary with the codes both of Hlothere and Eadric (*c.* 684) and of Wihtred (695). The major structural differences were that in Wessex there were two classes of nobility, of whom the superior had a blood-price six times that of the ceorl and the inferior three times (which was the Kentish ratio), but that there were no *laets*. The complicating factor is that the monetary system in Wessex was dissimilar to that of Kent, the shilling there being a mere unit of account reckoned at four silver pieces, described in the copy of Ine's laws that has come down to us as 'pennies'*.[96] The blood-prices of the two classes of West Saxon noble were 1,200 shillings and 600 shillings,[97] representing therefore 4,800 and 2,400 silver pieces, as against the 6,000 *sceattas* of the Kentish eorl; and the blood-price of the West Saxon ceorl was 200 shillings,[98] or 800 silver pieces, as compared to the 2,000 *sceattas* of the Kentish freemen. At first sight, therefore, it seems that blood-prices in Kent were higher at every level of society. But this assumes, as Chadwick did, that the 'penny' and the *sceatta* were identical coins;[99] whereas contemporary numismatists like Stewart Lyon believe that the penny of Ine's time resembled that of a hundred years later in being a larger coin of about twice the silver value and content.[100] There is nothing tangible to show this, but there is other evidence, examined in Appendix E, which tends on balance to support it and to suggest that the Kentish shilling was around two and a half times the value of the West Saxon, but no more. As may be seen from the Tables (below), the effect of this would be to make the blood-price of the Kentish eorl nearer to that of the inferior than of the superior noble of Wessex; and, while that of the Kentish ceorl would remain higher than of his Wessex counterpart, the margin would be greatly reduced.

CLASSES IN KENTISH AND WESSEX SOCIETY

Comparison of Status

Note: All values are converted to those of the Kentish shilling reckoned at two and a half times that of the shilling of Wessex

Leodgeld (Kent)		Wergeld (Wessex)			With addition of Lordship Money			
						Kent		Wessex
		Gesith (1)	480 s.				Gesith (1)	528 s.
Eorl	300 s.	Gesith (2)	240 s.		Eorl	350 s.	Gesith (2)	264 s.
Ceorl	100 s.				Ceorl	150 s.		
Laet (1)	80 s.	Ceorl	80 s.		Laet (1)	?		
Laet (2)	60 s.				Laet (2)	?	Ceorl	92s.
Laet (3)	40 s.				Laet (3)	?		

	Mund or Protective Rights			
	Kent		Wessex	
King	50 s.	King	49 s.	
		Gesith (1)	24 s.	
Eorl	12 s.	Gesith (2)	12 s.	
Ceorl	6 s.			
Laet (1)	?			
Laet (2)	?			
Laet (3)	?	Ceorl	2.5 s	

* The laws were appended to those of Alfred, some 200 years later, so that the term 'penny' may have been used anachronistically for what in fact was an earlier silver currency of the *sceatta*.

But the value of a man's life cannot be reckoned solely by the blood-price payable to his kindred; account has also to be taken of what was due to his lord, who in Kent was the king himself, but for ceorls in Wessex (and elsewhere) was usually a *gesith*, or noble. The Table shows that this factor makes little difference to the relative standing of the Kentish eorl, but it does to that of the ceorl; the full sum set upon his life is half as much again as on the life of the ordinary Wessex peasant.[101] And the disparities in *mund*, or protective rights, were even greater. The *mund* of the eorl was closer to that of the superior than of the inferior noble of Wessex, but that of the Kentish ceorl was more than twice that of his West Saxon counterpart.[102] There is nothing astonishing in all this, which is merely what one would expect from the contrasting land systems. The Kentish noble was not, in these early days, a territorial lord with his own retainers, as the *gesith* of Wessex usually was, and his status tended to be lower in consequence; but the ceorl, who ranked as the king's man and owed no other allegiance, was a singularly powerful and privileged individual. These direct ties between the king and his free subjects made for stability; in a true sense, and despite the numerous grades in its society, Kent was more homogeneous than the other kingdoms. And the study emphasizes again how wrong it is to regard the *laets* as a semi-servile people. They were, of course, tenants and not freeholders, but so generally were the ceorls of Wessex and Mercia, who were unlikely to have been better endowed or to have owed less in rents and services. Even if we had no knowledge of the *laets'* conditions of tenure the value set upon their lives would compel us to recognize that it was at this level that the closest comparison with the ceorls of Wessex and Mercia lay, and that the Kentish ceorls formed a superior class of yeomen farmers for which no exact equivalent existed elsewhere, except possibly in East Anglia (where the blood-prices are unknown).

The appearance in Æthelberht's laws of the standards of the golden shilling and the silver *sceatta* does not mean that these were current in every section of the community, still less that they were minted in Kent. A gold coin bearing the name of Liuthard has, in fact, been discovered at Canterbury, and appears from certain imperfections to have been struck locally; but this was pierced for wearing as a pendant and is regarded as a solitary venture of its kind,[103] and the Merovingian *tremisses* which found their way into Kent were more likely to have been treasured than used. The *sceattas* (of Frisian origin) were a different matter. While the laws show that compensation was still often — probably more often than not — paid in kind, they also specifically provide for the payment of *sceattas*.[104] The coin was, therefore, in circulation, and this implies a significant growth of overseas trade. On the Kentish side it could scarcely have been confined to the slave traffic, large as that no doubt was. We have suggested in the previous chapter that already in Eormenric's reign some primary products such as wool and salted fish and cheese had been exported, to which perhaps cereal surpluses were added from time to time, if only to make good shortfalls caused by poor continental harvests.

We have also suggested that, at the start, the bulk of the trade must have passed through the royal vills; and indeed well down into the 8th century such ports as Sarre and Fordwich, which had been associated with courts, continued to handle much of the continental traffic.[105] In the early days of the kingdom, before ecclesiastical and lay lordships had been built up by land grants, only the royal estates can have been large enough to yield substantial trading surpluses. There are indications that in Æthelberht's reign certain other places were beginning to share in the commercial prosperity;

notably Dover, where the burials at Buckland, dating from this time, show an unusually high proportion of swords to spears, suggesting a rich community.[106] Nevertheless the king must have been by far the chief beneficiary, and the bounty he was able to dispense, among his own subjects and (it is to be assumed) the other rulers who acknowledged his authority as *bretwalda*, became the very foundation of a power which could never have rested upon military resources alone. Æthelberht was supremely well equipped to maintain the state, and to fulfil all those obligations of generosity, that were expected of a great king.

The evidence of the fructifying effects of trade on Kentish society during Æthelberht's reign appears most of all in the splendour of the native craftsmanship, which had now absorbed, and often transcended, the earlier Frankish influences. Among men the most treasured possession at this time were the great double-edged swords, skilfully wrought by the method known as pattern-welding to make them more flexible, and with their pommels often quite elaborately decorated with parcel-gilding, chip-carving or niello-inlay.[107] A feature of these swords, quite common in France and the Rhineland but in England confined mostly to Kent, is the presence of a small ring attached to the pommel bar. The ring was traditionally a royal gift and these, it seems, were symbols of particular distinction or valour, the swords themselves having, perhaps, been presented by the king. Ring swords have been found at Faversham, Gilton, Sarre, Dover and Coombe near Eastry (an especially fine example). Judging from the ornamentation on the pommels, where this has survived, and from associated objects in the burials, they date from the last half of the 6th century, and seem, therefore, to represent gifts made by Æthelberht to the more valiant of the eorls who fought with him in the obscure battles by which he wrested the supremacy from Wessex. That they have mostly been found at, or in the close neighbourhood of, the royal vills is no coincidence; and that all have been found in north-east Kent emphasizes the predominance of this area in the early history of the kingdom.

The most superb examples of Kentish craftsmanship are, however, to be seen in the rich polychrome jewellery worn by women, and especially in the so-called composite brooches.[108] These were constructed of two silver or gold plates, bound together by strips or filigree and filled with a white clay-like substance. The Kingston Brooch, deposited *c.* 630 and apparently made in Æthelberht's reign, is generally regarded as the masterpiece in this genre, though six or seven other specimens have been found — one as far afield as Aylesford — and many more of a simpler, non-composite, i.e., single-plated, type which is especially well represented at Faversham. The polychrome ornament on the front of the brooches consists of gold or silver cloisons, stepped, square, semi-circular or triangular, enclosing garnets, blue or green glass, niello and various white materials, sometimes shell; and the plate is often slightly concave or convex to enhance the quality of the contrasting colours. The workmanship of the best of these brooches, particularly in the construction of the cloisons and the filigree, is of a very high standard. The designs are distinctive, showing a notable departure from, and improvement upon, earlier Frankish forms.

The graves of the period also contain large quantities of imported material such as amber, used for beads, and ivory for rings. Among the more uncommon articles are bronze tripod bowls with drop handles, of Rhenish provenance,[109] among the more common, wheel-turned Frankish pots, which were probably wine containers. There are also quantities of glass beakers, bottles and palm cups, most of which can be traced to manufacturing houses in Belgium, north France and the Rhineland, although it seems that some glass-ware was also produced at Faversham, the home of the distinctive 'bag beakers'. As D. B. Harden has pointed out, rich gold and garnet jewellery was often associated with glass, which was then very much of a luxury article.[110]

These goods, swords, jewellery, bowls, flasks and glass-ware are to be found widely distributed among the burial sites, especially in north-east Kent; mostly, no doubt, they were the possessions of eorls, but not exclusively so. Curiously, the two burials which have yielded the richest concentration of articles of Kentish design are at Taplow in Buckinghamshire and Broomfield in Essex, both within the Kingdom of Essex, which however was subordinate to Kent and deeply influenced by it.[111] It seems that these must have been the graves of people who were not merely nobles, but more in the nature of sub-kings, of whom there were none at this time in Kent itself, where Æthelberht maintained an undelegated authority. Taplow means Taeppa's *hlaw*, or burial place,[112] so that here the name of the individual concerned has been preserved, although nothing more is known to him. A particularly interesting feature of this burial is the discovery of mounts for two drinking horns, foreshadowing those found at Sutton Hoo.

Because Æthelberht died a Christian and was buried, as Bede tells us, in St Martin's Porch in the newly constructed Abbey of Saints Peter and Paul (later St Augustine's) at Canterbury,[113] he left no necropolis, rich in treasure to be discovered. Nevertheless, we can gain some impression of the style in which he lived from the Sutton Hoo burial, which has now been shown by Bruce-Mitford to have been that of his younger contemporary, and successor in the *bretwaldaship*, Raedwald of the East Angles,[114] who died within ten years of him, as a lapsed Christian or one who had merely added Christ to the pantheon of his gods. The connection between the two men was close, since it was Æthelberht who had brought Raedwald to Canterbury and persuaded him to be baptized,[115] and a number of the relics found at Sutton Hoo, notably a pair of silver spoons of classical design carrying the names of Saul and Paul in Greek characters, were no doubt presented to him on that occasion.[116] The magnificence, splendid workmanship, and eclectic character of the goods unearthed at Sutton Hoo are all the more remarkable because, this apart, the East Anglian cemeteries have produced nothing which can compare in quality with the material lavishly distributed in Kent. There is all the less reason to suppose that the state maintained by Raedwald, and the possessions he accumulated, surpassed those of Æthelberht. Kentish influences are apparent in much of the gold polychrome jewellery found at Sutton Hoo, though filigree work is less in evidence, there is a major innovation in the use of *millefiori* glass, and the cloisonne work is even more intricate and assured.[117] If, however, we allow for stronger Scandinavian connections with East Anglia and Frankish with Kent, there can have been little difference in the magnificence of the treasures amassed by these two rulers in the days of their supremacy.

Nothing has been found in Kent to match the splendid armour at Sutton Hoo, but the bulk of the other articles are of a sort that one would expect to have been seen at the Kentish court, allowing for local differences in the style and handiwork of the polychrome jewellery and its setting. Of special interest is the purse, of which the lid and clasp are adorned with cloisonne and garnet work carried to a standard of perfection which not even the Kingston brooch can rival,[118] and containing 37 gold *tremisses*, each from a different Frankish mint. In addition there was a quantity of foreign vessels and plate, mostly no doubt acquired by gift. Among these are three bronze Celtic hanging bowls,[119] such as have been found in a number of Kentish cemeteries; a circular silver dish of Byzantine origin, bearing the control stamps of the Emperor Anastasius (491–518); and other plate from the Mediterranean, including a fluted silver bowl, a silver ladle, a small cup, and ten hemispherical bowls with simple geometrical or floral designs.[120] Articles of this kind must have been familiar at the Kentish court, with its Frankish queen and royal connections; and no doubt they would also have featured among 'the small gifts' that Gregory the Great sent to Æthelberht in 601.[121] Some of those owned by Raedwald may well (like the baptismal spoons) have been gifts from Æthelberht himself; tokens of that generosity which a *bretwalda* would be expected to display to a king acknowledging his authority, just as the suzerainty which the Merovingian kings claimed over Kent would, if precedent is any guide, have been marked in the same munificent way.

Finally, there were two objects discovered at Sutton Hoo which appear to have been symbols of royalty. One of these is a stone shaft, two feet in length, which seems originally to have been surmounted by the figure of a stag, standing upon a ring, which was discovered close to the stone itself. That is thought to have been in the nature of a sceptre, to which certain magical or religious properties, wholly heathen in inspiration, may have clung.[122] The second of the royal emblems, however, harks back to a different tradition. This is an iron standard, some five feet six inches in height, with four short projecting arms at the top and a rectangular grill further down the haft, both the arms and the corners of the grille terminating in stylized ox heads; the base of the standard consisting of a short spike, with two volutes, which may have been used for planting the object either in the ground or in a leather frog to support it when carried.[123] It has been suggested that this standard, decked out with foliage, peacock feathers or the like, was a Roman-style *tufa*, such as (Bede tells us) was constantly carried in front of Edwin of Northumbria when he succeeded Raedwald as *bretwalda*.[124] It would seem, therefore, to have been a symbol not merely of royalty but of a High King, and from its Roman antecedents of a kind very likely to have been introduced by Æthelberht, to be borne before him, on formal occasions, by his *laadrincmannan*, or herald.

The discovery of a lyre at Sutton Hoo reminds us that this was a bardic society. As Michael Alexander has said, the poet was at the same time historian and priest, and his songs had a ritual significance.[125] Such knowledge as we have of the conquest of Kent comes, ultimately, from vanished sagas, but these were no more than an addition to a common stock of heroic tradition, known and celebrated throughout the Germanic world, into which those of the individual tribes were woven. The Swedish connections apparent at Sutton Hoo have prompted Bruce-Mitford to suggest that it was through the East Anglian court that the legend of *Beowulf* was transmitted into England;[126] but, by the same reasoning, it is to Kent that we should look for the source of the added ingredient to that epic which tells of the part played by the Jutes, as allies of the Frisians, in killing the Danish prince Hnaef, and of the revenge taken by Hengest. The depth of lore preserved in these sagas is shown by the earliest poem in the English language, *Widsith*, which has reached us from a 7th century Mercian source but has much older echoes, in which some have detected word forms suggesting a Kentish origin.[127] This poem, entirely heathen in inspiration, has as its theme the wanderings of the bard among the German tribes, of which nearly 70 are named, with as many rulers or heroes, some of whom are known to have lived as early as the 3rd century, a few — such as Theoderic the Frank — as late as the 6th, but none later. Great prominence is given to the Gothic king Eormenric, 'lord over cities' and to his wife Ealhhild, 'gold hung queen, gift-dealer'.[128] It is easy to understand from this why Eormenric's name should have been adopted into the Kentish royal house. Nothing illustrates more clearly than *Widsith* how close English society of the 6th century felt itself to be to its continental roots, and the hold exerted over it by the old heathen values.

This was the tradition in which Æthelberht had been steeped, and of which in the days of his supremacy he was a magnificent exemplar; and it was against this that the Christian influences in his own household had to contend. To transcend the old values by reaching out to the alien traditions of the Roman world was, however far-seeing, an act of great daring. It is not surprising that Æthelberht should have approached it warily, late in age, and only after his position as *bretwalda* had been secured. Events were to show that he came to it too late, and that while his own people were prepared to follow him, with whatever misgivings, his supremacy over the other English nations was not proof against it.

PART II:

THE CHRISTIAN ERA

Chapter Six

THE CONVERSION, 595-616

Æthelberht

THE STORY of the conversion which has imprinted itself upon popular history is that related by Bede. It tells of Gregory the Great's encounter, before he became Pope, with a group of slave boys of fair complexion who were being offered for sale in Rome. On asking who they were, and being told that they were Angles from Britain, he said that they had angelic faces, and on learning that they came from Deira, of which Aelle was then king, that they would be rescued *de ira* to the mercy of Christ and that their land would echo the praise of God in Alleluia. From this time on, Bede says, Gregory was intent upon the conversion of the English, but it was not until he had become Pope that he was able to put the matter in hand through the despatch, in 595-96, of St Augustine's mission.[1] Canterbury tradition adds certain adornments to this story. It places the encounter with the slave boys in the pontificate of Benedict I, which would make it as early as 575-79, and says that immediately afterwards Gregory himself set out for Britain, but was recalled by Benedict as indispensable.[2]

Bede says that Augustine and his companions, having started on their journey, became overcome by misgivings at being sent to so barbarous and fierce a nation as the English. Augustine thereupon returned to Rome to plead for the mission's recall, but was encouraged by Gregory to continue. The mission arrived in Thanet in 597 and immediately sent word of this to Æthelberht through Frankish interpreters whom they had brought with them. The king ordered that they should remain on the island, and be provided with necessities, while he considered what to do. After some days he came to the island himself to give them audience, taking care however that the meeting should be held in the open air for fear that magical arts might be practised upon him. Having listened to what Augustine had to say, and being convinced of his sincerity, he then settled the mission in Canterbury and gave it permission to preach. A number of converts were won over by the message and the exemplary lives of the company, and in due course Æthelberht himself was baptized, thenceforward becoming the church's champion and benefactor.[3]

This is history seen from the church's standpoint, in which Gregory appears as the sole initiator of a mission which arrived in Kent unbidden. Specifically, it is the version of events cherished at St Augustine's Abbey in Canterbury, since it was a head of that house, Albinus, who at some time after 709 encouraged Bede to embark upon his *History of the English Church and People* and provided much of the material for it.[4] Although Bede speaks nothing but good of Æthelberht — the third English king, he says, to hold sway over all the provinces south of the Humber and the first to enter the Kingdom of Heaven[5] — the account nevertheless diminishes him, and is open to question

109

THE LATER ESKINGS

A. The Ruling Line

```
                          (1) Bertha (of the          (2) Un-named
                              Merovingian line)

                     Æthelberht                                   Edwin, k. of Northumbria
                     (560–616)                                        =
                                                          d. Æthelburga
            Eadbald = (1)                                  (later Abbess at
            (616–640)                                      Lyminge)
                   = (2) Emma (of the
                          Merovingian line)

Oslafa = Eormenred                  Seaxburga = Eorcenberht        d. Eanswith        d. Eanfled = Oswy, k. of Northumbria
         (? of Northumbria)         (of East   (640–664)           (Abbess at
                                    Anglia, later                  Folkestone)
   See                              Abbess at
   Table B                          Sheppey)

Wulfhere, k. of = Eormenhilda       Egbert = Un-named              Hlothere = ?          d. Earcongeta
Mercia            (later Abbess     (664–673)                      (674–686)             (Nun in France)
                  at Sheppey)

                                Eadric                (1) Æthelburge = Wihtred = (2)   Werburga   ? Richard
                                (686–687)                              (691–725)                    (Priest in Italy)

                                Æthelberht II                         Eadberht = Un-named          Alric
                                (725–762)                             (725–762)                    (725– ?)

                                                                            Eardulf
                                                                    (sub-king 747; died before 762)
```

B. Eormenred's Descendants

```
                                        Eormenred = Oslafa

Merwald        ǂ Aebba        Æthelred, Æthelberht      d. Eormenburga = Ecgfrid, k. of     d. Eangyth
(Mercian         (later Abbess  (both murdered by        (later Abbess      Northumbria      = Centwine, k. of Wessex
sub-king)        at Minster)    Egbert)                  at Lyminge)

St Mildred (Abbess   d. Mildgyth        Oswine                   Eadburga      Wihtburga      d. Æthelthryth
at Minster)          (Nun in Kent)      (688–690)                (Abbess at    (Nun)          (Abbess at Lyminge)
                                                                 Minster)
                          ?
```

at a number of points. The story of Gregory's encounter with the English slave boys is altogether too pat; it has the colour of legend, and to do Bede justice he repeats it simply as a tradition. The origin of this may lie in a letter known to have been sent by Gregory in 595 to a priest in Gaul, instructing him to buy English slave boys of 17 or 18 to be educated in monasteries, evidently in preparation for the mission.[6] There must have been a good deal more to the meeting in Thanet than Bede recounts. Æthelberht was unlikely to have come to this unaccompanied, the pause before it was held being due to the need to summon the notables of the kingdom, whose advice he would be expected to seek on so important a matter. It is difficult to believe that Æthelberht himself, having been married for something like 40 years to a Christian wife with a bishop in her household as chaplain, should have had a superstitious fear of magic being practised on him by Augustine; but some of his notable may perhaps have felt this, so that there was need to reassure them. It seems, however, to have been customary for meetings to be held in the open air, as was that between Augustine and representatives of the Welsh church six years later;* and as the mission itself was forty strong, and Æthelberht would have been well attended, it is questionable whether the royal hall at Sarre would have been large enough to hold the assembly.

But the chief defect of the account is in what it omits. Bede does not say so, but Augustine carried with him to France a letter from Gregory to the Merovingian kings Theoderic and Theudebert saying that it had reached him that the English nation 'eagerly desired' to be converted but that the priests in the neighbourhood (i.e., in France) had neglected it, and that it was for this reason that he had despatched Augustine, whom he asked should be received and helped on his way.[7] It appears from this that Æthelberht had let it be known, presumably through Liuthard, that he would welcome a mission; but that the contacts with the Gallic church had come to nothing until Gregory had got word of the matter (evidently some time before 595) and had decided to take the initiative himself. Wallace-Hadrill has suggested that Æthelberht may have been reluctant to make direct overtures to the Merovingian kings, who already claimed paramountcy over England — as Gregory reminded them in his letter — for fear that any assistance they gave would have political conditions attached, but that a mission from Rome exactly suited his purpose.[8] He must have been prepared for it. There seems little doubt that his course of action had been carefully considered beforehand and that there was a good deal of play-acting in his reception of the mission.

According to Canterbury tradition Æthelberht's own baptism followed after what was no more than a decent interval; at Pentecost (1st June) in the same year as the arrival of the mission.[9] But Bede, when later recounting Æthelberht's death in February 5̶1̶6̶, 616 makes the remarkable statement that this was *'post XX et unum annos acceptae fidei'*[10] which implies that he had already embraced Christianity in 595, the year in which the mission first set out, or was prepared by Gregory. If *acceptae fidei* is intended to refer to Æthelberht's baptism then the passage is clearly erroneous; in which case, as Kenneth Harrison has suggested, the simplest emendation would be *XV (et unum)* for *XX*,[11] so placing the baptism in 599–600, nearly three years after St Augustine's landing. In support of this view Kenneth Harrison cites a letter sent by Gregory to the Patriarch of Alexandria reporting the mass baptisms which took place at Canterbury at Christmas

---

* The meeting was held at a place called Augustine's Oak (Bede, *Hist. Ecc.*, II, 2).

597,[12] but making no mention of the king, which he regards as a significant omission. Yet Bede clearly implies that it was the lead given by the king which brought people flocking to the faith,[13] and this is what one would have expected. Accepting that Bede was capable of error, and in this case the reference to 21 years may have been a mistranscription, or a confusion with the date on which the mission was despatched, the passage raises a more fundamental issue than chronology. The question is whether Æthelberht would have sought the mission at all unless his mind had already been made up. At the very least it argues a strong tendency towards Christianity (if not the 'eager desire' described in Gregory's letter to Theoderic and Theudebert), of which no evidence can be found among the general body of the people, who appear, on the contrary, to have been firmly wedded to the old religion. It is necessary to appreciate this if we are to understand the circumspection with which Æthelberht was compelled to act, and why the support of the mission was indispensable before he could publicly declare himself.

There is evidence enough of the ingrained paganism of the Cantware. Stenton has illustrated this by the number of place-names in Kent and Surrey which derive from heathen gods or refer to heathen shrines or temples;[14] and although his list has since been winnowed by Margaret Gelling[15] it still remains a sizeable one — Wye, Woodnesborough, Thunnor's Leap in Thanet, Thunderfield, Peper Harrow, Thursley, Willey and Tisley — of which the first was a royal court and the second directly associated with that of Eastry (near which, at Finglesham, a buckle has been discovered bearing the figure of the Horned God).[16] So entrenched were the old attitudes and customs in Kent that the practice of burial with grave-goods continued here until many years after the coming of Christianity, later indeed than almost anywhere in England. The conversion, when it came, was precarious and skin-deep. Æthelberht's own son and successor, Eadbald, was not a Christian at the beginning of his reign; his son Earconberht was the first who dared to order the destruction of idols and observance of Lent; and as late as 695 Wihtred still found it necessary to pass laws against idolatry.[17] While the Eskings themselves became staunch champions of the church, among the Cantware in general signs of Christian fervour were always singularly lacking. For all the benefits which the church brought to it, and of which its rulers were acutely aware, the kingdom contributed nothing to the distinguished company of early English missionaries and saints, except in its princesses, in whom piety was wedded to dynastic duty.

Unfortunately, we know very little about the old heathen cults. The Christian writers had no wish to dwell on them, and although they lingered on until well after the coming of the church they did so mostly in the form of debased superstitions. Tacitus' account of the worship of the earth goddess Nerthus by a group of German tribes, including the Angles and apparently also the Jutes, shows that fertility rites were a prominent feature,[18] and traces of this persisted, for instance in the practice, denounced by Archbishop Theodore nearly a hundred years after Augustine's time, of burning barley in a house where there had been a death for the protection of the living.[19] It seems that certain wells, trees and stones were considered sacred, and that magical properties were thought to reside in such animals as the auroch, the boar and the snake.[20] If place-names are a guide, the deities most venerated among the English were Woden the god of knowledge and wisdom, Thunnor the god of thunder and the elements, and Tiw the god of war; and their images were kept, with other sacred emblems, in temples such as there must once have been at Wye and that in which Raedwald of East Anglia also set up an altar to

Christ. Sacrificial feasts were held at certain seasons; on the first night of the heathen New Year (Christmas), which was known as 'the night of mothers', in the second month of the year, when cakes were offered to the gods, and in November, when beasts which could not be kept over the winter were slaughtered. The practice of burial with grave-goods suggests some belief in after-life, but it appears to have been a nebulous one. It was a religion almost devoid of theology, but abounding in taboos, charms and magical incantations, designed to ward off evil or ensure success in this life, with little thought beyond. The immortality sought by the heathen English was in the remembrance of heroic deeds.

By every empirical test the old religion had served the Cantware well. At a time when the kingdom was supreme and had never been more prosperous there was no reason why the Kentish freemen should believe that their gods had deserted them; and, while Æthelberht might associate Christianity with the splendour and achievements of the Merovingian kings, his subjects, from their more insular standpoint, would have been likelier to connect it with the British, a despised and defeated people. But there were deeper attachments than these. However theologically deficient the heathen cults may have been, they were shot through with magic and poetry; and while in themselves they may have been ethically barren they were a part of a complex of traditions which united the German people in a sense of shared values and of a common and heroic past. The old poems, such as *Widsith*, show how close the English felt to that world. It may be that the Cantware, with their Rhenish connections, had a clearer intimation than others of the different, imperial, ethos, and stood in some awe of it – a feeling expressed in a passage inserted later into *Widsith* which speaks of Caesar 'who was the wielder of wine-filled cities, and rent and riches, and the Roman domain' – but a whole style of life was bound up in their own beliefs, and they could not easily abandon them.

The contrast of traditions must have been present in Æthelberht's mind from the very beginning of his reign. On one side there was his upbringing, the values instilled into him from childhood, which pervaded his court, and were shared with his closest companions; on the other, the persuasion which Bertha and Liuthard must surely have exerted on him, the prestige of his connection with the Merovingian royal house, the resplendent example that it set, and the dawning realization of the practical, no less than the spiritial, advantages of the Christian faith. So powerful was this impulsion that it may seem surprising that it was only after he had been reigning for 30 years, and had been married for longer, that his first overtures to the church were made. There is little doubt that it was the winning of the *bretwaldaship* that finally tipped the scale. As a young man intent upon fame, and during the period of rivalry and conflict with Wessex, Æthelberht was acting entirely within the old traditions and values, and it was natural that he should have allowed himself to be carried along by them; but having won the prize the question became what use was to be made of it, in his own circumstances and those of his kingdom, and to this no truly satisfying answer was to be found in the prevailing ethos. The position he had gained in England must have brought the example of the Merovingian kings ever more clearly before him as the model for a supreme ruler who aspired to be more than a war leader.

There were also also considerations of practicality. To effect so momentous a change would require all the authority and prestige that Æthelberht could muster, and it is very doubtful whether he would have carried even his own people with him before the triumphant achievement of the *bretwaldaship* had made him an object of veneration to them. Even so his course was beset with difficulties. Gregory was later to chide Bertha for her dilatoriness in leading her husband to the faith,[21] but this was scarcely fair; it would have been folly, in such a society, for Æthelberht to appear to act upon the sole prompting of his wife, nor had he the resources and agents to carry through unaided the major undertaking required. A prestigious mission, to which he could respond after apparent hesitancy and misgivings, was vital to the whole enterprise, and it was for this, it seems, that he had been angling. Allowing for the unresponsiveness of the Gallic church, and the time taken for news of these overtures to reach Rome, the first of them must have been made shortly after the supremacy had been won. They amounted in themselves to a personal commitment, or something very near it. In a true sense the credit for Æthelberht's conversion (belated though it may have appeared) rests with Bertha and, more particularly perhaps, with Liuthard, who had for many years been a familiar figure at his court. It is unfortunate that we can never know what may have passed in quiet discussions between these two.

There are many reasons why Æthelberht should have sought Christianity; but nothing we know of him suggests that he would have been moved by an unreflecting piety. The spiritual benefits which the church had to offer, and which the old religion could not match, were an assurance of eternal life, a body of ethical teaching, and a sophisticated theology. For the magic and poetry of the heathen cults the church substituted its own profound mysteries, rituals and symbols, even its own talismans in sacred relics and holy water; and despite all its emphasis upon saintliness it left a large place for the exercise of the heroic virtues in defence of the community of God. As Wallace-Hadrill has commented,[22] 'One begins to see that the barbarian king might find his role in such a design without losing too much of what was traditional to him'. And Æthelberht was no mere barbarian but a ruler with a strong sense of majesty learned from his Merovingian relations. Behind the church there stood the whole imposing tradition of Imperial Rome, which, the more he learned of it, must have seemed to him the very fount of wisdom and enlightenment. We should expect that to a person of his disposition the truth of the Christian faith would have come less as a revelation than as a growing conviction, confirmed by the success of the Merovingian kings under the favour of God.

In practical terms, God's favour was manifested through the support of the church, the powerful ally of rulers. To fulfil its mission the church needed royal protection and an ordered framework of society; to construct which the king himself needed instruments of literacy which only the church, or those trained up by it, could supply. It may be true, as Margaret Deansley has suggested,[23] that even before St Augustine's arrival Æthelberht had obtained the services of a few Frankish notaries; but there is no proof of it, nor could the help of a handful of individuals, brought from overseas, compare with the resources which Augustine was able to put at his disposal, or serve as a substitute for the establishment within the kingdom of permanent centres of learning at which future generations could be schooled. The powers of king and church were thus interdependent and reinforced each other. In forming this partnership Æthelberht lacked the advantages of the Merovingian Clovis, who espoused a faith long established in his new dominions, and with a strong ecclesiastical hierarchy already in being; he had himself to break the ground from which the harvest was to be reaped. But the prospective rewards were great. We have described how, as a first fruit of this alliance, Æthelberht's code of laws enhanced the authority of the king by the very fact of its production, regardless of any innovations it might contain, because it set the royal seal upon custom, so entrusting it to the king's keeping. Moreover as patron and protector of the church the king acquired a standing in the religious life of the nation such as the old heathen cults, tended by their High Priests, could never have given him. To this was added the prestige of his dealings with Rome; the messages and gifts he received from Gregory; and the special veneration, transcending frontiers, which the church reserved for those who had befriended it. For many years the Eskings were able to profit from that fund of good will. As Wallace-Hadrill has said,[24] Christianity made for dynastic permanence. Conviction apart, that was unlikely to have escaped Æthelberht, a ruler who had won his position by political calculation.

There was another consideration that may also have been in his mind. It required no great perspicacity to see that in an heroic society which set its highest values upon military achievements and renown, and where able young men were attracted to the service of those who could offer them the best prospects of plunder and expropriation, the Cantware, who were blocked off from easy conquests by the frontier kingdoms, would be under a perpetual handicap, and that the ascendancy which Æthelberht had won for them would be precarious unless it could be placed upon some different foundation. The functions of the *bretwalda* could be reinterpreted as those of the supreme peace-keeper and mediator, but these rested upon personal qualities alone, and needed a firm moral backing. A Christian England proselytized from Kent, with a church offering new values which still left a place for the old, and which was centred within the Eskings' dominions under their special patronage, held out a more durable promise. There was a more tantalising prospect still. Such a church, with all the authority of Rome behind it, would have a strong claim upon the loyalties of the Christian Welsh, who might thus be drawn within the orbit of Kentish influence. Just how much of this had been grasped by Æthelberht it is impossible to say; but it is a mistake to under-estimate the comprehension of the early rulers. Æthelberht, whose overlordship included the recently conquered province of the Hwicce, in which it seems there was a considerable British remnant, must have known more about Welsh Christianity, and have had a clearer perception of its significance, than either St Augustine or Gregory, who showed a woeful lack of awareness on the subject. He must also have been conscious of the need to keep the metropolitan see firmly anchored at Canterbury, a prize which was rightly his and which he showed no disposition to forego.

Because the first overtures made by Æthelberht to the Gallic church had gone unheeded, the mission was belated and time had become pressing. On St Augustine's arrival Æthelberht had reigned in Kent for nearly 40 years and had been *bretwalda* for ten; he must already have been approaching (or past) 60. There was need, therefore, to act as quickly as possible, within the limits of prudence. The tradition that his baptism took place within a few months carries conviction; it was just enough to allow the ground to be tested, and after an interval no longer than appearances required; and he then threw the whole of his influence behind the work of the mission. Augustine, whose early fears had been so falsified, was elated by his success; he journeyed to Arles to be consecrated archbishop,[25] and was soon writing to Gregory to report how converts were flocking in — as many as 10,000, he claimed, had been baptized at Christmas of 597,[26] a palpable exaggeration since the figure cannot have been far short of the entire population of the kingdom. In 601 Gregory sent a number of helpers to join him, including Justus, Mellitus and Paulinus, who brought with them the archbishop's *pallium*, books, vestments and plate, letters of instruction and admonition for Augustine,[27] and a letter and gifts for Æthelberht.[28] The letters to Augustine dealt with the future organization of the church in Britain, answered a number of questions, largely on doctrinal matters, and while praising him for his achievements added a significant warning against pride and boastfulness. That to Æthelberht urged him to listen to Augustine's advice and to press ahead with all speed in helping to spread the faith among his people.

On the second point Æthelberht needed no encouragement. An old church, a relic of Roman times, was renovated in Canterbury to become the site of the episcopal see, and in 602 a start was made with the construction just outside the city of the Abbey of St Peter and St Paul (later St Augustine's).[29] Two years afterwards bishoprics were established for Justus in Rochester and Mellitus in London.[30] Although London was in the Kingdom of Essex the Anglo-Saxon Chronicle says, bluntly, that it was Æthelberht who installed the church there,[31] and this seems to have been near enough the truth. Essex was effectively under his control, and his nephew Saberht was prepared to adopt Christianity at his bidding. We have no information about the extent of these sees, but that of London was clearly designed to serve Essex and is unlikely, at this time, to have stretched into Æthelberht's own dominions south of the Thames. The boundary between the dioceses of Canterbury and Rochester later followed that between the lathes of Milton and Hollingbourne, on the eastern side, and Aylesford, on the western,[32] and this division of responsibility had probably persisted from the beginning, even if there was still no precise demarcation line. The balance between the two was not then so uneven as it became on the loss of Surrey to the kingdom, when the diocese was correspondingly curtailed; indeed the arrangement supplies further proof (if that were needed) that in Æthelberht's time Surrey was still treated as an integral part of Kent. Territorially, therefore, Rochester's portion must have been as large as that of Canterbury, or larger, though the population was almost certainly less. The choice of Rochester as the ecclesiastical seat of a diocese of which it occupied the extreme north-eastern corner was based, not upon considerations of convenience, but the fact that it had been a Roman town.

The association of the church with the old Roman cities followed, and must have been intended as an affirmation of, the Imperial tradition; strongly reinforced in this instance by the example of Merovingian France, where the cities had survived as strongholds of ecclesiastical power and influence. In heathen England it seems that they had been allowed to waste away, largely derelict and deserted, until the coming of Christianity led to their reoccupation. In Kent the expansion of trade had been bound in time to lead to some revival of urban life, and the germs of this must already have been present in the royal vills on Thamesside and in the north-east. The effect of the conversion was both to stimulate this development and to concentrate it upon the old Roman centres, which burgeoned as the church became established alongside the king as a major mercantile influence.

The impressive state maintained by the Roman Church (thoroughly understood and approved by Æthelberht) formed a large part of its appeal to the people. It had its own costly requirements in vestments and the gold braid that adorned them, in silver plate and jewelled crosses, in manuscripts, papyrus and parchment and everything that went to support its devotional needs, the dignity of its position, and the life of learning.

II. (*above left*) The Kingston brooch: early 7th century.

III. (*above*) Kentish polychrome round brooch from Faversham; early 7th-century.

IV. Kentish square headed brooch from Stowting: 6th cent▮

According to tradition preserved at Canterbury Æthelberht made a number of munificent gifts to St Augustine's Abbey on its first foundation, including a large silver pattern, a gold sceptre, a golden bit and a saddle adorned with gems.[33] Bede records the despatch by Gregory the Great of sacred vessels, altar coverings, vestments, relics, and a plenitude of books;[34] and an impressive catalogue of the Abbey's original possessions is contained in a history compiled at the beginning of the 15th century by one of its monks, drawing upon early traditions.[35] There was also a growing establishment to be fed and housed as the original mission was replenished from Rome; and the numbers must have constantly increased with new foundations and the progress of the conversion. Endowments were therefore needed. Whatever view is taken of the land grants ascribed to Æthelberht himself and his successor Eadbald – probably they rest upon authentic tradition, even if the surviving records are forgeries or botched copies – it is certain that by the close of the 7th century the church had become a major land-owner, particularly in north-east Kent, where to the original foundations of St Augustine's Abbey and Christchurch there had been added those of Reculver, Minster in Thanet (there was another in Sheppey), Dover, Folkestone and Lyminge,[36] with considerable estates attached. The religious houses had their own tenants and slaves, craftsmen and workshops, and surpluses to be disposed of in exchange for the many precious wares they needed.

A great part of this trade was drawn into the cities, where the appearance of a mercantile class inevitably attracted more from other sources. Although the church was expelled from London on Æthelberht's death[37] the initial impetus was renewed on the re-establishment of the see some 35 years later,[38] and from that time on the development of the city, opening on the narrow seas and lying at the hub of the road system bequeathed by the Romans, was rapid. Within 75 years of St Augustine's landing it had already become the great 'emporium' described by Bede, frequented by people of many nations,[39] and here, for all that it was in Essex, Hlothere of Kent maintained a royal hall and port-reeve,[40] a perpetuation – or, more likely, reaffirmation – of Kentish claims to influence in a city of which Æthelbert had been to all intents the second founder. In Kent itself Rochester had eclipsed the neighbouring vill of Milton Regis, and Canterbury that of Sturry, three miles distant, the haven of which – Fordwich – it had turned to its own use. By this time, it seems, the royal court had been moved to the city, and what had been the lathe of *Sturigao* was beginning to be known as that of the '*burh-ware*'.[41] The full name does not appear in written sources until the 9th century, because all the earlier references to the city were in Latin documents prepared by churchmen who, for traditional reasons, favoured the old Roman term *Durovernum*; but its inhabitants were already described as the '*burh-ware*' in a charter of 786,[42] and it is probable that the colloquial name of the place, testifying to its pre-eminence as 'the city of the Cantware', was acquired quite early in the 7th century. It was never the capital of the kingdom in the full sense, since it remained only one royal court among many, although doubtless the most important of them, a position it had usurped from Faversham. It was, however, the capital of the Roman Church in England, and as the seat of the archbishop (who was also the chief counsellor of the Kentish kings) exerted throughout the entire country an influence in which spiritual and political calculations were not always easy to disentangle.

This was the prize that Æthelberht had put in the hands of his successors, staked upon the triumph of Rome, which at the time of his death was still remote, and its chances apparently receding. The opportunity might have been lost from the beginning, since Gregory the Great had never envisaged Canterbury as the metropolitan see; his intention, formed against an Imperial background and coloured perhaps by the over-optimism of Augustine's reports, was that one archbishopric should be established in London and another at York.[43] The second was quite beyond the power of Æthelberht to accomplish; there were limits to what he could do, even within the sphere of his *bretwaldaship*, and Northumbria lay outside it. The first he could have achieved, but had good reasons to let go by default. Saberht's baptism was a formality, meaning little to his people, who were to show themselves obdurately heathen. While so much depended upon Æthelberht himself there was every cause to keep the see at Canterbury, within the security of his own dominions; and the advantages of London as a great centre of communications were nullified so long as Christianity was confined to Kent and, precariously, to Essex. There is no indication that Augustine ever seriously considered moving, and Æthelberht appears to have done all that was possible to make the church look upon Canterbury as its natural home. The foundation of the Abbey of St Peter and St Paul, in which Augustine came to be buried,[44] was a powerful bond, strengthened by the richness of its endowment. In the church's eyes the proof of Æthelberht's wisdom came immediately after his death, when Saberht's sons renounced Christianity and drove Mellitus from London. Essex then remained heathen for nearly 40 years, by the end of which the archiepiscopal seat had become firmly established in Canterbury. Later attempts by the Mercian king Cenwulf to move it to London, then under his control, foundered on the unwillingness of the Pope to break an attachment cherished by churchmen throughout England (*see* page 214 below).

From the time of Æthelberht's baptism the success of the mission had come to depend more upon his influence than on the proselytizing zeal of Augustine; and, for all Gregory's injunctions, the king was quite prepared to substitute his own judgement for the advice he was given. Among the questions which Augustine had put to Gregory was what punishment should be meted out to those who robbed churches; this evidently being prompted by Æthelberht's code of laws, then in preparation. Gregory's answer was that the punishment should depend on the circumstances of the offenders; some might be beaten, and some fined, but in the way of fatherly correction, not in anger; and that, while the stolen goods should be restored, the church should not (God forbid) recover them with interest.[45] Such an attitude of Christian charity was far from what Æthelberht considered expedient or consonant with the dignity of the church; it would be fatally unimpressive. (On the other hand, it would be a dire affront, in this society, for any freeman to be beaten). As we have seen, when the code was issued it provided 11-fold restitution for thefts from a bishop, and nine-fold from a priest, which was as much as for those from the king himself.[46] Considering the value of the church's goods, and the temptation they presented, there was a great deal of common-sense behind this; but most of all it must have been intended as a signal mark of royal respect.

This emphasis was all the more necessary because Æthelberht had rejected the use of compulsion, preferring instead to rely upon example and favour. Bede says that this was because he had learned from his instructors that the service of Christ should be accepted freely;[47] although, in fact, the suppression of idolatry and destruction of heathen shrines had been enjoined upon Æthelberht by Gregory,[48] who seems both to have underestimated the depth of the attachment to the old beliefs and to have credited the king with more autocratic powers than he possessed. It was impossible even for so great a king as Æthelberht to move so far in advance of opinion, and he was too wise to attempt it. Example and favour were potent influences, for a time. Some of the people may have followed their king purely out of respect or affection, others for the hope of rewards, which he was well able to give, and others because they were impressed by the ceremony of the church and the magnificence surrounding it. These, by themselves, were insecure foundations. There were, no doubt, many among the Cantware who believed that it was possible to accept a new god, with his particular magic, and to please the king by doing so, without abandoning all belief in the old ones, and who would test the new faith by the fortune it brought. Any serious set-back which weakened the king's authority, or his ability to bestow favours, would threatened a reversion. Æthelberht had a great fund of power and prestige to draw upon, but he was ageing, and his son Eadbald was still a heathen.

As the work of the mission progressed in Kent the question of the conversion of the other English kingdoms came increasingly to the fore, and, bound up with it, the relationship between Canterbury and the Welsh Church. Still less was Æthelberht able to compel the subordinate kings than his own people. It was easy enough to handle his nephew Saberht, but he could not expect the same subservience from the others. Among these the most prominent was now Raedwald of East Anglia, whose support it was, therefore, particularly important to win; and he was in fact, prevailed upon to come to Canterbury to be baptized, although he seems to have undergone the ceremony only in order to indulge Æthelberht and as a form of double insurance, reinforcing the rites of the old religion.[49] For the rest, the hope was to persuade the Christian Welsh to join with Augustine in a concerted campaign of evangelism.

It seems that the mission had set out uninstructed on this matter, because so great had the isolation of the Welsh become that Gregory was almost entirely ignorant of their affairs, and had little idea either of the pride they took in their own church, with its saints and martyrs — in Gildas' words 'lamps of exceeding brightness set alight for us, lest Britain should be involved in the thick darkness of pitchy night'[50] — or of the intensity of the hatred 'they harboured for the heathen but all-conquering English. Æthelberht, however, had every reason to be aware of the problem, and of the prospects which would be opened up if it could be successfully overcome. The conception of the Welsh church working under the guidance of an archbishop whose patron was the King of Kent in the conversion of the other English kingdoms was bold in the extreme; spiritual benefits apart, it would transform the whole political situation by bridging the gulf between the two races, and rewarding the Eskings with an influence far wider and more durable than it was within their military power to achieve. The *bretwalda* would them be a 'Britain ruler' in truth, and in the sense in which Æthelberht appears to have conceived his role, as a composer of differences and champion of enlightenment. None of this could have escaped a statesman of Æthelberht's calibre, but nor could he have underestimated the dangers and consequences of a failure which would appear as humiliating to him as to Augustine himself. The promotion of the enterprise depended upon Æthelberht, since it needed the exercise of his powers as *bretwalda* even to bring the two parties together, and he would be bound all the more to appear as its initiator to the other English kings, who would be watching the event and assessing its implications for themselves. He must have known, therefore, that he was putting his authority at stake, yet with so great a prize to be won he made no attempt to hold Augustine back, but set himself to forward the venture.

The issue was first raised by Augustine in the letter he sent to Gregory seeking instructions on a number of matters, which had come (or been brought) to his attention following his arrival; and he then linked it with the question of his relationship with the Gallic church, in which, it seems, he had detected a number of irregularities during his visit to Arles for consecration. In his reply Gregory dealt at some length with the second matter, making it clear that Augustine had no authority to correct abuses in the Gallic church, which he should content himself with reporting; but he then went on to dispose of the Welsh church in two cursory sentences, saying that all the bishops of Britain were committed to Augustine's charge, 'to instruct the unlearned, to strengthen the weak, and correct the misguided',[51] an uncharitable response which showed little understanding of the complexity of the problem, and was particularly unfortunate in touching the chord of arrogance in Augustine's nature. It seems that Gregory was less aware of the achievements of the Welsh church during its period of isolation than of its departure from orthodox practices in certain matters of organization and ritual, and in the calculation of Easter. Organizationally, the Celtic system was one of a loose monasticism, in which the bishops were subordinate to the abbots of the great houses; there were a number of differences of form and observance, such as in the clerical tonsure and the rite of baptism or confirmation; and while the British were no doubt aware — as the Irish were[52] — of the method of calculating Easter introduced by Pope Leo in 455 they had failed to adopt it, with the result that there could be a discrepancy of as much as 30 days between the dates on which they and the Roman Church celebrated the feast. There was nothing essentially doctrinal in this; all agreed that the festival should be held on the Sunday of the third week in the month in which the full moon fell on or after the vernal equinox; but the British took the equinox to be the 25th instead of the 21st of March.[53] The difference needed to be resolved if one community was not still to be observing the Lenten fast while the other was celebrating the feast, but that was a practical matter.

It seems that in arranging a meeting between the two sides Æthelberht used the people of the Hwice as intermediaries. The territory they occupied corresponded, broadly, to what are now the counties of Gloucestershire, Worcestershire and the south-western part of Warwickshire. It had been conquered for the English in Ceawlin's campaigns of 577 and 584 and so came under Æthelberht's overlordship as *bretwalda*, but it evidently still contained numbers of British Christians in communion with the Welsh church. The first meeting, which was preparatory, was held in 603, Bede says at a place later known as Augustine's Oak on the border between the Hwicce and Wessex,[54] that is somewhere on the eastern slope of the Cotswolds, perhaps near Wychwood in Oxfordshire (which means the Hwiccas' wood).[55] After a good deal of fruitless disputation the meeting ended, by Bede's account, in a contest to see who could restore sight to a blind Englishman, which was won by Augustine; on proof of whose miraculous powers the British agreed that another meeting should be held after they had had an opportunity to consult their own people more fully.[56] It was only at this stage, it seems, that the Welsh bishops and, more especially, the brethren of the famous monastery of Bangor-is-Coed (in Flint) were brought into the matter. The venue of the second meeting may have been on what was then the border between England and Wales, at Abberley in

Worcestershire, where tradition preserved the name of an ancient tree known as Apostle's Oak.[57] It was attended on the Welsh side by seven bishops and numerous learned monks, mainly from Bangor-is-Coed.

A story told by Bede,[58] which may be fictitious but goes to the heart of the issue, is that before coming to the meeting the Welsh ecclesiasts consulted a wise hermit, who advised them that their attitude should depend upon Augustine's demeanour, whether it was meek as befitted a true servant of Christ, or imperious; the test of which should be whether he rose from his chair on their arrival. In the event he remained seated, and all chance of agreement was at once destroyed. The demands made by Augustine on the Welsh had been reduced to three; that they should follow the Roman baptism or confirmation rites, observe the same dates for Easter, and join with him in the evangelization of the English. All these the Welsh utterly rejected. There seems little reason why the first two points, even the change of Easter, should not have been conceded, given good-will, but the touchstone was the third. Bede found the refusal of the Welsh to do anything for the salvation of the English deeply shocking. He recounts a prophesy by Augustine that if they refused to follow the path of peace with the English they would perish at their hands; saying that this was fulfilled within a few years when as a preliminary to a great victory won over the Welsh at Chester by the heathen Æthelfrid of Northumbria, he ordered the slaughter of a large company of monks from Bangor-is-Coed who had come to pray for the triumph of their people.[60] But the issue went a good deal deeper than Bede was prepared to admit. The question was whether the Welsh were being asked to co-operate with Augustine or to subordinate themselves to him, and through him, as they must well have realised, to his patron Æthelberht, King of Kent, overlord of southern England, and descendant of the barbarous Hengest. It was not only their cherished religious identity that was at stake but their political independence too, and in judging this Augustine's demeanour was indeed crucially important.[60] For all his antagonism to the Welsh, Bede was too good an historian to allow himself altogether to conceal the authoritarianism which must have shown in Augustine's attitude, the product of his own arrogance and Gregory's unfortunate miscomprehension. Augustine was a learned schoolman,[61] but success in this enterprise required someone of truly saintly character or else with supreme qualities of tact and diplomacy, and those he did not have.

It may well be asked why Æthelberht, who must have become aware of Augustine's limitations, nevertheless encouraged and supported him in a venture for which they unsuited him. No doubt events acquired their own momentum, and there must have come a stage when, whatever the risks, it was no longer possible to hold back. But Æthelberht may have been guilty of a grave misjudgement too. It must have been difficult for him, imbued as he had become with a sense of the majesty of Rome and the whole Imperial tradition behind it, to believe that in the last resort the Welsh, who were themselves heirs to that tradition, albeit at a remove, could bring themselves to reject the approach made to them, however recalcitrant they might be. For many years the Cantware had had few dealings with the Welsh, except as slaves; a king of Wessex or Northumbria might have known better. However, that may be, Æthelberht's own fortunes had become bound up in the venture and its failure was fatal to them. To say, as Wallace-Hadrill does, that Augustine's discomfiture was a defeat for Æthelberht as well[62] is to put the matter at its lowest. The church could, and eventually did, recover from the set-back; but there could be no recovery either for Æthelberht or for his kingdom. This is the watershed of Kentish history. In 603 the kingdom stood at the very height of its power; henceforth its story was to be one of slow but inexorable decline. It is not only that the failure of the design deprived Kent of the only firm foundation on which the supremacy won by Æthelberht might have been perpetuated but, more instantly than that, it destroyed his authority over the other English kingdoms. The position of bretwalda rested upon prestige, and Æthelberht had suffered a public rebuff, and at the hands of the despised Welsh. He was now entering upon old age, and had no longer the resilience to recover from such a humiliation.

Pope Gregory died in 605[63] and Augustine in the same year, or shortly after (there is an obscurity in Bede's account),[64] being succeeded by Laurentius, a member of the original mission. It is Æthelberht's tragedy to have outlived them by ten years, during which he had the capacity to achieve nothing, dying well on into his seventies or early eighties. Whether he formally retained the title of bretwalda we do not know, but if so it had become hollow. Although a certain respect seems to have clung to the old man, at any rate among his own people, for whom he had done so much, Bede makes it clear that before his death pre-eminence had already passed to Raedwald.[65] There was no early hope, after the Welsh fiasco, that any other English kings, Saberht apart, would adopt Christianity. In so far as Æthelberht had conceived it his duty to act as a mediator between the kingdoms, that restraining influence was removed, to be replaced by a contest for power, mostly it seems between East Anglia and Wessex. The Anglo-Saxon Chronicle records that in 607 Ceolwulf of Wessex was at war with Sussex, though why and with what result we do not know. It says approvingly of this king that he 'ever fought and made war either against the Angles, or against the Welsh, or' — difficult as it is to credit — 'against the Picts, or against the Scots',[66] the Angles referred to here presumably being not the Mercians, as would have been the case in later years, but the East Angles under the increasingly dominant Raedwald. Of Æthelberht we know only that on Bertha's death he had taken another wife, evidently young and presumably English, whom his son Eadbald coveted.[67] Ruled for ten years by a once great but now failing king, with a jealous son lacking his ability and convictions, the power of the Cantware seeped away. It cannot, at this time, have seemed to them that Christianity had been such a fortunate talisman after all.

Despite the impotence of his last years Æthelberht remains a towering figure, who casts a long shadow into history. In the work of the conversion, by which England was drawn back into the civilized world, it was he rather than Augustine who played the decisive part, royal influence counting for more than the message, and in doing so he set the English a new model of kingship. To his own people he was a munificent ruler, under whose patronage trade increased and the material arts flourished as never before, producing a jewellery of great beauty and distinction, which remains to delight us. Although he could find, in the end, no means of bequeathing his own power to his successors, he left them a valuable legacy with which to face the perils of the future; the partiality of the church and the prestige which clung to those who had first protected it, a wealth nourished by trade strengthening the foundations of royal authority, the use of letters and the makings of an administrative cadre, and a robust community proud of its inheritance and confirmed in its attachment to the dynasty.

Chapter Seven

THE VICTORY OF ROME

Eadbald and Earconberht, 616–664

FOR TEN YEARS after Æthelberht's death in 616 it must have seemed as though his work had been in vain; that the graft of Christianity would not take, and that the civilizing influences of the Mediterranean world would be rejected with it. During these years the church, driven from London, found its only refuge in Kent, and was imperilled even there, and supremacy passed to Raedwald of East Anglia, a warrior king in a familiar mould, matching Æthelbert in his magnificence but steeped in traditions that reached from across the North Sea and not the Channel.

The primacy of East Anglia was, however, as fleeting as that of all the kingdoms which were unable to enlarge themselves at the expense of the Picts or the British. Two new powers were entering upon the scene: Northumbria, in which the kingdoms of Bernicia and Deira had become fused, and which had broken the British containment that had kept it to the plain of York and the coastal lands between Humber and Tweed; and Mercia, the early stages of whose expansion from the frontier settlements on the middle Trent have gone unrecorded by history, but whose latent strength was now to be unleashed, not against the British, but in alliance with them against its fellow English. The middle years of the 7th century are marked by a bitter conflict between these powers; but also by the revival and triumph of Christianity, to which the Northumbrian kings acted as standard bearers, endowing it with the prestige of their own achievements, so that it came eventually to be accepted even by their Mercian enemies. The turning point may be said to have been reached *c.* 625 when, on the death of Raedwald, the *bretwaldaship* passed to Edwin of Northumbria, who had married a daughter of Æthelberht[1] and was shortly to be converted to Christianity through the zeal of Paulinus, her chaplain and mentor.

It is against this background that we have to consider the reigns of the two Kentish kings who followed Æthelberht; his son Eadbald (616–640) and his grandson Earconberht (640–664). In the history of Kent this period of nearly 50 years forms a precarious interlude of peace, during which a double contest of power was going on, the upshot of which would vitally affect the future security of the kingdom. In the military conflict between Northumbria and Mercia the Cantware played no direct part; they enjoyed, indeed, an exceptional immunity from the damage inflicted on others who were caught up in the struggle. Nevertheless the interests of Kent were deeply committed on the side of Northumbria. The kingdoms were drawn together, in the first place, by the shared aim of Christian propagation, which created a bond of mutual respect and sympathy between them, strengthened by inter-marriage between the royal houses; whereas throughout most of the period Mercia was ruled by the heathen Penda, a fighting man of singular ferocity, who was not positively hostile to Christianity but was himself an embodiment of the pagan ethic in its most savage form. It was the unbridled power of Mercia which all the southern kingdoms had most cause to dread. East Anglia was shattered by it, and Wessex — still suffering from divided rule and dissipated authority — forced into retreat beyond the Thames. Only Northumbria was capable, at this time, of holding Mercia in play. So long as this struggle was maintained, and the energies of Mercia diverted elsewhere, Kent in its corner of England could remain tolerably secure; but, by the end of the period, on Earconberht's death, the contest was approaching a stage of inanition, with Northumbria beginning to withdraw its interest from the south, leaving that field open to Mercia. The time was coming when Kent, like the other kingdoms, would be compelled to fight for its independence.

Although the second contest began as one between Christianity and heathenism, that issue was virtually settled from the time that Northumbria espoused the faith, since its Mercian enemies showed no countervailing religious passion; and it then developed into one between the Roman and Celtic Churches, the first having been displaced in Northumbria by the second (in its Scottish manifestation), which went on to spread its influence over much of England. In this rivalry the Kentish kings remained unswervingly on the side of Rome and played as great a part as any in securing its eventual victory, a debt more clearly acknowledged at the time than it appears to have become since. The decisive confrontation occurred at the Synod of Whitby in 664,[2] the very last year of Earconberht's reign, when Canterbury was confirmed as the centre of religious authority in an England which, on the surface at least, was now almost entirely Christian. What Æthelberht had initiated had thus, after many vicissitudes, been finally realised, but in a very different political setting. The alliance with the church could never restore Kent its lost supremacy, but it made it a power to be reckoned with and armed it to resist the now imminent threat of Mercia.

On Æthelberht's death in 616 not only was the kingdom already in decline, which his successors could only hope to mask, but the Christian mission was deprived of its one remaining champion who, even as his authority dwindled, had still been able to protect it by his prestige. The immediate expulsion of the church from London by Saberht's loutish sons[3] evoked no reaction from Eadbald, who probably sympathized with their action at the time; it was not this, but his inability to restore the situation when his own attitude had changed, that marked the first clear recession of Kentish power. Bede says that the offenders were swiftly punished by death in battle against Wessex.[4] It is unlikely that they were fighting in their own cause, as Essex never had the strength to pit against its larger neighbours, but was fated always to act as an instrument of whatever kingdom was dominant at the time, which was then East Anglia under Raedwald. Kent's loss of influence over Essex, which Æthelberht had treated almost as a satrapy, and more especially over a rapidly reviving London, was a most serious impairment to it.

Of Eadbald's character we know something and can deduce more. He was afflicted by periodic fits of madness, which Bede described as possession by an evil spirit and regarded as a punishment for his early contumacy.[5] This may have been epilepsy, or something worse. His behaviour at the beginning of his reign certainly seems to have betrayed a good deal of moodiness and instability. He was not a Christian, though he may have made some show of conformity during his father's lifetime. As a son of Bertha (married before 560) he must have been well over 30 at the time of his accession, and had all the more reason to find the delay frustrating because of the seepage of Kentish power under the ageing Æthelberht, and because he was intent upon marrying his young step-mother, which he did as soon as his father had died.[6] This action, of itself, put him outside the pale of the church, although it was acceptable under the old religion. Bede denounced it as fornication of a kind which the apostle Paul had described as unheard of even among the heathen;[7] but it had not, it seems, been unheard of among the German tribes – we have mentioned a previous example of it among the Warni (page 78) – nor can it have been uncommon in Kent or Augustine would scarcely have included it (as he did) among the issues which he submitted to Gregory for advice shortly after his arrival.[8] Equally, Gregory's uncompromising condemnation of it must have been known to Eadbald and have increased his sense of grievance against the church. The example set by the king had the effect that might have been expected in a community where the faith was still shallow rooted; it led to the defection of those who had followed Æthelberht not out of conviction but of fear or favour. So far did the reaction go that Justus was impelled to abandon his see in Rochester and join Mellitus on the continent, and Laurentius was on the point of doing the same, so closing down the mission entirely. According to Bede it was saved only at the last moment, and by a miracle. The story goes that on the very eve of his departure Laurentius was visited in his sleep by St Peter who upbraided and scourged him for deserting his post, and that next morning he showed the marks of the scourging to Eadbald, who was so deeply shaken that he forthwith renounced his idolatry, set aside his unlawful wife, accepted the Christian faith and was baptized.[9] Whatever actually happened, it seems – in Professor Finberg's apt description – that Laurentius had succeeded in putting the fear of God into him.[10] In Kent at least Christianity had been saved; Justus was restored to his see, and Mellitus recalled to succeed Laurentius on his death three years later.[11]

The church was adept at exacting retribution for misadventures of this kind. It seems that as a mark of his reconciliation Eadbald founded a house for secular canons within the precincts of the old Roman fortifications at Dover.[12] We are also confronted now with two more of those spurious charters which nevertheless appear to express substantial truths; recording the grant, supposedly in this same year, of Northbourne to St Augustine's Abbey and Adisham to Christchurch, Canterbury[13] – sizeable estates, which, at the time of Domesday Book, were assessed at 30 and 17 *sulungs* respectively (although more lands may by then have been added to them). The grant of Adisham has a particular claim to credibility even if no faith can be put in the document which purports to record it, because in later years it was constantly cited by Christchurch as a prototype for those that followed it, *libere sicut Adesham* becoming something of a stock phrase in the charters.[14]

From this time on Eadbald set himself to behave in every way as befitted a Kentish king. Although, no more than his father, did he attempt to suppress all heathen practices, since that would have been beyond his power, he did everything else he could to promote the welfare of the church. He married a Frankish princess, Imma (thought by some to have been a daughter of Theudebert of Austrasia),[15] and maintained the contacts with the continent which his predecessors had established; remarkably, his death was recorded in the annals of the church at Salzburg.[16] Kent now had become a beleagured bridgehead of the Roman world. For all his previous transgressions, a great deal was owed to Eadbald for helping to keep the faith alive during this period of its weakness and isolation, not least by the Cantware themselves, did they but recognize it. The church's fortunes were not, however to remain for long in eclipse. The turning point came in 625 when Edwin of Northumbria sought the hand of Eadbald's sister, Æthelburga, in marriage and the king made it a condition not only that she should be allowed to practise her own religion but should be accompanied by Paulinus as her spiritual adviser, together with a small body of priests.[17] It is ironical that Æthelburga, the vessel by which Christianity reached Northumbria, to be spread from there far and wide throughout England, should have been Æthelberht's daughter, not by Bertha, but by his second wife, with whom Eadbald later contracted his incestuous union. Although Bede avoids mentioning this (and never, at any time, mentions the woman's name) no other conclusion is possible from the date of Æthelburga's marriage, while still of child-bearing age. Her own name — 'the noble city' — strongly suggests that it had been given after the conversion, whether the reference was to the City of God, or to Rome, or was a more general expression of civic consciousness; but it is an insight into her character that she was also called by the affectionate diminutive Tata,[18] meaning 'merry'.[19]

The power of Northumbria, to which Edwin had succeeded, had been forged by Æthelfrid, King of Bernicia, who absorbed the neighbouring Kingdom of Deira, inflicted an exemplary defeat upon the Scots in 603,[20] and at some time between 613 and 616 annihilated a British force at Chester,[21] fulfilling in doing so the prophecy said to have been made by Augustine by slaughtering the monks of Bangor-is-Coed who had accompanied it.[22] Edwin himself had no part in this because, as heir to the royal line of Deira, he had been driven into exile, eventually taking refuge at the court of Raedwald, by whom he was restored to his kingdom (united with Bernicia) in a battle fought in 617 on the banks of the River Idle, in which Æthelfrid was killed.[23] This victory must have confirmed Raedwald in the *bretwaldaship*, if he had not already won it; and on his death it passed to Edwin, by then the most powerful king in England. Hitherto Northumbria had stood aloof from the other kingdoms, from which it was isolated by the large areas of marsh backing the Humber estuary,[24] but Edwin's exile had made him familiar with their affairs. He was a king in the high tradition, a great scourge of the British — he is said to have brought both Anglesey and the Isle of Man under his power — and an imposing and authoritative ruler within his own dominions. Bede says that everywhere he went, whether in war or peace, his *tufa*, or standard, was borne before him. He caused drinking vessels to be hung near streams on the highways, and because of the awe in which he was held nobody dare to remove them; and the story went that in his days a woman might carry her new-born babe across England from sea to sea without fear of harm.[25] His exile in the south, at a time when Æthelberht was still living, appears to have given him a respect for the Cantware and a hankering after wider horizons; and it was in keeping with this that when his first wife had died he should seek a daughter of Æthelberht for the second. His conception of the duties of a king among his own people, and the manner of his rule, made him in the fullest sense the heir of Æthelberht. When he had won the *bretwaldaship* he never sought to extend it to Kent, the one English kingdom over which he claimed no supremacy,[26] choosing instead to treat his brother-in-law Eadbald as his peer.

It is not our purpose to repeat in detail the account given by Bede of the conversion of Northumbria, which is one of the most eloquent and moving in his whole *History*.[27] Much was due to the missionary efforts of Paulinus, and something no doubt to the influence of Æthelburga, but it seems that Edwin himself must have been more than half inclined to accept the faith from the time he sought her in marriage. A daughter, Eanfled, was born at Easter of 626, on the very day, Bede says, that an attempt to assassinate the king, prompted by Cwichelm of Wessex, had miscarried through the self-sacrifice of one of Edwin's thanes, who flung himself in front of his master to take the dagger blow.[28] This was regarded as sign of divine providence. On his safe return from a punitive expedition into Wessex — in which, we are told, five (sub-)kings were killed,[29] an indication of the loosely organized state of that kingdom — Edwin agreed that Eanfled should be baptized, as he himself was a year later, following a council of notables at which the whole issue was debated and the heathen High Priest, Coifi, was won over by Paulinus' persuasion.[30] If the matter is to be judged on the evidence of place-names (and there is little else to go on) the old religion had never been as strong and deep-rooted in Northumbria as in the southern kingdoms,[31] and there were other reasons why the path was made easier for Edwin than it had been for Æthelberht, not least the illustrious example of Æthelberht himself. The impact of Edwin's conversion was all the greater because in the space of 30 years he was the second of those who had held the *bretwaldaship* to become a Christian, while a third, Raedwald, had at least gone through the form of baptism; a truly imposing model to the other English rulers. The rapid evangelization of Lindsey,[32] which was then as closely dependent upon Northumbria as Essex had once been upon Kent, was only to be expected, but Edwin also took advantage of his friendship with the East Anglian royal house to effect the conversion of Raedwald's son, Earpwald, whose brother and successor Sigberht had also become a Christian while an exile in France.[33] From this time on the East Anglian kings were among the staunchest champions of the Roman faith.

It was in the year after Edwin's baptism that Penda first appeared upon the scene, not yet as a king of Mercia but as a prince of its royal house bent upon conquests of his own. The Chronicle tells us that in 628 he fought at Cirencester against Cynegils and Cwichelm of Wessex; as a result of which (though this the Chronicle does not tell us) he seized the province of the Hwicce,[34] which became permanently attached to Mercia on his own accession to the throne in 633. Wessex must have been greatly weakened by the revenge taken upon it by Edwin, and it was this that had given Penda his opportunity. He was a predator, whose overmastering aim, pursued relentlessly throughout his career, was to destroy the ascendancy of Northumbria; not, it seems, because of any quarrel with Christianity but purely for reasons of dynastic rivalry. No royal house in England could claim a more illustrious ancestry than that of Mercia, which traced its lineage back through Icel, the founder of the kingdom,[35] to the ancient ruling line of Angel;[36] compared with which the Northumbrian dynasty was a mere upstart. The heartland of the kingdom was the upper Trent valley, Tamworth being its principal royal seat and Lichfield later its ecclesiastical centre, from which it had expanded north into the Peak District, west across Cannock towards the Wrekin, and south-west along the Warwickshire Avon.[37] Although this expansion had been at the expense of the British, any enmity they felt for the Mercians had now been submerged in their far greater hatred for Northumbria, which first under Æthelfrid, and later under Edwin, had constantly harried and humiliated them. By a startling reversal of policy for an English prince Penda now made common cause with Cadwallon of Gwynedd. In October 633 a combined force of Welsh and Mercians invaded Northumbria and defeated and killed Edwin in a battle fought at Hatfield, near Doncaster, in which Edwin's eldest son Osfrid also fell, while another was captured by Penda, who later made away with him.[38] At this stage, it seems, it was the Welsh who were in the lead; Mercian power was still in its infancy, and it appears from Bede's account that it was the campaign itself which brought Penda his kingship.[39]

For 12 months following the battle the victors despoiled Northumbria with merciless cruelty, so that Bede says that this year remained hateful and accursed to all good men.[40] It seems that Edwin, fearing the outcome, had entrusted to a faithful thane the care of Queen Æthelburga, her young daughter Eanfled, then seven years old, and an infant son (who died shortly after), all of whom were taken safely by sea to Kent, accompanied by Paulinus. They were honourably received by Eadbald and Archbishop Honorius, Paulinus being inducted into the vacant see at Rochester and Æthelburga ending her days as Abbess of a monastery at Lyminge which was founded and endowed for her.[41] The principle that a married woman retained the kin rights of her parents, who were responsible for her guardianship if she was widowed, applied to the royalty as well as to humbler classes of society; Æthelburga remained, first and foremost, an Esking, and the duty of protecting and providing for her would have fallen upon Eadbald even if any of Edwin's kin had survived the holocaust (page 99 above).

The means taken of providing for her was nevertheless a notable innovation. Æthelburga was the first of a long succession of Kentish consorts or princesses — and not Kentish alone — to adopt the religious life. The arrangements had a dual purpose. This was a convenient, and at the same time edifying, way of establishing royal widows or unmarried daughters in a position of dignity and comfort, and vested with all the authority that befitted their station; and it was a public testimony of the devotion of the Eskings to the church, whose interests, now thoroughly identified with those of the dynasty, it was the prime duty of the princesses to serve, whether through their influence as wives or by example. Eadbald was to make similar provision for his unmarried daughter Eanswith, who became the head of an Abbey at Folkestone*.[42] These places, and others such as Minster and Sheppey which were founded later, remained for many years preserves of royalty, so that the Eskings had, in effect, made themselves not only patrons and protectors of the church but shareholders in it. It has been suggested that Eadbald made use of the foundation of Lyminge to rid himself of the embarrassing presence at court of a daughter, Mildred, born of his incestuous union with his own stepmother and later confused in tradition with St Mildred of Minster.[43] It would have been an apt solution to consign this girl to the care of Æthelburga, who in the church's eyes would have been her aunt — though, looked at in another way, she would also have been her half-sister. There is an intrinsic plausibility about the story, but the evidence for the existence of the girl is too slight and inferential to inspire much confidence.

Following Gallic precedent, Lyminge and Folkestone were double houses, as later was Minster in Thanet; that is to say, although presided over by Abbesses, they contained men as well as women. Stenton considers it doubtful whether any houses for women alone were founded during the early years of the English church. Very little is known of the regime in these places, or the degree of separation effected between the sexes,

* Presumably after this time. As a child of Imma she could not have been more than 15 or 16 years old in 633.

which probably varied from one establishment to another, but appears to have been strict enough to avoid scandals.[44] At Lyminge the ground plan of the original Abbey church has been recovered, and is seen to have followed that of St Peter and St Paul (*aliter* St Augustine's) in Canterbury, which was later also adopted at Reculver, founded in 669, and was probably reproduced at Folkestone. The building consisted of an apsidal chancel divided from the nave by a triple arcade, and was flanked on either side by chambers used for keeping sacred vessels or as chapels for the burial of eminent people. The design, which has been found at only one site outside Kent, appears to have been of Italian inspiration; Roman brick was used to turn the arches; and surviving fragments, for instance at Reculver, show a skill in execution which suggests the employment of foreign craftsmen.[45] Except for the handful of ecclesiastical buildings there can, at the time, have been no stone-built structures in use in the kingdom; the royal halls, of which no traces have been left, apparently consisting entirely of timber, lath and plaster, and thatch.

Northumbria's tribulations were not to last for long. Its salvation came at the hands, not of Edwin's kin, but from the sons of Æthelfrid, of the royal line of Bernicia, who on their father's death had been driven into exile among the Scots, in the course of which they had been converted to the Christianity of the Celtic church. In 634 Oswald of Bernicia, at the head of a small army, utterly defeated the much larger forces of Cadwallon in a battle known as Heavenfield, fought near Hexham, in which Cadwallon himself was killed.[46] Northumbria was purged of its invaders and reunited under Oswald, who won back for it its previous supremacy.[47] He was a person of great sanctity of character, of whom many miracles are recounted;[48] but the Christianity he established in his kingdom was that, not of Rome, but of Iona, from which he brought Aidan to serve as his bishop, with Lindisfarne as his seat.[49] Between the Scottish and Roman churches there was at the beginning not so much a conflict as an incipient rivalry, which grew with time and needed, sooner or later, to be resolved, if only because of the incompatibility in the observance of Easter (though behind that there were deeper differences of approach and organization). Yet in Oswald's time the two movements worked together harmoniously in the common missionary endeavour. Oswald appears to have been on good terms with the Kentish kings, making no attempt to extend his *bretwaldaship* to them; and when in 635 Cynegils of Wessex accepted the Christian faith at the hands of Birinus, who had been sent from Rome, Oswald was present at his baptism, became his godfather and took his daughter in marriage.[50]

Eadbald's reign ended in 640[51] in an interval of deceptive calm, with Christianity in the ascendant, the Mercian threat apparently scotched, and Kent, although it was never to recover the position which Æthelberht had won for it, holding an honourable and influential place among the English kingdoms. To this he had made a worthy contribution; above all in confirming his dynasty as the foremost champions of the orthodox Roman faith. He left two sons, Eormenred and Earconberht, a daughter Eanswith, and his niece Eanfled, to whom he had acted as guardian and protector on the death of her father Edwin, and who was now growing to maturity at the Kentish court. He was succeeded not by his elder son but by the younger, Earconberht. The later monastic chroniclers differ as to how this came about. The Canterbury chronicler Thomas of Elmham, writing at the beginning of the 15th century, though on the basis of earlier traditions, says that it was because Eormenred had died;[52] the 12th and 13th century chroniclers, such as Simeon of Durham and Roger of Wendover, say that he was alive but had been 'craftily' dispossessed by Earconberht.[53] There seems no reason to doubt that he was still living; as the son of Imma, whom Eadbald could not have married before 617, he would have been still under 23 had he predeceased his father, yet he is known to have had five children (see Appendix G). To speak of dispossession is, however, to misapply the conceptions of later times to 7th century Kent, when there was no settled rule of primogeniture in kingly succession. (As we have said, there is no means of knowing whether any of the previous Kentish kings, from Oisc to Eadbald, were elder or younger sons, since no records whatever exist of the brothers which some of them must surely have had). The preference of Earconberht over Eormenred was most likely due to his father's belief, supported by a general consensus of opinion among the Kentish notables, that he was the better fitted to reign. For all we know Eormenred may have inherited his father's proneness to epilepsy or to whatever other mental illness it was that afflicted him. The choice was a good one which, although a cause of trouble in the next generation, passed unchallenged at the time; there is no hint that the succession was disputed.

Earconberht can scarcely have been 20 when he came to the throne and so was only in his early forties on his death in 664. He reigned during a period of increasing danger when the struggle between Mercia and Northumbria was savagely renewed, and by the end of which, while Northumbria remained undefeated, it no longer had the inclination or power to dispute the supremacy south of the Humber, to which Mercia was now free to turn its full attention. It was also during his reign that the rivalry between the Roman and Scottish churches came to a head, to be settled in the very year of his death in favour of Rome. Because throughout the whole of this period Kent contrived to remain at peace, apparently divorced from the great events which preoccupied the chroniclers, and because the final choice between the Scottish and Roman forms of observance was made by Oswy of Northumbria, it is easy to dismiss Earconberht as a minor and somewhat colourless figure; but the preservation of peace, unpurchased by the surrender either of land or of sovereignty, was itself an achievement in these critical days, and while Oswy was the instrument by which Rome gained its eventual victory as much was due to the single-minded advocacy of Earconberht and the influence he was able to exert at the Northumbrian court. Considering the pacific policies he pursued it may seem curious that he should have named his eldest son Egbert, 'the bright sword';[54] but it is a timely reminder that, whatever prudent statemanship might achieve, it was still the ultimate duty of a king to lead his people in battle if need arose, and his sons would be schooled to it.

Within two years of Earconberht's accession the stability founded by Oswald's victory at Heavenfield was shattered by his death at the hands of Penda, who appears never to have abandoned his resistance to Northumbria and to have provoked Oswald into a punitive expedition which ended disastrously.[55] It is eloquent of Penda's hatred, and typical of his barbarity, that after the battle he ordered that Oswald's head and hands should be severed from his body and hung on stakes.[56] The site of the engagement is named by Bede as Maserfelth,[57] and is generally supposed to have been at Oswestry — Oswald's tree[58] — which suggests that some Welsh forces may have been present, though there is no record of it. The alliance between Penda and the Welsh continued throughout his lifetime, but since Cadwallon's death it was he who had become the dominant partner.[59] For 13 years between 642 and 655 it seemed that there was no combination of powers capable of holding the Mercians in check. To the east Penda overran Lindsey and the province of the Middle Angles, of which he made his son Peada king,[60] and inflicted upon East Anglia wounds from which it never properly recovered; to the west, where the territory of the Hwicce had already been won, he annexed that of the Magonsaeta, comprising much of what is now Herefordshire and south Shropshire, whose king, Merwal, was said by the later chroniclers to have been another of his sons, but is thought by Stenton to have been of an independent dynasty;[61] and to the south he defeated Coenwalh of Wessex, who was driven for a while into exile,[62] and was hard pressed to defend his ancestral lands in the Thames basin. In this way the immense empire of Greater Mercia was built up, covering the whole of the midlands. On Oswald's death Northumbria broke into its original components; his brother Oswy maintaining control of Bernicia, but incapable of establishing more than a transient authority over Deira, which Penda used as a base for constant harassment.[63]

In 655 Penda determined to put an end to Oswy and destroy the last vestiges of Northumbrian power. With this object he assembled a great army in which 30 kings are supposed to have served; one of them being Æthelhere of East Anglia (whose brother, Anna, Penda had killed in the previous year),[64] others no doubt sub-kings of the various Mercian provinces, but most of them Welsh princelings, including Cadafael of Gwynedd.[65] According to Bede, Oswy tried vainly to buy off these enemies with large sums of money, but finally turned upon them in desperation to win an unexpected and overwhelming victory by the River Winwaed (near Leeds), where Penda, Æthelhere and many others were killed.[66] Welsh sources supply a fuller account. They say that the beleagured Oswy distributed his entire treasury to his enemies, including much that his predecessors had plundered from the Welsh, and that it was while they were straggling home encumbered by this booty (Cadafael having already abandoned the others) that Oswy fell upon and destroyed them.[67]

This battle, once again, caused an entire reversal of power. Oswy was now supreme in England, and for three years the Kindom of Mercia virtually ceased to exist. Penda's son, Peada, who had become a Christian and married into the Northumbrian royal house was allowed to keep a small part of his father's dominions, but was shortly assassinated through the treachery of his wife.[68] The situation could not, however, persist; Oswy's power, which extended as far north as the Forth, was seriously over-stretched, and it proved impossible to hold the Mercians in subjection. In 658, or thereabouts, three nobles who had kept hidden another son of Penda, Wulfhere, proclaimed him king,[69] and within a remarkably short time he had succeeded in winning back all the lands his father had held south of the Humber. By 664, when Earconberht died, Northumbria had been fenced off, East Anglia was impotent, and Wulfhere was poised for an advance to the Thames, pressing Wessex and threatening to overshadow Kent.

Throughout the whole of this period, irrespective of the fluctuating fortunes of war, the work of Christian proselytization had gone steadily ahead, without hindrance from Penda, who (Bede says) was indifferent to a person's religious views, provided they were sincerely held.[70] The chief impetus now came from the Scottish church, whose missionary efforts won over Peada, then ruling the Middle Angles, and Sigbert of Essex, a kingdom which for nearly 40 years since the expulsion of Mellitus had remained adamantly heathen.[71] Even before Penda's death Scottish missionaries were at work in Mercia, and not only Peada but his brother Wulfhere and Merwal, king of the

Magonsaeta, became Christians.[72] While there is no reason to doubt the genuineness of Wulfhere's convictions, it is clear that he recognized the political advantages to be won from championship of the faith. Like all the Mercian kings he was a redoubtable warrior, but with little of the sheer barbarity of his father. He became a friend of such churchmen as Wilfrid[73] and was an adroit tactician, adept at mingling statecraft with force in achieving his aims. Whether through the persuasion of Wilfrid, an instinct for authority, or political foresight, it was towards the Roman church that his inclinations were to lead him.

The strength of the Scottish church lay in its ascetism, scholarship and proselytizing zeal, and above all in the example of sanctity set by Aidan and his disciples; its weakness was its lack of coherent organization. Its ideals were monastic, and it was around the great abbeys, such as Lindisfarne, that its life was centred. Its bishops were themselves monks, and as such subject to the discipline of their abbots; Aidan combined in himself both functions. There were no defined episcopal sees, though as a result of circumstances the activities of a bishop, or a group of bishops, might be restricted to a particular kingdom.[74] The inherent qualities of the Roman church were its discipline and authority, its international range, and a depth of tradition which made the Celtic church, for all its achievements, look parochial by comparison; to which there were added an imposing ritual and a certain ostentation calculated to appeal to kings. But in England, at this time, these qualities were ineffectively displayed because of the increasing mediocrity of the survivors of the original mission, unreplenished from Rome, and (until the appearance of Wilfrid) a dearth of native ordinants capable of competing in fervour and force of personality with the products of Iona or Lindisfarne. Honorius, who succeeded Justus as archbishop in 627 and lived until 652, may have been of Augustine's company,[75] but neither he, nor his successor Deusdedit, an Englishman, was of much account. Canterbury had given some assistance to the East Anglian church in its early days, sending it books and teachers,[76] but it played almost no part in the conversion of Wessex, an independent venture by Birinus;[77] and its authority, even among those in communion with Rome, hardly extended beyond Kent itself. This deficiency it was left to the Kentish royal house to repair, as best it might.

At a time when Kent remained safely distanced from the depredations of Penda, still spreading his power throughout the midlands and pursuing his vendetta against Northumbria, Earconberht concentrated with unswerving fidelity upon forwarding the interests of Rome. He is best remembered as the first English king positively to order the destruction of idols and observance of Lent,[78] something which none of his contemporaries felt able to do — a reminder of the subterranean strength of the old religion, obscured by the chronicle of royal conversions. Indeed, even this edict must have been more of a manifesto than anything, or it would not have needed to be renewed by Wihtred 40 years later.[79] But it was on the judicious use of marriage alliances that Earconberht chiefly relied. At no time in the history of the kingdom was more expected of the royal princesses; every one of whom was destined to serve either as an exemplar or as an emissary of the Roman faith. The first need was to cement the religious alliance between Kent and East Anglia, the other main citadel of orthodoxy in England, and to foster the contacts with the Gallic church, whose counsel and assistance were to be vital. Earconberht himself married Seaxburga, daughter of Anna of East Anglia, a most devout and respected figure; one of the daughters of this marriage, Earcongeta, became a nun at the convent of Farmoutier-en-Brie, where she won fame for the great sanctity of her life, 'the golden coin', it was said, that had been brought from Kent. A daughter and step-daughter of Anna also entered this convent, of which both in time became Abbesses, while other girls of noble family entered those of Chelles and Andelys.[80] Earconberht himself was three-quarters Frankish by blood, of the Merovingian royal line, and it is indicative of the strength of that relationship that not only his daughter Earongeta but his younger son Hlothere bore Frankish names.[81] There may have been little political advantage to be gained from the association at this time, but the religious (and commercial links) were vital. The Kentish and East Anglian courts became the portals to the spiritual life of the continent.

There was also need to make the influence of Rome felt in Northumbria, where the Scottish church was now paramount. It is possible, from the alliteration of the name, that Oslaf(a), the wife of Earconberht's elder brother Eormenred[82] (who had been passed over for the succession) came from the Bernician royal house.[83] The really crucial part, however, was to be played by Eanfled, daughter of the great Edwin, who was married to King Oswy at some time before 646, perhaps as early as 643,[84] when she would have been 17. No doubt from Oswy's standpoint the prime object of the marriage was to preserve the union between Bernicia and Deira, then threatening to fall apart under the assaults of Penda. But to all intents it was a Kentish princess he was taking; a grand-daughter of Æthelberht, who had been baptized into the Roman church by Paulinus, who from the age of seven had come under the guardianship and protection of the Eskings, whose mother Æthelburga was now Abbess of the monastery of Lyminge, who had grown up at the Kentish court, and who went to Northumbria accompanied by a priest from Canterbury, Romanus.[85] Eanfled was a determined woman, with no doubt where her duty lay. She kept strictly to the Roman practice, although this meant that for nearly 20 years she and her husband observed the Lenten fast and celebrated Easter at different times,[86] and she became a rallying point for those of the orthodox persuasion in Northumbria, a few of whom, like James the Deacon, had remained from Edwin's time.[87] The use of her patronage is seen in her treatment of the youthful Wilfrid, whose promise she was the first to recognize. After arranging for his instruction at Lindisfarne she sent him to her cousin Earconberht in Kent, where he stayed for a year before going on, with the king's help, to Lyons and Rome,[88] from which he returned to become the most effective champion of the orthodox cause in the north, joining forces with others of the queen's entourage who, Bede says, had been trained in Kent and Gaul.[89] Wilfrid was not the only one who took the path through Kent to the continent; another was Benedict Biscop, the companion of Theodore of Tarsus and later Abbot of Wearmouth.[90]

The doctrinal differences within the royal family were increased by the attachment to Rome, through the persuasion of Wilfrid (and no doubt through the influence of his mother), of the king's eldest son Alchfrid, who had been placed in charge of Deira.[91] The growing strength of the Roman party, and the acute inconvenience caused by a conflict aggravated by the incompatibility of Easter dates, prompted Oswy to summon in 664 a synod at Whitby where the issues were to be finally resolved. The disputants at this conference came almost entirely from Northumbria, though among those of the Scottish persuasion was Cedd, bishop of the East Saxons, and of the orthodox faith Agilbert of Wessex, who was visiting at the time. It is indicative of the weakness of the archbishop's authority that he was neither present nor sent a representative. It was, however, through influence exerted over long years by the Kentish royal court that the ground had been prepared, and Bede tells us that it was from Wilfrid, the protege of Eanfled and Earconberht, that the decisive intervention came. It is likely that, in fact, Oswy's mind had already been made up. He pronounced in favour of the Roman party; Aidan's successor Colman retired to Scotland with others who were unwilling to subscribe to the new regime;[92] and the example set by Northumbria came to be followed everywhere in England. The ground had been captured for Rome; the need now was to consolidate it, and in particular to make the authority of Canterbury a reality. That was to be the work of Theodore of Tarsus.

During the last six years of Earconberht's reign, and while the issue in Northumbria was still in doubt, a new shift had been given to the balance of power, secular and ecclesiastical, by the rise to prominence of Wulfhere, a Christian. At some time during this period a double marriage alliance was arranged. Earconberht's daughter Eormenhilda was wed to Wulfhere,[93] and Aebba, the eldest daughter of Eormenred, to Merwal, King of the Magonsaeta (see Appendix G).[94] On Earconberht's side the motives are clear enough; in part it was a dynastic insurance against Mercian ambitions, now increasingly directed towards the south, and in part a continuance of the policy of installing Kentish princesses in positions of influence, where they could best serve the interests of Rome (which were also those of their own people). That Wulfhere should have sought his wife from the Eskings implies a firm wish on his part to gain the favour of the church and a realization that there could be no better way of doing it than through such a connection. Earconberht did not long outlive the event. He died, while still in his early forties, in an epidemic which was then sweeping the country.[95] Bede describes his reign as 'noble'.[96] This is not, perhaps, the first epithet that comes to mind; he might better be described in the words later used of his grandson Wihtred (who in many ways resembled him) as 'diligent' and 'devoted';[97] but in his prudent, conscientious and determined way he had served both his church and his kingdom well.

The period of Kentish history which ended with Earconberht was one of unimpaired independence and unexampled peace. One would like to know far more about the effects of this upon the community but the evidence is curiously unbalanced. Bede and the later chroniclers tells us a great deal about political, religious and military matters; and for no other period, before or after, have we such detailed genealogical particulars,[98] a testimony to the major part played in the affairs of the time by the women of the royal household, who in other generations the chroniclers hardly deign to mention. But all this is largely on the surface. As we have said, even the account of the spread of Christianity is chiefly one of the conversion of princes or the activities of bishops and saints, giving little inkling of the dark corners of heathenism that remained among the people, in Kent as elsewhere. No codes of law survive between those of Æthelberht (c. 603) and of Hlothere and Eadric (c. 684), and such charters as exist are clearly spurious, so that however much we may credit the traditions underlying them we are deprived of any reliable and revealing details. For Eadbald's reign we still have the archaeological evidence of the burial sites, since inhumation with grave goods continued to be extensively practised during the first three or four decades of the 7th century, and the finds are sufficient to show that much of the luxury and ostentation of Æthelberht's time persisted at the court of his successor. Merovingian coins associated with the rich graves of

Sibertswold and Barfreston assign these to a time after 630, and there is similar evidence for the late dating of many of the finds at, for instance, Sarre, Chartham Down and Kingston.[99] From the start of Earconberht's reign, however, the quality and quantity of the grave goods rapidly dwindled under the influence of Christianity; the small continuing deposits consisting mostly of such articles as beads, bronze buckles and diminutive brooches.[100] This does not necessarily mean that the old craft skills had died out or become debased; more likely thay were being turned to new uses, and especially those of the church. But whereas the wealth buried underground has tended to survive, that displayed in the great churches has mostly been plundered or lost; for instance, the rich gifts made by Æthelberht to St Augustine's Abbey are reputed to have been either looted by the Danes, or hidden from them and mislaid.[101] Yet despite the paucity of material in the burials they can still tell us something. The size of the cemeteries at such places as Holborough, Eccles and Polhill (near Otford) is,[102] for instance, eloquent of the growth of population in west Kent during this period of calm and stability.

There must also have been a steady expansion of trade, and it was probably during this period that the system of royal tolls was first instituted, although for evidence of that we have to wait for Hlothere's Laws, promulgated some 20 years after Earconberht's death. We are on somewhat surer ground in tracing the extent of settlement, because in this we have place-names to help us. We have argued in Chapter 4 (pages 84–86) that the sizeable class of names ending in -ham, which are recognized as being among the very earliest, continued to be formed, at least sporadically, until the close of the 7th century (Westerham being a late example), by which time they were coming to be replaced by new types of ending, notably -ton; but it is a reasonable supposition that the great bulk of those in Kent had come into being before Earconberht's death, which was occasioned by plague and followed by 30 years of acute danger and disruption which must have checked for a time the growth of population and consequent spread of cultivation. The distribution of -ham names shows that during the prolonged period of peace and well-being, now drawing to a close, settlements had been extended along the length of Holmesdale, reaching away from the river gates to such places as Wrotham, Ightham and Lenham, and had also begun to encroach upon both the crests and dipslopes of the Downs, as at Cudham, Meopham, Newnham, Waltham and Bodsham Green (Appendix D), where for all the poverty of the soil some of the amplitude of pasture was now being taken under the plough. The division of the original holdings had driven those less fortunate than others in the erratic lottery of partible inheritance to break away and open up new land, of which there was enough to spare without any significant stinting of coppice and grazing.

Place-names ending in -ton do not begin to appear in Kentish charters until the close of the 7th century, the first to be reliably documented being Wilmington, in a grant of 697.[103] In Æthelberht's laws the term had been used to denote a mere enclosure around a house or farmstead,[104] but in those of Hlothere and Eadric (c. 675) it had already taken on the larger meaning of a settlement,[105] and it must have been at about this time that it started to replace ham in the formation of place-names. The change coincided closely with another in the grammatical construction of patronymics, that is places called after their founders or occupiers. This was the abandonment of the old genitive plural case -inge(a), which appears as the middle element in such names as Gillingham (originally Gillingeham)[106] for a deceptively similar, but actually very different, form -ing, which appears, for instance, in Orpington (originally Orped*ing*tune)[107] and was nearer in sense to a genitive singular.[108] In Kent not a single instance is known in which *ham* is associated with the second type of construction or *ton* with the first. This change of usage was not confined to names of habitation, and it sheds a particularly interesting light upon early developments in the Weald. Here there is an abundance of patronymics of the later type, associated with woods, glades or uncharacterized pastures, for which the common term was *daenn*; but there is also a smaller number — it seems, nearly 20 in all — in which the earlier genitive plural construction appears, mostly in association with *baera*, which was synonymous with *daenn** and on this evidence the earlier term of the two. Some of these may have originated in the 6th century and none can be later than the 7th. They mark the first stages of a process by which small areas of supposedly common land became appropriated to the use of kin groups, who would return to the same places with their swine year after year during the acorn fall, until they were acknowledged as having established some sort of claim to them; a typical assertion of the Jutish preference for several over common rights. The names are to be found spanning the whole breadth of the Kentish Weald from Cobhambury (Cobb*inge*b'y, 1232) in the west, through Pembury (Pepp*inge*beria, *c.* 1100) and Sissinghurst (Sax*inge*herste, *c.* 1206) to Ægylbyrht*inga*hyrst (near Ingleden in Tenterden parish, and recorded in a grant of 833). The full list is contained in Appendix F. This was a significant development in the utilization of the forest, and there are enough of the names to allow us to form some idea of how deeply it had been penetrated by the herdsmen by the middle of the 7th century, or thereabouts. The conclusion is, as far as the first ridges of the High Weald, but still anything from five to ten miles short of what was ultimately to become the boundary with Sussex.

Finally, we come to a group of patronymics which have attracted more scholarly attention than any others, those which consist of proper names in the nominative plural case *-ingas-*, devoid of anything else; in other words the names of kin transferred unmodified to the places where they lived, much as (to adopt a modern analogy) the home of the Smith family might be described simply as 'the Smiths'. These, then, are patronymics of the purest sort, and they invariably denote settlement. An example is Hallingas, now Halling.[109] Place-names of this kind are almost entirely confined to eastern and south-eastern England, the areas of early conquest, and the proper names of which they are composed are often highly archaic; for which reasons it used to be thought that they lay at the deepest level of all, preceding even the *ham* names, and that the more versatile genitive plural constructions, which could be used to specify not only the homes of folk but also their pastures, woodlands and so on, developed naturally out of them.[110] Recently, however, the weaknesses of this argument have been exposed by John MacNiel Dodgson in an article published in 1966,[111] which was based upon a study of south-eastern England and demonstrated such a separation between the sites of the pagan cemeteries and those of the *-ingas* place-names that it remained almost impossible to believe that the names could have originated during the migration period. They appeared, instead, to mark a stage of later expansion and colonization. In short, instead of the genitive plural constructions having evolved out of the *-ingas* place-names the reverse

---

* A charter of 863 speaks of '*pascua porcorum que nostra lingua Saxhonica "denbera" nominamus*'. (CS 507).

had been the case. Specifically, there had been an abbreviation of names that would previously have ended in -ingaham, much as (to revert to our previous analogy) 'the Smiths' home' might in common parlance become whittled down to 'the Smiths' — a perfectly intelligible progression.

Yet Dodgson himself was reluctant to go all the way with the apparent logic of the evidence by assigning the formation of the -ingas names unequivocally to the Christian era. For a number of reasons he was inclined to place them rather at the end of the 6th century and beginning of the 7th, a proposition which made it necessary to assume the use by the still largely pagan communities concerned of burial sites which are now undiscoverable, perhaps because they became overlaid by Christian cemeteries. This is not the easiest of arguments to sustain, and Dodgson resorted to it on what appear to have been insufficient grounds. The first was the archaism of so many of the constituent proper names, which, with their continental analogues, often go right back to the time of the conquest. But that, after all, was true of the name of Oisc, whose descendants were still known as the Oiscingas when Bede wrote; and it is not unreasonable to assume that other patriarchal names were perpetuated in the same way, well down into Christian times, at the lower levels of a society in which the concept of kinship was deep-rooted and strong. The second reason was the need, as Dodgson saw it, to set the formation of the -ingas place-names sufficiently early to allow the settlements to have acquired 'the importance, venerability and recognition' which some of them had certainly attained by the 8th century. This argument is difficult to evaluate. It seems, however, to discount the possibility that the settlements sometimes originated from colonizing ventures carried out by kin, or groups of kin, who were already numerous when the movements were made. There is evidence of a migration on this scale into central Essex, where two kin groups, the Hrodingas and Ginges, each bequeathed their names to as many as eight places.[112] More generally, when one considers the strides made in the settlement of England during the first hundred years or so after Hengest's coming, which saw the formation from small beginnings of virtually all the later kingdoms, it is difficult to deny similar powers of rapid progress and expansion to these later migrant communities, such (notably) as those who established themselves around Hastings,[113] and had by 771 become a people sufficiently considerable for Offa of Mercia to launch a special expedition against them.[114] This area — the later Rape of Hastings, stretching along the coast from Bexhill to Rye and with a forest hinterland reaching as far as Heathfield and Ticehurst — provides a classic example of one in which a cluster of -ingas place-names is unaccompanied by a single known pagan burial site. It is difficult to resist the conclusion that Dodgson was being too conservative, and that while a few of the names may have originated late in the pagan era most belong to the early Christian times, with a median date perhaps around 650, and that their formation overlapped with that of the last of the ham names, especially those such as Westerham, Newnham and so on which were not patronymics.

In Kent the distribution of the -ingas names consorts with this conclusion but does little more than fill out the picture we already have. It confirms the increase of population in the lower Medway valley,[115] and shows how by the middle of the 7th century settlements had been extended upstream as far as Yalding, which, with Peckham neighbouring it and Rooting and Worten (originally Werting) on the upper Stour southwest of Ashford,[116] represent the first tentative encroachments of cultivation upon the fringes of the Weald — where another foothold appears to have been established even earlier at Freezingham, near where the Rother debouched from the forest (this being a true -*ham* name in the genitive plural construction: *see* Appendix D). But it is the opening up, at this time, of the coastal area around Hastings that chiefly concerns us, because there are good reasons for believing that the settlements here were made, partly perhaps from Sussex, but primarily from Kent. This was disputable territory; a no-man's-land where the Wealden forest reached right down to the shoreline, and offering little for cultivation except along the banks of the few streams — the Brede, Tillingham and others — that broke the wooded hills. Whatever superior authority the Haestingas might from time to time acknowledge they remained a large autonomous people, sheltered by their remoteness. We have seen that Offa, when in control of both Sussex and Kent, was compelled to mount a special expedition to subdue them, and as late as 1011 the Anglo-Saxon Chronicle distinguished the area from *Suthseaxe*.

Jolliffe has shown that a number of features of the Kentish land system were to be found at places in Sussex, but that in the Hastings area they were especially pronounced.[117] This was a country of scattered hamlet settlement, in which the manors, as they developed, took on the same disjointed character as in Kent, with forest pastures reaching deep into the hinterland. There is the appearance of partible inheritance, of tenures which in early times had actually been classified as *gavel-land*, and even of the typical Kentish distinction between *outland* and *inland*. It may be going too far to claim, as Jolliffe does, that we have only to probe beneath the surface to find 'not a Saxon land, but a province of *Cantia Irredenta*, complete in whole and members, the double of its eastern neighbour of the Lymeneware',[118] since this implies an improbable degree of formal organization and control from Kent; and no part of Jolliffe's argument is less convincing than that in which he attempts to demonstrate how an original fiscal structure on the Kentish basis of the *sulung* underlay the later Sussex assessment by *hides*. (There were certain peculiarities about the *hides* in the Hastings area, but Eleanor Searle has shown that these were a response to the physical environment rather than an adaptation of an earlier and alien system).[119] Nevertheless, the mode of settlement, and the customs and economy associated with it, bear a distinctly Kentish reflection; and there is an intriguing piece of evidence that the Haestingas, the most influential of the folk, who gave their name to the whole region, came originally from the area between Wye and Lyminge, where they left their name to the village of Hastingleigh (*Haestinga lege*, *c.* 993).[120] That some connection must have existed between this place and Hastings has long been recognized,[121] but it is only with the recent reappraisal of the dating of the two forms of name that it has become possible to understand what it was. Hastingleigh now appears as a hill pasture occupied by the Haestingas before, with other less-known folk, they left Kent for their new homeland in what was eventually to become a part of Sussex.

The occupation of the Hastings area deserves, therefore, to be remembered as the last pioneering venture of the Jutish people, induced by the pressure of population that built up in east Kent during the long years of peace; and the evidence we have previously cited, together with the demographic considerations, suggests that it was during Earconberht's reign that the bulk of the migration occurred. The arrival of these people on the virtually unoccupied sea-board between the old settled areas of Kent and Sussex, and competing claims to their allegiance, was bound to give rise to friction between the two kingdoms. We know that the issue had been decided by 740 or 741, when a grant by Æthelberht II of land near Lydd was described as bordering upon Sussex (in the neighbourhood of Camber, the very northern tip of Hastings Rape). Most likely it was decided in 685 when Hlothere fell in battle against a Sussex army that had been brought into Kent through the treachery of his nephew Eadric;[123] any later attempt by the Kentish kings to recover the loss being baulked because Sussex itself then shortly passed under the control of a revived Wessex. The evidence dovetails and the date fits. Yet, short as the period of political connection between the Haestingas and their native land may have been, they still kept the stamp of their origin in the distinction that clung to them, marking them off from the South Saxons, to whom they had become uncertainly united. There was a tradition in Kent, noted by Leland and later mentioned by Hasted,[124] that the Isle of Oxney had originally formed part of the territory of the Haestingas, but that the people there succeeded in retaining their allegiance to Kent, or that this was restored. The Isle had certainly been brought firmly within the Kentish dominions by 724,[125] perhaps as part of the general agreement reached thirty years previously between Wihtred and Ine of Wessex, then in control of Sussex.

The plague that carried off Earconberht heralded the end of the period of peaceful expansion. Just how serious its effects were we do not know, but they seem to have been felt most in Kent, where Archbishop Deusdedit also died,[126] and in Essex, where they provoked a heathen reaction.[127] Nor do we know what the infection was. The history of epidemiology shows long periods of relative stability, with diseases endemic to a society tending to lose their virulence, and sometimes to decline into mere childhood illnesses, as immunity to them grows and they themselves adapt to a more equable, parasitic role.[128] These, however, have been interspersed with other periods in which contacts established between societies hitherto strangers to each other have released on either side, with devastating results, infections against which no protection has been acquired. It seems that one such period began in the 2nd and 3rd centuries A.D. when the opening up of trade routes, by sea and land, between the Mediterranean and the ancient civilizations of India and China let loose upon the western world previously unfamiliar diseases, including probably measles and small-pox, which were followed in the 6th century by the onset of bubonic plague; catastrophes that some believe did as much as any external enemies to hasten the decline of Rome and destroy the recuperative powers of Byzantium.[129]

So far as can be judged, Britain until the middle of the 7th century had been a tolerably healthy place. Some earlier epidemics are known, such as the so-called Yellow Plague which, in 547 or thereabouts, killed Maelgwyn of Gwynedd,[130] but these seem to have been infrequent visitations. It was the renewed contacts with the Mediterranean world, strengthened by the Christian conversion and the growth of trade, that now exposed the people to diseases against which they had little or no acquired immunity, though the still sparsely settled and rural character of the country must have provided some defence. The epidemic which struck England in 664 may have been measles, small-pox or a form of influenza, but there is one small hint that it was, in fact, bubonic plague; Bede in his *Life of St Cuthbert* mentions that the saint once had a groin bubo and had suffered from the disease that 'carried off so many in his time'.[131] Flea infested rats were the vectors of plague, and they were ship travellers. It would be consistent with what little we know about the incidence of the epidemic that, having entered through the south-eastern ports, it should have established itself in the growing towns of London,

Canterbury, and already probably York, and that Essex and Kent should have been particularly afflicted by it.

Whatever the demographic effects of the outbreak, it had two major political conse-quences. The death of Deusdedit, and shortly after of his chosen successor Wighard, opened the way to the appointment by the Pope of Theodore of Tarsus,[132] and so to the great work of church reform which, in confirming the victory of Rome, also established Canterbury in a position of indisputable and effective ecclesiastical authority throughout England. The heathen revival in Essex led to the intervention there of Wulfhere, acting with the full approbation of the church;[133] the first, but by no means the last, occasion on which he was to use Christianity as a stalking horse for his temporal ends. Control over the rapidly expanding market of London must have added consider-ably to Wulfere's resources, besides giving him an invaluable fulcrum of power in the south-east. For the next 150 years, almost without intermission, Essex was to be a subservient client of Mercia. For Kent the presence of Mercian power directly across the Thames posed an imminent threat, and gave warning that it would soon no longer be possible for the kingdom to stand aloof from the military upheavals of the time.

Chapter Eight

THE DISRUPTION

Egbert I, Hlothere, Eadric and Oswine; 664–690

BY EARCONBERHT'S DEATH so great was the credit that the Eskings had acquired with the church that only internal weaknesses within the dynasty itself could offer a handle to Mercian intervention. It had hitherto been one of the great strengths of the kingdom that the throne had passed from father to chosen son with scarcely a hint of discord, but on Egbert's accession this harmony was disturbed by a challenge — or the fear of it — from the heirs of that Eormenred whose claims had been set aside a generation earlier. The murder of these conspirators (if that is what they were) threatened the moral authority of the dynasty, and although Egbert was quick to make amends, and the church — for its part — to accept them, it caused a cleavage in the royal house was was not properly repaired for another 60 years.

Even more damaging than this was Egbert's premature death after a reign of only nine years, when neither of his sons was of an age to rule. No better opportunity could have been offered to the Mercians, who seized upon it; and although Egbert's brother Hlothere was able to fight them off and establish his own claims this left a further legacy of weakness and bitterness, since it was now Egbert's sons who considered themselves to have been dispossessed. It was the treachery of the elder of these, Eadric, leading to Hlothere's death in battle in 685, that precipitated the worst of the calamities to befall the kingdom, plunging it into anarchy and leaving it as a cockpit in the struggle between Wessex and Mercia — in the course of which Eadric was killed and a grandson of Eormenred, named Oswine, made a brief and inglorious appearance as a creature of Mercia. This was the period during which, in Bede's words, 'various alien kings and usurpers plundered the kingdom for a while', until the younger of Egbert's sons, Wihtred, now grown to maturity, 'freed the nation from foreign invasion by his diligence and devotion', rallying the people to his support as Hlothere had once done.

It is with the period of stress and disaster between Earconberht's death in 664 and the emergence of Wihtred nearly 30 years later that we shall deal in this chapter. Paradoxically, it was in the worst of these times, when Kent was a battle-ground, that Theodore of Tarsus was engaged at Canterbury in his work of church reform, apparently unaffected by the political chaos surrounding him, and that the great renaissance of English scholarship began there under his guidance and that of his friend and collaborator Hadrian, Abbot of St Augustine's. Theodore's concern was with the whole of England; to achieve his aims he had to act as a mediator between the kingdoms, not as a partisan; but he gave what support he could to the legitimate line, and his influence can be discerned in a number of administrative innovations made by Hlothere during the short respite from foreign invasion which the Cantware had won under his leadership. The appointment of

141

Theodore, no less than the troubles which beset the nation, had its source in Egbert's reign.

Egbert was the elder of Earconberht's sons but not, it seems, the eldest of his children. Eormenhilda, who became Wulfhere's wife, appears to have been a few years older than him. A son of that marriage was already serving as a Mercian reeve, or sub-king, in 681.[1] This means that Eormenhilda must have been married during the last years of Earconberht's reign, and since Earconberht can only have been in his early forties when he died Egbert could scarcely have been older than his sister. As a second child he must, then, have been a very young man, probably still in his teens, when he came to the Kentish throne, with the plague raging and the smell of death about. In killing Archbishop Deusdedit as well as Earconberht the pestilence had created a vacancy at Canterbury, which was not to be filled for five years, so depriving Egbert of the mature moral counsel of which a young king stood in need — although some guidance may perhaps have been given by his mother, the devout Seaxburga, now established as Abbess of a monastery in Sheppey which had been founded for her.[2] It is easy to believe that in the fraught atmosphere of the time Egbert should have come under the influence of the more headstrong and unscrupulous of his companions. Yet in nominating a successor to Deusdedit he had the wisdom to consult Oswy of Northumbria,[3] the doyen of English kings whose unrivalled authority in ecclesiastical affairs had been demonstrated by the proceedings at Whitby. The choice fell upon a certain Wighard, who was recommended to the Pople for consecration but died shortly after his arrival in Rome. Pope Vitalian thereupon took the appointment into his own hands, first approaching Hadrian, Abbot of a monastery near Monte Cassino, who however modestly declined the offer but suggested Theodore of Tarsus and undertook to accompany him. These consultations had taken time, and Theodore was delayed on his journey to England. It was not until May 669 that this elderly man, then already 68, finally arrived at Canterbury[4] to take up the task which he was to continue with unflagging vigour until his death in 690.

Before Theodore's arrival Egbert's reign had been tarnished by an act of impetuous folly, the murder in the royal vill of Easty of his two cousins, Æthelred and Æthelberht, the sons of Eormenred; a crime which gave rise to one of the great legends of Kentish history. We do not know exactly when the deed was done, but it was probably at the very beginning of the reign, since it bears all the signs of a young man unsure of his position and if, in fact, the two princes had been conspiring against him this would have been the time for them to act, before Egbert had established himself and while the nation was unsettled by the plague. The legend in its final form, as retailed in the *Lives of the Kentish Royal Saints, c.* 1000[5] and adopted by later chroniclers such as Simeon of Durham,[6] emphasizes the youth and virginal purity of the victims and ascribes their death to a wicked minister called Thunnor, who first poisoned Egbert's mind against them and then cut short the king's hesitation by murdering them himself, hiding their bodies in the palace, where however they were revealed by a heavenly light. On discovery of the deed Egbert is said to have been overcome by remorse and to have offered restitution to the young mens' eldest sister Aebba, who chose to take it in the form of land on which to found a monastery of which she herself became Abbess by leave of her compliant and saintly husband Merwal, King of the Magonsaeta of Hereford. The land was in Thanet, and legend says that its extent was determined by releasing Aebba's pet stag and including everything it encompassed in the course of a day; an arrangement which so infuriated Thunnor that he spurred in chase of it, only for the ground to open up and swallow him at a place ever afterwards known as Thunnor's Hlaw (or, in later versions, Leap).[7] This, we are told, was the origin of the celebrated Abbey of Minster in Thanet.

The first comment to be made is that Bede, who had a taste for the miraculous and a close knowledge of Kentish affairs, made no mention of these events at all, although writing within 70 years of their supposed occurrence. The legend has, in fact, a number of different levels. It is easy enough to dismiss the stag story as the purest hagiography, and it is also difficult to believe in the existence of Thunnor. It would have been surprising, to say the least, for a royal reeve to have borne at this time the name of a heathen god; and it is clear that Thunnor's Hlaw did not take its name from him, but the other way round. *Hlaw* means a burial mound and this place-name must have originated in pagan times.[8] Thunnor, the reeve, appears as a mythical figure concocted to act as a scape-goat for Egbert, who later became a great benefactor of the church and had, therefore, so far as possible to be exonerated of the crime (which Bede preferred to pass over in silence). There seems little doubt that, whoever actually carried out the deed, Egbert was the true culprit. At the same time it is improbable that the victims were as young, chaste and innocent as legend came to suggest. Since they sprang from a senior branch of the royal family they are likely to have been somewhat older than Egbert himself — at least one would expect Æthelred to have been so — and there is good reason to believe that the mysterious individual named Oswine, who held a brief authority in Kent some 25 years later, was the son of one or other of them (*see* pages 155–156 below). The youths were the uncles of St Mildred (a daughter of Aebba's) with whose legend their own became bound up,[9] and the belief in their sanctity appears to have been fostered by the monks of St Augustine's, who had a vested interest in the matter because they had acquired St Mildred's relics.[10] Canterbury tradition records, disapprovingly, that Egbert's brother and eventual successor, Hlothere, laughed at the princes being described as martyrs.[11] This is a story one would like to believe; partly because it is in keeping with what we know of the robust character of Hlothere, and partly because common-sense suggests that the reaction was a sound one. The probability is that the young men were trouble-makers.

Given that the act was more impulsive than calculated, it certainly succeeded in scotching any internal disturbance. To all appearance the Cantware were quite unmoved by it; for many years they had been blessedly free of dynastic troubles, endemic in other kingdoms such as Wessex, and they no doubt shared Hlothere's view of the matter. But the effects were still extremely perilous, both because of the injury inflicted on the victim's kin, which involved the Mercian royal house through Aebba's husband Merwal, a dependent of Wulfhere, and because in the eyes of the church it was a deadly sin. Egbert had provoked powerful enemies while forfeiting moral support. It was fortunate for him that Wulfhere, besides having his hands full at the time in establishing himself in Essex, was also Egbert's brother-in-law and so in no position to side openly against him in a blood fued. It was urgently necessary nonetheless to make peace with the kin, and for this custom demanded the payment of a blood-price, or 'the fine for the murder' as the chronicler Thorne puts it.[12] This must have been a considerable sum. None of the Kentish laws tells us the *wer-geld* of a prince, or *atheling*, but in later years the price paid by Wihtred for the killing of a West Saxon prince, Mul, was 30,000 *sceattas* or silver pence,[13] which on a Kentish reckoning was five times that for a noble — and the compensation owed by Egbert was not for one prince, but two. Primarily it was owed to the sisters of the young men, and the grant of land to Aebba (also called Domneva, a conflation of Domina Aebba)[14] must have comprised a major element in it. It seems that the grant was made in Thanet because a large part of the lands which had been owned by the youths' father Eormenred had lain there,[15] and some of these may have been added. No charter or other detailed record has survived of the transaction, so that we do not know the size of the original foundation; at the time of Domesday Book the manor of Minster (which had then come into the ownership of St Augustine's Abbey) comprised 48 *sulungs* and 62 ploughlands, or rather more than half the Isle, but other grants had been made to it after Egbert's time. It must nevertheless have been a substantial estate from the beginning.

The vacancy at Canterbury meant that it was less easy for Egbert to make his peace with the church, which he had now become desperately anxious to do, no doubt for his own soul's sake as well as for the health and safety of the kingdom. He seems to have received some spiritual counsel from Wilfrid, the friend and protégé of his father, who officiated from time to time in Kent during the archbishop's absence,[16] but full absolution had to await the delayed arrival of Theodore. So eager was Egbert to hasten this that as soon as he heard that Theodore had reached France he sent his high reeve, or herald, Raedfrid to escort him across the Channel.[17] We learn from the Anglo-Saxon Chronicle that in 669 Egbert gave Reculver to Bass the priest for a monastery to be built there, and at the same time, or shortly after, he is known to have founded the Abbey of Chertsey in Surrey.[18] By these grants the crime had been expiated, and the process of exoneration, by which responsibility was shifted from him onto the mythical Thunnor, was shortly to begin.

The grant of Chertsey confirms that in Egbert's time the whole of Surrey was still in Kentish hands, despite the ever-present threat of Mercian power across the Thames. Although by this time Wulfhere may already have been acknowledged as *bretwalda*, or high king, of southern England, in which he had become by far the most powerful figure,[19] there is no indication that Egbert ever allowed him more than the strict dues of that office, and he himself seems to have been content for a while to leave Kent unmolested while he pursued other designs. That the two men were brothers-in-law was, no doubt, a factor in this, but it is questionable whether ir would have deterred Wulfhere had Egbert continued to forfeit the support of the church, which he had so dearly redeemed. For the time being Wulfhere's energies were directed against Wessex, which he had pressed back beyond the Thames; already in 661 he was raiding across the Bershire Downs,[20] and a charter of 674 shows him firmly in control of the area around Thame, where he had established a royal court.[21] He was also making use of Sussex to undermine Wessex on that side, posing again as the champion of the church in doing so. Bede tells us that it was he who persuaded Æthelwalh of Sussex to be baptized, standing as his god-father, and that he sealed the alliance by 'giving' him the Isle of Wight, another still heathen kingdom, together with the province of the Meonware on the mainland opposite, which was Wessex territory.[22] This marks the re-emergence of Sussex after nearly 200 years of complete obscurity; Æthelwalh is, in fact, the first of its kings of whom we have any knowledge since Aelle. His conversion appears to have made little impact upon the mass of his people, whose evangelization was finally undertaken by

Wilfrid some ten years later;[23] but it served Wulfhere's cause by allowing him to use Christianity as a means to his own ends, as he had previously done in Essex. An attack upon Kent would have been incompatible with this rôle, failing some respectable pretext, of which Egbert's reconciliation with the church had robbed him. Nevertheless Kent's position, held within the vice of Mercian power, in Essex on the one side and Sussex on the other, had now become extremely hazardous; all the more because the kingdom lacked the resilience of Wessex, which was able to compensate itself for the loss of its lands north of the Thames by a continuous expansion to the south-west against the British.[24] In the face of attack Kent would be cornered; its independence, if not its very existence, required internal unity and the cloak of the church's protection, both of which Egbert had contrived to retain. Any false move or dynastic mishap might destroy that tenuous immunity; but Egbert, now in his twenties, had recovered from his adolescent folly and was showing signs of maturing into a wise and capable ruler. In retrospect Bede was able to describe him, with Oswy of Northumbria, as the most noble of the English kings of the time.[25]

In July 673 disaster fell upon Kent with Egbert's untimely death,[26] we are not told from what cause, but almost certainly from illness. Of his two sons, Eadric must then still have been a child and Wihtred no more than an infant; the crisis does not appear to have been foreseen and no arrangement had been made for the succession. It is a remarkable fact, which may throw some light on the nature of the fatality, that absolutely nothing is known of Egbert's wife, not even her name, which would hardly have failed to come down to us had she survived him and been established, as had now become the practice with royal widows, as the head of some religious foundation. The likelihood is that husband and wife died together in some epidemic — it might have been a brief flare-up of the plague that had killed Earconberht nine years earlier — and that the children were left not only fatherless but orphaned. It is worth considering what would have happened to them. According to custom their guardianship would have passed to the paternal kin, that is primarily to Egbert's brother Hlothere, who would also (incongruous though it may seem) have inherited that of those other orphans of the royal house, the younger and still unmarried sisters of the two princes whom Egbert had murdered (see Appendix G). But Hlothere, preparing to stake his own claim to the throne, for which he would have to fight, was scarcely in a position at this time to undertake the safe-keeping of his wards. The natural arrangement would have been to entrust Eadric and Wihtred to the care of their grandmother Seaxburga in her Abbey at Sheppey, and the young girls to that of their elder sister Aebba at Minster in Thanet. That Seaxburga played a prominent part in the events of this time is shown by the garbled tradition in the *Lives of the Kentish Royal Saints* that she acted as regent for Hlothere at the beginning of his reign. This means, in all probability, that she used her influence as dowager queen to secure his acceptance by the Kentish nobility, perhaps on the understanding (which was honoured), that he would share his authority with Eadric when he came of age. There is also some reason to believe that, 17 years later, when Hlothere and Eadric had both been killed, Sheppey was the sanctuary from which the youthful Wihtred emerged to restore the kingdom from foreign invasion and anarchy (page 162 below).

The confusion into which the kingdom was thrown by the uncertainty of the succession provided the opportunity for intervention for which Wulfhere must have been waiting. Bede and the later chroniclers tell us almost nothing of this; but now, for the first time, we have an independent, and contemporary, source of evidence in the charters recording grants of land to the church, from which a great deal can be culled about the current political situation. The introduction of formal diplomas of grant is believed to have been inspired by Theodore of Tarsus.[27] Most of those we have are copies; but the use of parchment in place of papyrus means that some originals have survived, starting with a charter issued by Hlothere in 679,[28] and it is usually possible, by textual criticism, to separate the genuine copies from the forgeries. In dealing with the earlier of these diplomas, those of Theodore's own time, there is the difficulty that they are commonly dated, not by the Year of Grace, but by the year in the Indiction, which was a cycle of 15 years adopted for administrative purposes in Imperial times and used by the Papal chancery and had the additional complication that it was geared to 1 September.[29] It is generally easy to decide from the context of a charter in which cycle it should be placed; but this is not always so, with the result that one may be left with a choice of dates 15 years apart, a problem which we are about to encounter.

There are three charters to be considered here, all copies but held to be authentic. The first of these, issued by Hlothere in the April of a year which can be reliably converted from the Indiction reference to 675, is expressed as being given in the first year of his reign;[30] which shows that at least nine months, and possibly as many as 18, elapsed between Egbert's death in July 673 and the time when Hlothere felt strong enough to claim the throne. The second shows that during that interval Surrey had been detached from the kingdom and entrusted to a certain Frithewold, who had no connection with the Kentish royal house but was engaged in adding, with Wulfhere's leave, to the endowments of Egbert's foundation at Chertsey.[31] (This is the first record of Surrey, under that name; the term was certainly ancient, but exactly what it embraced is dubious; the places mentioned in this document all lay well to the west). The third is the one that raises the most acute problems of dating. It records the grant by a certain Suaebhard, as an underling of Mercia, and in the second year of his reign, of lands in Thanet, and was issued in Canterbury on 1 March either of 676 or of 691, according to which cycle of the Indiction is to be preferred.[32] Stenton opted for the earlier date, which would place Suaebhard's accession as a Mercian under-king in the last ten months of 674 or the first two of 675 and confirm the seizure by Wulfhere not only of Surrey but of the entire kingdom;[33] but Dorothy Whitelock in a recent lecture has argued strongly for the later, pointing out that Suaebhard is known to have been active in Kent in 692.[34] Kenneth Harrison, in supporting her view, has emphasized the improbability of his reappearance on a scene from which he had previously been expelled, and has suggested that Wulfhere himself may have been the effective ruler of Kent for about a year following Egbert's death[35] (after which the resistance under Hlothere would have begun).

This seems to be the better interpretation; but either way Wulfhere's seizure of Surrey in the immediate aftermath of Egbert's death is well enough established, and it is unlikely that his intervention would have stopped there. It was not a chance that he could be expected to let slip; but nor would naked annexation have been in keeping with what we know of his character. It had been his policy to subordinate, not to oust, the other dynasties, and there would have been no surer way of antagonizing the church, with whose favour he had prospered, than by supplanting completely the revered dynasty of the Eskings. Nor, for his purpose, would this have been necessary. He could claim a double interest in the future of Egbert's children, both as their uncle by marriage and as *bretwalda*,[36] a position that gave him a colourable right, in a confused period of interregnum, to protect Eadric's reversion to the throne. It would be enough for him to declare that he was holding the kingdom in trust for Eadric, who would later receive it from him as a client king, in every way as dependent upon Mercia as Sebbi of Essex and Æthelwalh of Sussex had become; while any attempt by Hlothere to take the throne could be denounced as usurpation. We cannot be sure that this is what happened, since within two years Wulfhere was dead and Mercian power in disarray; but it would not have been like him to act without respectable pretext, or to neglect such a good one.

An undertaking by Hlothere to associate Eadric with him on the throne when he came of age (as, in fact, was done) would have been the obvious counter. But the final say rested with the Cantware, a people jealous of their independence and within 18 months, probably less, they had turned to Hlothere to lead them against Mercian subversion. Their acknowledgement of him was an act of defiance, and in the circumstances a bold one. It was not only that Kent could not compare with Mercia in size or resources but that for more than 80 years, since Æthelberht had wrested the *bretwaldaship* from Wessex, the kingdom had been engaged in no serious warfare, and this prolonged period of peace must have deprived it of that cadre of experienced and committed fighting men, professionals in war, which the kings of Northumbria, Mercia and Wessex had assembled around themselves in the course of constant campaigning. There was a deceptive quality about Kentish society which may have misled Wulfhere, as it was later to do others. A kingdom with a petty nobility but with an exceptionally privileged body of ceorls — an aristocracy among freemen — may have lacked the urge to aggressive warfare, the time-honoured pursuit of the great nobles elsewhere, but could muster in its own defence a force of hardy and substantial farmers, men with a strong sense of their own identity and of partnership with a dynasty to which they were bound by direct ties of allegiance. These formed a reservoir of loyalty on which it seems that the Eskings could always rely. The Mercians were to find — and not for the last time — that in an age when permanent garrisoning was impossible there was no other means of countering the resistance of a determined nation than by resort to wide-scale plundering and devastation. But in defence of their own lands the Cantware were to show remarkable powers of resistance, against which these punitive measures were to fail.

By the spring of 675 Hlothere had won control of north-east Kent, the stronghold of the kingdom. In April of that year he was at Canterbury, where he granted certain neighbouring lands to St Augustine's Abbey, doing so as the sole lawful king of the Cantware — the first recorded instance of the use of that term.[37] Significantly, this grant was subscribed both by Archbishop Theodore and by Hadrian, an acknowledgement of Hlothere's rights which must have been of great service to him; and indeed at the Synod of Hatfield five years later Theodore was to refer to his reign as dating, not from 674 (or the early part of 675) which was the most that he himself claimed, but from 673, the time of Egbert's death, so implying that he had been the sole lawful king from the very beginning — an example that was to be followed by Bede.[38] Wulfhere was slow to respond to this threat, which he seems to have regarded as something that could be dealt with at leisure when more important matters had been settled. He was now at the height of his power. Disregarding small pockets of resistance, the Kentish coup had completed his supremacy over southern England, since it seems that a much harried Wessex had now been brought to acknowledge his overlordship. Although Bede withholds the title from him he was, in actuality, *bretwalda* of all the kingdoms south of the Humber.[39] It remained only to impose his authority upon Northumbria, now ruled by Oswy's son Ecgfrid, against whom Wulfhere assembled an army composed, as a contemporary chronicler expressly says, of 'all the southern nations'.[40] But, as so often before in this protracted duel, the outcome defied all expectations. Wulfhere was decisively defeated, and became a fugitive, vanishing completely from sight.[41] It might have been better for him had he relied entirely upon his own Mercians, since it is not to be supposed that contingents drawn from Wessex or East Anglia, any more than from the expropriated territories of Surrey and west Kent, would have fought in his cause with any enthusiasm. The hegemony that he had established now fell apart; Mercia itself was threatened; and to meet that threat the throne was given to Æthelred, a brother of Wulfhere and another son of the old warrior Penda.[42]

The Mercian defeat was Hlothere's opportunity, and he appears to have made good use of it. Immediately upon Wulfhere's disappearance his wife Eormenhilda, obeying the homing instincts implanted in all Kentish princesses, returned to her native land to assume the charge of the monastery of Sheppey (and with it, if we are right, of the young princes Eadric and Wihtred), her mother Seaxburga having left to join, and later to succeed, her sister at the Abbey of Ely in her own native country of East Anglia.[43] The arrangement shows that Hlothere was now in control of mid-Kent and it seems from what followed that he had gone on from there to recover Rochester and lands beyond. It must, moreover, have been at about this time that a marriage was arranged between Eormenburga, one of Eormenred's daughters and a royal ward, and Ecgfrid of Northumbria, whose first wife had deserted him for the religious life; while a little later another of the daughters, Eangyth, was married to Centwine of Wessex (*see* Appendix G). These were clearly political matches; the enemies of Mercia were being drawn together and Hlothere was at the centre of the design.

It was, no doubt, for this reason that Æthelred felt it necessary, in building up a front against Northumbria, to dispose first of the growing menace to his rear. Early in 676 he invaded Kent in force, ravaging the country as he went. Bede records with horror how his 'wicked soldiery' profaned churches and monasteries without fear of God or respect to religion, destroyed the City of Rochester and looted the cathedral church there, causing the bishop, Putta, to abandon his see in despair.[44] This cauterization was quite ineffective. It caused great offence to the church but did nothing to break the spirit of the Cantware. Given that the charter issued at Canterbury by the Mercian underling Suaebhard should be dated, not to 676 as Stenton thought, but 15 years later, there is no sign that the Mercian army ever penetrated into east Kent; and whether Æthelred was checked in battle or withdrew in the mistaken belief that he had done enough to keep the country quiet while he attended to the major threat from the north, it seems that Hlothere rapidly recovered whatever ground he had lost, and was soon to press his advantage still further by establishing a Kentish presence in London itself.

We do not know when it was that Hlothere first acquired this foothold in London, how it was brought about, or exactly what his presence there implied; but his Laws, issued in association with Eadric and so towards the end of his reign, show that he was then maintaining a royal hall in the city with a port-reeve to look after the affairs of Kentish folk[45] visiting this 'great emporium', as Bede describes it.[46] It may simply be that extra-territorial rights of the kind had persisted since the time of Æthelberht, and had been respected by the Essex kings and their Mercian overlords even when Kent had lost its political predominance; but even if that were all, the fact that Æthelred had been brought to acknowledge Hlothere as the legitimate holder of the rights would have been sufficiently remarkable, and could only have been achieved by force of arms. In fact, the appearance is that Hlothere had actually managed to displace Mercian influence in the city, from which it would also follow that he must have regained control at least of those parts of Surrey adjacent to it.

This reversal of fortune is the more striking because the Kentish presence in London survived a defeat inflicted on Northumbria in a battle fought on the River Trent in 679, which relieved Æthelred of all threat from that quarter and might have been expected to free him to turn once more upon Hlothere. But this seems to have been a singularly bloody engagement, leaving neither side with the stomach for more. The battle, in fact, marks the end of the memorable conflict between the two kingdoms, which were content henceforth to go their own ways without molesting each other. One of the casualties in it had been Elfwin, brother of Ecgfrid and also of Æthelred's wife, so that family blood had been spilt and demanded vengeance; but by Theodore's intercession the matter was composed by the payment to Ecgfrid of the customary blood-price for an *atheling*, or prince.[47] That the victor should have been willing to make this payment, and the loser to accept it and forego the feud, is some indication of the state of exhaustion to which both had been brought. The final withdrawal of Northumbria from southern concerns was ominous for the future, but so long as Hlothere was alive and the Cantware maintaining a united and resolute front Æthelred was evidently in no condition to try conclusions with them again. The Kentish influence in London remained and is attested by a story told by Bede.[48] A Northumbrian thegn, Imma, who had been wounded and captured by the Mercians at the battle on the Trent, was sold as a slave to a Frisian trader in the city, where he was able to reach Hlothere with an appeal for help (doubtless through the intermediary of his reeve there) and was redeemed by him. It was the miraculous elements in this story that impressed Bede — it was said that Imma could not be kept fettered, which made the slaver glad to be rid of him — but its interest to us is in the chivalrous light it throws on Hlothere's character.

This generosity was matched by his scrupulous dealings with Eadric. In 679, when the Mercians had been expelled from Kent, Hlothere had installed himself in London and his hold upon the kingdom was secure, he held a council at Reculver, attended by Theodore and a large number of notables, at which he granted the Abbey lands in the western part of Thanet, with all the pastures, marshes, woods and other easements belonging to them.[49] This grant is notable in a number of ways, not least because the document recording it is the first to have survived in the original from Anglo-Saxon times; but what concerns us here is that it was made expressly with the consent of Eadric, which shows that Hlothere had already acknowledged him as heir, and probably as prospective co-ruler, at a time when he can barely have become 15, which appears then to have been the age of majority for a boy.[50] (In the previous year a similar grant had been made of lands in the south of the Isle to the Abbey of Minster, but in the copy we have of this no mention of Eadric appears).[51] There is a tradition that Hlothere had a son, Richard, who later became a monk at Lucca in Italy,[52] but if there is any truth in this (which is doubtful) he must have been younger than Eadric and already passed over for the succession before he chose his vocation. By the time that Hlothere's laws were promulgated, that is shortly before his death in 685, he had gone further by actually associating Eadric with him in the kingship. This was the first time that joint rule had been introduced into Kent, and it was a perilous expedient, as events were to show. It failed to satisfy Eadric, who cannot have been much more than 15 years younger than his uncle, and therefore saw a long period of tutelage stretching in front of him before he could inherit the sole kingship which he believed to be his right.

That Hlothere was the true author of the laws cannot be doubted. The country needed to be set in order after the disturbances it had suffered; there had been changes in its society since Æthelberht's time, and new developments to be catered for, especially in trade; and there were also a number of administrative *lacunae* to be filled. The prominence given in the laws to procedural matters makes them an admirable and enlightening complement to those of Æthelberht, which had almost nothing to say on that aspect, and shows the strong practical bent of Hlothere's mind. It seems that he was now working in close harmony with that supreme administrator Theodore of Tarsus. The written diplomas of grant are one indication of this. We have also suggested in Chapter Three (page 57) that while the fiscal units of *hide* and ploughland may already have been familiar at the beginning of Hlothere's reign it was in the course of it, and under Theodore's influence, that the Kentish assessments first took the ordered form perpetuated in Domesday Book, since this matches the pattern of settlement of the period, as place-name evidence discloses it, and shows signs of having originally covered Surrey — or east Surrey at least — which was permanently lost to the kingdom after Hlothere's death. The laws were, therefore, only one aspect of a general re-ordering of the nation's affairs.

The first four clauses, which are concerned with killings by slaves, are not only an insight into the disturbed conditions through which the kingdom had passed but also provide, albeit incidentally, the clearest statement of the *wer-gelds* of the Kentish eorl and 'freeman', a term which we have taken — as most other writers have done — to be synonymous with ceorl (*see* Appendix E). No mention whatsoever is made of the *laets*, which might not be significant in itself but becomes so when it is realized that they make no appearance, in any source, after Æthelberht's time. It seems probable that, while the *outland* and *inland* holdings were still sharply differentiated, as they remained into the middle ages, the *laets* as a social class had already ceased to exist and had been absorbed into the general body of the ceorls. A system under which *outlands* could be bought and sold without hindrance and where partible inheritance might so diminish a ceorl's portion that he would be glad to sell what remained and take an *inland* tenancy if opportunity offered, could not fail to act as the solvent of a hereditary class structure based originally upon a distinction between freeholders and tenant farmers.

Specifically, these clauses provide that the owner of a homicide slave must surrender him (to vengeance) and pay in addition the value of three others if the slain is an eorl, or of one other if he is an ordinary freeman; if the killer escapes one further payment of the kind is to be due in the first case and two in the second. The slave's value is not given, presumably because it varied according to his function and ownership, as shown in Æthelberht's laws.[53] Seebohm was no doubt right in believing that the clauses were an innovation designed to relieve a slave's owner of complete responsibility for his acts, which would involve the payment of the full *wer-geld* of the slain man, a very much higher charge.[54] The special interest of the clauses, however, is that they require that where the slave has escaped his owner must clear himself of complicity with good 'oath-helpers', of whom one must be from his own *tun*, or community. Although the full number is not stipulated the later laws of Wihtred suggest it to have been three.[55] This is the first illustration in England of the general principle that issues were tried, not on any examination of the evidence, but upon the reputation of the accused, and whether enough people of the appropriate standing were prepared to vouch for him. (There is no mention in this, or in any other of the early Kentish codes, of the ordeal).

Other clauses define the procedure for settling disputes in general. Under these, once an accusation has been made the accused is required to give 'the judges of the Kentish people' sureties for his good behaviour should he meet the plaintiff at an assembly or other gathering; and the parties are then to agree upon an arbitrator within three days (or a longer period at the plaintiff's discretion) before whom the matter is to be settled either by the accused accepting the guilt and offering the appropriate compensation or by his clearing himself with the aid of 'oath-helpers'; failing either of which he is to pay 100 shillings, the equivalent of a full *wer-geld*. The arrangements are based, at every stage, upon the concept of enforcement in and by the community itself, without other intervention, and are an apt rejoinder to those who speak of the Kentish kings as being peculiarly autocratic.[56] On this, it should also be noted that every one of Hlothere's grants of land is expressed as being made with the consent of the notables — which Stenton sees no reason to regard as an idle phrase.[57]

A different element is, however, introduced by a provision that failure to give sureties where these are required shall be punished by the payment of 12 shillings to the king, whose authority is thus invoked to support that of the local elders; and there are a number of other provisions in the code which show a development since Æthelberht's time of the use of the royal *wite*, or fine, as a buttress to public order. It is charged at two rates, of which 12 shillings is the lower, imposed for acts of provocation liable to lead to violence, such as calling a man a perjurer or otherwise insulting him, snatching away his drinking vessel, or drawing a weapon on him.[58] The higher rate of 50 shillings is reserved for cases in which such actions result in actual bloodshed.[59] As Chadwick has pointed out, this figure is identical to that of the royal *mund*,[60] the deed being treated as a breach of the protective rights not only of the person in whose house it was committed but of the king himself, as though the whole realm were an extension of his household. The lower rate of the *wite* seems also to have been fixed by analogy to the *mund*, though this time of an eorl, the next step down on that scale. The clauses illustrate the development from what were essentially private rights, enjoyed by the ruler and all his subjects in their own degree, into the public remedy of the king's peace.

There are two provisions of a more miscellaneous kind. The first is an attempt to reconcile, in the case where a father has died, the claims of the mother and of the father's kin to the care and guardianship of the children. It provides, no doubt under the influence of the church, that in such circumstances it is right for the child to accompany the mother, but meets the interests of the paternal kin by placing his property in the trust of one among them, willing to act, until the child is ten years old (a surprisingly young age, which contradicts that appearing in Theodore's Penitentials;[61] Gordon Ward has suggested that an error has crept into the copying here,[62] which seems very likely). The second stipulates that anyone who accommodates and feeds for three nights or more a stranger to the kingdom, be he a trader or another, shall be responsible for his wrong-doings. This is indicative of the increase of trade across the frontiers, and an attempt to deal with the problem of itinerants, largely chapmen or merchants, with no kin to answer for their behaviour; the host being required, in effect, to assume the obligations of kinship.

Finally, there is a group of clauses which deal with 'vouching to warranty', that is the determination of cases in which property is alleged to have been stolen;[63] and it is in these that London features so largely. The general rule laid down is that where an individual claims that property in the possession of another has been stolen from him the possessor must vouch for his ownership before the king's court, and in particular produce the person from whom the property was obtained. Far more elaborate procedures apply, however, to property purchased in London, a great cosmopolitan market, much frequented by the Cantware, and well suited to the disposal of stolen goods of all kinds, but especially, no doubt, cattle. The laws require that any purchase made by a Kentish-man in London must be witnessed by two or three honest ceorls or by the king's reeve in the city; that if the property is then attached by someone claiming to be its rightful owner the purchaser shall, if he is able, produce at the king's hall the person who sold it to him; if we cannot do that he must declare at the altar with one of his witnesses, or with the king's reeve, that the purchase was openly made as a public transaction; failing which he must surrender it to the claimant.

The interest of these provisions lies not only in the light they throw on the uncertainties of lawful ownership in a time of disturbance when military plundering was liable to degenerate into sheer banditry or theft, or in the extent of the rights which Hlothere was able to enforce in London, but more generally in the terms in which the provisions are couched. London is described as *Lundenwic* and the king's reeve in the city as the *cyninges wicgerefa*, that is, as a royal official fulfilling the specialized function of a port, or market, officer. In early English the term *wic*, deriving from the Latin *vicus*, had Protean meanings. In its first manifestations, associated with *ham*, as in the common Wickhams, it seems to have denoted the site of a Roman village, whether left abandoned or resettled (Appendix B); and, standing on its own, as for instance at Wick in Headcorn, it often came to mean a dairy farm.[64] But in the context in which it is used here it meant a port, or market, subject to royal supervision and control.[65] Such were Dunwich in Suffolk and *Hamwih*, later Southampton, a port developed by the Wessex kings; and in Kent the major harbours of Sandwich and Fordwich (serving Canterbury). Vouching for warranty can have been only one aspect of the controls exercized at these places, which must from the beginning have included the collection of tolls.

Hlothere's Laws thus provide the first clear indication of the existence of a system which, even after the loss of London, must have provided a major source of profit to the Kentish kings, who commanded so much of the cross-Channel traffic. Royal tolls had, however, almost certainly been introduced well before this time. They were a feature of Imperial finance adopted early on by the new Germanic authorities in France, Spain and Italy,[66] and the practice of the Merovingian kings would not for long have passed unnoticed in Kent. But there was another consideration, which sprang more directly from native customs and concerns. Once foreign merchants appeared in the country in any numbers the regulation of trade became a necessary protective measure, both in their interests, since they had nobody but the king to look to, and in the interests of the community at large, which had every cause to be suspicious of wayfarers for whom nobody could vouch — a problem which Hlothere had been compelled to attend to and to which Wihtred[67] was to revert some ten years later. Protection and tallage went hand in hand, a duty which the king turned to his own advantage. The most striking evidence of the growth of commercial activity since Æthelberht's time is the discovery at Crondall in Hampshire of a hoard of 100 gold coins which are thought from their number to have constituted the *wer-geld* of a Kentish ceorl and have been dated to somewhere between 650 and 675, and so most likely to the reign of Egbert.[68] Some of these coins are Merovingian, but some are marked as having been minted in London, and others may have been struck at Canterbury. Given the origin of the hoard, they are, in any case, evidence that a native gold currency was now circulating in Kent and the south-east, and that the system of trade regulation also existed in Egbert's time is implied in the first recorded appearance then of the term *wic*, in its new connotation, in a reference to Sandwich (*Sandwicae*), where Wilfrid is said by a contemporary chronicler to have landed on his return from a visit to the continent.[69] The place seems to have developed as the harbour for the royal vill of Eastry, where the small sea channel that once reached to the town was now silting up.[70] Control over the revenues of London and the south-eastern ports was becoming a major factor in a power struggle in which Kent was a prize at which the Mercians were bound to snatch.

Within ten years of claiming the throne Hlothere had cleared the Mercians from the country, spun a web of alliances around them, restored and resettled the kingdom, and asserted its influence in London; a remarkable achievement which ranks him among the most successful (and estimable) of the Eskings. There was, however, a fatal flaw in his position; the envious ambition of Eadric, now 20 or approaching it, who considered himself dispossessed, was discontented with the subordinate role he had been given, and, since he could not hope to tamper with the nation's loyalty to Hlothere, turned instead to its enemies. Bede tells us that he conspired with Sussex, which sent an army against Hlothere.[71] The attack would not have been made purely in order to oblige Eadric. It is probable that friction had arisen between Sussex and Kent over the allegiance of the newly-established settlements around Hastings — the only bridge between the two kingdoms over the intervening waste of forest — but later events suggest that the conflict lay deeper than this and was precipitated also by developments at the other end of the Weald. The kingdoms had been drawn into opposing camps. Sussex was an ally of Mercia, of which Kent was a dedicated enemy, sharing in this a common cause with Wessex, from which Sussex had seized lands with Mercian encouragement and support.[72] A guerilla war, aimed at the recovery of these lands, was now being waged by Caedwalla, a prince of the Wessex royal house, using the Weald as his base;[73] very likely, it seems, with the connivance of Hlothere, who would have been able to open to him large areas of forest bordering Sussex along its most vulnerable flank. This would account for the readiness with which Sussex responded to Eadric's overtures, and also for the furious enmity which Caedwalla later showed towards him. If this was the background to the affair then it would be surprising if the Mercians, with their paramount influence over Sussex, were not also mixed up in it. The attack upon Hlothere should, therefore, be seen not as an isolated incident but as a move in the general power struggle which was taking place in south-eastern England; and Eadric was guilty of betraying not only Hlothere, who has treated him generously, but the true interests of his people, who were shortly to be driven by the anger of their abandoned allies into the waiting arms of their Mercian enemies.

In February 675 Hlothere met the Sussex army in battle and was mortally wounded, tradition says by an arrow,[74] which suggests that it was during the opening exchanges. We are told neither where the encounter took place, nor its outcome, which however, once Hlothere had fallen, could scarcely have been other than a defeat for his forces. In any event, the way was now clear for Eadric to take the throne, which he held for a mere 18 months, 'without the love or respect of the Kentish people' as Henry of Hunting-don says[75] (and we may well believe) before he himself died in circumstances brought about by his own treachery. It may be that during this period he made some effort to extricate himself from the consequences of his actions. In a charter of June 676 recording the sale to St Augustine's Abbey of lands at Stodmarsh he referred to Hlothere *sanctae memoriae*,[76] which betrays a guilty conscience or an attempt to propitiate a thoroughly alienated people; but within two or three months of this his reign was abruptly ended. According to some accounts he was expelled by the Cantware themselves, taking refuge on the continent;[77] but Bede, writing within 50 years of the event, says that he died,[78] and his death must have coincided with the invasion of Kent by Caedwalla which the Anglo-Saxon Chronicle tells us took place at this time, and which initiated a period of anarchy during which the unhappy, divided and leaderless kingdom was tossed between one usurper and another.

Caedwalla was one of those Wessex *athelings* who could trace his descent back to Cerdic,[79] and was so entitled, according to the conceptions of that kingdom, to make a bid for the throne if he felt strong enough to win it. His name, although conforming to the alliteration of the Wessex royal house, was British, which suggests that his mother had been so.[80] As a young man he had lived as an exile in 'the desert places of Chiltern and Weald',[81] gathering a band of warriors around him, with whose aid he embarked on warfare against Sussex, partly no doubt in the hope of carving out a principality for himself, but partly also in order to wrest back those lands in the Meon valley of Hampshire and on the Isle of Wight which had belonged to, or been claimed, by Wessex but which had been seized by Æthelwalh of Sussex, the protégé of Wulfhere. Caedwalla succeeded in killing Æthelwalh and for a while plundered his kingdom, from which, however, he was eventually driven by two of the late king's ealdormen, Berthun and Andhun (the same, no doubt, who invaded Kent at Eadric's invitation).[82] Undeterred by these reverses Caedwalla began to contend for the throne of Wessex, which he won in 685.[83] He then launched an attack on the Isle of Wight, with genocide as his aim, intending not only to destroy the dynasty (which he did) but so far as possible to exter-minate the Jutish inhabitants and replace them with West Saxons. The continuing heathenism of the Isle of Wight exposed it to treatment of this kind; and it was reckoned as an act of magnanimity by Caedwalla that before executing the two princes who were the last representatives of its royal line he allowed time for them to be converted and baptized.[84] (An instructive contrast to the horror aroused by the murder of Eormenred's sons: but they, besides having been brought up by Christians, were Egbert's own kin). In the course of all this he settled accounts with Sussex, killing his old enemy the eoldorman Berthun and reducing the kingdom to subjection;[85] and at some time, it seems in the late summer or autumn of 686, he descended upon Kent.[86] Whether Eadric was killed in battle, or obscurely in the débacle which followed the invasion, we do not know; but the

Cantware can have felt little incentive to support him and, torn in their loyalties, were confronted with the most ferocious fighting man whom Wessex had produced since Ceawlin. In gratitude for his victory, and to win the church's endorsement, Caedwalla founded a monastery at Hoo;[87] and he then left the conquered kingdom to the care — if that is the word — of his brother Mul.

The plight of the nation was now desperate. With Hlothere and Eadric both dead the legitimate claimant to the succession was Egbert's second son Wihtred who, however, must still have been too young to lead the resistance to a foreign rule which appears soon to have become intolerably oppressive. In these circumstances the Cantware acted on their own in a spontaneous uprising. In 687, within a year of Caedwalla's invasion, Mul with 12 of his companions was trapped and burned to death in a house[88] — tradition says at Canterbury where, in St Augustine's Abbey his remains were buried[89] — and it seems that this was followed by a general revolt against the West Saxon occupation. Caedwalla responded by again invading and laying waste the country, but to no lasting effect.[90] He was suffering from a serious wound received during his conquest of the Isle of Wight, and realized that his end was approaching;[91] in the following year he gave up his kingship and journeyed to Rome to be baptized by the Pope, dying seven days later.[92] The throne of Wessex then passed to Ine, an able ruler but of a very different stamp.

The abdication and death of Caedwalla could do no more than postpone the reckoning with Wessex; Mul's killing had touched a point of honour and left a debt of blood to be settled between the two peoples. The Cantware, in their leaderless, plundered and exhausted state, were incapable of maintaining a simultaneous resistance against two major powers, and were now driven into the waiting arms of their old enemy Æthelred of Mercia, who could at least offer them the sop of a ruler, Oswine, who came from their own royal house. Few scholars have bothered to enquire into Oswine's origins, and the obscurity surrounding his reign has been made all the greater because of the mistaken ascription of one of his charters to January 675, the date under which it appears in Birch's *Cartularium Saxonicum*,[93] but which Stenton shows to have been placed in the wrong Indiction and so 15 years too early.[94] Oswine was, therefore, ruling at the beginning of 690, and since the charter is expressed as being issued in the second year of his reign it follows that he came to the throne in 688, in the immediate aftermath of Mul's death and the revolt against Caedwalla. It is clear that he was a Mercian client, since one of his grants was confirmed by Æthelred as overlord,[95] and all were witnessed by Suaebhard, a son of Sebbi, King of Essex, and another of Æthelred's dependents.[96] Dorothy Whitelock believes that the two were, in fact, joint rulers;[97] in which case it seems that Oswine was placed in charge of east Kent, to which all his acts relate, and Suaebhard of west Kent, where (either at this time or later) he confirmed with Æthelred's approval the grant of the monastery of Hoo made originally by Caedwalla.[98]

Whether Suaebhard shared in the rule, or had been inserted by the Mercians to act as a power behind the throne, it is clear that Oswine was titularly the senior of the two. That he came from the Kentish royal line gave the arrangements a convenient air of legitimacy, and was no doubt intended to reconcile the Cantware to their loss of true independence. Gordon Ward has made out a persuasive case for believing that this 'forgotten ruler of Kent', as he calls him, was the son of one of the princes murdered by Egbert[99] (most likely the elder, Æthelred)[100] and the grandson of Eormenred. There are a number of pointers in that direction. Of the three charters known to have been issued by Oswine two were in favour of Minster Abbey, of which the princes' sister Aebba was still the head. One goes out of its way to express Oswine's gratitude at being restored to the kingdom of his fathers, and stresses that the lands conveyed had once belonged to Eormenred;[101] another says that the property granted (near Lyminge, and including an iron mine) had descended to Oswine from his parents;[102] and the third addresses Aebba as his close relative by blood.[103] The dates also fit this supposition. The two princes were of the same generation as their murderer, Egbert, and if anything slightly senior to him in age, so that Oswine himself, though still a young man, was likely to have been several years older than Wihtred, Egbert's younger son. He was, therefore, ready to be foisted upon the Cantware at a time when Wihtred was still adolescent.

It was a misjudgement of the Cantware to believe that they would for long be prepared to tolerate a king who was a mere figure-head of Mercia and whose claim to the throne stemmed from a grandfather, Eormenred, who had been passed over for the succession 50 years previously. For a brief period, however, Eormenred's kin were in the ascendant in Kent, and Oswine made good use of his opportunity. The partiality shown to his aunt Aebba was extended to two others; both of whom had been widowed in 685; Eormenburga through the death of Ecgfrid or Northumbria in battle against the Picts, and Eangyth when her husband Centwine had been driven from the throne of Wessex and killed by Caedwalla. These royal dowagers returned to Kent, where Eormenburga was installed as an Abbess, it seems of Lyminge, and Eangyth put in charge of a small offshoot of Minster, perhaps at Eastry (*see* Appendix G). The fissure between the two branches of the royal family had been reopened and was extending now to the religious houses, of which Sheppey was governed by Wihtred's aunt Eormenhilda, while his cause was also supported at Reculver, founded by his father Egbert and now ruled by Abbot Berhtwald,[104] who was to become his lifelong companion and friend. With each year that passed, as the country recovered from its ordeals and Wihtred grew to manhood, Oswine's position became progressively weaker. He was still able in 689 to assemble a respectable body of notables to witness a grant of land he made in that year to St Augustine's Abbey,[105] but could manage only a much smaller muster for a charter issued in the following January 'in the presence', it says, 'of those of our notables whom we are able to have with us, that is of the Kentish people whom we reach with our right and proper authority'.[106] This was Oswine's last known public act. It seems that, shortly after, his authority completely crumbled, and he simply vanished from the scene. There is no record that he was killed; more likely he fled the country; and the tradition (contradicted by Bede) that Eadric lingered on for many years as an exile on the continent may, in fact, have sprung from a confusion between Oswine's fate and his own. About Oswine himself the chroniclers, from Bede on, maintained a complete silence; only the charters have rescued him from oblivion. He was a 'forgotten king' indeed, rejected by the people with whom he had been so anxious to identify himself, discarded by his Mercian patrons, and rapidly buried by the hagiographers, who dwelt so much upon the youth and purity of his murdered father that they soon ceased to acknowledge the existence of a son at all.

The ousting of Oswine, by whatever means it was brought about, did not, however, dispose of Suaebhard, who with the support of his Mercian overlord Æthelred now proceeded to style himself as king over the whole people — *rex Cantuariarum*[107] — and to exercise, or to claim, authority over east as over west Kent. Two copies of charters of

Suaebhard have come down to us, both in favour of Aebba. The first of these, conveying land at Sturry and Bodsham, is undated and contains no statement of where it was issued.[108] The crucial evidence is provided by the second which on the face of it was issued at Canterbury on 1 March in the fourth year of the Indiction,[109] which would mean either 676 or in 691, but should clearly be assigned to the later period on the strength of Suaebhard's association with Oswine and a comment by Bede that he was still ruling in Kent in 692 (when Wihtred had also made his appearance).[110] There are, however, two difficulties about the date; first, the grant is expressed as being made with the consent of Archbishop Theodore, who died in 690;[111] and, second, it bears Æthelred's confirmation, said to have been given in January of the same year in which it was issued, which is an impossibility. For these reasons Dorothy Whitelock has concluded that the true date of issue was 690, the year of the Indiction having been altered by a minim to make it square with the confirmation clause by someone who had failed to notice that a different event was being dated.[112]

There is another notable feature about this charter, which is that the grant made in it was not new but a repetition, or reaffirmation, of one previously made by Hlothere in 678,[113] the wording of the two being identical in every respect except for the dating and the addition, in Suaebhard's charter, of the expressed approval of his father Sebbi, King of Essex, and of Æthelred. There is also a witness list which does not appear in the record we have of Hlothere's grant but contains six of the 11 names of notables who subscribed to a charter of his of 679,[114] four of whom also reappeared as witnesses to later grants made by Wihtred.[115] The inference is that in 690 Suaebhard was able to command the support, however reluctant, of many of those who had previously followed Hlothere, most of whom, however, transferred their allegiance to Wihtred when he emerged to stake his own claim to the throne. That was in 691, from which he dated his reign.[116] The appearance of the legitimate heir, untainted by the treachery of his brother Eadric or by subservience to Mercia, became a rallying point for the nation; but Bede tells us that in 692 Suaebhard was still ruling in Kent, or a part of it,[117] and it seems that he was not expelled for another two years, when the independence of the kingdom was finally restored in circumstances that will be described in the next chapter.

Theodore of Tarsus died in the year before Wihtred claimed the throne. Among his contemporaries he was renowned as much for his moral precepts, or judgements, as for his organizational reforms. In these matters of moral discipline Wihtred was his true disciple, as he also reaped the benefit of the great revival of learning at Canterbury (and elsewhere) which had been inspired by Theodore and his colleague and friend Hadrian, who outlived him by 17 years.[118] We shall reserve these subjects until later, dealing briefly here with the reorganization of the English church which Theodore put in hand shortly after his arrival and was mostly completed during Hlothere's time. Whereas all previous archbishops, hampered in their authority outside Kent, had been largely preoccupied with its affairs, Theodore's object from the beginning had been to make the primacy of Canterbury a reality; for which purpose it was vital that he should win the cooperation of all the English kings, and (so far as possible) compose the conflicts between them. This carefully temporizing spirit deterred him from adopting Wilfrid's part in the dispute which led in 677 to Ecgfrid of Northumbria expelling him from his see of York; although in this Theodore had his own aims to serve as well, since Wilfrid had been resisting the division of the see, with the diminution of authority which that implied, and the English church could not easily tolerate two such masterful personalities. In his own ecclesiastical sphere Theodore was determined to have his own way, and he achieved it.

His first great synod, held at Hertford in 672, was concerned to purge the church so far as possible of Celtic influences, for instance by insisting on the Roman method of calculating Easter, and to establish a proper discipline by requiring bishops to confine their activities to their own dioceses, and restraining monks and the clergy from wandering from place to place without leave of their superiors.[119] It was also agreed that regular gatherings should be held at a place called Clofeshoh, which some believe to have been Lubbenham in Leicestershire,[120] and which seems certainly to have been within the Mercian dominions. The synod was an affirmation of the essential unity of the English church under the authority of the archbishop. The question of the reorganization of the dioceses was also broached, though not at the time settled, owing to the absence and incipient hostility of Wilfrid. Nevertheless, in the following years Theodore took the matter in hand, and secured the reforms that he wanted. The situation, as he found it, was that outside Kent each kingdom constituted a single diocese, which therefore was often of inordinate size; more especially in Northumbria (York), Mercia (Lichfield) and Wessex (Winchester, to which the Mercian encroachments had caused the site of the see to be moved from Dorchester-on-Thames). The divisions which Theodore effected increased the number of sees from seven to 14, to which three more were to be added after his time. The banishment of Wilfrid removed the major obstacle to these plans in the north, where Theodore lost no time in creating three separate dioceses, one for Bernicia centring upon Lindisfarne or Hexham, one for Deira centring upon York, and one for Lindsey centring upon Lincoln.[121]

Wilfrid's estrangement from Ecgfrid of Northumbria began when he persuaded the king's first wife Ætheldreda, a daughter of the devout Anna of East Anglia (who had been killed nearly 20 years previously by the heathen Penda), first to remain a virgin and then to adopt the religious life.[122] The quarrel was inflamed by Ecgfrid's second wife, Eormenburga, who conceived a violent dislike for Wilfrid and played a large part in his expulsion from Northumbria in 677, at the same time making certain through her sister Eangyth, then married to Centwine of Wessex, that he was not received in that kingdom.[123] This was the third time in little more than 50 years that a Kentish princess had played a crucial role in the religious affairs of Northumbria, but there was nothing spiritual in the motive on this occasion. A contemporary chronicler ascribes Eormenburga's hatred of Wilfrid to his ostentatious and imperious manner, which threatened to eclipse the authority of the king himself,[124] but the cause may have been more deepseated than that. Wilfrid had acted as Egbert's spiritual adviser in Kent in the period following his murder of the two princes, Eormenburga's brothers:[125] she must have known him then, and may well have resented his familiarity with the murderer. In the absence of support from Theodore, who seems secretly to have welcomed the quarrel, Wilfrid journeyed to Rome to lay his case before the Pope, pausing in doing so to undertake missionary work among the Frisians; returned to Northumbria armed with the Pope's approval, only to be imprisoned and again expelled; and then settled down in Sussex to help the recently baptized Æthelwalh in the conversion of his heathen subjects, a work which he continued with the support of Caedwalla of Wessex after he had killed Æthelwalh and overrun his kingdom. The death of Ecgfrid in 685, and the return of

Eormenburga to Kent, opened the way to a reconciliation with the new Northumbrian king, Aldfrid, and with Theodore. Wilfrid was reinstated, though with diminished episcopal responsibilities, confined to Ripon and Hexham, and there seems to have been some understanding that he would succeed Theodore as archbishop, although nothing was to come of it.[126]

The legacy of authority that Theodore bequeathed to Canterbury, and the pervasive influence this gave to the Kentish kings, working with and through the church, were the fulfilment of Æthelberht's aspirations. It was not in Theodore's own time that Kent reaped the full advantage of it, since he himself, a cosmopolitan Greek picked by the Pope from an Italian monastery, and with a strong sense of mission, could transcend the concerns of a small kingdom suffering throughout most of his primacy from war, disruption or the displacement of legitimate rule. The union was perfected after his death between his successor Berhtwald and a securely established Wihtred. The archbishop, besides being primate of all England, was also 'the bishop of the Kentishmen's church',[127] to use the somewhat disparaging description applied to Berhtwald by the then Pope, and unless he was an exceptionally strong and independent character he could scarcely avoid taking on a Kentish complexion, which was liable to colour all his dealings. He was chosen as other bishops were, that is by his own clergy, in this case the community of Christchurch, and although the appointment was subject to Papal confirmation (expressed through the conferment of the *pallium*), and this was not entirely a formality,[128] approval seems in practice never to have been withheld. Once appointed he became, all else besides, the king's chief counsellor and spiritual adviser, a part of the establishment of the kingdom and deeply implicated in its policies. He was also a major landowner in Kent and so (like the heads of the other great religious houses there) had a direct stake in its fortunes. In all of this his situation did not differ in kind — though greatly in degree — from that of his suffragans. Their elections, too, were open to royal influences, and even if this fell short of turning them into the nominees of their respective kings they had at least to be acceptable to the court if they were to continue in office. Wulfhere had actually sold the see of London to Wini, who had previously been expelled from Winchester by Coenwalh of Wessex.[129] So long as they were required to act as the kings' advisers nothing else could be expected. The situation was well expresssed in a letter sent to Berhtwalf in 704–5 by Waldhere of London, who had been summoned to attend a meeting between his own king, Cenred of Mercia, and Ine of Wessex, at which an attempt was to be made to resolve the perennial differences dividing the two. It seems that at this gathering the rulers had required the attendance of 'ecclesiastics of both sides who share the direction of the government under them', and who had so, as Waldhere apologetically explained, become 'willy-nilly involved in this same dissension'.[130]

The appointment of bishops was, however, subject to the archbishop's confirmation. Theodore had taken matters very much into his own hands (though acting in concert with the local rulers);[131] and while his successors were not in so strong a position they nevertheless wielded a moral influence which reached to every part of England, could disturb other allegiances, and proceeded inevitably from a Kentish standpoint. It is never easy to disentangle Berhtwald's motives from those of Wihtred, so close was the understanding between the two men; and even when the dynasty had petered out the same influence was exerted on behalf of the Cantware and those who led them, notably by Archbishop Jaenberht, who was himself born of the Kentish nobility (*see* pages 203 to 208 below). This explains why the final conflict between Kent and Mercia at the close of the 8th century was fought out as much in terms of ecclesiastical control as of military power. For Kent to be subdued — which could be achieved only by methods of atrocity — this weapon had first to be struck from its hands, or turned against it.

How this was eventually done belongs to a later part of our story. But there was one advantage which Theodore had bequeathed to the Mercian kings; the choice of Clofeshoh as the venue for the regular ecclesiastical synods. No doubt the choice was guided by its central position, conveniently accessible from most parts of England; and it may also have been influenced by the fact that Wulfhere was *bretwalda* at this time (672) and had shown himself a champion of the church — to his own ends. It was natural that the Mercian kings, as hosts, should attend these assemblies, and a small step from that to appearing actually to preside at them. In later years a domineering king, like Offa, supported by the Mercian bishops and abbots, who formed the largest group at the gatherings, could use them to brow-beat the archbishop and impose his own wishes on essential points, while at the same time conveying the impression that he, and no other, was the true patron and protector of the English church.

The 30 troubled years which lay between Earconberht's death and the final triumph of Wihtred's cause in 694 altered the whole posture of the kingdom. Although the Cantware emerged from their ordeal with credit the kingdom had been materially weakened by it. The damage inflicted by Eadric's treachery was permanent, and Hlothere's death in battle may be said to mark the second major step in the kingdom's decline of power. Just as he himself, for all his achievements, could never aspire to the ascendancy which Æthelberht had won, so Wihtred could never hope to restore the grasp upon London and, worse than this, was compelled finally to relinquish Surrey. The boundaries of Kent had now been reduced very much to those that we know today. The kingdom still had reserves of strength which made it a redoubtable foe, but it no longer had the capacity to sustain unaided any prolonged contest with either Wessex or Mercia, and sooner or later would be forced to throw in its lot with one or the other. Events had already made this apparent, and the lesson was not lost upon Wihtred. The choice was to be crucial, not only for Kent itself, but because it would be enough in the end to tip the balance of ascendancy in England.

Chapter Nine

THE RESTORATION

Wihtred: 691–725

WIHTRED REIGNED for 34 years, of which the first three were spent in freeing the kingdom from foreign usurpers and the remainder in complete peace and independence. This period of calm, falling 100 years after St Augustine's mission, provides an admirable vantage point from which to survey the changes in Kentish society since the days of Æthelberht, when the kingdom was supreme, its pagan customs had still been little tinctured by Christian thought, and its institutions had not yet felt the impact of the church either as a spiritual or a temporal power.

The 7th century had also seen profound changes in the international setting. In France the Merovingian dynasty, with which the Eskings had once been so closely connected, had been reduced to a mere shadow through the seizure of power in 687 by Pippin, mayor of the palace in Austrasia, and was soon to be supplanted, in form as well as substance, by his Carolingian descendents.[1] The connection had meant little to Kent in political terms since the reign of Eadbald, nor, after Theodore's work and the revival of learning which he inspired, had the Gallic church as much to offer the English as it received from them. In a wider context still, the birth of Islam and the rapid Arab conquest of the whole southern seaboard of the Mediterranean had shaken the Imperial influence of Byzantium and disrupted the old maritime channels of commerce.[2] This is a large subject, covered by the great Belgian historian Henri Pirenne,[3] and it raises a host of disputable issues. It seems fair to say, however, that during the period which we are now considering the effects upon England, remote from these happenings, was still superficial. In the north the seaways were still open, and although the supply of gold had dried up (so that the minting of *tremisses* in England was abandoned almost as soon as it had begun)[4] and it is unlikely that such exotic treasures as the Byzantine dishes, Coptic bowls and other articles of Mediterranean provenance which appear in the Sutton Hoo burial continued to reach the courts of the English kings, nevertheless a flourishing trade was still being conducted with the continent and with Scandinavia through the medium of the Frisian carriers. If supplies of African ivory and of garnets were interrupted, walrus ivory, amber and other valuable products such as furs could be obtained from northern lands. While, therefore, Wihtred's court may have had little of the barbaric splendour of Æthelberht's, there can have been no lack of silver vessels and glassware, fine cloth and embroidery or of wine from the continent; and this was also a literate court (or largely so) frequented by such learned scholars as Hadrian and Tobias, with its own scribes and notaries, and familiar with manuscripts, though now produced on parchment rather than papyrus. In more than a figurative sense Æthelberht's reign was the age of gold in Kent, and Wihtred's that of silver.

The restoration of the dynasty was not achieved without serious sacrifices. Wihtred was very different from the secular-minded fighting man Hlothere, and in many ways less attractive; but he knew how to cut his losses, and to make the utmost of the advantages that remained. He was an intensely religious person, but with a firm grasp of political realities, a combination of qualities — 'diligence and devotion' to use Bede's words[5] — that exactly fitted the needs of the situation. Everything about him suggests a conventual rather than a court upbringing, which supports the supposition that he was reared as a child at the monastery of Sheppey, under the care of those devout women his grandmother Seaxburga and his aunt Eormenhilda. This is what one would expect from the circumstances of his orphanhood, and there are other pointers to it. He seems to have been a man with a marked partiality and respect for women, married twice (some would claim three times, but this rests on the evidence of a singularly dubious charter*), and, alone among the Eskings, associated his wives with him in a number of his public acts; his last wife, Werburga, appears to have had an influence on the succession. Moreover, again exceptionally among the Eskings, he was a man of mid-Kent. None of the three major enactments of his reign was executed at Canterbury; the sites chosen were Bearsted, *Cilling* and Bapchild, just outside the royal vills of Hollingbourne, Faversham and Milton Regis respectively.[6] There must certainly have been an element of policy in this, but we are nevertheless left with the impression that it was in this part of Kent — and especially in the countryside beside the Swale and surrounding Sheppey — that Wihtred best liked to be and felt most at home.

The death of his brother Eadric in 686 had left Wihtred, then probably in his teens, as the legitimate heir to the throne; still too young to lead the Cantware, but a growing embarrassment to the usurpers, from Caedwalla to Suaebhard, who were engaged, Bede says, in plundering the kingdom.[7] They must have been sorely tempted to get rid of him; but with Theodore of Tarsus at Canterbury, and all the odium which had surrounded Egbert's crime, the murder of a young Christian prince for dynastic reasons was not easy to contemplate. Nevertheless these were dangerous times during which Wihtred, if he remained in Kent at all, must have kept well away from the court, with Sheppey and Reculver — a house firmly committed to his branch of the royal line — as the natural sanctuaries. It is understandable that, in face of the incipient challenge from Wihtred, who was sheltered by the church's protection, Æthelred of Mercia should have attempted to subtract the loyalties of the Cantware from him by offering them, in Oswine, another prince of their own royal blood, though with inferior claims. But within three years Oswine had been rejected and Æthelred left with no other tool than Suaebhard, a more resolute person perhaps, but without a shadow of legitimacy. On Suaebhard's accession, coinciding with Theodore's death and a vacancy at Canterbury, the issue was forced. Wihtred's situation can never have been more perilous; he had now grown to manhood; and this was the time to make his appeal to the nation against what had become an undisguised annexation. In 691 he emerged to claim the throne,[8] the people welcomed him as they had previously done Hlothere, and the struggle to purge the country of the Mercian presence had begun.

*BCS 86 of A.D. 694 purporting to record a grant by Wihtred and his wife Kynigitha, of whom nothing more is heard. This charter and the existence of Kynigitha are dismissed by Haddan and Stubbs (*Councils* III, p. 242, n. 1). For Wihtred's wifes Æthelburga and Werburga BCS 91, 97 and 98 provide reliable documentary evidence.

In 692, Bede tells us, Wihtred and Suaebhard were both ruling in Kent; but in that year there occurred an event of great significance, the election as archbishop of Berhtwald, Abbot of Reculver.[9] It seems (as we have said) that the reversion had previously been promised, or half promised, to Wilfrid, but he had scarcely been restored to Northumbria before he re-opened the question of his jurisdiction, to the intense annoyance of the new king, Aldfrid, by whom he was again expelled in 691. His behaviour had, therefore, ruled him out of consideration.[10] The election has every appearance of having been politically inspired. In choosing a local man who could be expected to favour Wihtred's cause the community of Christchurch may have acted on its own initiative, but the likelihood is that Wihtred had by this time gained control of north-east Kent, always the centre of resistance to foreign domination, and had been able to bring his influence to bear. If this is right, Suaebhard must have fallen back upon west Kent, where he would be in close touch with his father Sebbi of Essex and with his Mercian sponsors, now once more firmly esconced in London.

The election of Berhtwald was a considerable coup; it meant that Wihtred could rely upon the justice of his cause being recognized by the church not only in Kent but outside it, and it gave a lead to the spontaneous affection felt by churchmen throughout England towards the dynasty of the Eskings. But it was not in itself enough. The key factor, as Wihtred well knew, was that he could not hope to dispose of Suaebhard, with his Mercian backing, while the feud with Wessex remained open. It was necessary to undo the effects of Eadric's treachery and Caedwalla's savagery by restoring an alliance that was in the interests of both countries in face of a greater threat than either presented to the other. It seems that Ine realized this as well as Wihtred; he cannot have wished to have been drawn into a debilitating struggle on his eastern frontier, from which Mercia was all too likely to pick up the pieces, when the interests of his kingdom lay in having a friendly nation at its back while it pursued its westward expansion at the expense of the British. The two rulers understood each other well enough, but the blood of Mul lay between them. Although Wihtred can have had nothing to do with that killing the guilt had devolved upon him with the kingship, and he now accepted and discharged it.

In 694, the Anglo-Saxon Chronicle tells us, 'the Kentishmen came to terms with Ine and gave him "thirty thousands" because they had burned Mul to death'. This has been treated as a humiliation inflicted upon them by Ine;[11] but that interpretation ignores both the circumstances of the time, and, more significantly, the precedent of the settlement reached in 679 between Æthelred and Ecgfrid of Northumbria, when the sum paid by Æthelred for the slaughter of Ecgfrid's brother in battle can have been no less, and was not made under duress. Theodore had been the mediator on that occasion, and Wihtred, as his disciple, must have had the example well in mind. There was, in fact, no other way in which the differences could be honourably composed without further bloodshed, and the sum was not arbitrarily fixed but the acknowledged wer-geld of an atheling, or prince. Although the Chronicle does not express it in terms of sceattas, or pence, that is clearly what was intended. On a Kentish reckoning it would have amounted to 1,500 shillings,[12] five times the wer-geld of a noble and 15 times that of a ceorl. Chadwick approaches the calculation from the other side, adopting the Wessex (or Mercian) standard of four pennies to a shilling of correspondingly lesser value, so arriving at a sum of 7,500 shillings, or six times the wer-geld or a Wessex noble (1,200 shillings), with some addition to compensate for loss in weighing.[13] Either way the conclusion is much the same. This was a sizeable payment but strictly what custom decreed, and well within the kingdom's means. To set it in perspective, if was five times the sum offered through Berhtwald c. 712 for the redemption of a Kentish girl (evidently of noble birth) who had been carried as a slave into Wessex; the money in this case having been got together by her brother.[14] The restitution made for Mul's death must be regarded as a small price to have been paid for settling so damaging a feud.

Although it is this payment that has attracted attention, it appears to have been part of a wider settlement. Ine is the first ruler outside Kent who produced a code of custom, or is known to have done so, and it can hardly have been coincidental that it dated from 694 when he was in contact with Wihtred on other matters. It seems that at some time during the course of this association he had had his attention drawn to the Kentish codes and was impressed by the example. Wihtred's own laws were issued in the following year, and must have been in contemplation at the time. This is not to say that the two codes resembled each other closely; they could not have done so when Kentish and Wessex customs, though based upon certain common Germanic conceptions, differed so much from each other in emphasis and detail; and Ine was making a start on the task of codification, whereas Wihtred was concerned only to embellish a body of written laws which his predecessors, notably Æthelberht and Hlothere, had left him. Nevertheless there are clear signs of cross-fertilization. This shows in such minor ways as Wihtred's use of the Wessex term *gesid* for a noble,[15] in place of the traditional Kentish term *eorl*; in certain common preoccupations, for instance with the proper observance of the Lord's Day and the condign punishment of thieves caught in the act;[16] and, most strikingly of all, in a provision on wayfarers which appears in both codes in almost identical words and was clearly based on a definite agreement reached between the two kingdoms on the behaviour expected of those travelling between them, whether on trade or other business, at a time when all strangers were liable to be taken for robbers.[17]

Most important of all was the territorial settlement. It seems that it must have been at this time that the boundary between Kent and Surrey took the shape that it has retained ever since (the Weald apart). We have said that the boundary was an artificial one, which cut across one of the early lathes. It has all the appearance of having been decided purely on the basis of *status quo*, the Surrey lands representing those which Caedwalla had been able to retain when he had been expelled from what was henceforward to remain as Kent. The lathe which the new border sundered had, like others, its own Wealden common, but for many years no precise division appears to have been made here, herdsmen from either side of the border continuing to inter-common their swine in the stretch of forest around Edenbridge and Lingfield.[18] Even at the time of Domesday Book, when the boundary had been projected into the Weald, a number of Surrey manors were still making use of pastures in Kent and *vice-versa*.[19] The old features of Jutish land use continued in Surrey (being particularly marked to the east), although they became overlaid by the Wessex standards of assessment, in which the *hide* was substituted for the *sullung*.[20] This final relinquishment of Surrey was the inescapable price which Kent paid for Eadric's treachery; and with it there necessarily vanished any hope of reassuming control over the Hastings area, which might have been recoverable from an independent Sussex, but not from one which had been conquered by Caedwalla and was now dominated by Ine. Here, too there seems to have been an agreement on the boundary, which was well known 50 years later[21] and left the Isle of Oxney as a remnant to Kent.[22]

Wihtred could not achieve as complete a restoration as Hlothere had done; but the agreement with Ine freed him to dispose of Suaebhard, which he did in short time, and deterred any further intervention by Mercia. In September of 695 (*Rugern*, the month of the rye harvest),[23] when Wihtred came to promulgate his own laws, the site at which he chose to do so was Bearsted,[24] directly on the boundary between the lathes of Hollingbourne and Aylesford and of the sees of Canterbury and Rochester,[25] and centrally situated so that it could be reached without too much inconvenience by notables from all parts of the kingdom, east and west; a venue which shows that by then Kent had been reunified, with Suaebhard completely banished from the scene. But the agreement had more permanent effects than this. Although whatever positive alliance there may have between between Kent and Wessex did not outlast the lives of those who made it, the underlying bond of common interest remained. The two kingdoms were never again to be at war with each other, and their eventual union under another Egbert, who had hereditary claims to both, was foreshadowed. Indeed those claims may have originated in a marriage contracted between a brother of Ine and a Kentish princess; but that is an obscure subject, to which we shall have to return in a later chapter.

Although the code of laws issued at Bearsted was said to have been drawn up by the notables of the kingdom with the consent of all orders of the church, it bears very much the stamp of Wihtred's own character, at once pious and severe. The code is in marked contrast to those of Æthelberht and of Hlothere, both in its preoccupation with ecclesiastical matters and because it introduces a sharply punitive element into a body of custom which had been based chiefly upon conceptions of restitution and the settlement of private wrongs. In a real sense the old customs, rooted in the pagan society of Kent, had constituted a form of civil law, under which the king had his own rights and a responsibility for seeing that the channels for agreement were kept open, in the interests of the general peace and well-being of the nation. Wihtred's main object, however, was to use the secular power to support the discipline and moral teachings of the church, as Theodore had pronounced them. There was a different emphasis, of sin and condemnation, and with this there went a more autocratic tone, which can be detected even in the terminology. Thus, the use of the word *gesid* for a nobleman, in place of the traditional Kentish word *eorl*, may have been a borrowing from Wessex, but it nevertheless carried a special connotation. *Gesid* means companion,[26] and although the reference was to a hereditary class identical with that of the *eorls*, the stress was now placed upon the function of attendance upon the king instead of upon an inherited status, in which such a duty may have been implicit but was not the first thing that mattered. More than that, the laws contain almost the first recorded use in English of the term 'king's thegn', which means literally 'the king's servant', and is contrasted here to the term ceorl (*ceorlisc man*) in such a way as to show that it was intended to apply to the whole of the nobility – an even more emphatic assertion of the king's claims upon their services.[27]

The laws dealt with three matters of purely secular concern. First, they gave effect to an agreement which had evidently been reached with Ine about the conduct of travellers from outside the kingdom, or from a distant part of it, by providing that if such a stranger left the road and neither shouted nor blew a horn to give warning of his presence he was to be assumed a thief and might either be killed or seized and redeemed as such.[28] Second, there was a useful tidying up provision about manumitted slaves, who, as they had no kin of their own, were to be treated as those of their liberators in matters of inheritance, *wer-geld* and protection, so that they should not be loosed upon society defenceless themselves and with nobody to answer for their actions.[29] Third, there were the measures against theft, the severity of which were a reflection of changing moral conceptions, but also of the general lawlessness induced by the troubled times through which the kingdom had passed.[30] Casual theft apart, there must have been left in the remoter areas of the countryside nests of robbers, escaped slaves or landless men, whose elimination was a matter of public concern. The most notable feature of the provisions is that they made the king himself the sole judge of the punishment, which was an autocratic innovation in Kentish law. The anarchy through which the kingdom had passed, and the debt owed to Wihtred for freeing the nation of it, had opened the way to a new authoritarianism.

A thief caught in the act might be killed without compensation, and if found with stolen goods on him was to be put to death, sold as a slave overseas or redeemed for his *wer-geld*, at the king's choice, the person taking him to be entitled to half the payments if his life was spared or to 70 shillings otherwise. If the thief was a slave the same sum of 70 shillings was required for his redemption. As Attenborough points out, this is an extraordinarily high figure in either case;[31] in the first well over half the normal *wer-geld* for a ceorl, so that it would have been to the positive advantage of the thief's taker that he should be killed, and in the second far more than the market value of a slave on any reckoning (*see* Appendix E). We can only guess at the considerations. It appears to have been the intention that offending slaves should be put to death, and although their masters were given the opportunity of redeeming them (usually there could be no-one else to do so) the price was set so high as to be a formidable deterrent. With a freeman there seems to be have been an inbuilt bias in the other direction, since it would be to the king's financial advantage to spare him and to take half his price (redeemed or enslaved) rather than to kill him and pay his capturer. It is to be supposed that only in an aggravated case would the death penalty be exacted, and then the capturer's reward would be deservedly great. Sale overseas was, nevertheless, an extremely harsh punishment, which contrasted with practice in Wessex, where Ine attempted to ban this traffic altogether.[32] The advantage was not only in the higher price to be obtained on the overseas market but even more, one supposes, in the assurance that even if the slave were later to recover his freedom he was unlikely ever again to be seen in the kingdom.

These provisions apart, the laws dealt almost exclusively with the privileges of the church and the enforcement of religious edicts and observances. The first article pronounced that the church was to be free from taxation,[33] a subject to which Wihtred was to return later, as we shall do; and the second stipulated that breach of the church's *mund* or protective rights (which would include sanctuary) was to be treated on a par with a similar offence against the king, demanding 50 shillings in compensation.[34] Nine articles were devoted to the subject of oath-giving, with the aim of establishing an equivalence between the different grades of the ecclesiastical hierarchy and of the classes of society.[35] The word of a bishop, as of the king, was to be incontrovertible, without need of an oath. The head of a religious house, a priest or a deacon was to clear himself by his own unsupported oath, solemnly given in due formula before the altar; and the same applied to a 'king's thegn' or to a stranger, i.e., a foreigner, who could have had no friends or neighbours to vouch for him and was obviously to be treated in this matter as under the king's special protection. A cleric was to purge himself with the witness of three others, and similarly a ceorl. A slave was to be cleared with the oath of his master, ecclesiastic or lay, except that in certain circumstances, and where his master was not a communicant, an oath-helper was required. While evidence played no part in all this, the awesomeness of the proceedings must usually have been substitute enough; it would take a bold person to perjure himself in God's presence.

The influence of Theodore's reforms is apparent in a provision that if a 'tonsured man' sought hospitality he was to be given it for one night, but for no more without leave.[36] This was obviously intended to reinforce the decrees of the Synod of Hertford against monks and priests wandering abroad without the sanction of their superiors (page 158 above); and a similar care for ecclesiastical discipline is seen in the pronouncement that a priest who countenanced an illicit union, or neglected the baptism of a sick person, or was too drunk to perform it, was to abstain from his administration pending the bishop's sentence.[37] But even greater concern was shown over the conduct of the laity; in particular with the need to stamp out idolatry, to secure the proper observance of the Lord's Day and fasts, and to put an end to irregular marriages.

The first two of these matters had been dealt with by Earconberht, in decrees that have been lost.[38] What Wihtred's laws added to these we cannot know, but they are a remarkable testimony to the persistence of heathen practices in Kent nearly a hundred years after St Augustine's landing. The penalty decreed by Wihtred for 'sacrificing to devils' was loss of a person's entire goods or his (or her) *healsfang*,[39] that is to say the first instalment of *wer-geld*, representing one fifth of the whole, which Æthelberht's laws stipulated should be paid at 'the open grave'.[40] In this matter husband and wife were each responsible for their own acts, but not for those of the other. Where the offender was a slave the penalty was six shillings, or a flogging;[41] a standard sanction, flogging being regarded as a degrading punishment, to which free men were never liable. Theodore's Penitentials provide some of the background to this and show (as might be expected) that women were the worst offenders, many of the practices amounting to little more than outmoded superstitions, or charms, deriving from the old nature cults. Apart from the major transgression of sacrificing to idols and eating the sacrificial meat, for which up to ten years penance might be exacted, they included the supposed cure for a feverish child of exposing it on the roof of a house or placing it in the oven (seven years' penance), and the practice of burning grain when a person had died for the protection of the living and of the home (five years' penance).[42]

The laws treated working on the Lord's Day or taking meat during fasts as seiously as idolatry. Once again, the penalty for a free man was payment of *healsfang*, with the rather unpleasant provision, where Sunday work was concerned, that half of this, and of the profit of the work, was to go to the informer.[43] A slave was liable to the full penalty of six shillings (payable to his master) or a flogging only if he worked on his own account or took meat of his own accord; if he worked on his master's account, though against his wishes, the penalty was reduced to 80 *sceattas* — the equivalent of four shillings — and if his master gave him meat he (the master) was responsible and had to redeem it with his *healsfang*.[44] The provisions confirm that slaves might contract for work in their spare time; Theodore had declared that it was wrong for a master to take from his slave money which he had earned by his own labour.[45]

Finally, five clauses were devoted to irregular marriages.[46] Where these already existed the offenders were to be excluded from the fellowship of the church until matters were put right, and, if foreigners, were to be expelled from the kingdom 'with their sins'; but there was no financial penalty. Where, however, such a marriage was contracted after the passage of the laws an offending nobleman was to pay his lord, i.e. the king, 100 shillings and an offending ceorl 50 shillings, and the union was to be dissolved. The fine represented the maximum *wite* for a public wrongdoing, which shows how seriously the trespass was regarded. The laws did not themselves specify what constituted an irregular marriage, but referred on this to the decree of the 'books', i.e. the ecclesiastical canons; and this opens up a large subject which had been treated by Theodore, whose judgements were at that time considered to be authoritative.

As Æthelberht's laws show, a pagan marriage was purely a contract between kin, with a purchase price and settlement agreed for the bride;[47] custom was lax enough to allow a man to marry his step-mother (as Eadbald did); and a union could be dissolved without difficulty on proper contractual terms, the observance of which it was the responsibility of the king to ensure. In Christian times it remained the practice for brides to be bought, and the betrothal, at which the settlement was sealed, was more important than the marriage ceremony itself, which did not even have to be conducted by a priest although an 11th-century account contained in the *Textus Roffensis* says that 'by rights' one should be present to unite the couple with God's blessing.[48] Theodore's Penitentials provided that at the age of 16 a girl should be free to dispose of herself, but until that time she remained under the authority of her parents, who could betroth her as they wished. If she found the chosen bridegroom utterly repugnant she could, in the last resort, reject him but might not then be offered elsewhere, and it seems to have been expected that she should enter a nunnery. In such circumstances the bride price was to be returned with the addition of a third; whereas if the man defaulted he was to forfeit it entirely.[49]

The chief concern of the church, however, was with the permitted degrees of consanguity in marriage, and with the circumstances in which separation and remarriage might be allowed. On the first matter, Gregory the Great had acknowledged, in replying to a query by St Augustine, that Roman law countenanced marriage between first cousins, but said that sacred law should condemn this practice, since (other considerations apart) such unions tended to be sterile.[50] Theodore was more specific. He pronounced that while existing unions within the fourth degree of consanguity (for instance between second cousins) need not be dissolved, marriages should not be newly arranged except within the fifth degree, or more.[51] This ruling appears to have been quite unrealistic for a rural community, and must often in practice have been breached, which doubtless accounts for the guarded wording of the script of the *Textus Roffensis*. This says of the ceremony 'it is well also to take care that one knows that they are not too closely related, lest one afterwards puts asunder what was previously wrongly joined together'.[52]

By contrast, the provisions on separation and remarriage were liberal, though with a marked bias in favour of the husband. A man might divorce his wife for adultery and remarry (though not on a second occasion) but a woman might do so only if the erring husband entered a monastery; and a wife set aside for this cause was liable to forfeit her entire inheritance, though she might herself marry again after five years, with due repentance. Desertion — again for a period of five years — was grounds for divorce by a husband, but not, it seems, by a wife; though a wife might get her marriage annulled on grounds of non-consummation. A union might be dissolved if either party was obdurately heathen, or (although there is some ambiguity about this) if one or other of them wished to adopt the religious life. But in many ways the most interesting provisions are those which deal with slavery, since they illustrate how large this institution loomed in early English society. If a man was reduced to penal slavery his wife might remarry after a year. If either partner was carried away as a slave in war, and could not be redeemed, the other might remarry after five years, and if the original spouse was later freed he or she might then do the same. Slaves might marry with their masters' leave, and if one was later set free, but not the other, he or she might then marry again. A marriage between a freeman and a slave was indissoluble. A master who seduced a slave girl was bound to free her, but not the child of the union.[53]

These laws were the first fruits of what was to be a long period of collaboration between Wihtred and Archbishop Berhtwald, who outlived him. The Pope's description of Berhtwald as 'the bishop of the Kentishmen's church'[54] may have reflected upon the circumstances of his appointment, but was occasioned by a renewed dispute over the future of Wilfrid. On his second expulsion from Northumbria in 691 Wilfrid had been welcomed by Æthelred of Mercia, with whom he remained for 11 years. He also appealed to Rome, where his earlier achievements had never been forgotten and his cause was strongly supported; and it was at the Pope's bidding that a council was held in 702, near Bawtry, to determine the issue.[55] This broke up in confusion, with Berhtwald and the Northumbrian bishops insisting that Wilfrid should subscribe to the principles of ecclesiastical organization laid down by Theodore and submit himself wholly to their judgement, and Wilfrid taking his stand upon the authority of the Pope, to whom he once more appealed. Accusations and counter-accusations were then lodged at Rome, which ended with Pope John commanding Berhtwald to convene another synod at which the matter should be settled for good and all, or else to appear in person at Rome to answer for it, under pain of excommunication.[56] The timely death of King Aldfrid in 705 finally opened the way to a settlement.[57] Wilfrid was received back in Northumbria, and given charge of the monasteries of Ripon and Hexham, but his claims to the bishopric of York were dropped and the division of the northern sees instituted by Theodore remained undisturbed.[58] Forty years had now elapsed since Wilfrid's great achievement at the Synod at Whitby; he had become an old man; and he died peacefully four years later at Oundle,[59] one of the monasteries that he had founded in Mercia.

The enmity felt towards Wilfrid in his native Northumbria is easily understandable; not only had his imperious manner antagonized two kings but his claims threatened the positions of every one of the northern bishops. It is also understandable that Berhtwald should have been driven to oppose him in defence of Theodore's reforms and the authority of Canterbury; and this hostility may have been sharpened by the knowledge that he had succeeded to a primacy that had at one time been marked out for Wilfrid. How far Berhtwald consulted Wihtred in the matter we cannot know, but it would be surprising if he did not; the two men were very close, their religious aims were identical, and this dispute touched upon the affairs of a king. The description of Berhtwald used by Pope John betrays a suspicion that he had abandoned the proper role of an archbishop for that of a Kentish prelate, and that this influence was bound to be hostile to Wilfrid's cause.

There were good reasons for such a fear. Wilfrid had begun his career as a protégé and friend of the Eskings, but after Theodore's arrival everything had changed. There was more to this than the conflict of ecclesiastical policy. Wilfrid had also contrived to alienate both branches of the Kentish royal house through his quarrel with Ecgfrid, whose second wife Eormenburga and her sister Eangyth had become his inveterate enemies (page 158 above). Both these royal dowagers had since returned to Kent to become abbesses. It was, in fact, unlikely (whatever the Pope might fear) that either Berhtwald or the king would have been unduly influenced by the feelings of these two survivors of Eormenred's kin, the aunts of the usurping Oswine by whom they had been installed in their abbeys. It was far more to the point that Wilfrid's rupture with Ecgfrid had cast him into the camp of the enemies of Kent and of its ruling line. Ecgfrid himself had been the ally of Hlothere; on his first expulsion Wilfrid had found a refuge in Sussex and then become the friend of Caedwalla of Wessex,[60] and on the second he had been received by Æthelred of Mercia; so that at every stage he had associated himself with the foes and despoilers of Kent, and the hatred felt towards them could not fail to rub off upon him. It may be unfair to Wihtred to believe that he would have allowed considerations of this kind to colour his attitude to Wilfrid to the exclusion of all else, any more than that Berhtwald would have let himself be governed by a purely personal rivalry and an uneasy consciousness of the invidious circumstances of his own appointment. Both men revered the memory of Theodore and had reasons of principle enough to withstand Wilfrid's pretensions, backed though they were by Rome. They were also more aware than the Pope of the political realities in England, and realized (none better) the practical impossibility of compelling a king to accept as his bishop and chief counsellor a person whom he heartily disliked. Nevertheless this was an antipathy which they must not only have understood but shared. The final solution was a just one; but while it may have been brought about by Papal pressure the aims it achieved were those of Canterbury.

The chief fruits of the partnership between Wihtred and Berhtwald are, however, to be seen in their ordering of the affairs of the church in Kent, in doing which they gave a lead to the whole country. The church had now become a major landowner, so that at the very time that the system of the lathes had achieved its fullest definition, with the creation of the fiscal network of the *sulungs* and the ploughlands, it was becoming fretted away by the growth of ecclesiastical estates within which the king himself was no longer the direct lord. The surrender of lands to the church had been as much enforced as voluntary. Eadbald and Egbert had had to pay dearly to redeem their sins of incest and murder, and during the period of invasion and disputed rule through which the kingdom had recently passed the various contenders for the throne had all attempted to purchase the favour of the church by granting lands to the religious houses. Wihtred himself, for all his piety, was sparing in this matter; after the settlement with Ine his position was secure and he had no need to squander the royal patrimony in order to reinforce it. He made a few modest grants — for instance to Lyminge Abbey in 697 of four ploughlands at Wilmington with sheep pastures on Romney Marsh attached[61] — and he reconstituted the Priory of Dover, moving it to a new site in the town,[62] but he established no new monastic houses. There were other ways in which he could benefit the church, most of all in defining its title and immunities, a task that needed to be done in order to set the ecclesiastical lordships in their proper place within the polity of the kingdom.

The first tentative step in this direction had been taken at Bearsted in the declaration that the church should be free of taxation; a principle that was reaffirmed in a charter issued in 699 at *Cilling*, near Faversham, at a gathering attended by all the principal ecclesiastical dignatories of the kingdom, including the three royal abbesses, Eormenhilda, Eormenburga and Aebba, and one other, Nerienda, of whom nothing further is known but who seems, by elimination, to have been the head of the mixed house at Folkestone.[63] This was an assembly of the older generation, and it must have been the last occasion on which many of them were to meet. Eormenhilda was to leave in this same year to succeed her mother Seaxburga in charge of Ely;[64] and both Eormenburga and Aebba were shortly to die, the first (it seems) to be followed at Lyminge by her younger sister Æthelthryth and the second at Minster by her daughter St Mildred (*see* Appendix G). The hereditary principle was becoming deeply ingrained, and control over such appointments was one of the matters to which Wihtred and Berhtwald were later to turn their attention. The *Cilling* charter was itself only the precursor of a far more elaborate instrument issued some years later at Bapchild (near Sittingbourne), which was copied many times and cited as a very foundation of the church's liberties.[65]

The exact date of the Bapchild council is uncertain, but by the time it was held all the abbesses had changed and Tobias had succeeded Gebemund as bishop of Rochester. The best clues, however, are to be found among the members of the royal family. It seems that Wihtred's first wife Æthelburga, who had been associated with him in the grants made to Lyminge Abbey in 697, had died before the proceedings at *Cilling*, which were attested neither by her nor by her successor Werburga. The latter, however, witnessed the Bapchild instrument both on her own behalf and that of her son Alric, evidently still a minor. Of the children of the first marriage Æthelberht was old enough to attest for himself, and did so also for his brother Eadberht, who was not. Taking 15 as the age of majority for a boy;[66] all this suggests a date somewhere between 705 and 710. A notable absence from among the witnesses was any representative of St Augustine's Abbey. This led Gordon Ward to conclude that the conference was held during the vacancy there between the death of Hadrian in January 708 and the appointment of his successor Albinus in the following April;[67] and that date would fit well enough with the other evidence.

Although, strictly, the council was concerned only with the church in Kent, and Wihtred had no authority to grant immunities extending beyond the kingdom, the problems dealt with had arisen, in one form or another, everywhere in England, and the principles propounded had all the greater force because they were agreed with the archbishop himself. None of the other kings could, therefore, afford to ignore them, and they came, in fact, to be generally accepted, although it was not until 749 that they were formally adopted in Mercia.[68] Wihtred must have been perfectly well aware that he was giving a lead to the entire country, just as Oswy had done at the Synod of Whitby more than 40 years earlier. In doing so he was enhancing his own prestige and compounding the already considerable debt owed by the church to his dynasty. While, therefore, the circumstances of his own kingdom may have been at the forefront of his mind, both he and Berhtwald must have been conscious throughout of the effects that their agreement would have elsewhere. It was, no doubt, their object to use just such a leverage.

The conference set out to establish three principles; of which the first was that land granted to the church should not later be taken back by the king or his successors, or be otherwise expropriated. At first sight there was little novel in this, except in the solemnity of its pronouncement; almost every diploma of grant had contained a similar injunction. But in Kent many of the more recent gifts had been made by usurpers — Caedwalla, Oswine, Suaebhard and Æthelred of Mercia himself — and the provision not only confirmed the church in its possession of these lands but laid down the principle for the future that such grants should be treated as inviolate, however disputable the title of the donors. The general significance of this provision was obvious at a time when, throughout England, territory was continually changing hands in internecine wars and it had become common practice for the victors to celebrate their triumphs by making grants to the church out of the conquered lands.

The second principle was that no layman, not even the king himself, should meddle in the affairs of religious houses, and, in particular, that the election of abbots and abbesses should in future be carried out in consultation with, and subject to the approval of, the bishop of the diocese, including the archbishop in his own. The primacy given to the bishops over the heads of the religious houses was in keeping with the organizational conceptions of the Roman, as opposed to the Celtic, church; but there were much deeper implications than that. The founders of monasteries were prone to regard the appointment of abbots and abbesses as a hereditary property, as the Eskings themselves had done; but while in the early, missionary, years it was kings who had been the founders and the church itself had approved the installation of princesses and royal widows, who had mostly shown themselves devout women well worthy of the office, the situation was now changing. There was a narrow dividing line between religious commitment and nepotism, and signs that this was often being over-passed. In Kent the two wealthy houses of Minster and Lyminge had virtually been captured by Eormenred's kin, who were no favourites of Wihtred, and this showed every sign of perpetuating itself; while Caedwalla's foundation of Hoo had later been taken over by Suaebhard and converted, with Æthelred's approval, into a daughter house of the Mercian monastery of Medeshamstede (Peterborough), so slipping into outside control.[69]

There was therefore need for Berhtwald and Wihtred (to all intents, one and the same) to assert their authority on their own home ground; and elsewhere the position was still less controlled because monasteries were being founded by many other people than kings. Wilfrid had established numerous houses, both in Northumbria and later in Mercia during the period of his second exile, over which he claimed an absolute jurisdiction,[70] so amassing to himself a power which was first resented by the Northumbrian kings and then became a major cause of aggravation in his dispute with Berhtwald and the ecclesiastical hierarchy, who had tried to insist (but with no support from the Pope) that he should surrender all of these houses before submitting himself to their jurisdiction.[71] On this issue, if no other, Wilfrid had finally got his way; but the time had come to repair the damage. There was all the more need to do so because monasteries were now beginning to be founded by ordinary laymen; and whereas those established by Wilfrid were reputable and well conducted places, into which he had introduced the Benedictine rule, the same could not be said of many of the others, which were often small and observed whatever rules pleased their founders, who managed the properties and were capable of making the most unsuitable appointments from among their own relatives. While this could amount to outright abuse, much of it was also due to ill-directed religious zeal.[72] The development seems to have been particularly marked in Northumbria, where the fervent influence of the Celtic church still lingered. Unsurprisingly, no evidence of the practice can be found in Kent; but Wihtred and Berhtwald were looking well beyond it.

The requirement of episcopal approval was thus intended, at one level, to correct abuses, and at another to support the authority of the hierarchy (with Canterbury at its apex) against such discordant elements as Wilfrid, who had defied the discipline of the English church and created an almost independent position for himself, as others might be tempted to do. Despite the disclaimers of royal interference in the elections the provision also strengthened the influence of the kings, given the close understanding which commonly subsisted between them and their bishops. This might be a matter of give and take, but between Berhtwald and Wihtred it is likely to have amounted to an almost complete identity of view. No doubt an obstacle had been set up to the grossest forms of royal nepotism; but rank still had its prerogatives and the arrangement did not preclude the appointment of suitable princesses, born to authority, but only of the obviously unsuitable. Under the Eskings this never became an issue; the test was to come 100 years later in the confrontation between a Mercian king who had seized power in Kent and was intent on treating the Abbeys there as appanages for totally undeserving relatives and a determined archbishop who was a Kentishman (pages 215–217 and 222–225 below).

The third principle, that the church should be free of financial and other exactions, was not merely stated but defined. The church was to be relieved of '*omni exactione publici tributi atque dispendio vel laesione*', a formula which concealed certain tacit reservations. The essential point about these provisions is that they treated the church primarily in its capacity as landlord, and the exactions at which they were particularly directed were no other than those rents in money and kind, and the work services, such as carting, ploughing and reaping, which had been owed to the king by ancient custom as an aid to the maintenance of the royal household and its retinue. These obligations had continued to attach to the holdings when they were transferred to church ownership, and the object of the immunities was to ensure that the whole benefit of them should be reserved to the ecclesiastical landlords, with no remaining lien by the king. Once again, the document probably did little more than confirm what had come to be regarded as correct practice. The religious communities must, from the beginning, have been reliant upon these rents and services; but the danger remained that the king would be tempted from time to time to divert them to his own use, or to impose them collaterally, so that a double burden fell upon the unfortunate tenants. The effect of the instrument was to establish – or more truly, perhaps, to recognize – the religious communities as fully autonomous economic entities, having the undisputed enjoyment on their own estates of all the advantages which elsewhere accrued to the king. This was the essence of lordship.

There was, however, a danger in the immunities. Within 25 years we find Bede writing to Egbert, then bishop, and shortly to become archbishop, of York, complaining of the abuse by which wealthy men, reeves or others, bought land from the king on which they founded spurious monasteries where they lived with their families, free from most secular burdens.[73] There was an impulse behind this development which it was difficult to resist; and the remedy was not, as Bede suggested, to close down the establishments but for the king to remove the religious pretence by granting lands to those whom he particularly wished to reward on the same terms as applied to church property. This system, the creating of *book-lands*, i.e. lands conveyed by royal charter with special immunities attached,[74] came increasingly into use during the 8th century, but needed to be applied with restraint if the royal resources were not to be dissipated. In Kent it seems that a few such grants may have been made to particular favourites by Wihtred's son and successor Æthelberht II (page 209 below), but it was not until the later period of Mercian domination that they became at all frequent, as part of the policy of spoiling the kingdom for the benefit of the intruders.

The immunities declared by Wihtred at the Bapchild council contained, however, certain implied reservations, which were referred to, without being specified, in a grant made by Æthelberht II in 732 to the monastery of Lyminge.[75] These must, it seems, have included royal tolls charged upon cargoes consigned to the religious houses, or there would otherwise have been no need for the special exemptions later granted to Minster and Reculver by Æthelberht's brother and co-ruler Eadberht.[76] But, as Nicholas Brooks has shown,[77] they were concerned chiefly with military obligations, that is with the fundamental right of the king to call upon the services in war of the free ceorls, whosoever's tenants they might be. Later instruments make this apparent. It seems that in order to combat the Danish raids which were developing at the end of the 8th century Offa of Mercia, who was then paramount in Kent, succeeded in 792 in persuading the Kentish churches to agree that their obligations should extend to providing fighting men to send against the raiders in Kent (and in Sussex if need be) and also to undertake a share of the work in the construction of fortifications and upkeep of bridges[78] — the latter being regarded as an integral element of defence, as is clear from a Kentish grant of 811, which reserves bridge-work *contra paganos*.[79] These three public duties, from which none of the lordships was exempt, were those which later became known as the *Trinodas Necessitas*. Nor did the matter end here. As the practice grew of buying off the Danes through the payment of *geld* this, too, became regarded as a public charge, the obverse of military service, binding upon the ecclesiastical estates (and the *book-lands* conveyed to laymen) as on the residue of lands over which the king remained the direct lord. But in Wihtred's time there were as yet none of these refinements. Service in the army was the sole, and immemorial, military obligation; exemption from which would have weakened the defence of the kingdom in measure with the growth of the ecclesiastical estates, and so seriously have deterred further grants.

It seems that, in England generally, every freeman was supposed to take up arms in defence of his own locality, but that for military expeditions forces were raised on the selective basis of one man from every five *hides* of land.[80] It would therefore appear from the so-called Tribal Hidage compiled by the Mercian kings in the middle of the 8th century that Wessex then had a potential fighting capacity of 20,000 men and greater Mercia itself little, if at all, less.[81] Kentish resources in no way compared with this, but the figures nevertheless give a misleading impression of relative military strength. The larger kingdoms could never have been able to bring their full potential to bear; it would have been quite impossible to raise, maintain and deploy such an unwieldy mass of men in a campaign, and only a proportion of those liable for service can have been summoned at any one time. Moreover, as Finberg has emphasized, warfare in these kingdoms had become typically the pursuit of men of noble birth, with the ordinary ceorl, or husbandman, fulfilling more of a supportive role.[82] It is, surely, going too far to say, as he does, that their place was in the commissariat and not in the fighting line; but it is clear all the same that it was chiefly in the professional warrior class of the nobility and in the retainers who surrounded the king (and some of the nobles as well) that the military strength of the larger kingdoms had come to reside, and that the influence of these men tended constantly to aggressive war.

The emphasis in Kentish society was different. For all that Wihtred may have rechristened them *gesids* and 'king's thegns' the eorls remained a petty nobility by the standard of the other kingdoms, and while reared in the same code of loyalty and honour as the nobility elsewhere lacked their fighting experience and accomplishment. This was a field in which Kent could not hope to compete, nor could it offer those prospects of conquest and plunder which attracted the more able and ambitious of the mercenaries. Yet, as recent events had shown, and was to be demonstrated even more strikingly in the later resistance to Offa at the very height of his power, this was an extremely difficult kingdom to subdue. There is little doubt that it was in the substantial class of the ceorls, and more especially the freeholders of the *outlands*, who regarded themselves as a people apart, that the true fighting capacity of the Cantware lay. We have said that in Kent, at this time, one ploughland was the equivalent of five *hides* elsewhere, on which reckoning the total armed muster of the kingdom, now bereft of Surrey, would have been around 3,000; but, in fact, the first line strength was considerably less, because in Kent full military obligations attached only to the *sulungs*,[83] the lands inherited from Hengest's warriors and which in later years were to bear the burden of such quasi-military duties as the payment of *geld* and upkeep of bridges.[84] Restricted to these *outland* holdings the muster would have produced some 1,225 men. This may seem a small number, but in the warfare of that time, and backed by an aroused countryside, it would have been enough to encounter an invading army whether in pitched battle or — more especially — in the sort of guerilla warfare on which it seems that Hlothere must largely have relied. These men were farmers, to whom battle was not a way of life, but they were hardy, well-found and with a good conceit of themselves, and in defence of their own country they could be formidable.

This was the reservoir of loyalty on which Wihtred had drawn to re-establish the dynasty, and he had rewarded it with a secure peace, which his dealings with the church were intended (among other things) to fortify. In those dealings Wihtred was concerned solely with the affairs of the monastic houses and of the two major religious communities of Canterbury and Rochester. The Bapchild instrument supplies no evidence of the development of a parochial system, though hints of this do appear in Theodore's Penitentials and a few chance references by Bede;[85] nor do we learn anything from it about the payment by the laity of any general ecclesiastical dues, though this is touched upon in Ine's laws.[86] It seems that, at this time, the parochial structure was still in its infancy. The situation — as William Page has described it[87] — is that each of the monastic houses was responsible for the spiritual care of its own tenants, and the bishop for that of the remainder of the population of the diocese, and that this was still normally done by sending out priests to conduct baptisms, services and other ceremonies. The letter addressed by Bede in 734 to Egbert, the bishop of York, emphasizes the need to appoint sufficient priests to visit outlying communities, which scarcely saw anyone in holy orders from one year's end to another.[88] Except for the cathedral churches and monasteries themselves there can have been few ecclesiastical buildings, the ceremonies often being conducted around a simple cross. It is probable that by Wihtred's time more permanent arrangements had been made by the religious houses for the tenants of their larger outlying estates, such as Adisham (Christchurch) and Northbourne (St Augustine's), with resident mass-priests and church buildings of a kind, mostly timber. Almost certainly the Eskings would have made similar provision at the royal vills for the welfare of the tenants and the use of themselves and their retinue during their periodic visits, and the *athelings* may also have done so on their own estates — at Ickham, for instance, which appears to have been the portion of Wihtred's son Æthelberht before he came to the throne (page 191 below). The parochial system was thus constructed piece-meal on the initiative of the great lords, whether the king himself, the religious houses, or — somewhat later — laymen; it grew commensurately with the grant of estates by the crown; and the mass-priests were essentially chaplains appointed by the lords, who maintained the patronage. Wihtred's pronouncement of ecclesiastical immunities did not extend to this field. The only compulsory church due (burial fees apart) appears to have been the church-scot, which is treated in Ine's laws,[89] and consisted of one load of grain levied, in Wessex, on each *hide* of land, and in Kent was presumably assessed by ploughlands. The tithe was still apparently a voluntary payment to be devoted to pilgrims, to churches or to the poor, and there were no signs yet of the later accumulation of dues like the plough-alms and Peter's Pence.[90] It took time for these to develop, and longer for them to be appropriated to parishes. We are in an era in which religious life was still dominated by the great ecclesiastical establishments, living largely off their own; and it was to their needs that the Bapchild instrument was directed.

The gatherings at Bearsted and Bapchild provide the model for the Kentish assembly in its fully developed form. These were not, however, gatherings of the whole of the free folk, who would in any case have been too numerous to bring together. When, 100 years previously Æthelberht had spoken of the king calling his 'people' – the *leode*[91] – to him he probably meant by this all his arms-bearing subjects, ceorls as well as eorls, of whom he was equally the sole lord; but it is unlikely that there was then any national muster, except in times of war, the ceorl's dealings with the king being otherwise conducted at the lathe courts during his periodic visits. Æthelberht's own code of laws was framed with the advice of the *sapientes* of the kingdom,[92] who were doubtless those referred to by Hlothere as 'the judges of the Kentish people',[93] and almost certainly consisted of the nobility, regarded as the leaders of their local communities in war and the custodians of custom in peace. Æthelberht's aim was not so much to make law as to declare it, and Hlothere's to adapt and reinterpret it in the light of changed circumstances; the customs remaining those of the folk as their leaders, the nobility, were prepared to endorse them. But Wihtred's laws, which placed upon custom the impress of the church, were innovatory; the notables whom he summoned were regarded (and described) as the king's servants and companions rather than as leaders of the community; and while it was important to obtain their advice on what was likely to be acceptable, they were in no sense mandated by the people. Also present at Bearsted were the archbishop, the bishop of Rochester and 'every order of the church'.[94] This, with the addition of the royal reeves, was very much the composition of the Bapchild council held some 12 years later;[95] the difference being that in the preparation of the laws, a temporal matter, the notables were supposed to be in the lead, with the churchmen advising and assenting, whereas in the proclamation of ecclesiastical immunities it was the other way round. We may be sure that on both occasions Wihtred and Berhtwald were the moving spirits. This was a long way from any conception of primitive democracy.

The appearance of the reeves at a deliberative assembly is significant, since these were officials appointed by, and answerable to, the king himself. In Æthelberht's time the only royal office-holder of whom we have knowledge was the *laadrincmannan*, messenger or herald, whose functions appear to have been largely ceremonial, and perhaps, ambassadorial.[96] Hlothere's laws speak of the *wic-gerefa* or port-reeves,[97] and it is probable that by his time reeves had also been appointed for the various lathes, these being *proacuratores* referred to in his charter of 679[98] and the *satrapes* summoned by Wihtred to Bapchild.[99] We hear of these men increasingly during the 8th century. Such, for instance, were Walhhun who in 747 had been engaged in a dispute with the bishop of Rochester about pannage rights in the Weald,[100] and Aldhun the reeve of Canterbury who in 776 played a major part in the resistance to Offa of Mercia (pages 204–206 below). They were intelligent and forceful men, not necessarily of noble birth, picked out by the king for their abilities and loyalty. Aldhun was a cousin of archbishop Jaenberht,[101] but the reeve Abba who died *c.* 840 a wealthy and well-rewarded man had a *wer-geld* of 2,000 pence, which was that of a ceorl.[102] No doubt the growth of population, the use of letters and the increasing complexity of public business had made the appointment of these functionaries inevitable, but it was another step in distancing the king from the ceorls, numbers of whom moreover were now no longer royal tenants but those of the church. The direct personal relationship which had existed between the king and every one of his freemen had become attenuated, but a bond of trust remained. The nation had passed through bitter times; and the ceorls, it seems, had no objection to an authoritative ruler provided he was not tyrannical. So long as the safety and well-being of the realm were assured, and their own liberties uninfringed, their loyalty to the dynasty could be relied upon.

All of Wihtred's major achievements were concentrated into the first half of his reign, the remainder of which passed uneventfully in complete peace and independence. The agreement with Ine remained the bedrock of this security, since it was strong enough to hold the line of the Thames against Mercian encroachments and freed both men to follow their own designs, which in Ine's case meant the pursuit of further conquests in the south-west, where the British were now hemmed into the Cornish peninsula,[103] and in Wihtred's the dissemination of Kentish influence through the medium of the church. That old antagonist Æthelred of Mercia found himself effectively baulked by this combination, and his successors Coenred (704-9) and Coelred (709-16) were of little account. On the latter's death, however, the throne was seized by a far more formidable character, Æthelbald, descended from a brother of Penda, and there are indications that shortly after this Ine had lost control over both Surrey and Sussex.[104] While this threat must have clouded the last years of Wihtred's life, his reputation was by then enough to preserve the integrity of the kingdom.

It was during the restored security and peace of Wihtred's reign that the new learning introduced by the church, and of which Northumbria and Kent were the principal centres, came to its fullest accomplishment. This is too large a subject to do more than glance at here. A spread of learning was to be expected once contacts were renewed with Rome and cross-fertilization had occurred with the intense scholasticism of the Celtic world, but the achievement had been delayed and it could not have been predicted that, when it came, it would be as splendid as it was. The delay had been caused by the early vicissitudes of the church, during which the original impetus given by St Augustine, himself a schoolman of some standing,[105] had languished, even though it had not entirely died away. The first signs of a renewal had come in Earconberht's reign, when the rivalry between the Roman and Celtic forms of observance had prompted numbers of eager young ordinants, won over to the Roman cause by Queen Eanfled's faction at the Northumbrian court, to take the path through Kent to the continent, Wilfrid and Benedict Biscop being the most prominent among them. To these men the splendour of Rome, and the great storehouse of learning opened up to them there, were an intoxication, and they returned not only fully committed to the Catholic cause but with whatever books they could lay their hands upon and an unquenchable thirst for knowledge of all kinds. It was to appease that thirst, as well as to consolidate the triumph won at the Synod of Whitby, that the Pope made the brilliant decision to send Theodore of Tarsus to Canterbury, accompanied by Hadrian, a unique combination of administrative skills and high scholasticism. Both were needed, to bring the English church under a proper discipline and to better the Celtic church on the very ground where it had previously excelled.

It was the second generation, reared at Canterbury and York and in the great centres of learning established by Benedict Biscop at Wearmouth and Jarrow,[106] which brought this work to its magnificent flowering; and the impulse originating in Kent and the north was felt throughout England in the activities of scholars such as Aldhelm, who developed at Malmesbury the skills he had learned under Hadrian at St Augustine's. Everywhere the libraries of the great churches were replenished with manuscripts, avidly sought from the continent. The range of knowledge was eclectic, including the study not only of the scriptures, but of music and prosody, history and chronology, versification, the science of astronomy, and also, it seems, Roman law. Bede says of Theodore and Hadrian that they were versed in secular as well as sacred literature and poured into the minds of their students 'the waters of wholesome knowledge, day by day',[107] and of Tobias, who became bishop of Rochester c. 700, that he understood Greek and Latin so thoroughly that they were as familiar to him as his own tongue[108] — which implies, so Stenton says, a standard of excellence at Canterbury unmatched anywhere in Europe north of the Alps at that time.[109] But it was Bede himself, in his treatises, histories and commentaries, and in particular in his great *History of the English Church and People*, who brought the literary renaissance to the summit of its achievement. At a time when politically Northumbria and Kent were drifting apart, and the power of both was in decline, the connections of scholarship between the two had never been more close. It was Albinus, Hadrian's successor at St Augustine's, who encouraged Bede to undertake his masterpiece and provided him with much of the early material for it;[110] which not only confirmed him in his partiality for Kent — that might have been expected in an ardent churchman steeped in the traditions of Rome — but explains his knowledge of its history, reaching back beyond the conversion and preserved in the sagas current at Æthelberht's court when St Augustine landed. Bede's reputation became international, and before his death in 735 the English Church was already repaying with interest, in scholarship and missionary endeavour, the debts which it owed to the continent and Rome.

It is in this ambience of enlightenment and religious zeal that Wihtred's reign must be set, though his is an austere reflection of it; it was to the moral, rather than the intellectual, teachings of Theodore that he appears to have responded. In this we can

again perhaps detect an upbringing by those devout women Seaxburga and Eormenhilda, in whom the influences of Earconberht, as husband and father, were still alive.
There is also something old fashioned for the time in what we know of the life of St
Mildred, who succeeded her mother Aebba in charge of Minster around 700[111] and seems
to have died in 733 or shortly after (the last charter in which she appears was of this
date).[112] She is the most renowned of the Kentish saints, Augustine apart, but on the
surface it is difficult to understand why. As a girl she went through the conventional
preparation of schooling at the Abbey of Chelles in France before returning to receive
the veil at the hands of Theodore;[113] from which time she was marked out to succeed
her mother. The miracles ascribed to her during her own lifetime can be discounted as
the stuff of hagiography; she seems to have had none of the intellectual distinction of
her cousin and successor Eadburga; and Bede, who was her exact contemporary, makes
no mention of her at all. A great impetus was given to her cult when, in 1030, her relics
were acquired by St Augustine's Abbey and translated to Canterbury. All sorts of
miracles then began to be associated with her shrine;[114] and it seems that the legends
surrounding her – and her kinsmen the two young princes murdered by Egbert – were
deliberately embroidered, because the custody of the relics had become a considerable
asset in an age of pilgrimage. Considerations of this kind were always very much in the
minds of the community of St Augustine's. They were, for instance, intensely jealous of
their right to the burial of the Kentish kings, and of the archbishops. The measures taken
by Archbishop Cuthbert (741–758) and his successor Bregowine (759–765) to ensure
that they should be buried among their own community of Christchurch caused immense
offence and fuelled the bitter rivalry between the two establishments.[115] By the 11th
century, when the Kentish royal house had been long extinct and the lien on the bodies
of the archbishops had been lost, possession of St Mildred's remains was an advantage
to be made the most of.

Nevertheless, the cult was already flourishing before this, as is attested in the *Lives
of the Kentish Royal Saints*, a document predating the removal of Mildred's remains;
and indeed as early as 948 we find, in a charter granting land at Wickhambreux, some
neighbouring property owned by Minster described as 'St Mildred's mark'.[116] Nor is there
any reason to doubt the tradition that when the monks of St Augustine's came to take
the remains from Thanet the local people tried to prevent it, pursuing the party with
staves and whatever other weapons they could lay their hands upon.[117] There was
evidently something about her which deeply impressed her contemporaries, and it seems
that the essence of it was simply an exceptional sweetness and selflessness of character.
The best judgement remains that of the writer of the *Lives*, who says of her:

'She was not, as nobly-born people now are, filled with arrogance, nor with worldly pride, nor
with insulting words; she was not quarrelsome nor contentious; she was not treacherous to any of
those who trusted her; she was the benefactor of widows and orphans and the comforter of all
the wretched and afflicted, and in all respects humble and gentle'.

The rift between the two branches of the royal house represented by Wihtred and
Mildred was not easily healed. Almost the last glimpse we get of Wihtred is in a letter
sent to St Boniface, some time around 720, by Eangyth and her daughter Eadburga in
which they complain, among other things, of the hostility shown to them by the king
and archbishop (his *alter ego*) and the hatred borne by the king to their last remaining

kinsman, because of his race.[118] In this Wihtred carried the burden of his father Egbert's crime, and he also, it seems, had unforgiving memories of Oswine's usurpation. There are, however signs that by the end of his life he had been won over by Mildred's qualities; to the extent at least that he was prepared to approve a handsome grant made to Minster Abbey in 724 by his son Æthelberht, who gave it from his own princely appanage.[119] Æthelberht was also to show himself a friend of Eadburga, and it was in his reign that the feud was finally laid to rest.

Piety is not now in favour, and there is little we know of Wihtred that makes us warm to him, as for instance to Hlothere. A hostile critic might say that he was priest-ridden, and also — bearing in mind the marks of his upbringing, his two marriages, and the arrangements he made for the succession (to which we shall come) — that he was unduly dominated by women. But this would do an injustice to the strength of his own convictions and the statesmanship that underlay his pious acts. Whether the Cantware warmed to him we cannot know, and may doubt, but they had every reason for gratitude. Not only did he restore the kingdom from anarchy but his means of doing so, and the policies he pursued, won it 70 years of unbroken peace and prosperity, the last it was fated to enjoy. He himself reigned for nearly 35 years with absolute authority and brought the alliance with the church to such a pitch as to make the kingdom virtually inviolate, so long as the dynasty endured. When he died, leaving three grown sons, no-one can have realized that the royal line was approaching its extinction or have foreseen the calamities that were to follow from that.

The Nydam boat: of the kind from which the conquest of Kent must have been launched.

2. (*left*) St Augustine's Cross, Ebbsfleet: possibly the site of Augustine's landing and probably that of Hengest's.

3. (*below*) Silver pennies of Egbert II (left) and Eadberht Pren (right) struck at Canterbury *c.*775 and *c.*797. Moneyers's names on reverse.

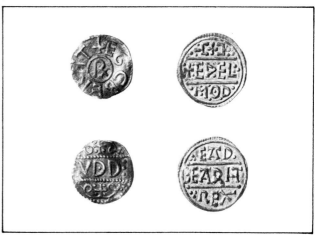

4. St Mary-in-Castro, Dover. Saxon church in unrestored state on site of Eadbald's foundation. Roman pharos to right.

5. Early print of St Pancras, within precincts of St Augustine's Abbey, Canterbury, showing 7th-century walling.

6. St Martin's Canterbury, where Queen Bertha worshipped and St Augustine first came.

7. The demolition of the abbey church, Reculver, in 1809.

8. Reculver; showing, concentrically, the ramparts of the Roman fort, the ruined medieval church and Norman towers and the ground plan of the 7th-century abbey church.

Chapter Ten

THE INDIAN SUMMER

Æthelberht II, Eadberht, Alric and Earduff, 725-762

BEDE DREW HIS *History of the English Church and People* to a close in 731, six years after Wihtred's death and within four of his own. Among his last entries were those recording that Wihtred's three sons, Æthelberht, Eadberht and Alric, had shared his inheritance between them; that all the kingdoms south of the Humber had become subject to Æthelbald of Mercia; and that many Northumbrians, both noble and simple, had laid aside their weapons to take monastic vows, with what consequences he could not predict.[1]

The way had been opened to Mercian supremacy over southern England by the removal within a year of each other of the two rulers whose alliance had previously withstood it, Ine having resigned the throne of Wessex in 726, after a reign of 37 years, to go on pilgrimage to Rome.[2] His successors were no match for Æthelbald, in whom the barbarous qualities latent in the Mercian royal house were present to an extreme degree. St. Boniface was to denounce him as an oppressor of the church and seducer of nuns;[3] and after more than 40 years of tyrannical rule he was killed in 757 by his own bodyguard, an almost unheard of breach of loyalty.[4] From Northumbria he had nothing to fear, and much of his reign was spent in plundering Wessex, from which he seized large parts of Berkshire, Somerset and Wiltshire, as well as Surrey, so that for long periods that kingdom was reduced, in Stenton's judgement, to little more than a large outlying province of Mercia.[5] Only Cuthred (752-756) offered any effective resistance to him.[6]

Yet, for all his savagery, and the violence of his appetites, Æthelbald was not immune to ecclesiastical pressures; there were limits to the offence which he could afford to cause the church, and in his more restrained, or contrite, moods he was capable of acting as its benefactor. It is no doubt this which accounts for the fact that, while he harried Wessex, Kent was left alone under the church's protection. It is, in fact, remarkable how little Æthelbald's supremacy appears to have impinged upon Kentish affairs. Only on one occasion, to our knowledge, did Æthelberht, the senior ruler, defer to him, and that was in 742 when the immunities granted to the Kentish church at Bapchild were submitted to Æthelbald for endorsement,[7] in the hope, it seems, of committing him to principles which he would then be bound to extend to his own dominions, as he in fact did seven years later.[8] This, clearly, was a move inspired by the church. For the rest, the Mercian overlordship appears to have meant almost nothing to the Cantware, content under the rule of their own kings. But the condition of this immunity remained that there should be no rift within the dynasty which would offer Æthelbald a pretext for intervention such as Wulfhere and Æthelred had taken advantage of in the past.

181

It may seem all the more surprising that Wihtred, who during the last years of his reign must have recognized the incipient threat of Æthelbald and have sensed the slackening of West Saxon power, should have chosen the perilous course of leaving the throne in commission among his sons. Divided rule had been the bane of Wessex, and on the one occasion when it had been resorted to in Kent — Hlothere's sharing of the kingship with Eadric — it had led to disaster. It is difficult to avoid the suspicion that Wihtred's decision had been influenced by the wish of his second wife Werburga that her own son Alric should be given some share of power; but this is unlikely to have been the only reason. The arrangement suggests some lack of trust in the ability of Æthelberht to govern effectively without the support of his brothers, especially perhaps that of the more worldly and industrious Eadberht. But one may guess that the chief object was to correct the neglect of west Kent by providing it with a ruler (albeit subordinate) of its own. North-east Kent, the seat of the archbishop and the cradle of the kingdom, had always dominated the affairs of the nation. From the beginning the see of Rochester had been overshadowed by Canterbury, and the loss of Surrey had increased the disparity. Bede tells us that after Rochester had been burned by Æthelred in his punitive expedition of 676, causing the bishop, Putta, to resign his position, the diocese had been left so poor that Theodore had found great difficulty in persuading anyone to take it;[9] and, although that damage had been repaired, half the original jurisdiction of the see had been lost. Wihtred, perhaps because of an early upbringing in Sheppey, appears to have been more conscious than any of his predecessors of the need to redress the balance between east and west, and to see that the people of the western lathes — who bore the first brunt of any foreign invasion — were given their proper place in the counsels of the kingdom; hence the unusual choice of Bearsted and Bapchild as the sites for his two major assemblies. If this was the object of the arrangement then it was achieved. Given a sub-king of his own, working in close collaboration with the bishop of Rochester, west Kent prospered, as did the affairs of the diocese. Moreover none of the internal trouble that might have been expected from divided rule occurred; a testimony to Wihtred's judgement of the characters of his sons, of the authority of the church and the temper of the people.

The closing of Bede's narrative is a serious deprivation, since it was succeeded by nothing in any way approaching it in accuracy, range and detail. In general, all we have left to go on are surviving charters, some genealogies, scraps of tradition gathered into later works, and the correspondence of eminent churchmen such as St Boniface. All this is fragmentary, and it can be positively misleading. Of the three brothers named by Bede no trace whatever can be found of Alric in any later source that is in the least contemporary; in particular, not a single charter issued or attested by him has survived. The 15th-century Canterbury chronicler Thomas of Elmham has an extraordinary story of his living to reign until 795,[10] and the same is implied by William of Malmesbury;[11] but besides making him around 90 at his death this would have had him ruling at a time when Kent was under the absolute dominance of Offa. Gordon Ward must be right in believing that the medieval chroniclers simply confused him with another Alric, of the Northumbrian royal house, who was killed in 798.[12] Our ignorance therefore remains complete. We can only assume that he very soon died or was shouldered aside by his elder half-brothers.

Of the other two we hear a good deal, but much of it is contradictory. It is clear that Æthelberht came to the throne the senior both in age and authority. He attested the Bapchild instrument on Eadberht's behalf as well as his own;[13] Bede names him first; he alone features among the Kentish kings in the collection of king lists prepared towards the close of the century;[14] and in 738 he is found insisting that a grant which had been made by Eadberht required his approval.[15] Up to 747, or thereabouts, he remains the leading figure, but he then drops completely from sight, to reappear briefly in 762 to conduct a trivial piece of business with St Augustine's Abbey.[16] This is followed before the year is out by a grant made to the Abbey by one of his companions, Dunwalh, saying that Æthelberht has been buried there and that he himself is about to set out to Rome to deliver to the shrines of the apostles some money which the king had entrusted to him for the purpose.[17] Every one of Æthelberht's deeds during the earlier period of his activity is concerned with east Kent. During this time Eadberht appears as a subordinate king in west Kent,[18] but in 747 his place there is taken by his son Eardulf[19] while he himself is found dealing with affairs in the east, as though filling a vacuum left by Æthelberht.[20] The last we hear of him is also in 762, when he is shown confirming, as senior king, a grant of lands in west Kent made, not by his son Eardulf who seems to have died, but by a certain Sigered,[21] apparently an outsider only indirectly connected with the royal line.

This is what we derive from the charters; but not one of them is an original, and it is often difficult to know what trust can be placed in the copies, more especially since the similarity between the names of Æthelberht and Eadberht is a constant source of potential confusion. This is compounded by two entries in the Anglo-Saxon Chronicle (made towards the close of the 9th century, and so nearly 150 years later) recording the death of Eadberht in 748 and of Æthelberht in 760 — which should be adjusted to 762 since the dating in the Chronicle is known to be two years adrift during this period.[22] To accept that Eadberht died in 748 would mean rejecting the testimony of at least four charters, most of which are thought by competent critics to be reliable. It would be easier to believe that it was Æthelberht who died then, and this indeed was Gordon Ward's conclusion.[23] But that would mean not only that the Anglo-Saxon Chronicle had got the names mixed, and that they had also been mixed in the charter of 762 ascribed to Æthelberht, but that it was 14 years after his death and burial before his companion Dunwalh — who features earlier as his cup-bearer[24] and was certainly his friend and not Eadberht's — set out with his bequest to Rome. All this is just possible, but there remains the major stumbling block that the collection of king lists prepared towards the end of the 8th century, and so close to the events, names Æthelberht and not Eadberht as the last in the Kentish line.[25] It seems to have omitted Eadberht because it was dealing only with those kings who were titulary the senior, and it could scarcely have done so had he in fact succeeded to this position, outliving Æthelberht by 14 years.

The only really tenable conclusion appears to be that both men lived until 762, dying within a few months of each other, when Æthelberht must have been approaching 70 and Eadberht only a little younger. This is what Stenton believed.[26] It is clear, however, that during the last 15 years or so of his life Æthelberht became something of a recluse, content to leave affairs very much to Eadberht and his son Eardulf, who had now come of an age to govern. Some intimation of this change must account for the thoroughly muddled entries in the Chronicle. Given that these were made nearly 150 years later, the error is understandable enough, on the assumption that neither of the brothers was a particularly memorable figure. This also is true of what we know of them. The Eskings, who had at first been the church's champions and defenders, and then its partners, appear in this last generation to have fallen under its tutelage; it was, above all, the influence of Canterbury which now guided the dynasty and shielded the kingdom.

That no serious friction developed between Æthelberht and Eadberht may be a testimony to family affection, or solidarity, or to the complementary temperaments of the two; but mostly, one suspects, it was due to consciousness of the Mercian threat and to the watchful attention of the archbishops. There are, however, signs that in the early years, while he was in charge of west Kent, Eadberht's subordination chafed him, and that at this time he made some attempt to assert his independence of Æthelberht's authority, the occasion being the grant in 737-8 of a large estate (ten ploughlands) at Hoo to the bishop of Rochester, a gift witnessed only by a number of court companions and their followers and for which Æthelberht's confirmation was not sought, as it should have been.[27] It is possible that he himself might have let this go unchallenged, but that was decidedly not the attitude of the archbishop, Nothelm. The unfortunate bishop of Rochester was compelled to answer for his own failure to obtain Nothelm's agreement, and both he and Eadberht were required to appear at Canterbury in April 738, so that the grant might be submitted and approved in proper form by both Æthelberht and the archbishop.[28] It seems that this rebuff was enough to check any further restiveness of the kind by Eadberht, who must have welcomed his later return to east Kent, where he was given greater scope for his energies.

This incident tells us something about Eadberht; but Æthelberht is a far more elusive character. As we shall see when we come to examine his grants, they are distinguished by their intelligence; but whether they were of his own design of the church's it is impossible to say. The impression we get from such documents as have survived is of a friendly disposed and rather indolent man, in whom the stern piety of his father had declined into a gentle quietism. There is a letter of his to St Boniface in Germany sending a number of gifts in the transparent hope (despite disclaimers) of receiving in return a couple of falcons of a kind found in that country but not in Kent and capable of killing herons.[29] It seems that Æthelberht was on good terms with the royal abbesses who were the last remnants of Eormenred's kin, and cherished none of Wihtred's grudges against this branch of the family. He was generous in his gifts to St Mildred[30] and used her cousin and successor Eadburga as his introduction to St Boniface in the important matter of the German falcons, mentioning that she had told him that on a recent visit to Rome she had sought the saint's prayers on his behalf (as one cannot imagine her doing on behalf of Wihtred, of whose treatment of her she had nothing but complaints).

The charge to be levelled against Æthelberht is that he failed his kingdom by neglecting to marry and ensure the survival of the dynasty. The charge cannot be substantiated absolutely, because this is a period during which information about royal wives and daughters is singularly lacking (we know nothing, for instance, about Eadberht's wife, nor about any child of his except Eardulf). All we can say with confidence is that if Æthelberht did marry he produced no son who grew to maturity, since had he done so we should have been bound, in one way or another, to have learned of him, as of Eardulf, to whom he would have been senior. There is at least a strong presumption that Æthelberht remained single. However much the church may have exalted the virtue of chastity this was a matter in which kings owed a duty to their people; and it was one to which the twice-married Wihtred, for all his piety, had shown no disinclination. It seems that Æthelberht was disinclined, and was content to leave the business to Eadberht, an altogether less complicated person, whose choice companions — so described in the offending charter of 737[31] — were the thegns who frequented his court with their followers. The closeness of Æthelberht's friendship with Dunwalh, his cup-bearer — a position occupied at the time of the first Æthelberht by the most favoured of female slaves — conveys to the modern mind at least a hint of homosexual inclinations. There is a suspicion, moreover, that pietism may have infected certain other members of the royal family. If Alric or Eardulf produced any offspring we do not know of it; and while both of them died young — it seems in their early thirties — and something must no doubt be allowed to the sheer mischance of infant mortality, or the birth of daughters instead of sons, nevertheless the suspicion remains. It seems that the long association of the Eskings with the church had now begun to touch them with the malady from which Northumbria was suffering, and which was to prove fatal not only to them but, through them, to the nation.

For a while, however, the kingdom was left to enjoy unmolested an Indian summer of peace and prosperity in which it reaped the benefit of Wihtred's accomplishment while the great events of the time passed it by. This was the era in which the English church became renowned throughout Europe not only for its learning but for its missionary work in Germany and Frisia, in which St Boniface was the outstanding figure.[32] In this development Kent played little part. St Boniface himself was a Wessex man, but the first impulse had come from Wilbrord and others in Northumbria. The Cantware had never been a fervent people — the princesses apart, saintliness was not much in their character, though they produced a number of ecclesiastical statesmen — and the prime concern of Canterbury was with the church in England. Here its responsibilities had been curtailed by the creation in 735 of a separate metropolitan see at York.[33] This gave effect, at long last, to Gregory the Great's original intention, which had first been frustrated by Edwin's death at the hands of Penda and the flight of Paulinus, and had then been delayed by the conflict between the Roman and Celtic churches, the requirements of the reform undertaken by Theodore, and the disputes surrounding Wilfrid. The separation was long overdue, since Canterbury's jurisdiction had become unmanageably large, but it emphasized the isolation of Northumbria from the rest of England, and by removing this northern influence was to weaken Canterbury in its dealings with the Mercian kings. For the time being, however, the loss was made good by the powerful support of St Boniface. Throughout the course of his missionary work in Germany, his visits to Rome, and the reform he undertook of the Frankish church at the invitation of the now dominant Carolingian house, St Boniface retained a keen interest in the ecclesiastical affairs of his native land, in which his word counted for more than that of the Pope himself, so great had his reputation become; and the whole weight of this authority was exerted to restrain the rapacity of Æthelbald.

Berhtwald died in 731,[34] at a great age; he had already been Abbot of Reculver in 679, when Hlothere addressed a charter to him,[35] and must have been well over 80 at his death. His successors are little remembered now, but they were not insignificant men. Both Tatwine (732-734) and Nothelm (735-739) were scholars of some distinction, the latter — then a priest in London — having helped Bede in the preparation of his *History* by visiting Rome to consult the Papal archives on his behalf.[36] Neither held the primacy long enough to make much impact, but Cuthbert (740-758) did. He had been Abbot of Lyminge[37] (a departure from the previous rule of abbesses over this mixed house) and was a confidant of St Boniface.[38] It must have been he who devised the scheme of getting Æthelbald, as overlord of southern England, to confirm the Bapchild instrument, a manoeuvre in which Æthelberht dutifully played his part;[39] and although this failed in its immediate object of securing the same privileges for the church in Mercia, that was achieved by the formidable intervention of Boniface, who not only wrote to Æthelbald admonishing him for his evil ways but got the German bishops to join him in doing so[40] and also enlisted the aid of Egbert, the archbishop of York[41] — a combined moral pressure which the king was unable to resist. The propitiatory state to which Æthelbald was reduced is shown by the handsome grant he made to Cuthbert of the monastery of Cookham in Berkshire, situated on lands snatched from Wessex.[42] Cuthbert was concerned to strengthen his own base at Christchurch, which was in danger of being put into the shade by the wealth and magnificence of St Augustine's Abbey, a foundation as old as it and enjoying the traditional right to the burial both of the archbishops and of the Kentish kings. The arrangements he made to break this tradition by securing his own burial at Christchurch aroused the fury of St Augustine's and brought the rivalry between the two establishments to a pitch of almost open enmity.[43] Cuthbert seems to have done nothing to discourage Æthelberht's withdrawal from affairs, and he developed a good understanding with Eadberht, who is said to have supported his plans in the matter of burial.

Among the closest of St Boniface's friends was Eadburga (also known by the diminutive Bugga: see Appendix G). It seems that the genesis of this friendship lay in Wessex, from which Eadburga's mother, Eangyth, had returned with her daughters on the deposition and death of her husband Centwine to take charge of a small mixed monastery (probably at Eastry) associated with the far more splendid establishment of Minster, a task in which Eadburga was helping her. The earliest correspondence, dating from around 720, when Eangyth must already have been approaching 70 and Eadburga herself 40 — a problematic age — is an outpouring of misery, couched in elaborate Latin and interspersed with quotations from the fathers and the *Aeniad*: and in it Eadburga does not hesitate to address Boniface as 'my beloved'.[44] The letters speak of intense sorrow and loneliness, caused by the death of her brother Oshere and the departure for Rome of her sister Wihtburga; lament the misfortunes of her mother's kin, of whom some (? the murdered princes) lay in 'the bitter earth' of their own country and others (? the unhappy Oswine) had been driven into exile abroad; express the inadequacy felt by her mother and herself in dealing with those, especially the men, committed to their spiritual care; and complain of the hostility shown towards them by the king (Wihtred) on account of their race. The object, consolation apart, was to beg for Boniface's help in arranging for them to visit Rome, 'once mistress of the world', so that they could see the holy places and pray forgiveness of their sins. We get little impression of Eangyth, except of decrepitude, but that given of Eadburga is of a highly intelligent woman desperate to escape from a situation in which she could see no future but to care for an aged mother in an impoverished establishment which provided no outlet for her abilities.

Boniface was moved by this appeal and responded to it, saying that he had entrusted the arrangements for the visit to Eadburga's sister Wihtburga, who would let her know when, in face of the Saracen threat, it could safely be made.[45] The later correspondence shows that Eadburga did, in fact, visit Rome;[46] but it was her choise as Abbess of Minster on the death of her cousin Mildred in 734, or shortly after,[47] that released her formidable talents. The deaths of Wihtred and Berhtwald no doubt helped to clear the way for an appointment which, although thoroughly merited, perpetuated the hereditary grasp upon the Abbey of Eormenred's descendants; but one may suspect that a great deal was also due to Boniface's influence with the scholarly archbishop Nothelm,[48] to whom Eadburga's qualities were in any case calculated to appeal. The strong bond of affection between Eadburga and Boniface remained the dominating feature in her life and enriched the whole of her rule at Minster, which she succeeded in making, for a time, a small but notable centre of the new humanistic learning. A younger woman, and even closer friend of Boniface, called Leafgyth (who later joined him in his work in Germany) in sending him some Latin verses composed 'according to the rules of poetic tradition' said that this was an art which she had learned from Eadburga 'who continues unceasingly to research into divine law'.[49] In 735-6 we find Boniface asking Eadburga to prepare for him an illuminated manuscript of St Peter's epistles, for which he sent her the gold;[50] and in 742-6, shortly before setting out on an expedition to Frisia, he wrote to her as one 'to be united with' him 'in a golden bond of spiritual love and by the pure and holy kiss of charity' seeking her prayers for his safety and for the success of his mission.[51] By later chroniclers she was remembered most for rebuilding Minster on a new site;[52] to her contemporaries she was clearly an imposing figure; and after her death she was canonized. We know that she was still governing Minster in 748,[53] but that shortly after this she abandoned her charge and retired to the contemplative life,[54] it seems at Lyminge, where she was buried.[55] The later Canterbury chroniclers say that she died in 751,[56] but that may have been when she retired (perhaps on reaching 70), since a letter sent by archbishop Bregowine to Boniface's successor Lul at some time between 759 and 764 implies that her death had been recent.[57] There is no other member of the Kentish royal line who speaks to us so directly. Through her we obtain our only insight into the lives of generations of princesses, from Eanswith on, who had followed the way of spiritual duty.

Meagre as the history of the kingdom may appear to have been during this period (and was in a political sense) the growth of population induced by the return of peaceful conditions led to a number of important economic developments, which can be traced partly in place-names and partly through the charters, and amounted to a quickening of the evolutionary processes. These developments bore especially upon the Weald and Romney Marsh, which were now being pioneered by settlers as well as being exploited more intensively and systematically than ever before as fattening grounds for swine and sheep. Custom in Kent, with its individualistic bias, favoured pioneering ventures. It was always possible for a freeman whose inheritance in north Kent had been diminished by partition to sell (without leave) such land as had been left him, buy what he needed, and take his chance in these frontier lands with their difficult terrain, their great expanses of wood and scrub, their bogs and inundations. On the Marsh reclamation work required co-operative effort, but in the Weald the first settlements were solitary affairs. While it seems that custom forbade the felling of timber, and especially 'the great oaks and beech' which were pannage trees, restricted enclosure, which would exclude the foraging swine, and regulated the amount of brushwood which might be taken for fuel, there was nothing to prevent the cultivation of open glades, of meadow lands along the river banks, or small cleared areas where the thorn and hazel thickets had been cut back, and here footholds could be established in the forest.[58]

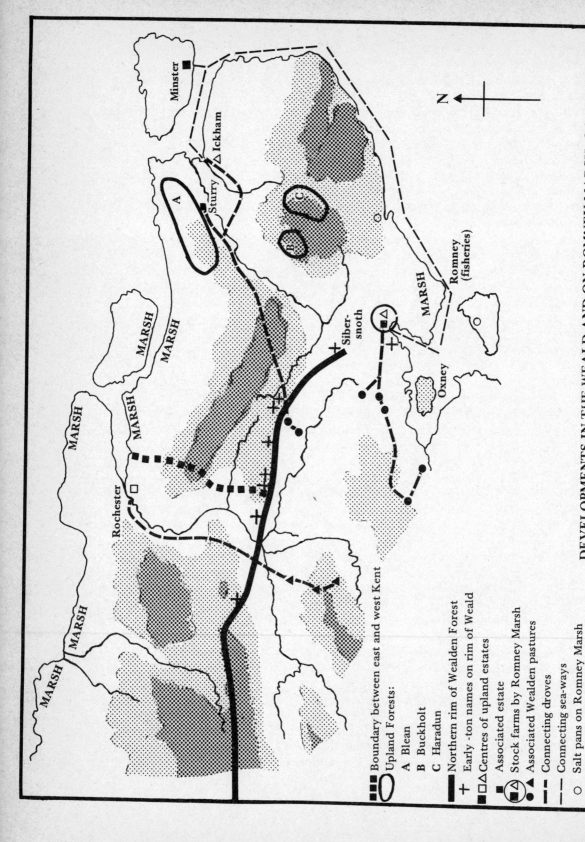

N

DEVELOPMENTS IN THE WEALD AND ON ROMNEY MARSH: 8th CENTURY

Boundary between east and west Kent
Upland Forests:
  A Blean
  B Buckholt
  C Haradun
Northern rim of Wealden Forest
Early-ton names on rim of Weald
□△Centres of upland estates
Associated estate
Stock farms by Romney Marsh
Associated Wealden pastures
Connecting droves
Connecting sea-ways
Salt pans on Romney Marsh

Scale: Approx 10 miles = 1 inch

Minster

Ickham

Sturry

A

B

C

Romney
(fisheries)

MARSH

MARSH

MARSH

MARSH

MARSH

MARSH

MARSH

Rochester

Siber-
snoth

Oxney

The process is revealed through the new types of place-name that were coming into use towards the close of the 7th century, overlapping the old ones, which by the 8th they had displaced. Notable among the names of settlement were those ending in *-ton*, which might still carry its original meaning as a farm enclosure but had also, as we have previously described, taken on the larger sense of a hamlet, commonly occupied by a family group (page 135 above). At the same time new forms were springing, out of the early *-ham* names, in particular *-hampton* and *-hamstead*, e.g. *Berghamstede*, or Bearsted, where Wihtred's laws of 695 were promulgated. The difficulty about the new types of name is that they continued to be formed for a very long time; indeed those ending in *-ton* sometimes as late as the 13th century, when, for instance, a perambulation of lands under the jurisdiction of Tonbridge Castle mentioned the messuage of William Scrufryn on a site which became known (and still is) as Scriventon.[59] But in certain constructions the use of the term can be more closely dated. Especially significant here are patronymics ending in *-ington*. The appearance in these of the participle *-ing-* instead of the old plural genitive case *-inga(e)-* associated with the early endings in *-ham* is a change of substance, which we have described at some length in Chapter 7 (pages 135–136 above). The new construction is to be found in all types of patronymic, whether names of habitation (*-ton*), of cultivation (*-lond*) or of pasture (*-daenn*). Judging by the charters it had become standard in the 8th and 9th centuries, though it originated a little earlier and doubtless continued for somewhat longer.

In Kent there is no more striking feature of the distribution of *-ton* names than the appearance of a whole series of them along the central and eastern sections of the Chart Hills — the woodlands of which merged into those of the Weald to the south — and also along the equally wooded stretch of country bordering the northern fringe of Romney Marsh.[60] The great majority of these are patronymics of the *-ington* type, such as Chilmington (*Ceolulfingtune*, 949),[61] and others, like Sutton (Valence) — simply 'the south settlement', on what was then the margin of habitation — are recorded early.[62] These fringe lands, previously neglected, were now being taken into cultivation, and there is little doubt that the process was well launched during the period of our present study. In the body of the Weald (devoid of *-ham* names) only two ending in *-ington* are to be found, and those at a short advance from the gateways of the Rother and Medway;[63] but there is a handful of other *-ton* names which betray an early origin, those in which the term stands entirely on its own (Townland in Woodchurch; *de la Tune*, 1240)[64] or in which it comes at the beginning of the word and not in the usual place at the end, as in Tonbridge and Tollhurst in Staplehurst parish (*Tunlafahirst*, 804),[65] settlements being so rare when these were founded that they either required no identification or could themselves be used as identifying features. There are also two *-hamstead* names, Whetsted in Capel (*Hwaetonstede*, 838)[66] and Hemsted in Benenden (*Haemstede*, 993)[67] — another settlement which needed no identifying adjective. Finally there are about a dozen names ending in *-gisel*, or *gisella* in the plural, a type which is almost exclusively Wealden. The term means a shack or collection of shacks and is commonly taken to refer to swine-herds shelters, but we have argued elsewhere (*The Jutish Forest*, 1976, pp. 113–114) that these were the first rough cabins, with their surrounding pens, established by the pioneer-ing settlers. The earliest noted is *Rindigsel*, now Ringden near Paddock Wood, which appears in a charter *c.* 763[68] and carries the origin of the term well back into the 8th century.

It seems, on the evidence, that it was during this century that the forest settlements began to appear, but they were still few and tentative, sited for the most part close to the river entries, on the terraces of the central Vale above the worst of the flood lands, or in the south-east within reach of the Rother tributaries, and almost always on one of the Roman roads or prehistoric tracks which formed the main droves used by the herdsmen and gave access to the outside world.[69] Hemsted, at the junction of two Roman roads and with the Rother only five miles distant, was the quintessential site. The choice of land was highly selective, as it had to be, with a preference for open meadow where the soil was sufficiently tractable to be worked with the light two-ox plough, which was all that the first pioneers, driven from north Kent by the poverty of their inheritance, and devoid of any neighbours to help them, could be expected to afford on their own. The settlement of the Kentish Weald did not begin as a community enterprise but, in the typically independent style of the Cantware, as the work of individuals.

These few acres of cultivation amid the vastness of the forest were the start of a long evolutionary process which was to end — but not for another 600 years — in displacing the herds altogether.[70] At this time they cannot have prejudiced in any serious way the primary use of the commons for pannage; which, on the contrary, had become intensified. The evidence for this is, again, to be found in toponymy. Whereas with names of habitation the typical transition was from -ingaham to -ington with those of the Wealden swine pastures as it was from -ingabaera to -ingdaenn, the new construction having coincided in this case also with a change of terminology, which appears to have been almost as abrupt, since in Kent -baera is never to be found preceded by -ing- nor (subject to one dubious exception)[71] -daenn by -inga-. Of the two forms of patronymic the second is by far the more frequent; it is, indeed, almost the stock nomenclature of the Kentish Weald, surviving today in the names of such villages as Biddenden, Benenden and Frittenden, as well as of numerous hamlets, farms and fields.[72] All these were originally lodgements made in the commons by the free ceorls — Bidda, Bynna, Frith and so on — whose names they perpetuate. The practice had begun probably as early as the 6th century, and certainly by the 7th, when it gave rise to the -ingabaera forms, but it had now become greatly accelerated.

This rapid increase in the appropriation of pastures no doubt owed something to the innate individualism of Kentish society, but it must also have been caused by a crowding of the commons which prompted the herdsmen to stake out their own claims. That the practice was especially marked in the eastern forest, where place-names of this kind preponderate, was due to the greater population pressures on this side, compounded by geography. Since the Weald is in south-west Kent the eastern lathes overlapped it, which meant that six of them had to make use of the forest on a front of some 20 miles, much the same length as that which, in the west, marched with only three. The eastern commons were therefore more cramped, which led to deeper penetration, but was only partly off-set by it, and caused a scramble for the more convenient and accessible sites. Nevertheless, the spread of the -ingdaenn names shows that the herdsmen were now reaching into the forest beyond Tenterden and Cranbrook towards Hawkhurst, a conclusion borne out by the appearance of such places as Sandhurst in 8th century charters; whereas in the ampler commons of the west there was no need to seek for pannage so far. The central core of the forest, including (in Kent) much of the present parishes of Hawkhurst, Goudhurst and Lamberhurst, is devoid of patronymics of this

type and seems not to have been approached until later.[73] Here the boundary with
Sussex was still open. It was probably not until the 10th or 11th centuries that it
became defined.

The lodgements made by the herdsmen, being a matter merely of use, did not
materially affect the integrity of the lathe commons; but in the 8th century we see, in a
grant made by Æthelberht to Minster Abbey, the beginning of a process that did.[74]
This charter is unusually interesting in a number of ways. The grant was made by
Æthelberht while he was still a prince, and so out of lands which his father must have
allotted to his use, with the rents, services and rights attaching to them, in the expecta-
tion that they would revert to the crown when he succeeded to it — a purely family
arrangement. They were not, therefore, *booklands* and he had no right to dispose of any
of them without leave, which explains why he sought consent to the grant both from
Wihtred and from Eadberht as prospective co-heir. The conveyance was of one ploughland by the Rother, which had previously been occupied by the inhabitants of Ickham
(east of Canterbury), and going with it three yokes of pastures at a place called
Hammespot, to which were added swine pastures in the northern forests of Blean and
Buckholt (south of Canterbury), on the Isle of Oxney, and in the eastern Weald. The
chief feature of the grant was its concentration upon pasture rights, which was obviously
intended to correct an imbalance in the agricultural economy of Minster. Although the
Abbey owned some lands at Sturry[75] the great bulk of its estates were in Thanet, which
was a corn country deficient in woods. Because of the great distance of this lathe from
the Weald it had no common of its own there; nor, it appears, were the marshes fringing
the Wantsum channel capable at this time of sustaining any really large flocks of sheep.

The places conveyed in the grant can be identified with some assurance. The
ploughland by the Rother must have been in the neighbourhood of Ruckinge,
which remained associated with Ickham right down until the time of Domesday
Book, and *Hammespot* seems to have been in the area of Romney Marsh south of
Ham Street,[76] where St Augustine's Abbey (ultimately the inheritor of the Minster
lands) is later known to have had property at Snave.[77] This, then, was sheep
pasture, the value of which as a source of cheese and wool was increasing the whole
time. Some 25 years earlier Wihtred, in granting Lyminge Abbey lands at Wilmington
in the lathe of Wye, had taken care to transfer with them pasture rights for a flock
of 300 sheep around Romney,[78] the south-eastern tip of the Marsh having for
many years constituted a common reserved to this lathe, which was land-locked
(*see* page 60 above). Similar provision was now being made for Minster, but with
the significant difference that it was being given rights in marshland common
attached to the lathe of Barham (in which Ickham lay) but where the Abbey itself had
no lands which might establish a claim to them. This was a prerogative act over-riding
custom.

The same point is illustrated even more clearly by the Wealden swine pastures
included in the conveyance. The Abbey, by virtue of its property at Sturry, had some
right to the use of the Canterbury common, *Burh-ware-weald*, in which it seems that one
of the pastures (Wick in Headcorn) was situated; but the other three, Broombourne in
High Halden, Tenterden, and Lossenham in Newenden,[79] were said specifically to have
been in the Wye and Lyminge commons, where it could have had no customary claims.
Moreover rights of use were one thing, but the subtraction of pastures for the exclusive

use of the Abbey, and to be held in prescriptive ownership, was quite another. What it amounted to was the creation of an entirely new common — albeit in separate parts — for the benefit not of the folk of a lathe but the tenants of a lordship. This was a departure of great significance; and significant also was the siting of the pastures. Wick in the Canterbury Weald could be reached without too much difficulty by drovers from Sturry, a place with which in later years it was particularly associated;[80] it would also have been possible, though laborious, to drive swine into the Wye or Lyminge commons from Minster, 40 miles distant, but to drive them back again the same way, taking perhaps a week to do so (swine are notoriously difficult to herd) would have been to prejudice the value of pannage in fattening them up for slaughter. Both commons were, however, readily accessible from Ruckinge on the Wealden fringe of the Marsh. It seems clear that the land near here (which formed the centre-piece of the grant) was intended to serve Minster as an outlying stock farm, with sheep pastured on the marshes to the south and swine sent to fatten in the oak woods to the west; the cheese, wool and pig carcases being transported — together no doubt with firewood — down the Rother and along the coast to Minster by boat, in those days by far the easiest and quickest method of carriage.

The precedent set in this charter was followed 60 years later by Offa when he granted Ickham to one of his thegns, so turning it into a small lay lordship.[81] It carried with it the lands at Ruckinge, and attached to the grant were three swine pastures, one at Southernden in Headcorn parish (and the Canterbury common) accessible to Ickham itself, and the others near Tenterden and at Sandhurst (both in the Lyminge common) accessible to Ruckinge.[82] So closely does the pattern resemble that of the Minster charter that it seems that this must have served as the actual model. Other examples are supplied by Adisham and Eastry. The first was one of the earliest of all the estates granted to Christchurch (page 125 above), and associated with it was Appledore on the eastern fringe of the Marsh, with a succession of swine pastures in the forest hinterland.[83] The stages by which the royal vill of Eastry came into the possession of Christchurch are difficult to trace; but in the outcome Eastry received lands on the Isle of Oxney, including sheep pastures on the surrounding Rother levels,[84] and swine pastures within reach of these in the area of Benenden and Hawkhurst.[85] In all these cases the circumstances were the same. The lordships were in the three north-eastern lathes of Thanet, Eastry and Barham which had no Wealden commons; they were now being given commons of their own in the form of discrete pastures, together with sheep runs on the Marsh; stock farms were being established to serve both and to relay their products by water; and the handicap of distance was thus overcome. The arrangements had about them that effective simplicity which marked each stage in the development of the agrarian economy of Kent; and to this day the traces of them remain in the succession of villages which ring the Marsh on the landward side along the line of the Royal Military Canal.

Over most of the kingdom, however, where the lathes were within herding range of the Weald and had old-established commons there, and where there was usually ample marsh within their own boundaries, for instance along the Thames estuary, no such exceptional dispensation was needed. Events here followed a different course, best illustrated by the rights given to the church of Rochester in the Aylesford common, called *Caester-ware-weald*. The story starts in 747 with the settlement by Eardulf of a dispute which had arisen between the reeve Walhhun and the bishop of Rochester over the pannaging of swine in the common:[86] the upshot of which was that the bishop was granted the exclusive use of three pastures, *Holanspic* (near Paddock Wood), Petteridge in Brenchley and Lindridge in Lamberhurst,[87] sited at intervals of three to four miles along a drove (originally a prehistoric iron track)[88] which ran from near the edge of the forest south towards Sussex. The herds owned by his tenants were thus being segregated from those of the general population of the lathe, the king's own tenants, who enjoyed the use of the remainder of the common. In later years, as the bishop's lands were increased by new grants, additional pastures were made over to him; four, for instance, accompanied the conveyance of Frindsbury in 762 and others came with Halling *c.* 780 and Trottescliffe in 788.[89] The general principle established by these grants, and adopted elsewhere, was that those tenancies of a lordship which lay in a particular lathe should be given their own pastures out of the lathe common. Thus when, in 804, lands at Lenham were made over to St Augustine's Abbey it received with them 13 small pastures in the common of Hollingbourne lathe, where Lenham was situated;[90] and many other examples of the kind could be cited. As, with the passage of time, the lordships grew in size and number, and the residual lands held directly from the king diminished, so the old commons became progressively parcelled out until only fragments of them survived for the king's remaining tenants, these royal lands themselves composing a lordship indistinguishable (except in origin) from any other. While the lathes retained a shadow of their original substance as administrative units, the commons had by the 10th century been obscured beneath congeries of pastures, a process which Æthelbert and Eardulf had set in train.[91]

These pastures were described as 'dens', like the small lodgements which preceded them, from which, however, they differed in scale, use and status. They acquired definite boundaries, and were often as much as a square mile or more in area. While the early dens had been staked out by individual families these were used by groups of tenants belonging to the several lordships, being in fact commons in microcosm, and they were held by prescriptive and not merely squatters' rights. The two systems persisted side by side for a while, but as time went on the early 'folk' dens, to which the occupants could claim no valid title, were progressively supplanted or absorbed; though more often than not they bequeathed their names, as familiar means of identification, to the new pastures which came to engross them. Commonly, the pastures belonging to a particular lordship were spaced at intervals along a drove penetrating into the heart of the forest, alternating with others in different ownership, the object being to allow the herds to be moved in easy stages from one to another, and back again at the end of the season, without having to pannage anywhere except on the lordship's own property. A single composite block of pasture would, if at a depth in the forest, have compelled the herds to pannage on the way at places where they had no entitlement, and, if on the outskirts, have placed a barrier in the path of others. As we have seen, the system was introduced at the very beginning with the grant to the bishop of Rochester of the three separate pastures of *Holanspic*, Petteridge and Lindridge. A good later example of it is shown in the conveyance in 814 with lands at Chart Sutton of a succession of ten pastures in the Hollingbourne common, spaced first along the Roman road which ran south through Staplehurst and then along a drove diverging from it to the south-west and ending at Bedgebury in Goudhurst, the last of the pastures named.[92] A happy consequence of this system is that it allows the droves to be traced in considerable detail and confirms that the present road pattern of the Kentish Weald was formed in Jutish times, being determined mostly by the course of the old iron ways through the forest, which the herdsmen adopted, and the relationship of the several commons to the lathes which they served. On no other basis is it, in fact, intelligible.[93]

Fish were also becoming an increasingly important supplement to the diet. In 740 Æthelberht granted Lyminge Abbey the use of a fishery at the mouth of the Rother, together with the land on which the fishermens' houses stood.[94] At this time the Rother had a number of different outlets, the Marsh being a great delta, but the fishermens' cottages were said to adjoin an oratory dedicated to St Martin, which suggest that the site was New Romney where St Martin's was one of a number of churches — four at least, and some say as many as eight — within the medieval town.[95] We see here the first, humble beginnings of this celebrated port, the wealth of which was founded upon the herring industry. The identification is supported by the grant, in the same charter, of pasture for 150 draught animals, i.e. oxen, at a place called Ripp, bordering upon Sussex, which must be West Ripe, just south of Lydd (there is also a Midrips in the neighbouring Sussex parish of Camber, previously Broomhill).[96] There were patches of rough grazing here, behind the shingle banks of Dungeness, and the passage is interesting in showing the use of the Marsh for cattle as well as sheep.

Pig carcases, cheese and fish all needed salt to cure them, and this was produced by evaporating sea water in pans situated on the coast. One such pan, at a place called *Sandtun* (later Sampton) in West Hythe was granted by Æthelberht to Lyminge Abbey in 732, together with an annual allowance of 120 laden wagons of wood to fuel it.[97] This was ideally placed to serve the needs not only of the Abbey itself, which was close at hand, but of stock farms and fisheries owned by others on the Marsh; and, equally important, it was close to its supply of fuel, which was cumbersome to transport and which the pans consumed in large quantities. Although the charter does not specify the source of this there can be little doubt that it was in the royal wood of *Sibersnoth* on the north-eastern rim of the Weald around Orlestone, at the entry to the Lyminge common,[98] and only six miles distant from West Hythe. The same combination of coastal saltings and woodland was found at Faversham, under the shadow of Blean Forest, and here too we learn of the existence of salt pans from a charter of 812.[99]

Not all of the wool, cheese and fish can have been for domestic consumption; the surpluses were readily exportable from Faversham, Hythe and other ports on the fringe of the Marsh or the Thames estuary, including no doubt Milton Regis. We know that English cheese (salted as a preservative) was in demand abroad, and, from a famous dispute which arose in 795–6 between Offa and Charlemagne, that woollen cloaks, known as *sagae*, were then a major item of English overseas commerce.[100] We should expect Kent, with its wealth of sheep pasture backing the Channel ports, to have been a prime source of both; and it is all the more interesting, therefore, to find that cloaks featured among the gifts sent by Æthelberht to St Boniface when soliciting the German falcons. It was not only the kingdom's position, but the richness of its resources, which gave it such a predominant share of the continental trade; and overseas demand must have been a factor in the attention pay to Romney Marsh during this period, before the Viking raids had begun and while the seaways were still unmolested. In this commerce, the religious houses played a large part both as producers and as importers, enjoying privileges not only in Kent but in London.

In 733 Æthelbald of Mercia confirmed to Mildred, as Abbess of Minster, the remission of toll on one ship a year in the port of London,[101] and in the following year endorsed a similar privilege for the bishop of Rochester.[102] That these rights were of long standing is evident from the preamble, common to both charters, which says that 'many, not without cause, seek to have the things which are known to have been conferred on them confirmed in a document'. Very likely they date from the time, some 50 years earlier, when Hlothere was in control of London and had his own port-reeve there, and in this case had persisted when Kentish influence over the city had lapsed. In 748 Æthelbald granted Mildred's successor Eadburga an additional remission of half the dues on a ship, making it clear that if it were wrecked or became unserviceable the privilege would be transferred to the new one replacing it.[103] The example was followed by Eadberht in another grant made to the Abbey towards the end of his reign, the remission this time being at Fordwich and Sarre.[104] There is a more dubious charter ascribed to him which purports to show the grant of privileges at Fordwich to Reculver Abbey;[105] but this, although dated to 747, is said to have been witnessed by Bregowine as archbishop, a position to which he did not attain until 759. If there is any substance behind the grant it has clearly been antedated by some 15 years, perhaps through mistaking the Indiction. Whatever is to be made of this charter, the documents as a whole reveal that tolls were now a well-established source of royal revenue, from which the religious houses enjoyed no general exemption, though they might be granted particular ones, and also that the larger of the houses were trading in their own ships. They mark what must have been very nearly the summit of commercial activity before the first Viking irruptions into the Narrow Seas.

Æthelberht played no part in these transactions, or indeed in any of which we are aware between 747 and 762, the last year of his life; although his correspondence with St Boniface may be dated to the earlier part of this period since the account given in it of his meeting with Eadburga implies, without definitely saying, that she had then retired. The affair with which Æthelberht concerned himself in the early months of 762 can scarcely be dignified with the name of public business; it concluded an arrangement by which half the usufruct of a mill at Great Chart was assigned to the royal vill of Wye, in return for which the miller and his heirs were given the right to pannage a herd of swine in the Weald 'for ever'.[106] This is the first surviving record of the use of water mills in England,[107] though there is some archæological evidence to show that they had already made an appearance some 50 years previously,[108] before which corn was still being ground by hand — hence the reference to the royal 'grinding women' in the laws of the first Æthelberht.[109] Interesting as this sidelight is, the arrangement was a purely domestic one, and Æthelberht must have died almost as soon as it had been completed, since before the year was out he had been buried at St Augustine's Abbey and his companion Dunwalh was preparing to leave for Rome with his bequest to the shrines of the apostles. It seems that hardly had Eardulf come of an age to share with Eadberht the responsibilities of government than Æthelberht retired into seclusion, perhaps at Wye, the most remote of the royal courts in east Kent. We may picture him — it is a pleasing fancy — flying his falcons on the downs above the vill, or in the fringes of the Wealden forest, in the company of a few devoted friends like Dunwalh, while Eadbert bustled about about in Canterbury enjoying his new-found responsibilities and Eardulf conscientiously administered the affairs of west Kent in co-operation with his namesake the Bishop of Rochester.

As Æthelberht and Eadberht aged it was on Eardulf that the hopes of the dynasty had come to rest, and it seems, from what little we learn of him, that he would have made a wise and dutiful ruler. We know that he was still alive at some time after 754 from a letter which he addressed to Lul, who had succeeded Boniface on his martyrdom in that year,[110] but this is the last trace that we have of him, and by 762 his place in west Kent had been taken by a certain Sigered, who acknowledged Eadberht's authority but whose antecedents are obscure. It is two grants made by Sigered, the first in 762 and the second apparently in the following year, which mark the extinction of the dynasty;[111] since while Eadberht countersigned the first of these the second was confirmed by an individual called Eanmund, who had then succeeded him as senior king but who seems to have had only an elective claim to the position — though very likely supported by some connections with the dynasty in the female line. The evidence is of a crisis in the succession which, despite every effort to resolve it, left the kingdom mortally weakened.

If, as it seems, Eadberht survived his brother Æthelberht it can only have been for a few months. He was the last of the Eskings and also, as the Canterbury chroniclers tell us, the only one since the time of the conversion to have been buried elsewhere than in St Augustine's.[112] This was a subject of such deep concern to the Abbey that their statement is to be believed, although they also paraded a charter, said to have been issued by Eadberht on 25 July in the 36th year of his reign, that is in 760,* in which he is shown granting them land at Mongeham near Deal in the express hope that both he and Æthelberht might be laid to rest with their fathers.[113] The Abbey were notorious forgers of documents;[114] this one survives only in late copies; and it is difficult to avoid the conclusion that it had been fabricated, or at least doctored, to conceal the unpalatable fact that it was Eadberht himself who rejected the Abbey as his burial place, just as he had supported archbishop Cuthbert's design to be buried not there but among his own community. We are told that Eadberht's tomb was at Reculver, a house which since its foundation, and more especially since Berhtwald's time, had always had particularly close association both with the ruling line and with Christchurch. In this way the feud between Eadberht and St Augustine's was carried into the grave, and it was on that discordant note, with far more serious problems impending, that the history of the Eskings drew to its close.

In 762 the kingdom had enjoyed nearly 70 years of unbroken peace. It must have been at the very height of its prosperity, with trade flourishing and the increase of population offset by a fuller and more systematic exploitation than ever before of the resources of forest, marsh and sea. The great variety of soil and terrain, which met every need of the agricultural economy, command of the seaways to the continent, and the safe harbourage of the great estuaries, made Kent an object of envy and covetousness; and therein lay its danger. Its security had come to depend upon the survival of a royal line which, over 300 years, had shown a remarkable stability, judged by the standards of the time; had produced a succession of able rulers, among whom the great Æthelberht was supreme, but all of whom, except Eadric and the pitiable Oswine, had a deservedly firm hold upon the loyalties of their people; and which by its consistent championship

---

* BCS 190. Birch ascribes the charter to the year 761, without explaining why; but according to Bede (V, 23) Wihtred died on 23 April 725, and Eadberht had presumably become king before 27 July in that year.

of the church had very nearly succeeded in setting the kingdom above the political struggle in England. Despite the crimes and failings of individual rulers — Eadbald's incest, the murderous impulse of the young Egbert, Eadric's treachery and the weakness and self-absorption of the second Æthelberht — the record of the Eskings is singularly free of tyranny, and in the church's eyes such sins as they had committed had been amply redeemed. The pride that the Cantware felt in their own identity, which had become focused upon the dynasty, was strong enough to outlast it, but their security could not. It now vanished at the very time when, following Æthelbald's murder in 757 and a period of civil war, the Mercian throne had been seized by Offa, a king of outstanding ability, matched by a total ruthlessness. Within 40 years, and despite the most valiant resistance, the nation which the Eskings had brought to such a happy state was to be utterly desolated.

Chapter Eleven

THE RESISTANCE TO MERCIA

Egbert II, Ealhmund and Eadberht Pren, A.D. 762–798

ON THE DEATH OF Eadberht the Cantware must have been acutely aware of the crisis that would face them unless the problem of the succession could be swiftly resolved in a way which offered no handle to Mercian ambitions. The hope was a forlorn one. There was nobody now with an unchallengeable right to the throne, and of the contenders some might be prepared to trade the independence of the kingdom for the powerful support of Offa. This, in fact, is what happened, but not before an attempt had been made to forestall it, by arrangements which Offa simply swept aside. Following this it took ten years for resistance to build up; but when it came it was so determined, and so charged with hatred of the Mercians, that it was to be another 25 years before it was finally suppressed, and then only by methods of the sheerest barbarity.

We have no narrative of what happened during the first, critical, period between 762 and 765, but we do have a succession of reliable charters (preserved mostly in the *Textus Roffensis*).[1] These tell us a good deal about the course of events, but nothing about the background of the rival claimants to the throne. In the whole history of the kingdom there is no more infuriating gap in our knowledge than this. The matter is too important to be passed over, and we are compelled, at whatever risk, to make what we can of such scraps of evidence as there are. The conclusions that emerge are that the rulers whom the Cantware first chose for themselves were princes from cadet branches of the Wessex royal house; that those who were later imposed upon the kingdom by Offa — including Egbert II, who was to rebel against him — came from the Kentish nobility itself; and that all could probably show some connection with the Eskings in the female line. If we are right in this, the obscurity surrounding their origins merely reflects the extraordinary dearth of information about Kentish consorts and princesses which begins with the failure of the chroniclers to record the name of the first Egbert's wife or whether he had any daughters, and which is in such marked contrast to the very full genealogical particulars we have for the previous period.

Of Egbert I's successors Hlothere is said, on dubious authority, to have had a son, but no mention is made of any other member of his family. Eadric died young, and perhaps unmarried, but we are told nothing about this either way. If we know the names of Wihtred's two wives it is only because, exceptionally for the time, they appear as witnesses to charters; there is no surviving record to show who they were or where they came from; and while they gave him three sons there is complete silence about the existence of any daughters. Of those sons, there is a strong presumption that Æthelberht remained unmarried, and an unverifiable suspicion that the same may have been true of Alric; but Eadberht certainly had a wife, whose name is unknown, and may well have had one or more daughters, equally anonymous. His son Eardulf is open to the same suspicion of celibacy as Alric, but there is little except the absence of a male heir to substantiate it. Four generations of the ruling line, spanning 100 years, are known to have produced six princes, and it is improbable that the number of princesses was much, if at all, less. Of these we get a hint of only one, in the letter sent by Eardulf and the bishop of Rochester to Lul at some time after 754,[2] seeking his prayers on behalf of three kinswomen of theirs — 'all virgins dedicated to God' — of whom two had names which suggest no connection with the royal family and were probably relatives of the bishop, but the third, *Irmiga*, that is presumably Eormengyth, seems unquestionably to have been an Esking (*see* Appendix G).

This letter, in fact, provides a clue to our ignorance. We learn of those princesses, but only those, who adopted the religious life, and this was a practice which, while it persisted among Eormenred's descendants, seems largely to have died out in the reigning branch of the Kentish royal family — which is to say that their daughters had been appropriately provided for in marriage, usually no doubt to *athelings* of other royal houses, but perhaps occasionally to the better born of the indigenous nobility. The offspring of these marriages, it may be several generations back, would have the strongest claims to the inheritance of the Eskings, even if their paternal origins lay outside the kingdom. A prince of the Wessex royal house, descended from a branch that had been ousted in one of the frequent internecine struggles in that country, might well be glad to take advantage of a maternal relationship to carve out a career for himself in Kent, and have been welcomed there because of the association and as a counter-poise to Mercian influence.

The first of the newcomers was Sigered, who already before Eadberht's death had been appointed as sub-king of west Kent,[3] and had very likely, therefore, been marked out by the Eskings themselves as their heir, following Eardulf's untimely death. It can scarcely have been a coincidence that at much the same time, or a little earlier, the prestigious position of Abbess of Minster, which had hitherto been the preserve of Eormenred's branch of the royal house, had passed to a certain Sigeburga,[4] from her name a connection of Sigered's and very likely his sister. These have the appearance of having been born to a Kentish princess — the dates suggest a daughter of Wihtred — married into some other dynasty. At first sight the alliteration of the names points to Essex, the last ruler of which was in fact called Sigered[5] (though he cannot have been the same person since he was still living at least as late as 823).[6] Essex had for many years been entirely subordinate to Mercia, so that this connection would imply that Offa had put pressure upon the ageing Eskings to adopt Sigered as their heir in order to prepare the way for his own contemplated take-over. But the events contradict this. In fact, Sigered was later deposed by Offa, to reappear some 15 years afterwards in the company of the Kentish rebels.[7] We must look for his origins among the enemies of Mercia, not its clients; and on this count the most likely association is with the Sigeberht who ruled briefly in Wessex between 756 and 757[8] and was perhaps an elder brother. It is significant, too, the Sigeburga, who we have suggested was a sister, should have taken over control of Minster from Eadburga, with her strong Wessex connections, who would certainly have been in a position to influence the choice of her successor. The dates fit, and the marriage of a daughter of Wihtred to a Wessex *atheling* would have been consistent with the policy of alliance in face of the Mercian threat which the two kingdoms had been pursuing at that time. It seems that it was this alliance which Æthelberht and Eadberht had been hoping, with good reason, to revive.

But while Sigered remained in charge of west Kent after Eadberht's death he never achieved a more senior position. The final decision on that matter rested with the inner core of notables whom we find acting as the chief councillors of the kingdom in 763-4.[9] This was a group committed to Kentish independence, but apparently with their own ideas of the most suitable leader. Curiously, the archbishop, Bregowine, does not appear among them; he seems never to have been a particularly forceful person, and he was now approaching the end of his life and may already have been ailing. The doyen of the group was a certain Balthard, whom we first encounter as a witness to a grant made in 727;[10] who acted a number of times later in the same capacity for Æthelberht when business concerning east Kent was being transacted; and who seems to have been the most prominent of the eorls in that part of the kingdom. In 762 he was among those who attested the gift made by Dunwalh to St Augustine's Abbey in remembrance of Æthelberht, a document in which, significantly, he styles himself as *dux*,[11] which was the Latin rendering of ealdorman. This is the first time that the rank is met in Kent; it was superior to that of reeve, and was in fact equivalent in authority, though not in birth-right, to that of a sub-king. It seems that during the period of the interregnum, while Sigered continued to administer west Kent, the east had been put in Balthard's safekeeping. He was thus acting very much as a regent when the critical question of the succession was decided. Among those associated with him were Hwaetred, the abbot of Reculver,[12] and a certain Aldhun, who was to become one of the most prominent figures in the Kentish resistance. He is known to have been a kinsman of another of the witnesses, Jaenberht,[13] who at this time was abbot of St Augustine's but was shortly to succeed Bregowine as archbishop, and from what we know of his character and later actions was almost certainly the moving spirit in the group.

These men, with three others of less account, were the signatories to a document by which a grant was made by Sigered of lands in west Kent was confirmed by Eanmund [sic], who had evidently been appointed as senior king.[14] Absolutely nothing else is known of Eanmund, under that name, but it seems very likely (as Stubbs, for one, believed) that it had been mistranscribed in the copies we have of the charter and was correctly Ealhmund, a person who played a major part in later events.[15] If this is so we are on much firmer ground, because we know from the Anglo-Saxon Chronicle that Ealhmund was a Wessex prince, a great-grandson of Ingeld, a brother of Ine.[16] The alliteration of Ealhmund's name conforms to that of the Kentish royal line, and there are already signs of a shift in that direction in those of his father Eafa and grandfather Eoppa, both recorded in the Chronicle. There is a suggestion in this that the association between this branch of the Wessex royal house and the Eskings may have arisen three generations back in a marriage between Ingeld and a Kentish princess, such as might very likely have been arranged to seal the settlement reached between Wihtred and Ine in 694. But this is problematical, and a more recent connection is perhaps likelier. Ealhmund, as the great-grandson of Ingeld, who did not die until 718,[17] cannot have been born much, if at all, before 740. He might therefore have been the offspring of a marriage between Eafa and a daughter of Eadberht, which would have marked him out more clearly for the succession.

If the identification is correct than it confirms that the purpose of the appointment must have been to shore up the defence against Offa by reviving the old association with Wessex, in which the chief hope for the independence of the kingdom now lay. But even if Eanmund was a different person, of whom nothing is known, or can be deduced except from the affinities of the name, the choice remained a provocation to Offa. A man of overriding ambition, he must have been meditating a descent upon Kent as soon as the deaths of Æthelberht and Eadberht had removed the last direct representatives of a line which the veneration of the church rendered almost inviolable. Control over Kent, besides greatly increasing his wealth and resources, would offer him mastery of the whole of the south-east, from which he could more easily dominate Wessex. There was need to act before the new rulers had time to establish themselves in the loyalties of the people, and there can have been no lack of pretexts for doing so. If, as it appears, both Eanmund (correctly Ealhmund) and Sigered were Wessex princes, then their claims to the throne could be dismissed as those of outsiders, who had been foisted upon the nation by a small clique; and since they came from a kingdom which was either actively or potentially hostile to Mercia it might seem reasonable enough that Offa should protect his own interests by supporting other claimants, who were Kentish. At this stage the full extent of his designs could be masked. Balthard, Jaenberht and their colleagues might see plainly enough what they were, but after 70 years of peace under an established dynasty the people in general must have been bewildered by the events that had overtaken them, and too uncertain to make a stand under unfamiliar leaders.

The intervention was swiftly accomplished and apparently met little resistance. In 764 Offa appeared at Canterbury to regrant in his own name, and with the concurrence of yet another Kentish king called Heaberht, the very lands which in the previous year had been given to the bishop of Rochester by Sigered with Ealhmund's approval,[18] the implication being that neither had enjoyed a legitimate authority. Shortly after a grant to the bishop by another newcomer, Egbert, who had displaced Sigered as sub-king of west Kent, was approved by Heaberht and submitted to Offa for endorsement.[19] It is clear that these two had been installed as dependents of Mercia. Exactly what claims they had to the kingship there is little to tell us. All we know of Heaberht's background is that in 762 he had been one of the witnesses to a charter issued by Sigered,[20] so that he was evidently a Kentish noble, and if — as Stubbs suggested[21] — his name was a variant of Eadberht, this at least hints at some connection with the Eskings. Egbert's name certainly does so, and it is clear that he came from the very heart of the Kentish establishment. His position as a Mercian underling was equivocal from the beginning, since his very first charter shows that he was already closely associated with the two individuals, Aldhun and Jaenberht, who were later to conspire with him against Mercia; it was witnessed by Aldhun, and Jaenberht was described in it as one dear to Egbert in all things.[22] Egbert was clearly a younger man than Heaberht, whom he outlasted. It would be a neat assumption (and in keeping with past practice) that he was Heaberht's son and owed his position to this relationship rather than to any more direct commitment to Offa; but, however that may be, it was a serious mistake by Offa to have countenanced the appointment. The ease of his intervention in Kent may have made him careless. He seems to have underestimated the latent pride of the Cantware in their nationhood and to have been blind to Egbert's ambition and qualities of leadership.

Offa was guilty of another, equally serious, default. In expelling Ean(Ealh)mund and Sigered he appears also to have got rid of the ealdorman Balthard, of whom nothing further is heard; but he could not deprive Jaenberht of his position, and whether through misjudgement, overconfidence or inadvertence, failed to prevent his election as arch-bishop on Bregowine's death in 765. Jaenberht was well capable of dissembling, and deceit was one of the charges which the Mercians were later to level at the Cantware in general. According to the later chroniclers Thorne and Thomas of Elmham, both brethren of St Augustine's, his election as archbishop was a direct, if back-handed, consequence of the dispute between the Abbey and the community of Christchurch over burial rights.[23] Their story is that Jaenberht, who had become Abbot in 760, was determined that Cuthbert's burial at Christchurch should not be allowed to set a precedent. Immediately upon hearing of Bregowine's death therefore he appeared at the cathedral with an armed band to take the body, only to find that the same trick had been played again, that the death had been concealed, and that he was too late. He thereupon prepared an appeal to the Pope, and it was in order to pre-empt this that the chapter of Christchurch elected him as Bregowine's successor. The obsession of the Abbey's chroniclers with the subject of burial rights adds nothing to the plausibility of this story, which is none the less true to the character of the man, and his intense loyalties. The interests of the community of Christchurch were inextricably bound up with those of the kingdom. Left to its own devices the community was always liable to choose a Kentish incumbent, and especially prone to do so when the times were threatening. Jaenberht was not only Abbot of St Augustine's but Kentish by birth — and almost certainly of noble stock — as his kinship with Aldhun shows. There could be no question of where his sympathies lay, his determination (and conspiratorial qualities), or of the use to which he would put the influence of his office.

But however much the Cantware may have resented the increasing autocratic attitude of Offa the time for resistance was not yet ripe, and Heaberht was too deeply com-promised to lead it, even if he had the inclination. His chief claim to memory is that he introduced into England a new type of silver penny, larger and thinner than the so-called *sceattas* previously in use, of a kind which had first been minted in France *c.* 755 and was later to be adopted by Egbert and developed by Offa into a coin of real elegance and distinction, the prototype of those used by the English kings.[24] These coins bore the king's name (later sometimes his effigy) on the obverse — which is how we know that Heaberht was their originator — and the name of the moneyer on the reverse, and they were evidently struck at Canterbury, although it appears that at some time *c.* 790 Offa also established a mint in East Anglia, another subject kingdom. Heaberht's moneyer, Eoba, later worked for Egbert with two others, Babba and Udd, and it seems that all three of these were among those minting for Offa's successor Cenwulf, who did not win control of Kent until the suppression of the second and last rebellion in 798. This has led C. E. Blunt to place the beginning of the coinage at some time between 775 and 780. Although the date cannot have been much earlier, Hearberht makes only a fleeting appearance in the charters and cannot be associated with the first rebellion which broke out *c.* 775.[25] It is unlikely that his reign lasted long beyond 770, and we suggest that it was then, or only a year or two after, that the new coins began to be struck.

With Kent apparently secured Offa continued his career of domination. Before 770 he had subjected most of Sussex, where he confirmed charters issued by two of the local kings,[26] and in the following year he completed his conquest of that country by subduing the men of Hastings.[27] East Anglia had, for many years, been overshadowed by Mercia, and after the extinction in 749 of the ancient dynasty of the Wuffingas[28] it lapsed into almost complete obscurity, becoming in due course a dependency of Offa. It seems that Wessex, too, was brought to acknowledge his overlordship, though only for a time. A charter of 772, which survives in a 13th century copy, much rewritten, but which Stenton believes, on the evidence of its witness list, to be substantially reliable, records a grant made by Offa to the bishop of Selsey of land near Bexhill and was subscribed, among others, by Cynewulf of Wessex, Egbert, Jaenberht and an obscure individual who had previously appeared as a king of Sussex but was now allowed the style only of *dux*, or ealdorman.[29] That Egbert should have been summoned to an occasion which was obviously intended to demonstrate the extent of Offa's dominion suggests that he had by then succeeded Heaberht in the senior position. He is described as king; but this is the last time that Offa is known to have accorded him any such title. The policy of demotion adopted in Sussex was shortly to be applied in Kent; it was to become a matter of outright annexation.

In 774 Offa issued two charters (the originals of which have survived) granting Jaenberht lands at Higham Upshire and at Lydd, without reference to Egbert or to any other civil authority in Kent, and styling himself as King of all the English.[30] We do not know the venue, but it appears to have been in Mercia, and the assembly was an imposing one, attended by Jaenberht himself, three bishops, five abbots and numerous nobles and officials. The bishops were those of Lichfield, Leicester and Lincoln;[31] none of the abbots was Kentish; but two of the nobles, Baban and Esni, may have been, since their names appear later among those of Egbert's adherents.[32] To all appearances this was a Mercian council disposing of Kentish lands; but in Offa's eyes it was probably intended to be more than that. He had moved beyond the conception of the *bretwaldaship* to that of direct and outright dominion over all the southern peoples, and in keeping with the title he had taken the assembly, for him, would have been tantamount to a council of England, lacking only the presence of certain rebels and dissidents who were still bold enough to deny his authority. He was asserting his claims against the opposition of Wessex, where Cynewulf had now renounced his allegiance and was engaged in a campaign to recover those lands to the south of the Thames which had been wrested from his predecessors,[33] and in total disregard of Egbert who, so far from being treated as a king (albeit a subordinate one), was not called upon to witness the grant in any capacity at all, but appears to have been entirely disowned with no-one substituted for him. It seems that something must have gone seriously wrong in Kent. Evidently Egbert had shown himself unwilling to sink to the position of ealdorman and had either been intriguing with Cynewulf or had already joined him in open defiance.

With the general poverty of information there is a danger of reading too much into the fragments that exist, but nevertheless it does seem that these two charters represent a definite climax in the course of affairs, and that Offa, with the threat of Cynewulf to deal with, was intent upon forcing the issue in Kent in the most brutal way possible, in the belief that he had only to assert himself in order to bring the people to heel. It must surely have been deliberate that the occasion he chose to parade the title King of all the English, and to dispense land without a shadow of agreement by any local ruler, was the grant to the archbishopric of two small estates in Kent. This would have the additional advantage of implicating Jaenberht, whose Kentish irredentism must by now have been well known, and forcing him apart from Egbert. For Jaenberht to reject these gifts to his church because of the terms in which they were couched would have been extraordinarily difficult, and would have forced him into a public declaration of enmity, an irretrievable act for which he cannot yet have been prepared; but by accepting them in those terms he would be seen as endorsing the autocratic principles surrounding them, and this at an imposing assembly in the presence of three of his own suffragans and other high ecclesiastical dignatories. Whatever mental reservations he might later plead, the moral authority he could exert in the Kentish cause would be prejudiced.

The issue had indeed been forced, but with results quite different from what Offa must have expected. For Egbert it had now become a question of outright resistance or nothing. However damaging the proceedings may have been for Jaenberht, if Offa thought that he could be persuaded to swallow this humiliation and abandon his loyalties in return for more tangible benefits he misjudged him. But above all he appears to have misjudged the reaction of the Cantware at this affront to their nationhood — following upon who knows what others. It must have seemed to them that the last tatters of independence were being removed from them, leaving them exposed to the exploitation of a singularly ruthless king. From this time on Egbert was assured of all the support which the Eskings had previously commanded from their people; without which his rebellion could never have prospered. It seems, from what followed, that Egbert simply assumed control of the entire kingdom, acting in concert with Wessex. It was one thing for Offa to disown him, but he now had to be ejected.

We have no detailed narrative of events; but when, two years later, the clash occurred the Kentish forces were standing on the defensive. The respite was no doubt due to Offa's entanglement with Wessex, but it gave Egbert time to complete his preparations. In this his right-hand man was Aldhun, whom he made reeve of Canterbury,[34] where he acted as the indispensable link between the king and Jaenberht, his own kinsman. It is to this period that we should best assign Egbert's sale to Jaenberht, 'for a recompense of great riches', of extensive lands at Charing and Great Chart, and his gift to Aldhun of a small estate at Bishopsbourne; transactions which cannot be precisely dated because we learn of them only retrospectively after Offa, once more in control of the kingdom, had annulled them.[35] It seems that the purpose of the sale must have been to finance the resistance — which explains the violence of Offa's feelings about it. There was no reason to doubt the steadfastness of the Kentish levies, who were to do all that was expected of them and more; but, as in the past, the military weakness of the kingdom was in the lack of professional fighting men. The Kentish kings must, like others, have had their own retainers, and indeed Eadberht's charter of 737 shows that so did a number of their court companions;[36] but 70 years of unbroken peace, followed by ten during which the kingdom had been reduced to clienthood, can have done little to attract to it the more proficient of those mercenaries and adventurers who had now become the indispensable nucleus of the Anglo-Saxon armies. Men of this kind could expect far greater rewards in the service of Offa or Cynewulf, but without their experience the quality of the Kentish levies could not be made to tell properly in pitched battle. Money was needed to hire this support, and the generous payment made by Jaenberht for the lands at Charing and Great Chart amounted, in effect, to investing the funds of Christchurch in the rebellion. Aldhun was at the very centre of the conspiracy, on the success of which his own future was staked; and the estate at Bishopsbourne, comprising four ploughlands, or a nominal 800 acres, was a modest recognition of his services. Offa's fury at these arrangements was directed as much at Jaenberht as at Egbert, and it was he and his community who were later penalized by having the estates reft from them without compensation; an extreme act, since it was contrary to all the canons to confiscate property from the church, however it had been acquired.

The Anglo-Saxon Chronicle says that in 773 (correctly 776; the chronology is three years wrong at this point) a red cross appeared in the sky after sunset and the Mercians and the Kentish men fought at Otford. The attack had evidently come from Surrey along the Harroway, with Egbert's forces defending the crossing of the Darent. The Chronicle neglects to say who won the battle, and the medieval writers, not unnaturally, assumed that it must have been Offa; though (according to Henry of Huntingdon) only after a terrible slaughter on both sides.[37] No doubt mutual hatred made this a bloody encounter; but, as Stenton has pointed out, subsequent events suggest a decisive victory by the Cantware.[38] For nine years after the battle Offa exercised no authority in Kent, where the charters show that first Egbert and then Ealhmund reigned in complete independence of him.[39] The vindictive hatred which he later expressed for Jaenberht and the Cantware[40] no doubt sprang from the humiliation of this defeat. Considering the relative resources of Mercia and Kent, and making due allowances for the inroads that Cynewulf of Wessex had made into Mercian power, this victory must rank as the greatest single feat of arms performed by the Cantware as an independent people.

The absence of any comprehensive Mercian narrative, and the neglect of the Chronicle, means that little more is known of Egbert than that he was still reigning in 779, when he made a grant of land to the bishop of Rochester, following one of the previous year which was issued at Canterbury,[41] where the mint was also striking silver pennies in his name.[42] Evidently he was in control of the entire kingdom, shared the throne with nobody, but maintained an undivided rule. During this period he must have been in alliance with Cynewulf of Wessex, with whose fortunes those of Kent were intimately bound up, and this appears to have brought a reconciliation with those Wessex princes whom, 15 years earlier, he and Heaberht had displaced. His own position, which now rested upon the strongest of all possible foundations, victory in battle, was unassailable, and he could have felt no qualms in welcoming back, and making some restitution to, these earliest victims of Offa's aggression. The Sigered who appears as a witness to his charter of 778[43] (another which has survived in the original) can scarcely have been other than the earlier ruler. Ealhmund became his heir, and gave the name Egbert to his own son — who lived until 839,[44] which suggests that he was born at about this time.

In 779 the tide of battle turned. In that year Offa defeated Cynewulf at Bensington[45] and was free once more to turn his attention to Kent, which nevertheless continued to resist for five more years; at some time during the course of which it seems that Egbert died or was killed in battle, leaving the throne to Ealhmund, who, deprived of allies, was faced with a task that was beyond him. Only a single charter of his can be attributed to this period, and that is of doubtful authenticity; it is dated to 784,[46] the year in which the Chronicle says that he was ruling in Kent. Although this is an interpolated entry, the interest focused upon Ealhmund's line, from which the kings of England sprang, makes it highly unlikely that the tradition behind the insertion was wrong; and it is supported by the vendetta carried on by Offa against his son, who in later years was to win the throne of Wessex and claim Kent as his patrimony. Yet this interest has also detracted from the memory of that other Egbert, the victor of Otford,[47] whose achievements, outshining those of Ealhmund, the chroniclers with their strong West Saxon bias had little concern to commemorate. There is an ambiguity about his character which the sparseness of the records does little to dispel; but whatever else he may have been he was a great leader in his time, who should not be allowed to slip into oblivion because the future belonged to others.

By 785 Kentish resistance had finally crumbled or been beaten down, leaving the nation exposed to the vengeance of Offa. Ealhmund himself was probably killed, since we hear no more of him; but it seems that his son, that other Egbert, was taken to safety in Wessex, his father's native land. Many of those who had been most prominent in the rebellion must have fled abroad; Charlemagne's correspondence shows that his empire had become a refuge for fugitive Englishmen,* and escape was easier from Kent than from elsewhere. We know that Aldhun went overseas, taking care before doing so to leave his estate at Bishopsbourne to Jaenberht,[48] in the mistaken belief that by consigning it to the church he would keep it out of Offa's hands. Jaenberht's own position may have seemed secure, since it would have been an extreme measure, even for Offa, to attempt to depose an archbishop. There were, however, other ways of dealing with him, and Offa was not a man to leave scores unsettled.

In 776, for the first time since St Augustine's landing, the Pope despatched a legantine mission to Britain. There seems little doubt that he had been part cajoled and part threatened into doing so by Offa whose virtual conquest of southern England, where even Wessex had been beaten into temporary submission, had made him a power to be reckoned with in European affairs. (There is a letter from Pope Hadrian to Charlemagne rather pitifully disclaiming rumours that Offa had suggested his — the Pope's — deposition).[49] There were, in any case, good reasons for a mission. From Theodore's time the province of Canterbury — as also of York since its inception — had been governed by a succession of native archbishops, who appear to have sought and received little guidance from Rome, the chief influence during this period having been that of St Boniface, himself an Englishman. There was need for Papal authority to be reasserted; all the more, no doubt, because Jaenberht's passionate commitment to the Kentish cause must have had a profoundly disturbing effect, particularly in the dioceses under Mercian control, where the bishops were torn between their loyalty to Canterbury, the duty they owed to their own king, and their fear of him. Ostensibly the mission was concerned with canonical matters rather than with organization, but Offa had other plans for it. His object, which he evidently pursued with the legates in informal discussions, was the creation of a new province centring upon Lichfield, which would halve the authority of Canterbury and deprive it of influence over the church in greater Mercia.

On their arrival in England the legates, the bishops of Ostia and Todi, first met Jaenberht and then attended a council with Offa and Cynewulf of Wessex, the only other ruler in southern England whom Offa now acknowledged as having any sort of

---

* A letter sent by Charlemagne in 793–6 to Archbishop Æthelhard asks him to intercede with Offa on behalf of a group of Englishmen who had followed their lord Hringstan (since dead) into exile: see EHD I, p. 780. The letter does not say from where this group of exiles came. They may not have been Cantware but East Anglians, since that nation had also been in revolt. But it is clear that Charlemagne's dominions had become a general place of refuge from Offa's vengeance.

independent standing. The mission then divided, the bishop of Todi going on to Mercia and Wales, and the bishop of Ostia to Northumbria, where a further council was held with King Ælfwald, the archbishop of York and leading churchmen, and a number of canons were agreed. These were taken south to be endorsed at a final assembly by Offa, Jaenberht, all 12 bishops of the province of Canterbury, and four Mercian abbots, including Æthelhard, who five years later was to become Jaenberht's successor.[50] In themselves the canons contained little that was startling, or even novel. Half of them were concerned purely with matters of doctrine, ecclesiastical practice and discipline; and many of those addressed to the laity, enjoining obedience to the bishops, justice for the poor, the suppression of violence and of heathen practices, the payment of ecclestical dues, observance of oaths, and so on, were platitudinous. This was ground that had been covered by Theodore.[51] More pointed was a clause which forbade bishops to concern themselves with secular affairs. Much attention was paid to the position of kings, who were to be chosen by the priests and elders of the people, with bastards excluded from the succession. Anathemas were pronounced upon anyone who should dare to kill one of the 'Lord's annointed'; an emphasis upon the sacred character of the kingship which Offa was to take very much to himself, though he paid scant regard to it in others. There was a condemnation of fashions in dress and hair styles copied from the heathen (presumably the Norsemen), and other practices denounced as barbarous were eating horse flesh, binding the ears of horses together, slitting their nostrils and bobbing their tails.

The hidden purpose of the mission was not revealed until after the legates had returned to Rome. In 787 a proposal to divide the province of Canterbury was put by Offa to a synod at Chelsea which the Anglo-Saxon Chronicle describes as 'contentious'.[52] This was to be expected. There was a deep traditional reverence in the church for the premier see, made illustrious by the work of Augustine and Theodore, and if we know anything of Jaenberht's character he would not have been so cowed as to be incapable of defending his prerogatives, whether openly or by intrigue. Nevertheless, Offa finally got the formal consent he needed, and in the following year Pope Hadrian, to whom the event can have come as no surprise, sent an archbishop's *pallium* to Hygeberht of Lichfield. The most respectable argument for the change was that the province of Canterbury, with 12 suffragan bishops, was unusually large by the standards of the time; but Offa is also said to have assured Hadrian that it was generally welcome to the English churchmen,[53] which was manifestly untrue. The real reason, or combination of reasons, appears in the admission made by his successor Cenwulf that the action had been prompted by hatred for Jaenberht and the Kentish people,[54] and in the judgement by Alcuin, writing shortly after Offa's death, that it had been caused by 'a certain desire for power'.[55] No doubt there was a great deal of sheer vindictiveness in the matter, but there was policy too. The political influence which Jaenberht had been able to exert by virtue of his spiritual office must have been seriously damaging, and Offa was determined that never again should the loytalties of the Mercian clergy be tampered with in this way by a 'bishop of the Kentishmen's church' — to revert to a description which had never been more apposite than now.

Jaenberht was allowed to retain formal seniority over Hygeberht, but only because his had been the earlier appointment. The last years of his life were a time of increasing tension between Offa and Charlemagne, and the story is told by Mathew Paris that

Jaenberht invited Charlemagne to invade England.[56] It is likely enough that some sort of intrigue was carried on with the continent, where Aldhun and other of the Kentish rebels were now living in exile, but if so nothing came of it. Jaenberht died in 791,[57] true to his old loyalties to the last, since he insisted on being buried at St Augustine's,[58] a decision which could hardly have endeared him to the community of Christchurch which he had governed for 25 stormy years. Offa had learned enough not to repeat his previous omission of 765; he made certain of the election of a candidate of his own choice, Æthelhard, Abbot of the monastery of Louth in Lincolnshire,[59] whose Mercian sympathies could be relied upon.

Kent was now treated as a conquered province in the fullest sense,[60] being brought under the direct rule of Offa himself. We have no knowledge of the appointment even of ealdormen; to all appearances the day-to-day administration was carried on through the reeves of the various lathes, those *ministri* — Mercians or Kentish defectors — mentioned in contemporary charters.[61] Grants of land in Kent were now commonly made at councils held outside it — Chelsea being a favourite venue[62] — attended by Offa and his queen, his son Ecgfrid whom he had associated with him in the kingship, and often a whole assembly of bishops, as well as a number of notables, the most prominent of whom appear to have been Mercians (for instance Brorda and Beorhtwold, who appear as witnesses to other grants by Offa, in Worcester and elsewhere, some made during the period when he had lost control of Kent).[63] The assemblies over which Offa presided, including, as they did, churchmen from all over southern England, every one of whom he thus treated as his own adviser, constituted to all intents the council of a single nation, in which there was only one true ruler, although the title of king was still acknowledged to exist here and there, notably in Wessex, as a matter more of grace than anything. Beorhtric, who succeeded to the throne of Wessex in 786, and married Offa's daughter,[64] was a mere cipher, exercising little more independent authority than an ealdorman. To Kent, as also it seems to East Anglia, no concessions were made whatever; it was as though these kingdoms had never been.

Bitter as these humiliations were, they could scarcely have been enough in themselves to account for the intensity of the hatred stored up among the Cantware. No doubt the retaking of the country had been a bloody business, with the usual accompaniments of pillage and enslavement, but it seems to have been followed by wide-scale expropriation, as Offa rewarded his thegns out of the conquered lands. No more than the echoes of this have reached us because charters granted to the laity were not preserved and copied with the same assiduous care as those issued to the religious communities, and have therefore tended to survive only when the lands later came into ecclesiastical ownership and the records into the muniment rooms of the great churches. It is because of this that we learn of the grants made by Offa to two of his thegns of estates at Ickham and Eastry, which ultimately came into the possession of Christchurch; and (some 15 years after the event) of another such grant of 12 ploughlands at St Mary Cray which featured in a later exchange with the archbishop.[65] Most instructive of all, however, is what happened to the lands at Charing and Great Chart which Egbert had sold to Jaenberht, and those at Bishopsbourne which Aldhun had left him before fleeing the country, all of which Offa confiscated and distributed to his own followers on the grounds that 'it was not right for a man to grant away land which his lord had given him, without his lord's assent',[66] by which he meant that it was he who had first made Egbert king. Stenton has cited this as the most uncompromising assertion of an overlord's authority that has come down to us from the whole Anglo-Saxon period.[67] This is true enough, but it ignores the background to the affair — the apparent purpose of the sale to finance rebellion, the hatred which Offa felt for all the parties, who had combined to inflict upon him the most serious defeat of his career, and the need to justify the expropriation of church property to which that hatred impelled him. These estates alone comprised 44 ploughlands, or close on 8,000 acres by Kentish reckoning, with appurtenant meadows, pastures and woods; and we know of the transaction only because, like the grants at Ickham and Eastry, it was of direct concern to Christchurch. It must represent only a sample, though a major one, of the lands which Offa made over to his followers, the bulk of which, no doubt, were those that exiles had abandoned.

A feature of the Mercian domination, which became even more pronounced under Offa's successor Cenwulf, was the multiplication of secular lordships, as a means either of reward, or of raising money, from the resources of a conquered province. These were *booklands*, granted by charter, and with the same privileges and immunities — always saving the obligations for military service, repair of bridges and upkeep of fortifications — as attached to the ecclesiastical estates.[68] It was this status, conferred on them by royal grant, which distinguished them from other lands accumulated by inheritance, marriage or purchase. From the time of the first settlement the Gavelkind customs of Kent, coupled with the free market in land, must have led to increasing disparities in wealth, so that while some freemen were reduced to selling the small plots which had come down to them and striking out on new pioneering ventures, or eking out their means by craftsmanship or hired labour, there must have been a number — ceorls as well as eorls — who had acquired sizeable properties worked by slaves or paid hands, and partly, it may be, let to tenants of their own. But however extensive the property, and in whatever way it was managed, this was still *folkland* — the term is met in a Kentish charter, of 858[69] — to which the customary rules of inheritance applied and owing stipulated rents and work services to the king, of which the *booklands* were free.

It seems that until the 8th century *bookland* was almost entirely confined to the church, for whose benefit the privileges and immunities going with it were confirmed by Wihtred at the Bapchild council. The absence of comprehensive records makes it difficult to say when in Kent, the creation of secular lordships began, but it seems that a few, modest, grants of *bookland* were made by the last of the Eskings to particularly valued officials or companions. The small property in Canterbury which Æthelberht gave to his cup-bearer Dunwalh (who later bequeathed it to St Augustine's) must have been of this kind,[70] as was Aldhun's estate at Bishopsbourne; a Christchurch account, speaking of the confiscation of this estate, makes that clear when it says it was as though Egbert were not allowed 'to bestow by charter lands by hereditary right'.[71] Since, however, every such grant involved the loss of rents and services in perpetuity, the Kentish kings were sparing of the privilege. The Mercians felt no such inhibition. To them the royal patrimony of Kent was disposable and could be used to win or reward loyalty, or (more especially in Cenwulf's case) sold for a quick profit. The tenants or under tenants of lands included in these conveyances, some of them ceorls and others occupiers of what had been royal *inlands*, now found themselves answerable for their rents and services to lords who were the servants of the hated usupers and might themselves be Mercians.

Offa's grant in 785, on the very eve of the reconquest, of an estate at Ickham to his thegn Ealdbeorht and a sister Selethryth (Kentish defectors whom we shall meet again) serves as an admirable model of the kind,[72] because the lands remained as an entity down to Norman times and were anatomized in Domesday Book. They consisted then of 12 ploughlands — there had been 14 at the time of the original grant — of which about two were in demesne,[73] four were *sulungs*, i.e. free *outland* holdings, and the remainder were *inland* tenancies; a well-balanced composition, indeed an appanage which some 60 years earlier the young Æthelberht had held as a prince (page 191 above). With these lands there went — as described in the last chapter — sheep runs at Ruckinge on Romney Marsh and three swine pastures in the Wealden hinterland. There were also woodlands in the local forests of Blean, Buckholt and Haradun, with a right to pasture swine in the royal *snade* there and to take building timber and firewood for domestic use or for salt pans, and carefully-defined fishing privileges at an unidentified weir, perhaps on the Little Stour which ran by the property. This, then, was a self-sufficient agricultural unit, with virtually every need provided, although small in comparison to the ecclesiastical lordships such as those of Christchurch, St Augustine's and Minster, which had been built up by a whole succession of grants. It was, in fact, already a prototype of the manor which it had become at the time of Domesday Book, a form to which other secular lordships, created out of single grants on much the same scale, were easily to take. It is perhaps even more significant that when, in due course, Ickham and its appurtenances passed into the ownership of Christchurch they continued to be administered as a separate unit. The amorphous ecclesiastical lordships were each beginning to crystallize into a number of defined estates with marshlands, woodlands and Wealden pastures apportioned between them; a devolution which completed the transition to a manorial system. The period of Mercian occupation marks a notable advance towards this, and the establishment of secular lordships was an important stage in the process.

With the reconquest of Kent Offa was at the height of his power. In 786 Cynewulf of Wessex was surprised and killed by a rival claimant to the throne, Cynheard, while on a visit to his mistress, an episode made famous because, on the king's death, his retainers refused all offers of mercy and fought to the last man, an example of loyalty followed by Cynheard's own retainers when he, too, had been killed by forces sent to avenge the king's death.[74] The throne of Wessex was now taken by Beorhtric, who was completely subservient to Offa and at his wish expelled the young Egbert, Ealhmund's son, who became for a time another refugee at Charlemagne's court.[75] The oppression in Kent appears to have been paralleled in East Anglia which broke into revolt *c.* 792 under a king called Æthelberht, who for a short time assumed control of the mint there, where a few coins were struck in his name;[76] but this rebellion was rapidly suppressed and Æthelberht was taken and beheaded.[77] Although Offa's influence extended to Northumbria he was wise enough not to embroil himself too deeply in the affairs of that country which had in the past so often been the ruin of Mercian hopes and was now rapidly degenerating into anarchy and chaos.[78] South of the Humber his control was absolute, and in order to perpetuate it in his line he had his son Ecgfrid anointed as joint king with him, the first recorded instance of royal consecration in England, but modelled upon Frankish practice followed by Charlemagne, with whom Offa aspired to be regarded as an equal.[79]

It was this, it seems, which caused the quarrel between the two men. Despite the uneasy situation created by the sanctuary given by Charlemagne to English fugitives he wished to be on friendly terms with Offa, and in or about 789 suggested that his son Charles should marry one of Offa's daughters. Offa's response to this was to suggest that his own son Ecgfrid should marry Charlemagne's daughter Bertha, a proposal that caused great offence.[80] Relations between the two men were broken off and Charlemagne closed his ports to English traders. They were eventually reopened after protracted negotiations largely conducted, on Charlemagne's behalf, by the Northumbrian expatriate Alcuin, and ending in what Stenton has described as the first commercial treaty in English history, by which it was agreed that traders from either country should be protected by the public authorities of the other and have access to the king in case of trouble.[81] The dispute reveals the magnitude of cross-Channel trade at the close of the 8th century, and the correspondence also shows, incidentally, that *sagae*, or woollen cloaks, were among the major English exports. With much of this traffic passing through Kentish ports and yielding a rich harvest in tolls, control over the kingdom had become more than ever a factor in the bid for English supremacy.

Offa died in 796 and his son Ecgfrid within a few months of him; a judgement, Alcuin suggested, for all the blood his father had shed.[82] Offa's greatness is indisputable, and the extraordinary achievement of his Dyke, constructed with an exact eye to topography along 70 miles of difficult border country, remains as visible testimony to it. No king in England had ever exercised power so ruthlessly, or made such an impact upon the international scene; as Stenton has said, English diplomatic history begins with him.[83] His reign presaged the end of what has been described as the heptarchy, because it crushed out the smaller kingdoms; but the detestation it aroused, and which was compounded by the barbarity of his successor Cenwulf, left the benefit to be reaped, 30 years later, by Egbert of Wessex, who was welcomed throughout the south as a liberator from Mercian oppression. On the very eve of Offa's death the Cantware, goaded beyond endurance, had once more risen in rebellion, defying without allies the power not only of Mercia but of the church, from which the appointment of Æthelhard as archbishop had estranged them.

The leader of this rebellion, Eadberht Pren, had been in holy orders.[84] He was no upstart, but almost certainly of royal blood. Henry of Huntingdon says that he was a kinsman of Egbert of Wessex and describes his later deposition as an unjust act,[85] a verdict echoed by the Norwich chronicler Bartholomew Cotton.[86] We cannot be sure that this represented a genuine tradition. It might have been an attempt to rationalize Egbert's claim to the Kentish throne; which, however, rested independently upon the reign of his father Ealhmund. Leaving aside the connections suggested by Eadberht's name, it is difficult to conceive that the Cantware would have turned to a priest to lead them had he not been of royal descent; and it is certain that even before the rebellion broke out Offa regarded him as a threat and Charlemagne a person to take account of. The web of inter-relationships created (it seems) by the past marriages of the Kentish princesses means that Egbert II of Kent and Ealhmund may well have been kin in at least some degree, and it is an intriguing possibility that Eadberht was a son of the elder Egbert, the victor of Otford, which would amply account both for the loyalty of the Cantware and Offa's hostility to him. Whatever the relationship, it seems clear that he had a respectable claim to the Kentish throne, or would have done so but for his calling.

Stubbs has suggested that he may have been forcibly inducted into the priesthood to pre-empt these claims,[87] a practice that was common at the time – in 790, for instance, a Northumbrian king, Osred, had been deposed and tonsured in this way.[88] Among so much that is uncertain the one thing that is clear is that he had the temperament, not of a priest, but of an embittered *atheling*. Whereas the future of the younger Egbert now lay in Wessex his own lot remained cast in Kent, where his presence must have acted as a focus for the loyalties of the Cantware.

In 796 we find Charlemagne writing to Offa about the arrival at his court of the priest Odberht (the Frankish form of Eadberht) together with 'other exiles who in fear of death have taken refuge under the wings of our protection'.[89] The letter was tactfully phrased but it is clear that Offa had come to regard Eadberht as a menace, and it seems, reading between the lines, that Æthelhard had been prevailed upon to threaten, harass and so get rid of this survivor of the rebel stock in much the same way as Beorhtric had been persuaded to expel the young Egbert. Charlemagne informed Offa that he had despatched Eadberht and his companions to Rome so that their cause, and Æthelhard's rejoinders, could be heard by the Pope; but if they ever started on this journey it is doubtful whether they completed it. The rebellion, which broke out before the end of the year, must already have been plotted, and one object of Egbert's audience with Charlemagne may well have been to feel out the possibilities of his support; the time for which, however, had passed since Charlemagne's breach with Offa had been healed and he was at pains in his letter to disclaim any sinister intentions. With or without support, the Cantware were now determined to act, and Eadberht returned, or was called, to lead them, renouncing his priesthood. Æthelhard's position at Canterbury had become perilous, and he was already contemplating flight, against which Alcuin urged him, but to no avail.[90] His abandonment of the see was an inglorious act, for which Alcuin was to suggest that he owed penance, but he himself was later to claim that he had been advised to it by the community of Christchurch.[91] This is very likely. He had been imposed upon the community and his presence in Canterbury at this time must have been an acute embarrassment to them. Had he stayed he could not possibly have acknowledged Eadberht and would have been courting martyrdom. The community, unhappily divided from their people and harrowed by the course of events, must have dreaded the prospect of the Cantware adding this sin to the guilt of Eadberht's appointment.

In an age without garrisons or standing armies a popular uprising of this kind was bound to be successful in the initial phase; the question was whether the Mercian counterattack could be resisted when it came. Those of Offa's thegns who had received estates in Kent must have been given short shrift; it is significant that the lands at Charing, Great Chart and Bishopsbourne became vacant so that Cenwulf was able to redispose of them when he eventually regained control of the country.[92] Isolated as the Cantware were, without a single ally to turn to, Offa's death, followed so shortly by that of Ecgfrid, was a singular stroke of fortune for them; because Cenwulf, coming unexpectedly to the Mercian throne, needed some time to establish himself before trying conclusions with Kent. Eadberht Pren was now installed at Canterbury, where he had taken the kingship. No charters of his have survived, and none could have been issued with ecclesiastical assent; but the Canterbury mint was striking silver pennies in his name and he is known to have employed no fewer than five moneyers, one of whom, Æthelnoth, used the same reverse die with obverses in the names of Offa and Eadberht respectively.[93] The rift between the Cantware and the church was not only a crippling weakness to the rebels but deeply disturbing to conservative churchmen like Alcuin, who can have had no illusions about Offa, and whose traditional sympathies inclined him towards Kent, but who realized the disastrous course on which the country was now set. In 797 he issued a remarkable appeal to the clergy and nobles of Kent (it seems that he could not bring himself to address Eadberht) urging them to recall Æthelhard and submit to his spiritual authority.[94]

The appeal was addressed to 'the most noble and praiseworthy people and the imperial kingdom of the Cantware'. It extolled the nation as the origin of imperial influence, the catholic faith, and of learning and prosperity in Britain; recalling the greatness of its teachers, the wisdom and dignity of its kings, the prowess of its people in war, their piety, fair judgements and honourable demeanour. This was flattery to a purpose; but it nevertheless expressed, however fulsomely, the esteem which generations of English churchmen had cherished for the kingdom of the Eskings, and was nowhere more sincere than in its lament that scarcely anywhere in England had the ancient royal lines survived. It was not only the flight of Æthelhard and the appearance on the Kentish throne of a renegade priest that perturbed Alcuin; he was also concerned at the disunity of the English people in the face of the new threat presented by the Norsemen. In 793 Lindisfarne had been plundered by these raiders,[95] a deed which had deeply shocked churchmen everywhere, and which Alcuin rightly regarded as a portent.[96] That south-eastern England had also been exposed to attack is clear from the agreement reached by Offa in 792 about the employment of Kentish levies against heathen pirates, not only in their own country, but in Sussex if need be (page 174 above). The attacks still appear to have been tentative, hit-and-run affairs, to which the coastal monasteries were especially vulnerable, and the Cantware must have regarded them as little more than a distraction compared to their major quarrel with the Mercians, but they were nevertheless a persistent threat in the background to the rebellion.

To the Kentish clergy Alcuin's appeal was superfluous. Much as they must have hated the Mercians, who had tyrannized over the people and debased the dignity of Canterbury, it was clearly impossible for them to support Eadberht Pren. Their sentiments must have been exactly those of Alcuin. There may also have been some among the nobles who needed no reminder of the hopelessness and untimeliness of this rebellion and what were all too likely to be its consequences. But among the Cantware in general the appeal went entirely unheeded. They were not, and had never been, the pious folk described in Alcuin's letter. The special relationship with the church had been the achievement of the Eskings, whom they had followed in loyalty and affection, and there was now nobody left to tend it. In this last extremity, left to their own devices, they were prepared to sacrifice every other consideration to the claims of nationhood. They were moved by more primitive feelings than Christianity could approve, a sense of injury and outraged pride which defied all prudence and overrode any responsibilities to a church which under Æthelhard's rule had appeared to abandon them. Eadberht Pren, in his own actions, had identified himself with the feelings of the nation; he embodied their qualities and failings; and they were prepared to follow him, to whatever uncertain or bitter end.

Cenwulf, too, can have had no illusions about what was at stake. His own authority depended upon crushing the Kentish revolt so mercilessly that no embers of resistance were left. For this the ground had to be thoroughly prepared, not only militarily but diplomatically. The first need was to settle his own differences with the church so that Kentish contumacy could be even more fully exposed. The English clergy had never reconciled themselves to the division of the province of Canterbury and the slight this had cast upon St Augustine's see; and with the menacing presence of Offa removed the controversy over this had evidently revived. Cenwulf, therefore, entered into correspondence with Pope Leo, freely admitting that Offa's true motives in the matter had been hatred of Jaenberht and the Kentishmen; hinting at the same time that an acceptable solution would be to reunite the province but to move the metropolitan seat from Canterbury to London, which would be in keeping with Gregory the Great's original intentions[97] (and also, although this he did not say, ensure Mercian control over it). In his reply Leo showed that he understood Cenwulf's intentions perfectly. He was not willing to break with long-established tradition by moving the see, but he announced that he was prepared to anathematize Eadberht Pren as an apostate priest and call upon all the English people to assist in ousting him.[98]

The isolation of Kent was now complete and its cause hopeless. Cenwulf had no need to risk another disaster like the battle of Otford, since he was in a position to bring an overwhelming strength to bear. The Anglo-Saxon Chronicle records that in 796 (correctly 798) he harried the Kentishmen as far as the land of the Merscware, that is Romney Marsh. Simeon of Durham has a more graphic account.[99]

'In these times' he says, 'Cenwulf, king of the Mercians, invaded the province of the people of Kent with the whole strength of his army, and mightily devastated it with a grievous pillaging almost to its utter destruction'.

We can only guess at the desperate nature of the resistance which provoked this treatment, towards which Cenwulf would, in any event, have needed little prompting, so great was the hatred between the two peoples. It was, it seems, as merciless a harrying as that to which, many years before, Penda and his Welsh allies had subjected Northumbria after Edwin had been killed (page 128 above); an exposure of the enduring savagery of the Mercian royal house who, for all their achievements of power, inflicted in their time immense damage and misery upon the English, and by doing so unfitted themselves for the supremacy to which they aspired. There can have been nothing heroic in this campaign against a cornered nation, but a story of slaughter and enslavement, the pillaging of stock and wastage of crops, from one end of the country to the other; and in it the independence of the Cantware was finally extinguished.

For Eadberht Pren there could be no escape. There was nowhere in the Christian world where he would have been received. He was driven to find hiding places in his own country until he was run down and led as a slave into Mercia,[100] where his hands were chopped off and his eyes put out. He suffered, Simeon of Durham tells us, 'because of the deceit and pride of these people"; words which may stand as a fair statement of the Mercian case. William of Malmesbury says that he was later manumitted by Cenwulf at the founding of Winchelcumbe Abbey.[101] This is another of those stories that one would like to believe. It may be wondered what value his freedom could have been to him in his mutilated state, but at least it would have restored to him a last shred of dignity and have meant that, at the end, he had made his peace with the church.

Epilogue

THE UNION WITH WESSEX

Egbert, son of Ealhmund, 798–825

ALTHOUGH THE CANTWARE survived the blood-letting of 798 it destroyed all hope of armed resistance for a generation. For more than 20 years the country was subjected to Cenwulf, who regarded it chiefly as a source of profit for himself and his family. His brother Cuthred was made king, a position he held until 807;[1] but he was given almost no independent authority, deferring to Cenwulf in everything he did, and was not replaced on his death, the appointment apparently having little other object than to put him in possession of the royal revenues. When the abbacy of St Augustine's fell vacant in 803 Cenwulf secured the election of another relative of his, Cunred;[2] and at about the same time, or a little earlier, his daughter Cwoenthryth was made Abbess of Minster in Thanet,* in succession to Sigeburga, who is said to have died in 797.

Effective control over the kingdom was exercised not so much through Cuthred as through ealdormen, of whom it seems that two had now been appointed, one for east and one for west Kent. The ealdorman of east Kent, Oswulf (so described in the adjudication of his will)[3] already held that rank on the very eve of the conquest.[4] He was a powerful and unscrupulous man, apparently a Kentish defector who had once been an adherent of Egbert II,[5] but who later made his peace with Offa, survived the uprising of Eadberht Pren, and profited greatly from his service to the Mercians, amassing large estates in Lyminge lathe on the fringe of Romney Marsh. The thegn Ealdebeorht and his sister Selethryth, to whom Offa had granted Ickham in 786,[6] were relatives of his,[7] who also gained handsomely from the Mercian connection, Selethryth becoming Abbess of Lyminge. The ealdorman of west Kent was a less important figure; the existence of the office is to be inferred from Oswulf's title, but there is no clear indication of its holder.

Yet in the five years that followed the conquest of Kent, the period of its deepest prostration, two events occurred of the greatest significance and hope for the future. In 802 Beorhtric of Wessex died and Egbert was recalled from exile to take the throne.[8] There must have been a number of *athelings* descended from the line of Cerdic[9] whose claims were as strong as his; but the rule of Beorhtric and his hated wife, Eadburh, daughter of Offa,[10] had sickened the people with the Mercians, and the choice of Egbert was a reassertion of their independence. On the very day that Egbert was installed a

---

* Probably in 798. According to Thomas of Elmham the Abbess Sigeburga died in the previous year (*Hist. Mon. S. Aug. Cant.* p. 221). Elmham says that she was succeeded by Siledretha, but this is clearly a confusion with Selethryth, who was Abbess of Lyminge at the time (CS 317); which is all the more evident because he then goes on to ascribe to Siledretha the dispute with Archbishop Wulfred over the possession of Minster lands in which Cweonthryth is known to have been the true protagonist (CS 378 and 384).

force from the Mercian province of the Hwicce crossed the Thames and invaded the country, but was met and defeated by the men of Wiltshire.[11] Cenwulf made no further attempt to interfere, a sign that his power did not reach as far as Offa's had done. But Egbert had none of the rashness of Eadberht Pren. He offered no immediate challenge to Cenwulf but for more than 20 years was content to bide his time, engaging in the traditional pursuit of the Wessex kings, campaigning against the British of the south-west, now hemmed into their ultimate stronghold of Cornwall.[12]

In the year of Egbert's return Canterbury was restored to its full metropolitan dignity, an event made inevitable by Cenwulf's admissions in his correspondence with Pope Leo and delayed only by the difficulties which Leo had been experiencing with his own enemies. In 801 Æthelhard visited Rome to discuss the matter; early in 802 he received a papal privilege confirming him in authority over all the English churches which had previously been subject to the see of Canterbury; and this was endorsed in the following year at a council at Clofeshoh, Hygeberht of Lichfield having retired uncomplainingly from the scene.[13] Æthelhard did not long survive this, dying in 805. For whatever reason, Cenwulf neglected the precaution of securing the see for another Mercian; and the community of Christchurch, moved no doubt by the wish to see their own welfare protected in a dangerous and unhappy time, elected one of their own number, Wulfred, who had been archdeacon of the diocese.[14] He was also, like Jaenberht, a Kentishman, with sizeable hereditary estates of his own, mostly in the lathe of Eastry.[15] No better choice could have been made. Gervase of Canterbury describes him as a 'most wise man' who 'in all his works . . . considered the advantage and peace of the church of Canterbury which he ruled'.[16] In defending the interests of his community, and the privileges of the church in general, he was led, step by step, into a duel with Cenwulf, whom he encountered with great resolution. Although he came to be on friendly terms with the Emperor Lewis, Charlemagne's heir, and was known and respected in Rome, his sympathies remained deeply rooted in his own soil. It was as though this descendant of the Kentish nobility had been called to act as caretaker for his people until in due course Egbert could claim his own.

There were two interwoven strands which ran through the whole of Wulfred's dealings with Cenwulf. The first was the attempt to combat the gross nepotism practised by the king in appointments to the abbacies; and the second a determination to increase, at every opportunity, the territorial lordship of Christchurch, so as to set the archbishop's own authority upon a firm material foundation. For this the circumstances were propitious. Cenwulf's avarice made him very ready to sell property the rents and services of which had been husbanded by the Kentish kings, and the immense devastation wreaked upon Kent in the reconquest of 798 meant that they could be acquired cheaply. Cenwulf's attitude was one of plunder; Wulfred's that of a trustee for a great institution. If the patrimony of the Eskings was to be squandered it was as well to gather as much as possible into the keeping of Christchurch, a more fitting repository for Kentish lands than Cenwulf's relatives or a host of adventurers and time-servers. It was impossible to separate this issue from that of control over the great monasteries. At the beginning of the 9th century St Augustine's and Minster must each have owned lands as extensive as those of Christchurch itself, and Lyminge and Reculver cannot have been far behind. The question was whether these foundations, the wealth and prestige of which already made them difficult subjects of the archbishop's authority, were now to be virtually subtracted from it, serving little better purpose than to provide rich livings for such as Cwoenthryth, who appears to have inherited all the worst characteristics of her father.

As we have seen, the issue of control over the monasteries had a long history behind it. The principle affirmed by Wihtred that there should be no royal interference in appointments, which should be made subject to the advice and confirmation of the bishops of the respective dioceses (including the archbishop in his own), had been endorsed by Æthelbald of Mercia and paid at least lip service by his successors (pages 172 and 186 above). It did not rule out all accommodations. Throughout the 8th century Minster in Thanet, for instance, had continued to be governed by abbesses of royal blood or connections; but nobody could question the fitness of Mildred and Eadburga, and Sigeburga was also described by the later chroniclers as 'blessed',[17] which must mean, if nothing more, that she took her religious duties seriously. But professions of principle meant little to the Mercian kings, who were able to make their power felt in Rome and whose good-will the Popes were anxious to retain. Offa succeeded in extracting from the insecure Hadrian a hereditary right of appointment to all the monasteries which he himself founded,[18] and a similar privilege was obtained by Cenwulf for his own great foundation at Winchelcumbe.[19] But Cenwulf went much further than this. In 798, when he appeared as the champion of the fugitive Æthelhard and enemy of the apostate Eadberht Pren, he was able so far to draw upon his credit with Pope Leo as to obtain for his son Kenelm the extraordinary privilege of making appointments to Glastonbury Abbey, the most prestigious of all the Wessex houses — an arrangement to which the abject Beorhtric was prepared to subscribe. The monastery of Cookham in Berkshire, which Æthelbald of Mercia had originally granted to Christchurch, but control over which had changed hands during the fighting between Cynewulf and Offa, was now made the dower of Offa's widow Cynthryth, Christchurch being given in exchange lands at Northfleet, Teynham and in the Cray valley,[20] which were supposed to be equivalent but in practice were not (as we shall show). It was entirely in keeping with this that Minster in Thanet and St Augustine's Abbey itself should have been treated as little more than spoils of conquest; although no more unsuitable incumbent for Minster could have been found than Cwoenthryth, and the best that can be said of Cunred, the heir to such illustrious predecessors as Hadrian, and placed in charge of the prime monastic foundation in England, is that nothing positive is known against him.

Æthelhard, restored to his see by Mercian arms, was in little position to challenge appointments of this kind, however much he may have deplored them; but so flagrant did they become that they exhausted the tolerance of Pope Leo. It seems that the matter must have been discussed during Æthelhard's visit to Rome in 801 because on his return the principles declared by Wihtred were reaffirmed, specifically at the Pope's bidding, at the ecclesiastical council held in 803 at Cloveshoh.[21] There was a significant absence, among the Kentish clergy who witnessed this document, of any of Cenwulf's nominees; but it was attested by Wulfred as archdeacon, and by the abbots Æthelheah and Feologeld, of whom the first seems to have been the incumbent at Reculver and the second of the small foundation of Dover.[22] These were survivors of the earlier order, and Feologeld was to become Wulfred's successor as archbishop (though only for a few months) which suggests that he was a confidant of his.[23] Whatever the Pope might enjoin, in Kent itself the damage had been largely done, but there were still ways in which it might be alleviated. Wulfred, on his election to Canterbury, was prepared to carry the fight beyond the question of appointments, acting upon the principle that the religious houses, independent foundations though they may have been, were as much subject to his authority as was Christchurch itself, to the extent indeed that their lands were at his disposal; a doctrine which he applied in 811 by transferring five ploughlands in Eastry lathe from the ownership of Reculver to that of Christchurch.[24] The monastery of Reculver, founded by Egbert I at the instance of Theodore of Tarsus, and over which Berhtwald had once presided, had always had particularly close connections with Christchurch. The same compliance could not be expected of Minster, where Cwoenthryth ruled with the backing of her father. Wulfred appears to have become embroiled with Cwoenthryth from the very beginning, and so inevitably with Cenwulf, a dispute which underlay all of their other dealings and was to lead in 817 to a complete rupture between them. It was as ferocious a quarrel as that between Offa and Jaenberht, and although a number of factors contributed to it control over the monastic lands was the central issue.

By the time Wulfred succeeded to the archbishopric it was already apparent that Christchurch could expect few favours from the king, whose generosity was reserved for his own thegns and kinsmen. Records survive of certain grants of land, near Cooling and at Chart Sutton, made to his companions,[25] and while a part of Oswulf's estate at Aldington may have been accumulated by purchase much of it was no doubt obtained for services rendered. The most munificent of all Cenwulf's gifts – 20 ploughlands at Lenham with 13 Wealden dens attached – was made to St Augustine's in 804,[26] the year after Cunred had become Abbot. The king's behaviour to Christchurch was grudging from the very beginning. Leaving aside the haggling over Cookham, in which Christchurch interests were given second place to those of the royal family, the most striking illustration of this was the handling of the estates at Charing, Great Chart and Bishopsbourne which Offa had confiscated. It was customary for a great victory, such as the reconquest of Kent, to be celebrated by some notable offering to the church, and Cenwulf did, indeed, restore these estates in thanksgiving for the triumph of his 'most dear Mercian people'; but in doing so he could not forbear to impose a charge of 100 *mancuses*,[27] a weight in gold equivalent in value to 3,000 of the new silver pennies,[28] or 6,000 of the earlier *sceattas*, and so to the *wer-geld* of a Kentish noble, which meant that, in effect, Christchurch was still being penalized for its dealings with Egbert II more than 20 years previously.

Æthelhard is not known to have received any other gifts from the king.* His pronouncement on the matter of ecclesiastical privileges, although avowedly inspired by the Pope, can have done nothing to endear him to Cenwulf, and he himself appears to have become disenchanted with the Mercian house. Any archbishop, whatever his antecedents, was liable insensibly to take on a Kentish complexion, and it looks as though during the last years of his life Æthelhard had come increasingly under the influence of Wulfred, whom he must have envisaged as his successor. Nevertheless it is curious to find this nominee of Offa, whom the Cantware had chased from his see, referring in the last years of his life to Aldhun, that earlier rebel and co-conspirator with Jaenberht and

---

* There is a record, apparently in a late 10th or early 11th century copy, of the grant to Christchurch in 799 of four ploughlands at Giddinge and Wootton (CS 296), but these are identical with the lands said in another document of no less reliability to have been granted by Caedwalla of Wessex in 687 (CS 69). It seems, therefore, that this was a restoration of property, at the best.

Egbert II, as 'a good man'.[29] If Æthelhard had been shabbily treated Wulfred could certainly expect no better. It was, however, possible to take advantage of the king's avarice by buying up lands from him, and this was the policy which Wulfred set himself to pursue. It is remarkable that throughout the 12 years of deepening hostility which preceded the final rupture between the two men this process of chaffering went on. Only at the end did the king take alarm at the steadily strengthening resources of Christchurch. He had become a victim of his own cupidity, and the realization of this appears to have added to the fury which the dispute over the control of the monasteries had provoked.

Never had there been a better opportunity to invest in land, or a greater need to bring it into secure stewardship. As any prudent person might have foreseen, this was an asset which was bound to appreciate. The vicious harrying of Kent had left a wasted and grievously depopulated countryside, with stocks lifted, crops destroyed and buildings burned, so that many of the tenements could no longer be properly worked nor yield the customary rents and services. We need not rely upon Simeon of Durham's account for this;[30] it shows clearly in the assessment of yield. The actual prices paid for the land are of little use as a guide. Commonly the payments were made in a weight of gold or silver – the *mancus* or the pound of coin – and although these can be converted to a common standard of the silver penny, at a rate of about 30 to the golden *mancus* and 240 to the pound,[31] we are still left with no reliable basis for comparison whether in place or time. There is, however, evidence of a different kind. The key document here is a charter of 812 which recounts an exchange between Wulfred and Cenwulf of a small property at Swarling (in Petham) for another at Graveney near Faversham;[32] the significant feature of which is the equation struck between one *sulung*, in the Kentish reckoning, and two *hides*, in the Mercian. These, as we have seen, were units of assessment, regulating the obligations of the tenants in areas defined for that purpose (in Kent considerably larger than in Mercia), and a conversion was necessary because, rents and agricultural services apart, it was in terms of the *hide* that such public duties as military service, the repair of bridges and upkeep of fortifications were apportioned throughout the Mercian dominions. But the relationship expressed in this charter was not, as has been commonly supposed, a stable one which had always applied. We have given reasons in Chapter Three for believing that in Bede's time, and later in the 8th century, a Kentish ploughland (of which the *sulung* was a special kind) was considered the equivalent of five *hides*; and, indeed, this appears to have been the relationship adopted in assessing the compensation to be given to Christchurch, in Kent, for the loss of the lands at Cookham Abbey, outside it,* not surprisingly perhaps, since the effect was to short-change Christchurch by ignoring the devastation of the Kentish lands in the valuation. It seems, however, that by 812 there had been a tardy recognition of the very sharp decline which had occurred in the value of property in Kent, measured by what could be exacted from the tenants; and this could not fail to be reflected in its price. There is also some evidence, to which we shall come later, which suggests that the value

---

* The account of the transaction (CS 291) shows the allotment to Christchurch of what was supposed to be the equivalent of 110 *hides*; 60 at Northfleet, 30 at Teynham and 20 in the Cray valley. Northfleet provides the clearest comparison. Domesday Book shows that the archbishop owned 14 ploughlands here, which accords closely to the formula of five *hides* to one ploughland, assuming a small addition of land in the intervening years. The formula of two *hides* to one ploughland (or *sulung*) comes nowhere near the mark.

recovered as the scars of the Mercian conquest healed, a new generation grew up, and the land was restocked. And this is precisely what might have been expected.

While circumstances may have impelled the quarrel between Wulfred and Cenwulf its violence also suggests a deep personal antipathy. Wulfred as a churchman, and Æthelhard's archdeacon at that, can have had nothing to do with the rebellion of Eadberht Pren, which could only have caused him the same acute distress and conflict of feeling as it did Alcuin. But no civilized man, much less a Kentishman, could have felt anything but abhorrence for the cruelty with which the rebellion was suppressed. As archbishop, Wulfred had become the last repository of the dignity and independence of his people. It was one of the privileges of his office to mint his own silver coins at Canterbury, and it has been noted that whereas Æthelhard dutifully stamped the name of the Mercian king on the obverse Wulfred did not;[33] a straw in the wind, perhaps, but indicative nonetheless. There were ways in which ecclesiastical influence could be used on behalf of the victims of Cenwulf's savagery. If the chroniclers' account of the manumission of Eadberht Pren at the founding of Winchelcumbe Abbey is to be believed[34] it must have been done at the intercession of the church, and that it was the work of Wulfred rather than Æthelhard appears from the only record we have of the event, which shows his presence as archbishop, together with Cuthred.[35] The record itself is a late and obviously faulty one (not least in its dating of the event to 811, whereas for both Wulfred and Cuthred to have been present in must have occurred between 805 and 807) but Haddan and Stubbs believe it to have been concocted out of a true tradition, which the chroniclers preserved.[36] Wulfred's intercession would certainly have been in keeping. Christian charity apart, he must have known Eadberht Pren not only at the time of his rebellion but in the earlier days of his priesthood at Canterbury.

While Cuthred was alive he provided some sort of buffer between Wulfred and the king. Even on his death there existed a rudimentary council of Kent, over which Wulfred presided by virtue of his office, and although in Cenwulf's eyes it may have had no other function than to endorse what he dictated it was nevertheless a forum in which the archbishop's influence could be brought to bear upon the leading men of the country. These were mostly remnants of the old Kentish nobility, men who were prepared to serve a Mercian king but shared a common background with Wulfred. We have a brief glimpse of this body in action in 810 when a land transaction between Cenwulf and Wulfred, which had been approved by a Mercian council, was sent to be endorsced by the Kentish 'satraps', a number of whom bore such evocative names as Wihtred, Eadberht and Esne.[37] Wulfred's personality, in which great firmness was combined with diplomatic skills, was bound to impress itself upon this company, and he must very early on have begun to acquire that moral leadership among his own people which was to become so apparent later, and which his office alone could not have earned him. Cenwulf's omission to replace Cuthred may have been due to a suspicion that anyone appointed as sub-king was liableto become infected with Kentish sympathies; but the effect was to surrender this field of influence to Wulfred.

Already by 808 the hostility between the two men was sufficiently notorious for Pope Leo to deplore it in a letter to Charlemagne.[38] All else apart, Cwoenthryth's activities had become a major provocation. According to a later account by Wulfred himself they descended to the outright theft of a property at Easole (in Nonnington) which had been bequeathed to Christchurch by Ealdebeorht and his sister the Abbess Selethryth, on whose deaths, however, the deeds were stolen by their kinsman Oswulf and handed to Cwoenthryth, who refused to release either them or the land.[39] The event can be dated to this period because it is known that Selethryth was still alive in 804 and that Ealdebeorht survived her,[40] and because Oswulf had died by 810, when a dispute arose over his own will.[41] Whether he was trying to ingratiate himself with Cwoenthryth, or was acting as ealdorman on instructions from the king, it is impossible to say; but it seems that at the end of his life he repented of his conduct towards Christchurch, or feared that it had imperilled his soul, since he gave the community the reversion of the whole of his large estate at Aldington after the deaths of the immediate heirs, a son and daughter, on condition that prayers should be said for him. The deed was contested but it finally became effective in 844.[42].

The growing animosity between Wulfred and Cenwulf did not interrupt the land dealings, in which each was pursuing his own ends. By 811 Wulfred had acquired for Christchurch, by purchase or exchange, sizeable properties at Barham, Petham, Rainham and Graveney, at several others places near Faversham, and in the Snargate area of Romney Marsh.[43] The period also saw the beginning of that division between the property of the archbishop and his community which was to be completed and systematized by Lanfranc 250 years later.[44] Partly this was due to the fact that Wulfred was a considerable landowner in his own right. In 811 he came to an agreement with the community by which he made over to them four ploughlands from his own inheritance in Eastry lathe, in return for the estate at Bishopsbourne which had originally belonged to Aldhun but had suffered so many vicissitudes since;[45] and in 824 he made a similar exchange of five ploughlands at Eythorne and Langdon for the equivalent at Barham (neighbouring Bishopsbourne).[46] The object of these transactions is plain. Wulfred's private estates were too far from Canterbury for him to have the full enjoyment of them. Bishopsbourne, only five miles distant and situated on the banks of the little Stour with a backing of downland and wood, was admirably placed for leisure and recreation — which is no doubt why it had previously been awarded to Aldhun when he had been Egbert's reeve in Canterbury. On Wulfred's death the property remained with his successors, becoming the archbishop's own manor, a principle of separation which in later years was to be carried much further.

All this was accompanied by internal reforms at Christchurch.[47] This was not a monastic community; indeed St Augustine's companions, whom he had ordained as clerks, had been released by him from their monastic obligations, and a number of the boys whom he trained to the church were allowed to marry, remain in minor orders, and receive stipends. Nevertheless it was expected that the Archbishop's *familia* should live a communal life. In the course of time there had been a departure from this strict régime; presbyters were now to be found living in their own houses and enjoying stipends, a practice which St Boniface had deplored as uncanonical. Wulfred set himself to restore the old order and discipline, and in particular the sense of community which was needed if religious life was to flourish and the institution to hold its own against the great monastic establishments like St Augustine's, always its rival. Whatever else they may have achieved, however, these reforms came too late to arrest the catastrophic decline in scholarship which began during the years of Mercian domination and is marked by the increasing clumsiness and flawed grammar of the Latin texts of the period, until some 50 years later the syntactical struggle was abandoned altogether for use of the vernacular.[48] No doubt the disturbed conditions of the kingdom had been the prime cause of this, but it must also have been aggravated by the nepotism of the Mercian kings (the contrast between Minster under the rule of Eadburga and of Cwoenthryth is especially striking); and the Viking attacks, from which the monasteries were among the first to suffer, hastened the degeneration.

The years 812–814 saw a significant shift in the relationship between Wulfred and the king. During this period, quite uncharacteristically, Cenwulf made certain free grants of land to Christchurch; 22 yokes (five and a half ploughlands) near Faversham, 30 yokes (seven and a half ploughlands) near Canterbury, and ten ploughlands at Bexley with five Wealden dens annexed.[49] This generosity is all the more puzzling because at the end of the period Wulfred visited Rome, accompanied by the bishop of Sherborne (in whose see Glastonbury lay)[50] almost certainly, it seems — and all the more clearly in the light of later events — to complain to the Pope about the infractions of ecclesiastical privilege caused by the activities of Cwoenthryth, and of Kenelm in Wessex. It looks very much as though Cenwulf had been trying during the two preceding years to head off these complaints, or he may already have been planning to take control of Reculver and its estates and was hoping to purchase Wulfred's acquiescence. If so, the attempt failed. Nevertheless the Pope must have been able to exercise some mediating influence, which postponed the final rupture for three years. In 815 the haggling was resumed with the sale by Cenwulf to the archbishop of a small portion of land near Faversham for a gold ring of 23 *mancuses*;[51] and early in 817 Wulfred attended a Mercian council to witness certain grants of land to the see of Worcester.[52]

It was later in that year that the hostility between the two men broke into open enmity. It is probable, as Haddan and Stubbs surmised, that Cenwulf had by then become thoroughly jealous of the friendship that had developed between Wulfred and the Emperor Lewis,[53] and he may well also have been alarmed at the position of influence and strength that Wulfred had built up for himself in Kent; but, according to a later account, the issue which precipitated the quarrel was control over the monasteries of Minster and Reculver.[54] Wulfred could scarcely have hoped to exercise any effective authority over Minster while Cwoenthryth was there; but Reculver had hitherto been kept out of the king's hands and firmly within his own. There is no evidence that the abbot of the time, Beornwine,[55] was a Mercian nominee, and he had (as we have seen) concurred in 811 to the transfer of some of the Abbey's lands to Christchurch. This action was probably not as arbitrary as it may seem, but prompted by a decline in the size of the community, for which the reason is not far to seek. The raids of the Norsemen were becoming more frequent, and bolder; the charters show, significantly, that the duty of constructing fortifications against the heathen pirates had now been extended to include the destruction of those which they themselves had built.[56] The coastal monasteries were particularly easy and tempting targets. Already there is a complete and ominous silence about those at Sheppey and Hoo, and by 804 it had been found necessary to provide the nuns of Lyminge with a place of refuge in Canterbury.[57] Reculver, cut off by the Wantsum channel on one side and hemmed in by Blean Forest on the other, was exceptionally isolated and exposed, and only the truly dedicated can have chosen to remain there. It was reasonable to redistribute lands that were no longer needed to sustain a shrinking community, which may well have become unable to manage them properly. The question was by whom this was to be done, and to whose advantage.

As Stenton has pointed out, the only account we have of the dispute is an *ex parte* one written from Wulfred's standpoint and couched in such execrable Latin that at important points it becomes almost impossible to construe.[58] What appears to have happened, however, is that Cenwulf claimed the full right to the disposal of Reculver's property and revenues, much of which he assumed himself or transferred to his daughter Cwoenthryth at Minster. In doing so he must have realized that Wulfred was bound to respond to this challenge, and it looks as though the issue had been deliberately forced as a means of undermining his authority for good and all; to ensure which, and as a pre-emptive measure, Cenwulf lodged certain unrecorded, but evidently serious, charges against him at Rome (we may guess, of peculation, to which Wulfred's financial pre-occupations exposed him). The result was that for four years, as these charges were being considered and answered, Wulfred was prevented from exercising his office. We can discount, as a palpable exaggeration, the later claim that because of this the English race were deprived of baptisms,[59] but the effect on the life of the church must have been serious enough without this. Cenwulf may have hoped that he had got rid of this troublesome priest for good, but however protracted the proceedings Wulfred evidently succeeded in winning the support of the Emperor Lewis and eventually also of Pope Paschal. In these circumstances the king resorted to naked force. In 821 he summoned Wulfred to London and confronted him with an ultimatum. Either he was to surrender an estate of 300 *hides* and pay a fine of £120 — in which case the king would withdraw the charges he had made — or else he would be stripped of all he had and the king would refuse to take him back, 'whatever the Pope, the Emperor or anyone else might say'.[60] For the time Wulfred had been left powerless and had no choice but to comply with the terms dictated to him.

The fine inflicted upon Wulfred (converting to 28,800 silver pennies) was equivalent to the *wer-geld* of a Mercian *atheling*,[61] and compares with the payment made by Wihtred to Ine for the killing of the Wessex prince Mul. To add to this the forfeit of what must, on any reckoning, have been a very large estate was no doubt intended to be crippling; it would destroy the basis of material power which Wulfred had so assiduously built up. But the reckoning is important, and it is relevant to this to identify the estate, if that can be done. It must have been in Kent, since Christchurch at this time had very few properties outside, and certainly none of this magnitude. If we were to adopt the equation used in 811 then the 300 *hides* would convert, in Kentish terms, to 150 *sulungs*, or ploughlands. The estate is described in the record as *Iognes hamme*, and Du Boulay has suggested that 'just possibly' it might have been Ickham.[62] But the number of ploughlands at Ickham was only 14,[63] and at the time of Domesday Book, when the lands owned by the archbishop and Christchurch had been greatly augmented, there was not one of their manors which approached 150 ploughlands in size. If, however, we assume that with the passage of nearly 25 years since the conquest of Kent the country had recovered sufficiently for the old norm of one *sulung*, or ploughland, to five *hides* to have beome reinstated we are left with the much more credible total of 60 plough-lands. This is still larger than any of the estates that Christchurch is known to have owned at this time, but it can be matched with three or four of those appearing in Domesday Book. Of these Aldington, Lyminge and Otford must all be dismissed, not only because their names in no way resemble *Iognes hamme*, but because there is clear evidence that they were obtained after 821. There remains Wingham (*Uuigincgga ham*,

824),[64] which shows what is perhaps sufficient similarity of name, given the general illiteracy of the document; which was one of the largest of the archbishop's manors in Norman times; but the origin of which is wrapped in mystery since no record of its acquisition survives. It might, in fact, have been one of the first grants made to Christchurch by the Kentish kings. But it is perhaps foolhardy to venture any identification. The significant point is the return to the earlier valuation, and what that implies.

The same point can be illustrated from another document some ten years later in date. When Wulfred died in 832 he left much of his newly acquired land to his nephew Werhard, a priest, with a reversion to Christchurch; and Werhard's own will, made in the same year to honour this agreement, defines the various estates in *hides*, since not all were in Kent.[65] Once again, if we try to convert the figures for the Kentish estates into ploughlands we find that they are too high to be reconciled with the 2 : 1 ratio but fit with a ratio of 5 : 1. The clearest example is provided by a property at Barham which Wulfred had acquired in 824, when it was said to consist of five ploughlands,[66] and which was entered in Werhard's will as 32 *hides*. This conforms closely to the 5 : 1 standard if we allow for a small unrecorded addition, whereas the 2 : 1 standard would imply that the estate had more than trebled in size over a period of eight years; and on the same criterion the figures given for the other Kentish properties would show an equally improbable expansion.

Cenwulf died in the same year that he imposed his sanction upon Wulfred, and if the penalty was ever exacted it was soon made good. The nemesis of the Mercian royal house was now approaching, a collapse that began through its own internal rottenness. Cenwulf's son Kenelm was murdered, a deed in which the chroniclers say that Cwoenthryth had a hand;[67] an unjust accusation perhaps, but illustrating her evil reputation. The throne was then taken by her uncle Ceolwulf, who held it for less than two years before he was himself deposed and replaced by a certain Beornwulf, who appears to have been one of the less distinguished Mercian ealdormen.[68] This was the end of the illustrious line of the *Icelingas*, descended, so tradition said, from the ancient kings of Angel; and it carried the power of Mercia down with it. Neither Ceolwulf, nor his successor Beornwulf, can have felt secure in his position, and least of all in Kent; a situation reflected in the current coinage. Of the six mints then operating at Canterbury only two struck coins in Ceolwulf's name, the others resorting to the ambiguous practice of replacing the king's name on the obverse with that of the moneyer and naming the mint itself on the reverse; and none of them struck any coins at all for Beornwulf.[69] Both men were anxious to placate Wulfred, who as archbishop remained the one stable element in the shifting scene, and whose influence was now paramount in a rapidly reviving Kent. During the twilight years of Mercian rule Wulfred rounded off his policy of acquisition by two important purchases from Ceolwulf; five ploughlands near Kemsing with three Wealden dens attached,[70] which were to form the nucleus of what later became the great manor of Otford, and 30 yokes (the equivalent of seven and a half ploughlands) in Canterbury, for which he gave 'a choice dish of gold and silver estimated at £5½'.[71] He received from the propitiatory Beornwulf the gift of eight ploughlands at Godmersham.[72] And he settled accounts with Cwoenthryth, who on Ceolwulf's deposition was deprived of the protection of royal kinsmen. She was summoned to an ecclesiastical council at Clofeshoh, attended by Beornwulf, to answer as Cenwulf's heir for the violence and rapacity of his dealings, and, while remaining abbess of Minster, was compelled to surrender to Christchurch in compensation for them considerable lands in Harrow and elsewhere in Middlesex, besides restoring the property at Easole the deeds of which Oswulf had stolen.[73] Beornwulf's eagerness to ingratiate himself with Wulfred suggests that already a rival claimant — Baldred — had appeared in Kent, and that he recognized, as others did, that the Cantware would now follow where Wulfred led.

The first 20 years of Wulfred's archiepiscopacy, which were to be the last of Mercian domination, mark the watershed in the passage of Kent from the relatively simple community of Æthelberht's time, in which the king was sole territorial lord, to the involved hierarchical society displayed in Domesday Book. The scale on which the Mercian kings divested themselves of land will never be precisely known because, while their dealings with Christchurch and the other ecclesiastical establishments are on record, only a few scraps of information survive about their transactions with the laity; such, for instance, as Cuthred's sale in 805 to Æthelnoth, the reeve of Eastry lathe, of four ploughlands at Eythorne, for the price of 3,000 silver pence.[74] An indication of the amount of property which had passed to private individuals is to be found in the multiplication of bequests, since the very fact that land was capable of being freely willed shows that it had been obtained by the 'book'. In addition to the bequests made by such powerful figures as Oswulf and Ealdebeorht, favourites of the king, we find, for example, that the reeve Abba, whose *wer-geld* was only that of a ceorl, was able in 835 to dispose of the income of considerable lands, mostly at Challock and Chillenden, which had doubtless been amassed during this time.[75] Wulfred can have been by no means the only one to take advantage of a buyer's market. Although at the end of the period most of Kent may still have been in the king's own lordship he can now have been left with only a minority holding in the old lathe of Thanet, and a bare majority, if that, in those of Eastry, Canterbury and Lyminge, while significant inroads had also been made on most of the other lathes, even such a small and remote one as Hollingbourne (with the disposal of Lenham and Chart Sutton). But Wulfred's careful husbandry had ensured that of all the ecclesiastical and lay lordships that of the archbishop and the community of Christchurch had become, as it was to remain, pre-eminent. The principle of ecclesiastical authority for which he had fought was also to bring its reward. One the eventual destruction of the coastal monasteries by the Danes the lands of Minster were to pass to St Augustine's Abbey, but those of Lyminge, Reculver and, for a time, Folkestone to Christchurch;[76] a considerable accretion of wealth.

A large stride had therefore been taken along the road which led, by the Norman Conquest, to something like a third of all the lands in Kent belonging either to the archbishop or the community of Christchurch, while those of the king had dwindled to less than ten per cent, with nothing at all remaining in the north-east except the port of Fordwich (a last remnant of the once royal vill of Sturry) and an estate of Barham, which was itself in the archbishop's occupation.[77] Whereas the lordship of St Augustine's was virtually confined to east Kent,[78] and that of the bishop of Rochester entirely to west, the Canterbury lands extended to every part of the county, and beyond into Surrey, Middlesex and Sussex, and even as far afield as Buckinghamshire and Suffolk.[79] This rested upon the foundation of Wulfred's work, improved by his successors. The period also witnessed the distillation of the lordships into what can properly be described as manors. We have shown in the previous chapter how the small lay lordships were virtually indistinguishable from manors from their inception, and how the great ecclesiastical lordships were becoming congeries of individual estates, each separately administered and with its own appurtenances of marshland, wood or Wealden dens. The shrinkage of the royal lands completed this process, because the residue left in any lathe became, in effect, a manor little different, except perhaps in size, from those surrounding it. When, towards the end of his life, Wulfred made a gift to Christchurch of some of his hereditary land near Wingham he defined it by reference to neighbouring estates, among which 'the king's land which belongs to Eastry' featured as the eastern boundary exactly as though it were any other property.[80] While the basis of Kentish society — the terms on which the individual husbandman held his land — still endured the whole superstructure was changing.

Another, equally momentous change was in preparation. The disarray in Mercia caused by the deaths of Cenwulf and Kenelm, the deposition of Ceowulf, and the succession of a hitherto obscure ealdorman, gave Egbert of Wessex the opportunity for which he had evidently been waiting. In 825 the Mercian army, led by Beornwulf, was defeated at Ellendun[81] (Wroughton, a little way to the south of Swindon)[82] in that border country on the fringe of the White Horse Vale which had long been contested between the two kingdoms. For 200 years, ever since Penda had seized the province of the Hwicce, they had fought for possession of the lands astride the Thames, with the balance of advantage passing steadily to Mercia despite momentary rallies by Wessex, as in Ine's time. At first sight there might seem little reason why Ellendun should prove any different from all the previous battles in this fluctuating conflict; but, in fact, it was conclusive. Partly, no doubt, this was because the extinction of the royal line of the *Icelingas* had deprived Mercia of an effective rallying point; but chiefly it was that after Cenwulf's rule, following upon those of Offa and Æthelbald, it needed only a single jolt for the whole structure of Mercian power to collapse under the weight of its own oppression. Throughout all south-eastern England, and in East Anglia too, the people had been waiting for the deliverance that this victory promised.

The battle precipitated a break-up of the Mercian empire which seems to have begun a little before it. In Kent this was associated with the fleeting appearance of a king called Baldred. Some of the chroniclers, such as Roger of Wendover, suggest that he had succeeded Cuthred as sub-king in 807,[83] but there is absolutely no warrant for this. He appears nowhere as a witness to the numerous charters issued by Cenwulf, nor to those of Ceolwulf, who styled himself uncompromisingly 'King of the Mercians and of the Kentishmen';[84] nor even was he present at the council of Clofeshoh in 825 when Beornwulf presided over the adjudication of the dispute between Wulfred and Cwoenthryth. All we know of him is that he held power sufficiently long for some silver pennies to be struck at Canterbury in his name; that Egbert drove him out; and that in the very moment of his flight he issued a charter granting Christchurch a large estate at Malling, near Lewes in Sussex, with swine pastures reaching as deep into the Weald as Wadhurst.[85] That he had already made his appearance before the battle of Ellendun must follow from the statement of the Anglo-Saxon Chronicle that Egbert intervened in Kent immediately after it;[86] and the fact that the Canterbury mints produced coins for him, but none for Beornwulf,[87] suggests that, whatever authority Beornwulf may have claimed over Kent (for instance in the proceedings at Clofeshoh) it had effectively passed into Baldred's control from the time of Ceowulf's deposition in 823. The probability is that Baldred, too, was an ealdorman, perhaps from Sussex, who recognized the weakness of Beornwulf's position and decided to carve out a kingdom for himself, trading upon the hatred of Mercian rule felt everywhere in the south-east; and that for a brief spell he succeeded in uniting under his authority Kent, Sussex and Surrey, from all of which Egbert was to expel him.

The battle of Ellendun was as much as disaster for Baldred as for Beornwulf: it brought into the field an adversary who was not only more powerfully backed but had a much stronger claim upon the loyalties of the Cantware. A reinvigorated Kent, because of its reputation and resources, and as the seat of ecclesiastical authority, was the key to the whole of the south-east, and more. Whereas Mercia had despoiled it, it might be honourably united with Wessex, and the strength of that union would make the verdict of Ellendun irreversible. This prize was now within Egbert's reach, and we can believe the Chronicle when it says that his first concern after the battle was to grasp it. We are told that he immediately detached from his levies his son Æthelwulf with a large force and sent him into Kent, accompanied by Eahlstan, the bishop of Sherborne, where he drove Baldred north over the Thames; and that the Kentishmen, and the men of Surrey, Sussex and Essex submitted to him (Egbert) 'because formerly they had been wrongly forced away from his kinsmen'.[88] That both contenders recognized the decisive influence wielded by Wulfred among his own countrymen is shown by Egbert's despatch of the bishop of Sherborne with his army, and by Baldred's hasty gift of the lands at Malling to Christchurch, a last minute attempt to buy support, or a promissory note to be redeemed if he should regain the kingdom. But the decision can never have been seriously in doubt. In Egbert the Cantware were receiving their lawful king, the son of Ealhmund who had once ruled them and the head of the only surviving branch which had sprung from the stock of the Eskings. There can have been little thought of resistance in favour of the adventurer Baldred, however much me may have tried to woo them. Egbert's claims to Surrey and Sussex were also well founded, since both had belonged to his predecessor Ine. His right to Essex was far more debatable. The only possible cause to be made out was that it had once, more than 200 years previously, been a dependency of the Eskings, whose heir Egbert had become; but Essex had always been the prize of the dominant power of the time, and legalities mattered less than control over London.

It was not only the south-east that was now wrested from Mercia. The Chronicle tells us that 'the king of the East Angles' (whoever he may have been) 'and the court turned to Egbert as their protector and guardian against the fear of Mercian aggression; and the same year the East Angles slew Beornwulf, king of the Mercians'.[89] The triumph of Wessex was complete. For a brief period Mercia ceased to exist and although it was to recover its independence under a certain Wiglaf[90] it was never again in a position to contest the supremacy of England, and 40 years later was to be overwhelmed by the Danes, whom Wessex alone had the strength to resist. Of Baldred nothing more is heard. Wulfred lived for seven years longer, in high respect and in harmony with Egbert, but with the events of 825 the greater part of his work had been done. The privileges of the church had been upheld, Kent delivered, and his own community of Christchurch immeasurably strengthened; even the estate of Malling, which had come to him in such dubious circumstances, was to be confirmed to his successors.

Although the enlarged Kingdom of Wessex was regarded as a unity it was the practice, during the earlier years, for the presumptive heir to be put in charge of the four south-eastern provinces with the title King of Kent. Æthelwulf held this position until he succeeded his father Egbert, and returned to it again at the end of his life when he had resigned the throne of Wessex. Three of his five sons — Æthelstan, Æthelbald and Æthelberht (note the names) — each in his turn took the title before its eventual abandonment in 860.[91] By that time the Danish onslaughts had firmly welded Kent into the Kingdom of Wessex, and the loyalty of the Cantware to its ruling line, which preserved the last connection with their own and whose kings bore in their very names the hall-mark of the Eskings, had become absolute. It was upon Kent that the brunt of the first Danish attacks fell;[92] and when Alfred (Ælfred), the youngest of Æthelwulf's sons, came to the throne of Wessex in 871 the fate of Kent was involved with that of the whole of southern England in a single struggle for survival.

During the 350 years of its independent existence Kent, one of the smallest of the kingdoms, had contributed as greatly as any to the formation of England; and at the very end it had the casting vote in deciding the contest for mastery between Mercia and Wessex. It had shown, more clearly than any of the kingdoms, that England could not endure Mercian rule, and in Egbert had united the prestige of its own royal house with that of the *Gewissae*. This was not a matter merely of dynastic chance; the choice had been foreshadowed as early as 694 in the agreement reached between Wihtred and Ine, and although after that the two nations had from time to time drifted — or been forced — apart, they were always in the end to return to an alliance of which the dynastic connection was not the cause, but an effect. For Kent the stake had at first been its independence, and later, when hope of that had vanished, the pride and integrity of its people.

The triumph of Egbert and the onset of the Danish wars effectively marked the end of what has become known as the heptarchy. There is a tendency to interpret the events of the time in purely geopolitical terms, by which it is made to seem inevitable that the supremacy, which passed in their day to the rulers of six separate nations, would come to rest on one of the expanding border kingdoms of Northumbria, Mercia or Wessex, among which Wessex had the advantage that in dealing with the British of the south-west it had an encompassable task, unlike that which confronted the Mercians in Wales or the Northumbrians in the north. There may be a large element of truth in this generalization, but there is also a great deal of hindsight, which ignores personality, chance, the expediency of kings and the temper of their peoples.

The end might have been very different. Among the nations whose rulers at one time or another held the *bretwaldaship* Sussex was too small and remote ever to have had a serious chance of maintaining the lead which the military prowess of Aelle briefly gained for it. It is easy, however, to imagine circumstances in which (but for a fatal loss of momentum) the ascendancy won by Æthelberht might have been perpetuated through the moral authority of the Christian mission backed by the magnificence and wealth of the Kentish court. There was a time at the beginning of the 7th century when it seemed that East Anglia, which under the rule of Raedwald had broken out of its geographical isolation, might have captured the middle ground of England before the power of Mercia had begun to emerge. Northumbria's withdrawal from the contest after producing three *bretwaldas* in succession, and its decline into anarchy, was not only due to the fact that its military ambitions tore it in two directions, north and south, but that the very splendour of its spiritual and intellectual achievement contained in it destructive seeds of pietism implanted by the Celtic church; and that withdrawal profoundly affected the security of the southern kingdoms by removing the counterpoise to Mercian aggression. That Wessex took so long to realize its potential after the start that Ceawlin's campaigns against the British had given it seems to have been due, as much as anything, to a conception of kingship which made for divided rule, a weakness which Æthelberht was the first to recognize and exploit. To consider what might have happened had this or that gone differently is deplored by most historians as pointless, and so no doubt it usually is, but it can sometimes have a value in correcting too determinist a philosophy.

There is one contrast that needs to be emphasized, because so much stemmed from it. Never throughout this period did Wessex desist from campaigning against the British. But when Mercia emerged as a power in the second quarter of the 7th century it was in alliance with the Welsh, and despite occasional forays and expeditions the object of its later rulers was not to conquer Wales — which would have led them into a quicksand — but to fence it off, a policy most strikingly exemplified by Offa's Dyke. The alliance made by Penda in 633 had evil consequences. It imported into domestic wars between the English kingdoms a savagery which they had previously reserved for their Celtic enemies; and although Penda's sons Wulfhere and Æthelred appear in retrospect to have been relatively civilized and humane men their successors resorted to atrocity whenever it suited their ends. The interests of Mercia — that pike among the kingdoms — were turned in upon England. While by the end of the 7th century it had abandoned its attempts against Northumbria, the two powers having fought themselves to a standstill, it was determined to grasp the whole of the south; and in order to dispose of its chief rival Wessex it needed first to subdue the smaller eastern kingdoms. Of these Essex was easily reduced to clienthood and Sussex was first lured and then trapped by the bait of lands belonging to Wessex. But East Anglia and Kent were kingdoms with a proud history and they would not willingly become subordinates. By 655 East Anglia had been battered almost into insensibility, with the splendid promise of its earlier years destroyed; but Kent remained, fortified so long as the dynasty lasted by the bond between it and the church, whose authority not even the Mercian kings could afford openly to flout.

The course taken by Wessex was very different. Throughout almost the entire period its preoccupation with conquests in the south-west, coupled with dynastic instability, surrendered the initiative to Mercia; but it also gave it great resilience, as losses along the Thames were compensated by gains in Somerset, Devon and Cornwall. These were a warrior people, who had learned how to absorb, and win the loyalties of, the subject British. There was a short spell, towards the close of the 7th century, when Caedwalla of Wessex adopted the same predatory approach as Mercia, and pursued it with equal atrocity; but while these methods served to subdue the Isle of Wight and Sussex they failed in Kent, where they thrust the Cantware temporarily into the arms of Mercia. But this was a passing aberration. On the early death of Caedwalla, the succession of Ine in Wessex and the appearance of Wihtred in Kent the natural alliance between the two kingdoms asserted itself. Kent needed the support, or at least the benevolent neutrality, of Wessex to withstand the Mercian threat directed at it from London, and to compensate for the withdrawal of Northumbria, with which he had previously had a close understanding, a harmony of religious and political aims. Wessex needed a friendly power at its back while it completed its conquests in the south-west, to help it block off Mercia at the Thames, and to isolate an always unreliable and potentially hostile Sussex. Even when these defences crumbled under the assaults of Æthelbald and Offa the underlying bond of common interest remained. At the end, when the balance between Mercia and Wessex turned upon secure possession of the south-east, to which Kent was the key, the choice before it was between subservience and an honourable partnership, and there could be no question what the answer would be; and much the same choice confronted East Anglia, where hatred of the Mercians had continued to smoulder. These ancient kingdoms could not be beaten into permanent submission, but there was a liberality about Wessex to which they could respond.

The Cantware, who had contributed so much to the common stock of English experience, carried with them into the future two legacies of their own. The first was the great church of Canterbury, which the Eskings had founded, protected and endowed, and which had now been restored to its full authority and dignity. The second, an inheritance from their Jutish ancestors, was that unique body of custom, later to be known as *Gavelkind*, which governed the lives of the ordinary husbandmen and persisted beneath all the paraphernalia of the lordships and the manors. This was the guarantee of the liberties which they continued to enjoy throughout the feudal age; it was the object of their pride and the source of their distinction. They were a people who never lost their sense of identity, nor — some would say — their conceit of themselves.

APPENDIX A

Supposed Parallels between the Kentish and Roman or Celtic Land Systems

Roman Models

The belief that the Kentish land system rested upon a Roman foundation derives primarily from the studies carried out by H. L. Gray of the land divisions known as *yokes* which were used in medieval Kent to assign rents and services between tenants of the various manors.[1] In theory these were units of 40-50 acres, but in practice their sizes were far from uniform. If they had ever coincided with actual land holdings or fields they had long ceased to do so, becoming, as a later writer has expressed it, 'not topographical realities but fiscal artificialities' superimposed upon the pattern of the countryside.[2] Gray found that at Gillingham the *yokes* were severely rectangular in shape, and he thought that the same was true in Kent generally. In his belief they represented the land holdings of the early settlement period which had become broken up over the generations by division between heirs and the sale or alienation of different portions, until where the obligations had originally fallen upon a single occupant of a compact tenement they had since come to be shared among a medley of successors. The shape of the *yokes* suggested to him that at the beginning the land settlements had been fitted into a Roman framework.

This theory was taken up and developed, in different ways, by later writers. Gordon Ward saw in the *yokes* a reflection of the Roman *juga* introduced into parts of the Empire at the close of the 3rd century precisely in order to provide a simple and rapid means of assessing tax contributions from land; the size of these units varying according to the fertility of the soil but having much the same range as that of the Kentish *yokes*.[3] Gilbert Slater believed that the shape of the *yokes* was evidence of the continued use in Kent of the Roman light plough, which only scratched the surface of the soil and so necessitated cross-ploughing, instead of the heavy plough, common among the Anglo-Saxons and thought to have been first introduced by them, which turned the furrow, dispensed with cross-ploughing and so encouraged the layout of plots in long strips which reduced the shuttling of the plough-teams.[4] The very term *yoke* denotes a single pairing of oxen, whereas four pairs were usually needed to draw a heavy plough. Others have attempted, specifically, to derive the Kentish land settlements from the Roman system of *centuriation* by which the property attached to the *coloniae* where time-served soldiers were settled, and sometimes also to cities, was apportioned in family plots laid out in a regular grid-iron pattern; and H. M. Nightingale has claimed that traces of such a pattern are still detectable at Cliffe near Rochester.[5]

As a model, *centuriation* can be dismissed. In the opinion of such experts as I. A. Richmond no unimpeachable example of this system can be discovered anywhere in Roman Britain; although the search has, he says, 'proved a will o' the wisp to many antiquaries'.[6] In any case the standard plots laid out on this design were of rather less than two acres, and so very much smaller than the Kentish *yokes*.[7] A rectangular layout on a larger pattern might well, however, have been in more general use in Roman Britain with the prevalence of the light plough (although archaeological evidence has shown that the heavy plough was, in fact, known at this time, even if its use was restricted to the larger villa estates).[8] A much more serious objection to Gray's theory is that his belief that the rectangular shape of the *yokes* found at Gillingham was typical of Kent as a whole appears to have been mistaken; Helen Muhlfeld's researches have shown that those at Wye, for instance, conformed to no such pattern.[9] Nor was the use of a fiscal network, or mesh, for apportioning tenurial obligations in any way peculiar to Kent; much the same purpose was served by the *caracutes* in East Anglia and the *hides* in Wessex and Mercia (*see* Chapter 3, page 67). It was simply that in this matter, as in others, the standard used in Kent was different, and so was the nomenclature.

The original Kentish standard seems, in fact, to have been the *sulung*, or ploughland, nominally of 160-200 acres, out of which the *yoke* developed as a quarter fraction.[10] The term *sulung* means a heavy

231

plough, and the unit was supposed, notionally, to represent the amount of land which could be cultivated by such a plough in the course of a year. It was natural to adopt the term *yoke* for the quarter fraction, as representing one out of the four pairs of oxen in a full plough-team, and also very likely (after knowledge of the old Imperial tradition had been revived by the Christian conversion) by analogy with earlier Roman practice. However that may be, the pre-conquest charters provide clear evidence that the *sulung* (or ploughland) was the prime unit of computation in Kent; it was still used everywhere in the county at the time of Domesday Book; and it persisted in north-east Kent throughout the Middle Ages, although the *yoke* had then come to replace it over most of mid and west Kent. The reason for this change appears to have been that the growth of population and multiplication of holdings made a finer fiscal mesh expedient; and in a few places the process was taken even further with the introduction of a quarter *yoke*, or *virgate*, notionally of some 10–12 acres.[11] No doubt the *sulungs* and ploughlands by which Gillingham, like all the other Kentish manors, was assessed in Domesday Book were as rectangular as the *yokes* that were later formed out of them; for an artificial demarcation of this sort that pattern was as convenient as any, though others might be used elsewhere. That the *sulungs* could never have borne any exact relationship to the land holdings is apparent from their distribution among the lathes in round figures ranging from 60 to 240. The size and shape of the lathes were determined by topography, so that it is clear that the *sulungs* had been adapted to them and not the other way round (Chapter Three, pages 55-61).

It is not in the *sulungs* and *yokes* that traces of the original holdings should be sought but in the open fields, which in medieval times had themselves come to be divided between numerous different occupiers, and which the fiscal divisions cut across.[12] The early charters refer to these as *londs*, and they often bore the names of individuals or families, who appear to have been the early occupants, e.g. Folcwininglond, Wynnheardinglond and Babbinglond, all from a charter of 811.[13] These have not yet received the attention they deserve. As time went on they no doubt became frayed, or eaten away, by small crofts or enclosures, but the studies at Wye and Gillingham show that in the 13th and 14th centuries they were irregular in shape,[14] and probably they had always been so.

Celtic Models

The analogies between the society of Kent and that of the *gwelyau*, or free clan units, or medieval Wales have been considered in Chapter One, where they have been shown to be irrelevant to the migration period.

The model proposed by Glanville Jones is the different one of the Welsh bond communities, or *maenors*, as they existed *c.* 1100.[15] The features to which he draws particular attention are the discrete, that is the scattered and intermingled, nature of these settlement groups, which resemble in this the dispersed hamlet pattern of Kent; the attachment to each group of its own common pastures, much as Wealden and marsh pastures were attached to the several Kent lathes; and the fact that the groups often centred upon royal vills, as the lathes did.

Leslie Adcock, in rejecting this model,[16] is especially critical of the assumption that the Welsh system existing around 1100 had undergone no significant change over the preceding six or seven hundred years, and so mirrored that found during the 5th century in the very different environment of south-eastern England. The comparisons drawn with Kent are highly selective. There appears, for instance, to have been no counterpart among the *maenors* to the distinction between *outland* and *inland* which was fundamental to the Kentish system (*see* Chapter Three); and indeed it would be a contradiction to expect it, when the Kentish *outlands* were completely free holdings. In the *maenors* cultivation was carried out in common,[17] whereas in Kent each man worked his own land, or if he co-operated with his neighbours did so voluntarily. The contrast goes much further than this, since so servile were the conditions in the Welsh bond communities that the lord's overseer allotted (and frequently re-allotted) the holdings, dictated the crops to be grown, and assigned each cultivator his role;[18] a state of affairs which could not have been further removed from that in Kent, where even the tenant farmer of the *inlands* was free to crop his land as he pleased and was secure in his possession of it so long as he did not default on his rents and services, and the *outland* ceorl could not only sell his land without seeking leave from anyone but if he defaulted on his obligations could be evicted only with extreme difficulty and after every opportunity had been given to him to make proper restitution (Chapter Three, page 65).

In the face of this, such similarities as existed between the Welsh *maenors* and the Kentish lathes (or the manors which later emanated from them) appear incidental and trivial. There were some resemblances of structures, but almost none of custom or status. Indeed, it is difficult to see how any useful comparison can be made between entirely bond communities and the highly differentiated society shown in the early Kentish laws,[19] in which there was a sub-stratum of slaves but freeholders and tenant farmers predominated.

APPENDIX B

Latin Loan Words in Kentish Place-names

Wickham names (*vicus*, a village)

Margaret Gelling has demonstrated a particularly close connection between names in this group and Roman roads. Of the 28 examples known in England no fewer than 24 are either on, or closely associated with, such roads, and of these five are in Kent (Wickhambreux, West Wickham, East Wickham in Bexley, Wickham in Strood and Wickham Bushes in Lydden).[1]

The very distribution of the names suggests that they were not those of surviving British communities; in so far as such communities existed in Kent it would have been remarkable if they had been confined to the neighbourhood of Roman roads. The distribution would, however, be consistent with the view that these places were small mercenary camps, established before the conquest of Kent, and that the descriptions had been passed on by the forces stationed there, who joined in the conquest under Hengest. The position of Wickhambreux is particularly instructive, since it neighbours the early cemeteries of Westbere and Howletts, which were first used by Jutish mercenaries (Chapter One, pages 26-27). Alternatively, the places may simply have been small ruined Roman settlements, or stations, and the descriptions of them obtained from British slaves, like those of the major rivers and other features of the landscape.

Campus names (*campus*, a field or plain)

There are five place-names in Kent, and one in east Surrey, in which the last element derives from the Latin *campus*. Margaret Gelling has endeavoured to establish a relationship between these and Roman roads,[2] but her demonstration is unconvincing. Swanscombe and Addiscombe are both on Roman roads, but of the other examples she cites Balcombe in Frittenden (a Wealden parish) is no nearer than two miles to a road, and Maplescombe in Farningham and Comp in Wrotham are both a good deal farther away than that. So, too, is *Gelecancamp*, a Wealden example which she has overlooked, but which is named in a charter of 939[3] and appears to have been in the neighbourhood of Golden Green near Tonbridge.[4]

The term may not have been a direct borrowing from Latin at all, since, as Margaret Gelling herself says, it had found its way into the Frisian dialect,[5] which strongly influenced the Kentish. In any case it is a purely topographical term, with no connotations of settlement. Judging from the Kentish examples it seems to have denoted an open tract of country, marsh, common or plain.

Faversham (*faber*, a smith)

As we have said, Faversham was the site of a pre-conquest mercenary camp. It also later became a royal court of the Kentish kings, which, significantly, was the great craft centre of the kingdom in pagan times. It may well be that in the early days a number of British slaves were employed here as smiths; but if so they contributed little to the great flowering of the Kentish crafts in jewellery and glass-ware, from which Celtic influences are notably absent. (The argument advanced by Kendrick in 1933[6] that the splendid Kentish brooches ornamented with garnets, blue glass, cloisonne and filigree work were the product of British craftsmen, or others working under their influence, is now no longer accepted; the brooches can be dated mainly to Æthelberht's reign and are seen to have been a native development from earlier Frankish themes).[7]

Eccles (*ecclesia*, a church)

Eccles names are particularly a feature of north-west England, where they are supposed to derive from the Welsh *egles*. They are very rare in the east, but there is one example in Kent. Margaret Gelling's suggestion that this comes directly from the Latin *ecclesia*[8] is almost certainly right. The place is less than a mile from the royal court of Aylesford, and seems to represent an abandoned Romano-British church refurbished, as St Martin's in Canterbury was, for the use of Æthelberht's Christian wife Bertha,[9] or perhaps for the use of the King himself after the conversion.

Croydon (the *crocus*, or saffron plant)

Margaret Gelling has traced the derivation of this name from the saffron plant used as a yellow dye, and probably a Roman introduction.[10] It is a purely topographical term of a kind particularly likely, because of the striking and unfamiliary nature of its appearance to the Saxon newcomers, to have been picked up from British slaves.

APPENDIX C

The Early Lathes: Nomenclature, and those in north-east Kent

Nomenclature

It is unfortunate, but necessary, that any detailed enquiry into the identity of the early lathes has to be prefaced by a brief word on nomenclature. This is because since the intemperate attack launched upon Jolliffe's work by Gordon Ward in 1933[1] disproportionate attention has been concentrated upon this aspect.

In this book we have used the term *lathe* for the primary divisions of Kent because that is the term used in Domesday Book and which became familiar later. It is true that it is not encountered in any written document before 975[2] and we do not know exactly when it originated; but as it is a vernacular term we should not, in any case, expect to find it in any of the charters or diplomas before 850, or thereabouts, until when all these documents were in Latin. But, whatever certain critics may imply, this question of usage has no bearing at all on the antiquity of the units themselves, however described. In fact, they seem first to have been described by the Frankish term *ge*, equivalent to the German *gau*, which survives in the place-names Lyminge, Eastry and Sturry,[3] which are among the very earliest recorded, and of which the first two were adopted by Domesday Book lathes and the last means 'the Stour district', the inference being plain. It really does not matter when the one term gave place to the other; and if we have used *lathe* that is simply because it is the more intelligible today.

The rendering in the early Latin documents was usually *regio*. In many instances the reference is unmistakeably to a lathe, as for example where the charters speak of land *in regione Eastrgena* (A.D. 788) or, more elaborately, *in regione suburbana ad oppidum regis quod ab incolis ibi Fefresham appellatur* (A.D. 811: roughly translated, 'the region attached, or subordinate, to the royal town of Faversham').[4] Jolliffe was undoubtedly at fault in implying that the term was used exclusively in this sense, since it was sometimes also applied to tracts of country like Romney Marsh, or the Chart woods fringing the Weald, or the peninsula of Hoo,[5] which were not lathes. So, too, with the term *ware*, which was commonly employed for the folk of a lathe, as in Domesday Book and — much earlier — in the description of the Wealden commons (compare, e.g. *Wi-Ware-let* in Domesday Book with the *Weowera wealde* of 724);[6] but which sometimes denoted the inhabitants of a geographical area like Hoo or Romney Marsh.[7] The intention is usually clear from the context. None of our own conclusions has been based upon the appearance of the term *regio*; but in certain contexts the term *ware* can provide a valuable clue, as we shall show.

The chief evidence on which we have relied is that of the Wealden commons, supplemented by the fiscal assessments of the *sulungs*. The first fails us in north-east Kent, where the lathes were too far distant from the Weald to have had any commons there, although a few manors later acquired Wealden dens, it seems at second-hand (*see* Chapter Ten, pages 191-192 above). The assessments, however, still come to our aid, and are supported by an accumulation of other evidence pointing to the existence in this area of three lathes, those of Eastry, Thanet and Barham (or Kingston).

Eastry

This presents no problem. It was still a distinct lathe at the time of Domesday Book, its name means 'the eastern region', and Eastry manor (or town) was a royal vill in early times.

The Isle of Thanet

Thanet is a distinct geographical entity, It was included in the lathe of Borowart, or Canterbury, by Domesday Book, but appears as an awkward appendage to it.

The people of Thanet were known as the *Tenet-ware*, a description which persists in the name of Tenterden.[8] The term was evidently used here in contradistinction to the *Buhrware*, or inhabitants of Canterbury lathe, who left their name to the den of Boresisle, immediately adjoining Tenterden[9] — so it seems that it, too, must have been intended to denote the folk of a lathe, not merely of a geographical area, and harks back to a time before the two lathes had been combined.

Jolliffe in his article *The Hidation of Kent*, published in 1929,[10] concluded that Thanet had once been a separate lathe because the number of *sulungs* on the island came to the round figure of 80; but his calculation of the figure mistakenly included land at *Estursete* (Westgate) near Canterbury, for which reason he later recanted the opinion.[11] In fact, although his premise was wrong the sum he arrived at was right. At the time of Edward the Confessor the two major manors on Thanet, Minster and Monkton, had no more than 68 *sulungs* between them; but to this figure there should be added another 11½ *sulungs* owned on the island by the mainland manors of Chislet (6),[12] Reculver (4)[13] and Northwood (1½),[14] giving a total within the merest fraction of 80.

The number of ploughlands on Thanet cannot be computed so exactly. Minster and Monkton had 93 between them but it is impossible to say how the ploughlands owned by Chislet, Reculver and Northwood divided between Thanet and the mainland. If they divided in the same proportion as the *sulungs* the number on Thanet would have been 33, making a total for the island of 126. On the other hand, if the proportion of *sulungs* to ploughlands in Minster and Monkton could be taken as typical of the island as a whole we should arrive at a total of about 110. Particularly significant here is Bede's statement that the island contained 600 *hides*,[15] which we have suggested in Chapter Three, page 67, can be reconciled with the Kentish forms of assessment only on the assumption that he was converting 120 ploughlands, each nomimally of 200 acres (the standard applying in north-east Kent) into five times as many *hides*, each nominally of 40 acres (the standard for the 'short' *hide* met in other parts of England where that unit of account was adopted). In any case Bede's statement confirms that at the beginning of the 8th century Thanet was assessed in round figures for fiscal purposes.

In my work *The Jutish Forest* I suggested that the royal court of the lathe was at Reculver, just outside the island but always closely associated with it.[16] I now withdraw this suggestion, for three reasons, of which two are negative. They are, first, that the computation of 80 *sulungs* allows for none on the mainland and, second, that it would have been unique for a royal court to be sited in a Roman city or fortress, which the Eskings appear deliberately to have shunned until St Augustine's mission and the conversion led to the reoccupation of some, and then as ecclesiastical and mercantile rather than royal centres. There is a positive reason for believing that the court was at Sarre, the main harbourage of the island, where c. 761 the king was enjoying rights of toll (as also at Fordwich, the port associated with the once royal vill of Sturry and itself still in royal possession at the time of Domesday Book).[17] Besides this, the very early, prolific, and richly furnished cemetery at Sarre picks it out (Chapter One, pages 26–27), and so does its position on a tidal estuary and a Roman road, but away from any Roman settlement — exactly the choice made for other courts in the neighbourhood, such as Eastry and Sturry.

The Little Stour Valley

This area is defined by the Domesday Book Hundreds of Downhamford, Bridge, Petham, Kinghamford and Barham, which form a geographical entity. At the time of Edward the Confessor their combined number of *sulungs* amounted to 59¼ — again within a fraction of a round figure.

Although Domesday Book included the area in the lathe of Borowart, or Canterbury, there is clear evidence for the existence of a royal court at Kingston in Barham, which, in fact, means 'the king's farm'. The pagan cemetery on Kingston Down, though relatively late, was peculiarly rich in the jewellery it produced, including the finest single specimen of the distinctive Kentish style of composite brooch.[18] The manor remained in royal hands right down to Edward the Confessor's reign. Domesday Book says of it 'This manor Archbishop Stigand held, but it was not part' (of the fief) 'of the archbishopric but belonged to the demesne farm of King E' (Edward).

We have described in Chapter Three, pages 61-62, how the great preponderance of demesne and *inland* at Barham, to the one side of Kingston, and at Bishopsbourne, to the other, suggests that there was a royal vill here from early times. A charter of 799 speaks of Bishopsbourne as lying in 'the western part of Barham',[19] a form of wording which seems to imply that Barham was either still a lathe at that time or was remembered as having been one.

Finally, although the Little Stour area does not appear to have had a common in the Weald, there are indications that it had its own common in the north-western segment of Romney Marsh. Thus Ruckinge, on the edge of the marsh, was attached to Ickham, in Downhamford Hundred, in 786;[20] Appledore is recorded as a limb of Adisham, in the same hundred, in 1006;[21] and Bishopsbourne is also known to have had pastures on the marsh at this time.[22]

APPENDIX D

Identification and Classification of Place-names in *-ham*

Dodgson in his survey of *-ham* place-names in south-eastern England[1] includes names ending in *-hamsted* and *-hampton*. No account has been taken of these in Chapter Four, in the belief that they are significantly later in origin than the *-ham* names proper. The order in which the elements appear in the names suggests so. Moreover a small number of the names are to be found in the body of the Weald — for instance at Hemsted in Benenden and Whetsted[2] in Capel — which seems to indicate an origin in the 8th, rather than the 7th, let alone the 6th, century. And, finally, the names betray a shift of meaning, since they no longer refer to a constellation of settlements but take on much more of the modern sense of a homestead, or a home farm, as the case may be.

Identification

The major problem is to distinguish the true *-ham* names from those which originally ended in *-hamm* or *-hamme*, the simplest rendering of which is 'water meadow'. Dodgson suggests four conditions which should be met in picking out a true *-ham* name from these others. They are that no *-hamm* form should appear anywhere in the early spellings; that the place should be an ancient manor or parish; that it should be on record before 1300–1350 as something more than a field name or boundary point; and that the site should not have a topography which might be that of a *hamm*. Excellent general working rules though these are, in combination they are extremely strict and there is danger in applying them too inflexibly. In fact, Dodgson's own choice of *-ham* names departs from there here and there, usually with good reason.

We suggest a number of alterations to Dodgson's list, specifically:

(a)   The addition of the downland sites of Petham (Piteham, 1086)[3] and Newnham (Newenham, 1177).[4] Dodgson omits these because they are in valley bottoms; but so is Alkham, which he includes; these are dry chalk valleys, not the natural sites for water meadows. Admittedly, the water table has been falling; but at the time of Domesday Book mills were to be found wherever there was a trickle of running water which could be ponded, and there was no mill at Petham. For Newnham evidence is lacking; but the first element in the name — simply 'new' — consorts with settlement rather than a meadow.

(b)   The addition of Aylesham (Elisham, 1367),[5] which Dodgson excludes because it never gave its name to a parish or manor and is late recorded. Nevertheless the site, on a dry chalk wold, is the antithesis to that of a *hamm*, nor does that ending appear in any of the early spellings.

(c)   The further addition of Freezingham[6] (Rolvenden parish, on the south-eastern fringe of the Weald). This is on the strength of evidence cited by Wallenberg that French Hay and Frenchurst in the neighbouring parishes of Tenterden and Sandhurst respectively are names from the same stock, suggesting the early presence in this area of a folk known as the Frisingas,[7] whose chief settlements would then seem to have been at Freezingham. Once again, no *-hamm* endings appear in any of the early forms.

(d)   The omission of Engeham in Woodchurch parish. Dodgson seems guilty here of disregarding his own precepts, since the name first appears in 1278 as Eading*hame*.[8] Moreover the site is on the bank of a river, the Beult, and indeed within a pronounced bend of the river. In construing this as a *-ham* name Dodgson appears to have been over-influenced by the fact that it was on a Roman road. For the same reason he was tempted to include in his list Langham in Rolvenden parish, taking the site to have been at Halden Place (also on a Roman road), though he

239

eventually decided against doing so. In fact, the original site appears to have been near Forsham on the banks of the Hexden Channel,[9] and the place is first mentioned in a charter of 833 as Langeburnan, a palpable meadow name.

Taking account of these amendments the full revised list of -ham in Kent would be as follows:

(i)   Compounded with the names of individuals:

Adisham, Aylesham, Barham, Bodsham Green, Chilham, Cudham, Eltham, Fawkham, Godmersham, Ightham, Lenham, Lewisham, Meopham, Offham, Otham, Rodmersham, *Andscohesham* (now Stoke),[10] Teynham, Tutsham (in West Farleigh), Wouldham, Wrotham = 21.

(ii) Compounded with the names of folk:

Farningham, Freezingham (in Rolvenden), Gillingham, Islingham (in Frindsbury), Mongeham,[11] Rainham,[12] Terlingham (in Hawkinge), Wingham[13] = 8.

(iii) Compounded with descriptive terms:

Alkham, Burham, Chartham, Dalham (in High Halstow), Downham (in Littlebourne), Faversham, Finglesham (by Eastry), Higham, Hougham, Ickham, Newnham, Peckham, Petham, Shoreham, Thurnham, Waltham, Westerham, Wicham (in Strood), East Wickham (in Bexley), West Wickham, Wickham Bushes (in Lydden), Wickhambreux = 22. *Total* 51.

Classification

The broad classification is as indicated above. Of those in group (iii), the Wickhams and Faversham, the first elements of which consist of Latin loan words, are certainly early, perhaps of the 5th century (Appendix B, page 234); if Alkham derives from a heathen temple, as Stenton believed[14] but Margaret Gelling apparently does not,[15] it is unlikely to be any later than the 6th; and Finglesham, 'the prince's *ham*',[16] neighbouring the royal vill of Eastry and with a well furnished cemetery going back to the beginning of the 6th century,[17] may well have acquired its name by that time. But pointers of this kind are exceptional, and the sample they provide is too small to be of much help. The group as a whole is very heterogeneous, and it seems impossible to generalize about it. Westerham, for instance, is certainly late, for reasons that have been explained in Chapter Four (page 86), and so apparently is Newnham, from its very meaning. Usually there is no way of telling whether a *ham* name associated with some purely descriptive term dates from the late 5th century, the late 7th, or somewhere in between.

More can perhaps be learned from the patronymics. In most of them the first element consists of the name of an individual in the singular possessive case, as with Godmersham (Godmeresham, 822);[18] but sometimes it is that of a kin in the old genitive plural case, -inga(e) as with Gillingham (Gillingeham, 975).[19] Constructions of this kind are often found with other endings than -ham for instance, -leag a glade, -baera a pasture, or -hyrste a wood.[20] There is obviously a connection between them and that class of names which end in -ingas, the old nominative plural case, which are those of folk applied directly to the places where they lived — Hastings, which means 'Haesta's people', and nothing more, being an example.[21] When it was thought that the -ingas names were the earliest of all the patronymics, dating from the migration period, compounds of the -ingaham type were seen as a development from them, but now it is legitimate to consider whether the reverse may not have been the case.

Both Barry Cox[22] and Dodgson[23] believe that, among the various types of -ham names, those ending in -ingham come relatively late, but the reasons they give for this view are questionable. Barry Cox's reason is that they appear to be less closely associated with the Roman roads than are the generality of -ham names; but this rests on the assumption, which we have disputed in Chapter Four (page 85), that the attraction which the Roman roads exerted on the settlements was present — and predominant — at the very beginning, instead of developing later. Dodgson's reason is that compounds of this kind are to be found in the body of the Weald; but this argument loses its force when it is realized that there they end almost exclusively in -leag, -hyrste or -baera,* terms which imply, not settlement, but merely

* But not in -denn. Subject to one, dubious, exception (Beginge den, *Liber de Hyda*, 933: *see* Wallenberg, 1931, p. 337), names with this ending are always of a later type of construction. While *baera* and *denn* were synonymous — a charter of 863 (CS 507) speaks of 'swine pastures which in our Saxon tongue we call *denbera*' — the former was clearly the older expression of the two.

merely the seasonal use of pastures or woods, so that the names might have originated with the Wealden commons themselves, almost from the foundation of the kingdom. Nevertheless, there are *a priori* grounds for suggesting that, in general, *-ham* names associated with those of individuals preceded those compounded with the names of folk, just as they preceded the pure *-ingas* names; and some supporting evidence can be found for both of these propositions.

It is reasonable to assume that the first settlements, founded in the aftermath of the conquest when the leaders of the bands who accompanied Hengest and Oisc were still living or fresh in the memory of their kin or followers, would be known by the leaders' individual names; that with the passage of two or three generations the folk would come to describe themselves generically by their descent from, or connection with, these patriarchal figures, so that the *-inga-* compounds would come into being; and that, finally, the simple *-ingas* names would develop from this, by a process equivalent (to use a modern analogy) to substituting for 'the Smiths' home' merely 'the Smiths' — a perfectly intelligible progression. Examples can be cited to illustrate each of these transitions. Teynham near Faversham (*Teneham*, 798)[24] is typical of a *-ham-* name linked to that of an individual and is appropriately situated in an area of primary settlement, on the rich soils of the Thames foreshore. Some five miles to the south, on the poor flinty land of the Downs, is Timbold Hill, which appears in 850 as *Teninge faledun*, meaning 'the clearing of the Teningas',[25] and which seems plainly to mark a colony established from Teynham. On the Downs to the north of Ashford another such compound appears in the name of the village of Hastingleigh (*Haestinga lege*, 995)[26] denoting, it seems, a hill pasture once used by the Haestingas, the folk from whom the name of Hastings originated, and who appear to have migrated from Kent at some time during the 7th century.

If this argument were valid the different types of patronymics could be set in some sort of time-scale, allowing for all the vagaries of usage and the probability of overlap; but the problem cannot be resolved on evidence from Kent alone and more work needs to be done on it. We believe that, until it has been done, there is a strict limit to what the distribution of *-ham* names can teach us. They show how far settlement had spread by 700, or thereabouts, but are of little use in monitoring the stages in its progress up to that time.

APPENDIX E

The Status of the Kentish Ceorl

Blood-price

Finberg has made a point of emphasizing that, despite 'frequent statements to the contrary by historians of repute', none of the Kentish codes specifically states the blood-price of the ceorl.[1] Strictly, he is right. In Æthelberht's laws 100 shillings is cited as the 'ordinary' blood-price[2] and in the laws of Hlothere and Eadric as that of the 'freeman';[3] but since the codes tell us — specifically — that the blood-price of the eorl was 300 shillings[4] and those of the three classes of *laet* were 80, 60 and 40 shillings,[5] it appears that 100 shillings cannot have been other than the ceorl's. It seems that Æthelberht described it as the 'ordinary' blood-price because in his code it was used as the standard against which sums of compensation for lesser injuries than death were measured and quoted; these being intended to be scaled up or down proportionately for the eorls and *laets*.

The meaning of 'freeman'

What Finberg intended to imply was that the blood-price of the 'freeman' and the ceorl were not necessarily identical, the 'freeman' — in his words — being a class 'seemingly distinct from the ceorls, but perhaps including some of them'.[6] But if the blood-price of the 'freeman' was 100 shillings, and of the superior class of *laet* 80 shillings, there is virtually no room left between the two for the inferior class of ceorl that he postulates. (Nowhere are blood-prices graded in units of less than 20 shillings). The aim of the argument is to detract from the provision in Æthelberht's laws that when any 'freeman' was killed 50 shillings became payable to the king in 'lord-ring'.[7] The plain interpretation of that provision is that the king was directly the lord of every ceorl (at least), and it seems impossible to evade it.

The laws of Hlothere and Eadric, by citing 100 shillings as the blood-price of the 'freeman', do appear to exclude the *laets* from that definition. But it is only in Æthelberht's laws that the *laets* make any appearance at all; and we have suggested in Chapter Eight that by the time those of Hlothere and Eadric were promulgated, 80 years later, they may have ceased to exist as a separate social class and become merged into the general body of the ceorls. In Æthelberht's laws the term 'freeman' is used in numerous contexts which suggest that it was intended to embrace everyone who was not a slave — in other words, who was personally free, whether or not he was also a freeholder (like the ceorl) or merely a tenant farmer (like the *laet*). Thus the provisions referring to 'freemen' are paralleled, or contrasted, with others dealing with slaves; for instance, a 'freeman' is to make a three-fold restitution for theft and a slave a two-fold one.[8] In this there is no mention of the *laets*, who seem therefore to have been treated under the description of 'freemen'. A free-born woman is said to be distinguished by wearing her hair long,[9] with the implication that a slave woman (but surely not one of the *laet* class) was supposed to have her's cropped. But most significant of all is the clause providing a forfeit of 20 shillings for anyone laying bonds on, that is attempting to enslave, a freeman;[10] which is paralleled by a clause in Wihtred's laws (c. 695) that a manumitted slave is to be 'folk-free', or in other words to have the rights of a freeman of the people.[11] In these instances, and others, the terms 'freeman', 'free-born' and 'folk-free' appear to be used in their natural meanings, the contrast being with the slaves alone and no intermediate class. The inference, then is that the *laets* too were accounted among those who, in Æthelberht's time, had the king as their lord, and no other; which is not surprising since most, if not all, of them were tenants of the royal estate.

242

The relative standing of the ceorl in Kent and Wessex

In comparing the blood-price of the Kentish ceorl (100 shillings or 2,000 *sceattas*)[12] with that of the West Saxon (200 shillings or 800 'pennies')[13] the crucial question is whether the *sceatta* and 'penny' were identical coins, or whether the first had only half the value of the second — in other words, whether a shilling had five times the value in Kent as in Wessex or only two and a half times. On this the numismatic evidence is suggestive rather than conclusive.[14] It remains to consider what clues can be gleaned by comparing other provisions in the two bodies of law.

The most topical comparison is perhaps to be found in those clauses in the laws of Wihtred of Kent (*c.* 695) and Ine of Wessex (694) which prescribe penalties for working on the Lord's Day, since they were novelties which have the appearance of having been concerted, and although the approaches in the two kingdoms were different the effects might be expected to have been much the same. In Kent the penalty was the payment of a sum equivalent to the offender's *healsfang*, or first instalment of blood-price, which for the ceorl was 20 shillings.[15] In Wessex the offender was to forfeit his freedom or redeem it by paying the worth of a slave, which was 60 shillings.[16] Assuming some correspondence between the penalties, this suggests that the Kentish shilling was nearer two and a half than five times the value of the West Saxon.

But a comparison between the values set on slaves (a commodity trafficked between kingdoms) suggests the reverse. In Kent, unlike Wessex, the slave had no single value; the sum payable for killing a male slave varied according to the standing of his master, being six shillings if he was a ceorl, 12 shillings if he was an eorl, and 20 shillings if he was the king himself.[17] The approach is so different that it may invalidate comparison altogether; if not, we should be bound to conclude that the Kentish shilling was worth at least five times that of Wessex.

Perhaps the royal *mund*, or the value set upon the king's protective rights, is the best indicator of all, because in both kingdoms this also governed the maximum rate of the *wite*, or fine for public offences,[18] and the sum paid to the king for killing a man of whom he was the lord (in Wessex this meant a noble only). It had, therefore, an especially wide application, and was moreover an expression of the royal dignity, which cannot have been much differently rated in the two kingdoms. In Kent the figure was 50 shillings[19] and in Wessex 120,[20] which brings us back to the 1 : 2½ ratio. Lower down the social scale the *mund* of the Kentish eorl was 12 shillings,[21] as compared to 36 shillings and 18 shillings for the two classes of Wessex noble[22] — a ratio which is not altogether out of keeping. But the ceorl's *mund* was six shillings in both kingdoms.[23] This means that, on any reckoning, it must have had more than twice the value in Kent than in Wessex; it would be stretching things too far to believe that it had five times the value.

On balance this evidence supports the view of the numismatists that the Wessex penny was worth twice the Kentish *sceatta*, and that accordingly the Kentish shilling was worth two and a half, and not five times, the shilling in Wessex. On this basis the blood-price of the West Saxon ceorl would have amounted to 80 per cent of that of his Kentish counterpart. But if we take into the calculation the sum paid to the lord — the king himself in Kent but usually a noble in Wessex — the position changes dramatically; since in Kent this was more than four times as much (50 shillings compared with 30, or 12 in equivalent value). The full sum payable, to kindred and lord, for killing a West Saxon ceorl was thus only about 60 per cent of that for killing a ceorl in Kent; and, as we have seen, the discrepancy in the values of the *mund* — very much an indication of status — was even greater.

APPENDIX F

Place-names in *-inga(e)-* in the Kentish Weald

The following list has been given by John MacNiel Dodgson,[1] relying for his sources upon Wallenburg's *Kentish Place-Names* (1931) and *The Place-Names of Kent* (1934).

Aegylbyrhtingahyrst (lost, Biddenden)	KPN 172
Bardingley (Sutton Valence)	KPN 128; PNK 232
Brandenbury (Yalding)	PNK 169
Cobhambury (Edenbridge)	PNK 73
Dorningbury (lost, Chart Sutton)	KPN 127; PNK 210
French Hay (Tenterden)	KPN 89; PNK 357
Frenchurst (Sandhurst)	KPN 89; PNK 344
Glassenbury (Cranbrook)	PNK 320
(Hallinghurst (lost, Smarden)	PNK 399)
Hawkenbury (Headcorn)	KPN 129; PNK 21
Kensham (Rolvenden)	KPN 120, 460; PNK 353
Pembury	PNK 185
Stokenbury (lost, East Peckham)	PNK 166
Tatlingbury (Capel)	PNK 174
Trillinghurst (Goudhurst)	PNK 313

We have not included in this list Freezingham (Rolvenden: KPN 89; PNK 352) because this was a name of settlement; but we have included Frenchurst in Sandhurst, about which Dodgson was dubious, because this was a wood associated with it, the name clearly being coeval. Hallinghurst in Smarden ought, however, to be omitted; Dodgson is relying upon the form Hallingehurst, which appears in 1254, but both he and Wallenburg have overlooked the first appearance of the name in 940 as Holenhyrst, a toponymic meaning 'the holly wood' (BCS 753). As a matter of identification, Aegylbyrhtingahyrst was not in Biddenden parish, but near Ingleden in Tenterden, which preserves echoes of the name;[2] Stokenbury was at The Pound in East Peckham; and Dorningbury is Dunbury in Chart Sutton.[3]

To Dodgson's list it seems that we can add:

Angley (Cranbrook; Anglingele, 1278)	PNK 318
Downingbury (Pembury; Dudingeber'. 1291)	PNK 186
Etchinghill (Goudhurst; Tottingehol, 1254)	PNK 312
Sissinghurst (Saxingeherste, *c.* 1206)	PNK 323

and possibly also two names which end, exceptionally, in *den* viz.:

Crittenden (Brenchley: (West)oteringeden, 1202–3)	PNK 190
Begingeden (993; probably Bevenden in Great Chart)	KPN 342

244

APPENDIX G

Eormenred's Descendants

The First Generation

The earliest accounts appear in the texts variously described as the *Kentish Royal Legend* or the *Lives of the Kentish Royal Saints*, which can be shown on internal evidence to date between 974 and 1030,[1] but are still some 300 years later than the life-times of those with whom they deal and betray a good deal of confusion. Among later chroniclers the fullest account is given by Florence of Worcester, who seems to have had access to some independent source of information. He names, in addition to the murdered princes Æthelred and Æthelberht, four sisters, Eormenbeorh (*alias* Domneva), Eormenburh, Eormengyth and Æthelthryth[2] — being the only one to mention the last.

(1) All agree that the eldest sister was the first married to Merwald, King of the Magonsaeta. When she became Abbess of Minster she was known as Aebba, which is how the numerous contemporary charters refer to her.[3] Domneva is merely a conflation of Domina Aebba, or — more exactly — of the popular equivalent, 'Domne Eafa',[4] That her original name was Eormenbeorh (and Aebba, by inference, a religious name) rests upon the testimony of the *Lives of the Kentish Royal Saints*. It is, however, highly improbable that two of Eormenred's daughters should have been given names identical except in a small matter of spelling; and since we know that there was a Kentish abbess called Eormenburh, or Eormenburga, contemporary with, but distinct from, Aebba — both appear, for instance in a charter issued by Wihtred at *Cilling* in 699[5] — it seems that the two became confused in later legend. It follows that Aebba was the eldest sister's given name, not an assumed one. If, as it seems, the two princes, her brothers, were murdered *c.* 665, and she herself became Abbess of Minster not later than 670, by which time she had had four children (*see* later), she must certainly have been the senior member of the family.

(2) The real Eormenburga is identifiable through the contemporary chronicler Eddius as the second wife of Ecgfrid of Northumbria and the inveterate enemy of St Wilfrid.[6] Eddius tells us that after Ecgfrid's death, which was in 685,[7] she became an abbess, and she appears as such in the *Cilling* charter of 699, a document that confirms her connection with Kent, with whose royal house her name in any case associates her. She could not have been Abbess either of Minster or of Sheppey, which at that time were in the charge of Aebba and Eormenhilda (her cousin) respectively.[8] There remain, of the mixed houses, only Lyminge and Folkestone. The better choice is Lyminge, both because Eormenred had owned land there[9] and because of the connections which other of her kin had with this house.[10] Her marriage with Ecgfrid occurred at some time after 672 (which, it seems, is when his first wife left him)[11] and before 677, when she played a major part in the expulsion of Wilfrid from Northumbria; the most likely date is 674-5, when Hlothere was building up his system of alliances against Mercia. She was still alive in 699,[12] but had died by the time of the Bapchild Council, *c.* 708.[13] It seems that she must have been younger than the two princes.

(3) We know from Eddius that at the time of Wilfrid's expulsion a sister of Eormenburga was married to Centwine of Wessex.[14] He does not name her, but if we can believe the Canterbury chroniclers she would have been Eormengyth, who later took religious vows and lived with her daughter Eadburga in the neighbourhood of Minster, where she came to be buried.[15] In fact, however, it seems that the chroniclers had confused her name, which was correctly *Eangyth*. The key document here is a letter sent to St Boniface *c.* 720 by a mother and daughter calling themselves Eangyth and Heaburg [*sic*], of whom the second also described herself as Bugga (a diminutive).[16] Given the volatility of capital H in early spelling and pronunciation, there is little doubt that 'Heaburg' was simply a rendering of Eadburga; and this is strongly reinforced by another letter sent to St Boniface by Æthelbehrt II in 748-54, in which he mentions Bugga as a Kentish abbess, a blood relation of his own, and a close friend

of Boniface, who had met him in Rome[17] — all of which exactly fits Eadburga. To complete the chain of evidence we have a poem preserved among Alcuin's papers which says that Eadburga was the daughter of Eutwine [sic], which Stubbs takes to be a corruption of Centwine. He comments that if the identification of Eadburga with Bugga or Heaburga is allowed then Eangyth must have been the widow of Centwine and sister of Eormenburga.[18]

There was an *Eormengyth*, of the royal blood, living at a somewhat later time, and that the chroniclers should have confused *Eangyth* with her is understandable. It was natural that they should assume from the first element in the name that this was Eormenred's daughter, although in fact the prefix was also used in the other, ruling, branch of the Eskings, descended through Earconberht, appearing for instance in the name of his eldest child Eormenhilda. There were also similarities of circumstance. It seems from the correspondence with St Boniface that, after the death of her husband, Eangyth returned to Kent to take charge of a small religious house, apparently associated with Minster,[19] of which her daughter Eadburga later became Abbess. The Eormengyth for whom she was mistaken also adopted the religious life and according to the *Kentish Royal Legend* was buried near Minster; which suggests that the confusion between the two originated very early on. There is, however, one contemporary, or near contemporary, reference to this Eormengyth which exposes the error. It appears in a letter sent by Eardulf, then ruling in west Kent, to Boniface's successor Lul at some time after 754, in which he solicits Lul's prayers on behalf of a kinswoman Irmiga [sic; a rendering of Eormengyth*) whom he describes as a 'virgin dedicated to God'.[20] Not only does the letter imply that Eormengyth came from the ruling branch of the family, to which Eardulf himself belonged, and was still alive at the time or only recently dead, which means that she could not credibly have been a daughter of Eormenred, but the reference to her virginity shows that, whoever she was, she was not Centwine's widow and the mother of Eadburga. It seems possible, judging by the generation, that she was a daughter of Wihtred, and so Eardulf's aunt; but that remains surmise.

(4) Although Florence of Worcester is the only one to tell us that Eormenred had yet another daughter called Æthelthryth it is significant that a Kentish abbess of this name appears in the record of the Bapchild Council c. 708.[21] It is a reasonable supposition that she, like others of her family, had taken the veil and had lived with one of her sisters, whom she had in due course succeeded; and it seems that this could only have been Eormenburga. That Æthelthryth was the youngest of the family is implied by Florence of Worcester through the order in which he names her; and she can perhaps be identified as the sole surviving sister mentioned by Eangyth, in the letter which she sent to St Boniface c. 720. (Aebba and Eormenburga having then been long since dead).

The Second Generation

(1) We have given evidence in Chapter Eight (pages 155-156) for believing that Oswine, who ruled in Kent from 687-90 and addressed Aebba as his close relative by blood, was a son of one of the murdered princes, most likely the elder, whom the *Lives of the Kentish Royal Saints* shows to have been Æthelred.

(2) Aebba is said by Florence of Worcester to have had one son Meresin, who apparently died young, and three saintly daughters, Mildburg, Mildred and Mildgyth. The first remained with her father's people in Mercia. Those of concern to us are St Mildred, who accompanied her mother to Minster and succeeded her as Abbess there at some time between 699 and 708,[22] and Mildgyth, who (we are told) also came to Kent and died as a nun at Eastry.[23] This mention of Eastry suggests that it was the site of the Sudmynstre named in the account of the Bapchild proceedings, c. 708 independently of Upmynster[24] (later North Mynstre),[25] which was the main Abbey. It is also likely that this off-shoot of the parent foundation was the one of which Eangyth and Eadburga were in charge c. 720.

(3) Eormenburga is not known to have had any children. Her husband Ecgfrid of Northumbria was succeeded there by a brother, Aldfrid.[26]

(4) Eangyth seems to have had two children besides Eadburga. A letter sent by Eadburga to St Boniface between 716 and 720 laments the death of a brother Oshere and the departure to Rome of a

---

* Thus Bede (*Hist. Ecc.* II, 5) writes the name of Eormenric the father of the great Æthelberht, as Irminric.

sister Wethburg [*sic*].[27] Of these Oshere, born a Wessex *atheling*, is of no direct concern to us. Wethburg appears at first to have accompanied her mother Eangyth to Kent. She seems to be identical with the nun Withburg(a) who features in the early legends; the same whose uncorrupted remains the Anglo-Saxon Chronicle says were discovered at Dereham in 798, having lain in the earth for 55 years; and whose final resting place was at Ely. The fact that the remains were removed to Ely seems to have prompted the suggestion in the *Lives of the Kentish Royal Saints* that she was a daughter of the pious Anna of East Anglia, whose two undoubted daughters Ætheldreda and Seaxburga were both buried there.[28] But that would mean that she had no blood connection with the Eskings and was not, in fact, a Kentish royal saint at all. Leaving that aside, since Anna was killed in 654[29] it is very difficult to conceive that the Wihtburga who died in 743 could have been his child. The date of her death shows her to have been a contemporary of Eadburga, and supports the view that she was indeed her sister, and so a daughter of Centwine of Wessex — which would also explain why the Anglo-Saxon Chronicle, compiled in Wessex, should have gone out of its way to record the miraculous preservation of her body. She seems to have been a recluse and a wanderer, who retired to East Anglia after leaving Rome.

(5) There is no record that Æthelthryth ever married.

BIBLIOGRAPHY

I. Journals, Collections and Works of Reference

A. JOURNALS

	Abbrev. where used
Anglo-Saxon England	A-SE
Antiquaries Journal	Ant.J.
Antiquity	Ant.
Archaeologia	Arch.
Archaeologia Cantiana	Arch.Cant.
Archaeological Journal	Arch. J.
Bulletin of the Board of Celtic Studies	Bull.Celt.St.
Economic History Review	Econ.H.R.
English Historical Review	EHR
Historical Journal	Hist.J.
History	Hist.
Mediaeval Archaeology	Med.Arch.
Proceedings of the British Academy	Proc.Br.A.
Transactions of London and Middlesex Archaeological Society	Tr.L. and M.Arch.S.
Transactions of Royal Historical Society	T.R.Hist.S.
Welsh History Review	WHR

B. COLLECTIONS

Agrarian History of England and Wales, Vol. I (II), 1972, ed. H. P. R. Finberg	Ag.Hist.I(II)
Anglo-Saxon Coins. Historical Studies Presented to Sir Frank Stenton ed. R. H. M. Dolley	A-S Coins
Cambridge Mediaeval History, 2nd ed., Vol. I, 1924, and Vol. II, 1967	CMH I and II
Dark Age Britain, ed. D. B. Harden, 1956	DAB
Early Mediaeval Kingship, ed. P. H. Sawyer and I. N. Wood, 1977	E.Med.King.
England Before the Conquest, ed. Peter Clemoes and Kathleen Hughes, 1971	
Essays in Mediaeval History Presented to Thomas Frederick Tout, 1925	Ess.Med.Hist.
Introduction to the Survey of English Place-Names, English Place-Name Society, Vol. I, Part I, 1933	Int.Sur.Eng.Pl.N.
Preparatory to Anglo-Saxon England, Collected Papers of Frank Merry Stenton, ed. Doris Mary Stenton, 1970	P.A-S.E.
Victoria County History of Kent, Vol. I, 1908, Vol. II, 1926 and Vol. III, 1932	VCHK I, II and III

C. WORKS OF REFERENCE

Anglo-Saxon Bishops, Kings and Nobles, compiled W. G. Searle, 1899	Bishops, Kings and Nobles
Concise Oxford Dictionary of English Place-Names, ed. Eilert Ekwall, 4th ed., 1960	Dic.Eng.Pl-N.

C. WORKS OF REFERENCE – *continued*   *Abbrev.*

Dictionary of Christian Biography, ed. William Smith and Henry Wace,
    Vol. I, 1877, and II, 1880 . . . .   Dic.Chr.B.
Dictionary of National Biography, ed. Leslie Stephen and Sidney Lee,
    Vol. 6, reprint 1921–22 . . . .   Dic.Nat.B.
Gazeteer of Early Anglo-Saxon Burial Sites, compiled Audrey Meaney,
    1964 . . . .   Gaz. A-S. Bur.
Oxford Dictionary of English Christian Names, ed. E. G. Withycombe,
    3rd Ed., 1977 . . . .   Dic.Eng.Chr.N.
Student's Dictionary of Anglo-Saxon, ed. Henry Sweet, 1896 . .   Dic. A-S

II. Primary Sources

A. CONTEMPORARY DOCUMENTS, PRINTED AND COLLECTED

Anglo-Saxon Charters, ed. P. H. Sawyer, 1968 . . . .   S
Beowulf, trans. with notes Michael Alexander, Penguin Classics, 1973
Black Book of St Augustine's, ed. with introduction G. J. Turner and
    H. E. Salter, Part I, 1915 . . . .   B.Bk.S.Aug.
Cartularium Saxonicum, ed. W. de G. Birch, 3 vols., 1885–93 . .   CS
Codex Diplomaticus Aevi Saxonici, ed. J. M. Kemble, 6 vols., 1839–48   CD
*Councils and Ecclesiastical Documents relating to Great Britain and
    Ireland*, ed. A. W. Haddan and W. Stubbs, Vol. III, 1871 . .   Councils
Domesday Monarchorum, ed. Nellie Nielson, VCHK III, 1932, pp.
    253–69 . . . .   Dom.Mon.
Earliest English Poems, trans. with introduction and notes Michael
    Alexander, Penguin Classics, 2nd ed., 1977 . . . .   Poems
English Correspondence of St Boniface, ed. Edward Kylie, New York,
    1966 . . . .   Corr.S.Bon.
English Historical Documents, Vol. I, ed. Dorothy Whitelock, 1955 .   EHD I
Inquisitiones Post Mortem, Folkestone, Arch.Cant.3, 1860, p. 255 .   IPM
Kent Domesday, Text, ed. with introduction F. W. Ragg, VCHK III,
    1932, pp. 203–52 . . . .   K.Dom.
Kentish Book of Aid for Knighting of Black Prince, ed. James
    Greenstreet, Arch.Cant.10, 1876, pp. 99–162 . .   KBA
Laws of the Earliest English Kings, trans. with notes F. L. Atten-
    borough, 1925. . . . .   Attenborough
Liber de Hyda, printed by J. K. Wallenberg (*Kentish Place-Names*,
    1931, Uppsala, pp. 336–51) . . . . . .   Lib.de H
Monumenta Germanica Historica: Auctores Antiquissimi, ed T.
    Mommsen, Vols. IV, 1881; IX, 1892; and XIII, 1898 . .   Mon.Ger.Hist.
Poenitentiale Theodori, printed in Councils, ed. A. W. Haddan and
    Stubbs (*see above*), Vol. III, pp. 173–203 . . . .   Poen.Th.
Recueil des Historiens des Gaules et de la France, ed. Dom. Martin
    Bouquet, Vol. IV, 1869 (*Rerum Gallicarum et Francorum
    Scriptores*) . . . .   Recueil
Textus Roffensis, extracts in EHD I (*see above*), p. 431 . .   Text.Roff.

B. EARLY ANNALS, CHRONICLES AND LIVES

Anglo-Saxon Chronicle, ed. G. N. Garmonsway, Dent paperback, 1972   A-SC
Asser, *Life of King Alfred*, ed. W. H. Stevenson, New impression by
    Dorothy Whitelock, 1959

B. EARLY ANNALS ETC. – *continued*   *Abbrev.*

Bartholomew Cotton, *Historia Anglicana*, ed. Henry Richard Luard, 1859
Bede, *Historia Ecclesiastica*, ed. C. Plummer, 1896 .   .   .   .   Bede, Hist.Ecc.
——,   *Life of St Cuthbert*, ed. B. Colgrave (*Two Lives of St Cuthbert*,
        1940)
Constantius of Lyon, *Life of St Germanus of Auxerre*, ed. R. Borius,
        1965.
Eddius, Stephanus, *Life of Bishop Wilfrid*, ed. B. Colgrave, 1927
Felix, *Life of St Guthlac*, ed. B. Colgrave, 1955
Florence of Worcester, *Chronicon ex Chronicis*, ed. B. Thorpe, 2 vols.
        1848–49
Gervase of Canterbury, *Actus Pontificum*, ed. William Stubbs (*The Historical
        Works of Gervase of Canterbury*, Vol. II, 1880)
Gildas, *De excidio et conquestu Britanniae*, ed. Joseph Stevenson, 1838.
Gregory of Tours, *History of the Franks*, trans. with introduction
        O. M. Dalton, 1927
Henry of Huntingdon, *Historia Anglorum*, ed. Thomas Arnold, 1879
Lives of the Kentish Royal Saints, trans. M. J. Swanton in *A
        Fragmentary Life of St Mildred and the Kentish Royal Saints*,
        Arch.Cant.91 (1975), pp. 15–27
Mathew Paris, *Vitae Duorum Offarum*, ed. Wats
Nennius, *Historia Brittonum*, ed. with commentary Ferdinand Lot
        (*Nennius et L'Historia Brittonum*, Paris, 1934)
Procopius of Caesarea, *De Bello Gothico*,
Roger of Wendover, *Flores Historiarum*, ed. Henry O. Cox, Vol. I, 1841
Simeon of Durham, *Historia Regum*, ed. Thomas Arnold, 1885
Tacitus, *Germania*,
Thomas of Elmham, *Historia Monasterii S. Augustini Cantuariensis*, ed.
        Charles Hardwick, 1858
William of Malmesbury, *Gesta Pontificum Anglorum*, ed. N. E. S. A.
        Hamilton, 1870 .   .   .   .   Malmesbury G.P.
——, *Gesta Regum Anglorum*, ed. Duffus Hardy, 1840 .   .   .   Malmesbury G.R.
William Thorne, *William Thorne's Chronicle of St Augustine's Abbey,
        Canterbury*, trans A. H. Davis, 1934

III. Secondary Sources

Aberg, N., 1926. *The Anglo-Saxons in England during the Early Centuries after the Invasion*,
        Uppsala.
Alcock, Leslie, 1962. Article in Ant.63, *Notes and News*, pp. 51–55, with commentary by Jones,
        Glanville.
——, 1973. *Arthur's Britain*, Pelican paperback.
Applebaum, S., 1972. *Roman Britain*, Ag.Hist.I(II), pp. 3–277.
Attenborough, F. L., 1925, *see* under II.A. above.
Baker, Alan R. H., 1964. *Open Fields and Partible Inheritance on a Kent Manor*, Econ.H.R., 2nd ser.,
        17, pp. 1–23.
Becker, C.H., 1967. *The Expansion of the Saracens*, CMH II, pp. 366–90.
Blair, Peter Hunter, 1977. *An Introduction to Anglo-Saxon England*, 2nd ed.
Blunt, C. E., 1961. *The Coinage of Offa*, A-S. Coins, pp. 39-62.
Brooks, Nicholas, 1971. *The development of military obligations in eighth- and ninth-century England*,
        printed in *England before the Conquest*, pp. 69–84.
Bruce-Mitford, Rupert, 1979. *The Sutton Hoo Ship Burial, a Handbook*, British Museum, 3rd ed.
Campbell, A., 1973. *Charters of Rochester*.

Chadwick, H. M., 1905. *Studies on Anglo-Saxon Institutions.*

—, 1907. *The Origin of the English Nation.*

Chadwick, S. E., 1958. *The Anglo-Saxon Cemetery at Finglesham, Kent; a Reconsideration,* Med. Arch.2, pp. 1–71.

Charles, Dennis and Stoyel, Anthony, 1975. *Otford in Kent.*

Collingwood, R. G.,1937. *Roman Britain,* Oxford History of England, Vol. I, Books I–IV, 2nd ed.

Cox, Barry, 1972-3. *The Significance of the Distribution of English Place-Names in 'ham' in the Midlands and East Anglia,* English Place-Names Society Journal, 5, pp. 15–73.

Davidson, Hilda R. Ellis and Webster, Leslie, 1967. *The Anglo-Saxon Burial at Coombe (Woodnesborough), Kent,* Med.Arch.11, pp. 1–41.

Deansley, Margaret, 1925. *The Familia of Christchurch, Canterbury,* Ess.Med.Hist., pp. 1–13.

—, 1941. *Canterbury and Paris in the Reign of Aethelberht,* Hist.26, pp. 97–104.

Derolez, A., 1974. *Cross-Channel Language Ties,* A-SE 3, pp. 1–14.

Detsicas, A. P., 1973-4. *Excavations at Aylesford, 1972 and 1973,* Arch. Cant. 88, pp. 73–80 and 89, pp. 119–34.

Dodgson, John McN., 1966. *The Significance of the Distribution of the English Place-Name in -ingas-, -inga-, in South-East England,* Med.Arch.10, pp. 1–29.

—, 1973. *Place-Names from 'ham', distinguished from 'hamm' names, in relation to the settlement of Kent, Surrey and Sussex,* A-SE 2, pp. 1–50.

Du Boulay, F. R. H., 1961. *Denns, Droving and Danger,* Arch.Cant.76, pp. 75–87.

—, 1966. *The Lordship of Canterbury.*

Dumville, David, 1974. *Some Aspects of the Chronology of the Historia Brittonum,* Bull.Celt.St., 25, pp. 439–45.

—, 1976. *The Anglian Collection of Royal Genealogies and Regnal Lists,* A-SE 5, pp. 23–50.

—, 1977. *Kingship, Genealogies and Regnal Lists,* E.Med.King., pp. 72–104.

—, 1977. *Sub-Roman Britain: History and Legend,* Hist.62, pp. 173-92.

Ekwall, Eilert, 1920. *Englische Studien,* Lund.

—, 1923. *English Place-Names in -Ing,* Lund.

Evans, John H., 1953. *Archaeological Horizons in the North Kent Marshes,* Arch.Cant.66, pp. 103–46.

Evison, V. I. 1956. *An Anglo-Saxon Cemetery at Holborough, Kent,* Arch.Cant.70, pp. 84–141.

—, 1965. *The Fifth-Century Invasions South of the Thames.*

Finberg, H. P. R., 1972. *Anglo-Saxon England to 1042,* Ag.Hist.I(II). pp. 385–532.

—, 1976. *The Formation of England, 550–1042,* Paladin History of England.

Fletcher (Lord) and Meates, G. W., 1969 and 1977. *The Ruined Church of Stone-by-Faversham,* Ant.J. 49, pp. 273–94 and 57, pp. 67–72.

Forster, Max, 1921. *Keltisches Wortgut in Englischen,* Halle.

Fowler, H. P. R., *Religious Houses of Kent,* VCHK II, pp. 112-240.

Furley, Robert, 1871-4. *A History of the Weald of Kent,* 2 vols.

Garmonsway, G. M., 1972. *Introduction to Anglo-Saxon Chronicle,* Dent paperback.

Gelling, Margaret, 1967. *English Place-Names Derived from the compound 'wicham'* Med.Arch.II, pp. 87–104.

—, 1978. *Signposts to the Past.*

Gray, H. L., 1915. *English Field Systems,* 1959 ed.

Grierson, Philip, 1959. *Commerce in the Dark Ages: a Critique of the Evidence,* T.R.Hist.S., Fifth ser., pp. 123-40.

Grove, L. R. A., 1952. *The Whiteheath Excavations: The Beale Poste MSS.,* Arch.Cant.65, pp. 160–66.

Harden, D. B., 1956. *Glass Vessels in Britain and Ireland, A.D. 400–1000,* DAB, pp. 132–67.

Harris, John, 1719. *The History of Kent.*

Harrison, Kenneth, 1971. *Early Wessex Annals in the Anglo-Saxon Chronicle,* EHR 86, pp. 527-33.

—, 1973. *The Primitive Anglo-Saxon Calendar,* Ant.47, pp. 284–87.

—. 1976. *The Framework of Anglo-Saxon History to A.D. 900.*

Hasted, Edward, 1797–1801. *History and Topographical Survey of Kent,* 2nd ed., 12 vols.

Havighurst, F., 1958. *The Pirenne Thesis,* Boston.

Hawkes, C. F. C. 1956. *The Jutes of Kent,* DAB, pp. 91–111.

Hawkes, S. C., 1961. *The Jutish Style: A Study of Germanic Art in Southern England in the Fifth Century, A.D.*, Arch.98, pp. 27–74.

—, 1975. *The Anglo-Saxon Cemetery at Monkton, Thanet*, Arch.Cant.89, pp. 49–89.

—, and Dunning, G. C. 1961. *Soldiers and Settlers in Britain, Fourth to Fifth Century*, Med.Arch.5, pp. 1–70.

—, and Grove, L. R. A. 1963. *Finds from a Seventh Century Anglo-Saxon Cemetery at Milton Regis*, Arch.Cant.78, pp. 22–38.

Hill, P. V., 1958. *Anglo-Frisian Trade in the Light of Eighth Century Coins*, Tr.L. and M.Arch.S. 19, pp. 138–46.

Hinton, David A., 1977. *Alfred's Kingdom, Wessex and the South, 800–1500.*

Hodgkin, R. H., 1952. *History of the Anglo-Saxons*, 3rd ed., 2 vols.

Hollister, C. Warren, 1962. *Anglo-Saxon Military Institutions.*

Homans, G. C., 1957. *The Frisians in East Anglia*, Econ.H.R., 2nd ser. 10, pp. 189–206.

Hughes, Kathleen, 1973. *The Welsh Latin Chronicles: Annales Cambriae and Related Texts*, Proc.Br.A., 59, pp. 233–58.

Jackson, K. H., 1939. *The Goddodin of Aneirin*, Ant. 13, pp. 25–34.

—, 1953. *Language and History in Early Britain.*

Jenkins, Robert C., 1860. *On the Connection between the Monasteries of Kent in the Saxon Period*, Arch.Cant.3, pp. 19–34.

Jessup, Frank W., 1978. *A History of Kent.*

Jessup, R. F., 1946. *An Anglo-Saxon Cemetery at Westbere, Kent*, Ant.J. 26, pp. 11–21.

—, 1974. *Anglo-Saxon Jewellery*, Shire Publication.

Johnson, Stephen, 1977. *Roman Fortifications on the 'Saxon Shore'*, H.M. Stationery Office.

Jolliffe, J. E. A., 1920. *The Hidation of Kent*, EHR 44, pp. 613–14.

—, 1933. *Pre-Feudal England. The Jutes.*

Jones, Glanville, 1961. *The Tribal System in Wales; a Reassessment in the Light of Settlement Studies*, WHR 1, pp. 111–32.

—, 1961. *Settlement Patterns in Anglo-Saxon England*, Ant.35, pp. 221–32.

—, 1964. *The Distribution of Bond Settlements in North-West Wales*, WHR 2, pp. 19–36.

Kendrick, T. D., 1933. *Polychrome Jewellery in Kent*, Ant.7, pp. 429–52.

Kent, J. P. C., 1961. *From Roman Britain to Saxon England*, A.-S. Coins, pp. 1–22.

Kirby, D. P., 1968. *Vortigern*, Bull. Celt.St. 23, pp. 429–52.

Knocker, Herbert W., 1932. *The Evolution of Holmesdale. No. 3. The Manor of Sundrish*, Arch.Cant.44, pp. 189–210.

Lambarde, William, 1576. *A Perambulation of Kent* (edition of 1826).

Leeds, E. T., 1913. *The Archaeology of the Anglo-Saxon Settlements* (reprint 1970).

—, 1933. *The Early Saxon Penetration of the Upper Thames Area*, Ant.J.13, pp. 229-51.

—, 1935. *Early Anglo-Saxon Art and Archaeology.*

—, 1946. *Denmark and Early England*, Ant.J.26, pp. 22–37.

Lennard, R. V., 1942. *The Character of the Anglo-Saxon Conquests*, Ant.18, pp. 204–14.

Levison, William, 1946. *England and the Continent in the Eighth Century.*

Lieberman, F., 1916. *Die Gesetze der Angelsachsen*, Vol. III, Halle.

—, 1925. *Nennius. The Author of the Historia Brittonum*, Ess.Med.Hist., pp. 25–44.

Livett, G. M., 1926. *Ecclesiastical History of Kent*, VCHK II, pp. 1–111.

Lloyd, J. E., 1913. *A History of Wales from Earliest Times to the Edwardian Conquest*, 2nd ed., Vol. I.

Lot, Ferdinand, 1934. *Nennius et L'Historia Brittonum*, Paris.

Loyn, H. R., 1953. *The Term Ealdorman in the Translations prepared at the time of King Alfred*, EHR 68, pp. 513–24.

—, 1970. *Anglo-Saxon England and the Norman Conquest*, Longman paperback.

—, 1974. *Kingship in Anglo-Saxon England*, A-SE 3, pp. 197–209.

Lyon, Stewart, 1976. *Some Problems in Interpreting Anglo-Saxon Coinage*, A-SE 5, pp. 173–224.

McNeill, William H., 1979. *Plagues and Peoples*, Peregrine Books.

Morris, C., 1971. *The Plague in Britain*, review article, Hist.J.14, Pt. i., pp. 205–15.

Morris, John, 1977. *The Age of Arthur*, rev. ed.

Morris, Richard, 1966. *The Dialect of Kent in the Fourteenth Century*, Arch.Cant.6, pp. 135–56.

Muhlfeld, Helen, 1933. *A Survey of the Manor of Wye*.

Murray, Walter J. C., 1972. *Romney Marsh*, 2nd ed.

Myres, J. N. L., 1933. Review of Jolliffe, 1933, in Arch.J.90, pp. 156-60.

—, 1937, *The English Settlements*, Oxford History of England, Vol. I, Book V, 2nd edn.

—, 1942. *Cremation and Inhumation in the Anglo-Saxon Cemeteries*, Ant. 16, pp. 330–41.

—, 1956. *Romano-Saxon Pottery*, DAB, pp. 16-39.

—, 1966. Review of Evison, 1965, in EHR 81, pp. 340–45.

—, 1969. *Anglo-Saxon Pottery and the Settlement of England*.

—, 1970. *The Angles, the Saxons and the Jutes*, Proc.Br.A., 56, pp. 145–74.

Nightingale, M. D. and Stevens, C. E., 1952. *A Roman Land Settlement near Rochester*, Arch.Cant.65, pp. 150–59.

Page, William, 1915. *Some Remarks on the Churches of the Domesday Survey*, Arch.66, pp. 61-102.

Pfister, M. Christian, 1924. *The Franks before Clovis*, CMH I, 2nd ed., pp. 292-303.

—, 1967. *Gaul under the Merovingian Franks*, CMH II, 2nd ed., pp. 132–58.

Pollock, Frederick and Maitland, Frederic W., 1911. *The History of English Law before the time of Edward I*, 2nd ed.

Reaney, P. H., 1960. *The Origin of English Place-Names*.

—, 1961. *Place-Names and Early Settlement in Kent*, Arch.Cant.76, pp. 58-74.

Richmond, I. A., 1963. *Roman Britain*, Pelican History of England, 2nd ed.

Rollason, D. W., 1978. *Lists of saints resting-places in Anglo-Saxon England*, A-SE 7, pp. 61–93.

Rollister, C. Warren, 1962. *Anglo-Saxon Military Institutions*.

Romano-British Kent, 1932. Composite article in VCHK III. pp. 1–175.

Sawyer, P. H., 1977. *Kings and Merchants*, E.Med.King., pp. 139–58.

Searle, Eleanor, 1963. *Hides, Virgates and Tenant Settlement at Battle Abbey*, Econ.H.R., 2nd ser., 16, pp. 290–300.

Seebohm, Frederic, 1911. *Tribal Custom in Anglo-Saxon Law*.

Shaw, William Francis, 1870. *Memorials of the Royal Ville and Parish of Eastry*.

Sisam, Kenneth, 1953. *Anglo-Saxon Royal Genealogies*, Proc.Br.A., 39, pp. 287–346.

Slater, Gilbert, 1932. *Social and Economic History* (of Kent), VCHK III, pp. 319-55.

Stamp, L. Dudley, 1943. *The Land of Britain (Report of the Land Utilization Survey of Britain), Part 85. Kent*.

Stenton, F. M., 1918. *The Supremacy of the Mercian Kings*, P.A-S.E, pp. 48-66.

—, 1926. *The foundations of English history*, T.R.Hist.S. 4th ser., 9, pp. 159–73.

—, 1933. *The English Element*, Int. Sur.Eng.Pl.N., Vol. I, Part I, pp. 36–54.

—, 1940. *Presidential Address*, T.R.Hist.S., 4th ser., 22, pp. 9–11.

—, 1941. *The Historical Bearing of Place-Name Studies: Anglo-Saxon Heathenism*, T.R.Hist.S., 4th ser., 23, 1-24.

—, 1955. *The Latin Charters of the Anglo-Saxon Period*.

—, 1971. *Anglo-Saxon England*, Oxford History of England, Vol. II, 3rd ed.

Stubbs, William, 1877. *Bugga*, contribution in Dic.Chr.B., I, pp. 355–56.

—, 1880. *Eadberht Pren*, contribution in Dic.Chr.B.,II,pp. 4-5.

—, 1880. *Eahlmund*, contribution in Dic.Chr.B., II, p. 11.

—, 1880. *Eangitha*, contribution in Dic.Chr.B., II, p. 16.

Swanton, M. J., 1975. *A Fragmentary Life of St. Mildred and other Kentish Royal Saints*, Arch.Cant. 91, pp. 15-27.

Tait, J., 1904. *Large Hides and Small Hides*, EHR 17, pp. 282–86.

Teichman-Derville, M., 1936. *The Level and the Liberty of Romney Marsh*.

Tester, P. J., 1958. *An Anglo-Saxon Cemetery at Orpington*, Arch.Cant.83, pp. 125-50.

Turner, G. J., 1915. *Introduction to B.Bk.S.Aug.* Part I, pp. xiii-xliv.

Vinogradoff, Paul, 1904. *Sulung and Hide*, EHR 19, pp. 282–86.

Wallace-Hadrill, J. M., 1971. *Early Germanic Kingship in England and on the Continent*.

Wallenberg, J. K., 1931. *Kentish Place-Names*, Uppsala.

—, 1934. *The Place-Names of Kent*, Uppsala.

Ward, Gordon, 1930. *A Note on the Yokes of Otford*, Arch.Cant.42, pp. 147-56.

—— 1933. Review of Jolliffe, 1933,in Arch.Cant.42, pp. 147-56.

Ward, Gordon, 1934. *The Topography of Some Charters Relating to the Faversham District*, Arch. Cant.46, pp. 123-36.

—, 1938. *King Oswin — A Forgotten Ruler of Kent*, Arch.Cant.50, pp. 60-65.

—, 1939. *Eadberht, Son of King Wihtred*, Arch.Cant.51, pp. 9-26.

—, 1940. *The Wi-Wara-Wics*, Arch.Cant.53, pp. 24-8.

—, 1946. *Saxon Abbots of Dover and Reculver*, Arch.Cant.59, pp. 19-28.

—, 1947. *King Wihtred's Charter of A.D. 699*, Arch.Cant.60, pp. 1-14.

—, 1954. *King Hlothere*, Arch.Cant.68, pp. 91-100.

Warhurst, Alan, 1955. *The Jutish Cemetery at Lyminge*, Arch.Cant.69, pp. 1-40.

Whitelock, Dorothy, 1954. *The Beginnings of English Society*, Pelican History of England, 2nd ed.

—, 1976. Lecture published by Kenneth Harrison in *The Framework of Anglo-Saxon History to A.D. 900*, App. I, pp. 142-46.

Witney, K. P., 1976. *The Jutish Forest*.

Wood, Ian, 1977. *Kings, Kingdoms and Consent*, E.Med.King., pp. 6-29.

Woolf, Rosemary, 1976. *The ideal of men dying for their lord in the Germania and in the Battle of Maldon*, A-SE 5, pp. 63-81.

NOTES TO CHAPTERS

Chapter One

1. For a general account of the end of Roman rule and its aftermath, *see*, in particular, Collingwood, 1937, pp. 248–319; Hodgkin, 1952, pp. 37–73; and Alcock, 1973, pp. 89–113.
2. Johnson, 1977.
3. Hawkes and Dunning, 1961.
4. Myres, 1969, pp. 71–7.
5. Alcock, 1973, pp. 96-8.
6. Myres, 1969, pp. 71–7.
7. Hawkes and Dunning, 1961; and Myres, 1969, pp. 87–9.
8. Bede, *Hist. Ecc.*, I. 15.
9. On the evidence of the late Romano–British style military belt buckles and pottery vessels; *see*, in particular, Alcock, 1973, pp. 182–84.
10. For a general account of the soil and topography of Kent *see* Stamp, 1943. For Romney Marsh and a somewhat conjectural outline of the coast of Kent *c.* A.D. 450, *see* Murray, 1972, pp. 16–40 and Jessup, Frank W., 1958, maps facing pp. 21 and 22· also Evans, 1953. For the extent of the Wealden forest at this time, *see* Witney, 1976, pp. 7–10.
11. For Roman Kent in general *see* Collingwood, 1937, pp. 208-209, 217 and 359-60; *Romano-British Kent*, VCHK III, 1932; and Applebaum, 1972, pp. 69–72.
12. Alcock, 1973, p. 194.
13. Collingwood, 1937, pp. 208–209.
14. Alcock, 1973, pp. 182–84.
15. Bede, *Hist.Ecc.* I, 15.
16. *See*, e.g. Myres, 1937, pp. 436–37; Loyn, 1970, pp. 29–9; and Jessup, Frank W., 1958, p. 29.
17. The term first occurs in two charters issued by Hlothere in 675 and 679 (CS 35 and 45), of which there may be some doubt about the first but the second is an original (S. 7 and 8).
18. Florence of Worcester, II, pp. 44–5.
19. A-SC sub. A.D. 508–534.
20. Bede, *Hist.Ecc.*, I, 15.
21. *See* note by Stevenson, W. H. to Asser's *Life of King Alfred* (1959), pp. 166–70.
22. Stenton, 1971, p. 14.
23. *See*, e.g. Hodgkin, 1952, I, pp. 1–19.
24. *Germania*, 40.
25. Compare Chadwick, H.M., 1907, p.193 and 198n.
26. *De Bello Gothico*, IV, 20.
27. Bouquet, IV (1869), p. 59.
28. *See*, e.g. Gregory of Tours, II, 5 and II, 8.
29. *De Bello Gothico*, IV, 20.
30. *Ibid.*, II, 15 and III, 35.
31. Mon.Ger.Hist., IX, i, 73, p. 203.
32. Myres, 1937, p. 345, n. 1.
33. Ed. Michael Alexander, 1973, pp. 84–7 and Notes, p. 163.
34. *Ibid.*, Introduction, p. 11.
35. *Ibid.*, pp. 153–55.
36. *De Bello Gothico*, IV, 20.

37. Ed. Michael Alexander, 1977; *see*, in particular, Introductory note, pp. 32-5. On possible Kentish origin *see also* Wallace-Hadrill, 1971, p. 38.

38. Chadwick, H. M., 1907, pp. 65-7; and Derolez, 1974.

39. Slater, 1932, p. 334; and Morris, Richard, 1866.

40. Derolez, 1974.

41. Forster, 1921; and Ekwall, 1920, p. 102. ff.

42. Jackson, 1953, in particular pp. 220-23.

43. CS 346. (S. 175).

44. Jolliffe, 1933, pp. 98-120.

45. CS 41.

46. CS 97 and 98. (S. 19).

47. Hlothere and Eadric, Laws, cap. 1 and 3; Æthelberht, Laws, cap. 26.

48. Æthelberht, Laws, cap. 21-3; and *see also* Attenborough, 1922, note on p. 175.

49. Chadwick, H. M., 1907, pp. 81-3 and 1905, p. 402.

50. Hodgkin, 1952, I, pp. 93-4.

51. Pfister, 1924.

52. *Ibid.*

53. Jolliffe, 1933, pp. 117-18.

54. Homans, 1957.

55. *See*, in particular, Myres, 1933.

56. Gildas, c. 24 and c. 25.

57. A-SC sub. A.D. 456 and 473.

58. Æthelberht, Laws, in particular cap. 26.

59. Cf. Loyn, 1962, pp. 40-2.

60. Slater, 1932.

61. Jones, Glanville, 1961 (WHR 1), pp. 111-32 and 1964, pp. 19-36.

62. Jones, Glanville, 1961 (Ant. 35) pp. 221-32.

63. Alcock, 1962.

64. Wallenberg, 1934, p. 577.

65. Dic.Eng.Pl.N., p. 493.

66. Wallenberg, 1934, pp. 318, 323 and 326.

67. Gelling, 1967.

68. Wallenberg, 1931, p. 117.

69. Gelling, 1978, pp. 63-86.

70. *Romano-British Kent*, VCHK III, 1932.

71. Alcock, 1973, p. 194.

72. A charter of A.D. 811 (CS 335; S. 168) mentions the 'royal town' of *Roegingaham*.

73. Bede, *Hist.Ecc.*, I, 26.

74. Gelling, 1978, pp. 82-3.

75. Fletcher and Meates, 1969 and 1977.

76. Finberg, 1972, p. 391.

77. Ine, Laws, cap. 32.

78. Æthelberht, Laws, ca-21 and 26; and Hlothere and Eadric, Laws, cap. 3.

79. Chadwick, H. M., 1905, pp. 113-114.

80. Chadwick, H. M., 1907, pp. 77-83.

81. Æthelberht, Laws, cap. 10-12, 14 and 16.

82. As, for instance, at Chatham Lines; *see* Gaz.A-S.Bur., pp. 114-15.

83. As at Faversham and Dover; *see* Leeds, 1935, pp. 8-13 and, for the nature of the finds as loot, Alcock, 1973, pp. 234-46.

84. As at Barfreston and Sibertswold; *see* Leeds, 1935, pp. 106-07.

85. *See* Alcock, 1973, pp. 142-65, for a critique of the limitations of the typological method and the uncertainty of the dating of archaeological material for this period.

86. Myres, 1969 and 1970.

87. *Germania*, 27.

88. Myres, 1937, pp. 361-2, 369-70 and 377; Leeds, 1913, pp. 115-16; and, for a more recent discovery, Tester, 1968.

89. Jessup, R. F., 1946.
90. Leeds, 1935, pp. 46–7.
91. Leeds, 1913, pp. 121–38.
92. Jolliffe, 1933, p. 102.
93. Harden, 1956. Ten in Kent, at Bifrons (3), Faversham (2), Westbere (2), Eastry, Howletts and Milton Regis. One at Mitcham, Surrey.
94. Cf. Leeds, 1935, pp. 43–4; and Hawkes, S. C., 1975.
95. Aberg, 1926, in particular pp. 30–2.
96. For a convenient summary of the finds of cruciform brooches in Kent, *see* Hawkes, C. F. C., 1956. Finds at Bifrons (3), Howletts (2), Sarre, Faversham, Westbere, Milton Regis, Lyminge and Gilton (Eastry).
97. Myres, 1969, pp. 95–7, and 1970.
98. Gaz.A-S. Bur., 1964, pp. 116-17 and 127.
99. Grove, 1952.
100. Myres, 1969, p. 97.
101. *Ibid.*
102. *Ibid.* p. 95.
103. For Monkton, *see* Hawkes, S. C., 1975; and for other major sites Leeds, 1935, pp. 43–4.
104. Notably at Eastry itself (Buttsole), Ash and Gilton.
105. Myres, 1969, pp. 96–7.
106. Bede, *Hist.Ecc.*, I, 15.
107. A-SC.
108. *Ibid. See also* Harrison, 1971.
109. Chadwick, S. E., 1958.
110. Evison, 1965, pp. 18–30 and 33–37.
111. Leeds, 1935, pp. 1–7.
112. Hawkes, S. C., 1961.
113. Evison, 1965, pp. 46–78.
114. Myres, 1966.
115. Cf. Myres, 1969, p. 109.
116. Gaz.A-S.Bur. (1964); but a more up-to-date plot of the sites in east and mid-Kent is given by Hawkes, S. C., 1975 (map).
117. Myres, 1933.
118. At Lyminge, as at Faversham, the burial sites were concentrated; *see* Warhurst, 1955. At Milton, as at Eastry, they were scattered; *see* Hawkes and Grove, 1963, in particular pp. 36–8.
119. Leeds, 1935, pp. 42–58.
120. Hawkes, C. F. C., 1956.
121. *De Bello Gothico*, IV, 20.
122. Leeds, 1946.
123. Hodgkin, 1952, I, p. 101.

Chapter Two

1. Harrison, 1971, 1973 and 1976, pp. 1–14.
2. Harrison, 1971.
3. Bede, *Hist.Ecc.*, II, 5.
4. Alcock, 1973; but *see also* Chapter 5, pp. 117–118.
5. Bede, *Hist.Ecc.*, II, 5.
6. Harrison, 1976, p. 124.
7. *Ibid.*, p. 33. *See also* Alcock, 1973, pp. 5–9.
8. Harrison, 1976, p. 33.
9. *Ibid.*, pp. 30–51. *See also* Alcock, 1973, pp. 17–18.
10. Ed. Borius R., 1965.

11. Mon.Ger.Hist., ed. T. Mommsen, Vol. IX, 1892, in particular, p. 660.
12. Cf. Lennard, 1942. For different interpretations of the meaning of these entries, *see* Alcock, 1973, pp. 105–107, and Hawkes, C. F. C., 1956.
13. Harrison, 1976, pp. 26–27.
14. Ed. Joseph Stevenson, 1838.
15. For critique of Gildas' work, *see* Stenton, 1971, pp. 2–4; Hodgkin, 1952, I, pp. 76–8; Alcock, 1973, pp. 105–107; and Harrison, 1976, pp. 21–4.
16. Cf. summary of relevant considerations in Myers, 1937, pp. 460–61; but for a possible different interpretation of the dating, *see* Alcock, 1973, pp. 53–5.
17. Bede, *Hist.Ecc.*, I, 15.
18. Stenton, 1926; and Harrison, 1976, pp. 134–45.
19. Harrison, 1976, pp. 121–23.
20. Councils, III, pp. 17–18.
21. Harrison, 1976, pp. 121–23.
22. *Ibid.*, p. 123.
23. Stenton, 1971, pp. 16–17.
24. Dumville, 1977 (Hist.).
25. Bede, *Hist.Ecc.*, II, 5.
26. Wallace-Hadrill, 1971, pp. 34–9.
27. Bede, *Hist.Ecc.*, II, 5.
28. Bede, *Hist.Ecc.*, I, 15.
29. Harrison, 1976, pp. 21–6.
30. *Ibid.*
31. *Ibid.* pp. 123-26.
32. *Ibid.*
33. Dumville, 1974.
34. E.g., Garmonsway, 1972, pp. xxi–xxii.
35. Harrison, 1971 and 1976, App. 2, pp. 147–50.
36. Harrison, 1976, pp. 11–12.
37. *Ibid.*, App. 2, pp. 147–50.
38. E.g., Alcock, 1973, p. 43.
39. E.g., Hodgkin, 1952, I, pp. 79–81; Myres, 1937, pp. 329–30; Stenton, 1971, Bibliography, 2, p. 694; Alcock, 1973, pp. 33–4; and for a still more critical verdict Lot, 1934, *passim*.
40. Morris, John, 1973, p. 37.
41. Dumville, 1977 (Hist.).
42. For a recent evaluation of this part of the *Historia Brittonum, see* Alcock, 1973, pp. 55–73; but not everyone would share the trust he places in it.
43. Hughes, 1973.
44. *Ibid.*
45. Alcock, 1973, Preface, p. xvii.
46. Harrison, 1971.
47. Alcock, 1973, pp. 104–109.
48. Dumville, 1974.
49. Woolf, 1976.
50. Gildas, c. 23.
51. Hawkes, C. F. C., 1956.
52. Nennius, c. 31.
53. Gildas, writing in Wales, appears to have overemphasized the early menace from the Picts and Scots in comparison to that from the Germans; *see* Harrison, 1976, p. 25.
54. A-SC sub. A.D. 449.
55. Cf. Hodgkin, 1952, I, pp. 22–4.
56. Alcock, 1973, pp. 274–81 and 301.
57. *De Bello Gothico*, IV, 20.
58. A-SC sub. A.D. 455.
59. CS 502. (S. 327).

60. Bede, *Hist.Ecc.*, I, 15.
61. Myres, 1937, p. 358, n. 1.
62. Nennius, c. 38.
63. Bede, *Hist.Ecc.*, II, 5.
64. A-SC sub. A.D. 449.
65. CD 758.
66. Wallenberg, 1931, p. 320.
67. Nennius, c. 43.
68. Liebermann, 1925.
69. For a description of Kits Coty, *see* VCHK I (1908), pp. 318-319.
70. Nennius, c. 37.
71. Gildas, c. 23.
72. Collingwood, 1937, pp. 179-80. *See also* Alcock, 1973, pp. 310-311.
73. Alcock, 1973, pp. 324-25.
74. *See*, in particular Gaz.A-S.Bur.; and for a summary of the evidence Alcock, 1973, pp. 327-34.
75. Leeds, 1935, p. 46.
76. Evison, 1965, p. 26.
77. Gildas, c. 24.
78. A-SC sub. A.D. 491.
79. *De Bello Gothico*, IV, 20.
80. Jackson, 1939.
81. Gildas, c. 23.
82. Bede, *Hist.Ecc.*, II, 5.
83. On the identification of *Crecganford* the considerations are well summarized by Wallenberg, 1931, pp. 83-4.
84. The term Surrey is used by Bede (*Hist.Ecc.*, IV, 6) but first appears in a charter of 672-4 (CS 34). For derivation, *see* Myres, 1937, p. 371 and Stenton, 1971, pp. 54-5.
85. Myres, 1969, pp. 96 and 111.
86. *Ibid.*, pp. 104-105.
87. Myres, 1969, pp. 101-102 and 114; and Leeds, 1933.
88. A-SC sub. A.D. 501, 530, 534 and 554.
89. Lot, 1934, p. 66.
90. Hawkes and Dunning, 1961. In addition Richborough shows a quantity of hand-modelled pots of degenerate Roman form, evidently dating from the sub-Roman period; *see* Myres, 1956.
91. Gildas, c. 24.
92. Bede, *Hist.Ecc.*, II, 5.
93. Leeds, 1935, pp. 13-14.
94. Cf. Myres, 1937, pp. 368-69.
95. Evison, 1965, *passim*.
96. Gregory of Tours, II, 13. *See also* Lennard, 1942.
97. Alcock, 1973, pp. 55-73; and Dumville, 1977 (Hist.).
98. Dumville, 1977 (Hist.).
99. Hodgkin, 1952, I, pp. 121-23.
100. Alcock, 1973, pp. 67-71.
101. Morris, John, 1973, pp. 112-113.
102. Dumville, 1977 (Hist.).
103. Nennius, c. 56.
104. Alcock, 1973, pp. 59-60.
105. Myres, 1937, pp. 380-81.
106. Evison, 1965, *passim*.
107. *See*, e.g., Alcock, 1973, p. 71 and Collingwood, 1937, p. 322.
108. Myres, 1969, p. 115.
109. *Ibid.*, pp. 110-111 and 115.

Chapter Three

1. Cf. Chadwick, H. M., 1907, pp. 65-7.
2. Cf. Harris, 1719, p. 399.
3. Levison, 1946, App. 1, pp. 174-225.
4. Turner, 1915; and Stenton, 1955, p. 4 with n. 1 and pp. 19-22.
5. CS 6 (S. 4).
6. Witney, 1976, pp. 49-55 and 60-64.
7. Jolliffe, 1933, pp. 82-90.
8. *Ibid.*, pp. 73-82.
9. Bede, *Hist.Ecc.*, I. 19.
10. Jolliffe, 1933, heading to Chapter II, p. 73.
11. Witney, 1976, pp. 49-55.
12. CS 459 (S. 300).
13. CS 1321 and 1322.
14. Æthelberht, Laws, cap. 6. And *see* Chapter 5, pp. 125-27.
15. Cf. Bede, *Hist.Ecc.*, I, 25, though the terminology he uses is that employed not in Kent itself, but outside it.
16. For the nature of these entities, *see* Jolliffe, 1933, pp. 19-39.
17. *Ibid.*, p. 44.
18. Du Boulay, 1966, p. 206.
19. Jolliffe, 1933, p. 43.
20. Du Boulay, 1966, p. 118.
21. *See*, e.g. Baker, 1964.
22. Hasted, Vol. X, 1800, p. 220.
23. CS 214 (S. 111).
24. Jolliffe, 1933, pp. 19-39.
25. *Ibid.*, pp. 41-43. *See also* Lambarde, 1826 ed., pp. 344-46 for the distribution by sulungs of the charges for the upkeep of Rochester Bridge.
26. Jolliffe, 1933, pp. 39-72, more especially pp. 44-46.
27. Ward, 1933, for a particularly ungracious criticism.
28. Bede, *Hist.Ecc.*, II, 9.
29. Finberg, 1972, pp. 412-413.
30. CS 34 and 36 (S. 1165 and 7).
31. Witney, 1976; for the Wealden commons and the lathes to which they belonged pp. 31-55, and for the processes by which the commons were broken up into a medley of manorial dens, pp. 78-103.
32. Wallenberg, 1934, pp. 355-56.
33. Witney, 1976, p. 45.
34. Cf. Ward, 1940.
35. Murray, 1972, pp. 16-40 for an excellent summary of the evolution of Romney Marsh.
36. *Note*, e.g., the lands around Dymchurch later owned by the manors of Monks Horton and Newington near Hythe, and those in the north-east corner of Romney Marsh by the manor of Street in Lympne; Teichman-Derville, 1936, App.III, pp. 99-112. Also, a charter ascribed to A.D. 616-18 (CS 837) mentions land to the south of Burmarsh owned by men of Folkestone; and although this document is in itself spurious the information it gives probably represents genuine tradition.
37. Murray, 1972, pp. 16-40; in particular pp. 30-1.
38. Wallenberg, 1931, pp. 269-70.
39. CS 248 and 263, of A.D. 786 and 791 (S. 125 and 1614). Ruckinge was still accounted an appendage of Ickham at the time of Domesday Book.
40. CD 715 (S. 914).
41. Hasted, Vol. VIII, p. 481.
42. CS 469 (S. 328). For identifications of the lands,*see* Ward, 1940.
43. Jolliffe, 1933, survey of Wye lands pp. 1-8 and map.
44. Witney, 1976, p. 37 and pp. 249-53.

45. CS 247 and 328 (S. 123 and 164); and for identity of *Haradun* Wallenberg, 1931, pp. 67–8.
46. Æthelberht, Laws, cap. 2.
47. Leeds, 1935, pp. 123–24.
48. Cf. Æthelberht, Laws, cap. 7.
49. *Ibid.*, cap. 75.
50. Witney, 1976, pp. 60–64.
51. Cf. CS 418, 459 and 507 (S. 280, 300 and 328).
52. Wallenberg, 1931, p. 169.
53. Chadwick, S. E., 1958.
54. Witney, 1976, pp. 59–64.
55. Du Boulay, 1966, in particular pp. 194–218.
56. Muhlfeld, 1933. But Miss Muhlfeld, in recounting (Introduction, p. xxiii) a survey of 1312 which values a number of large fields and other properties in Wye fails to recognize, what is evident on the face of the valuation, that these were demesne lands; one of the fields surveyed was, in fact, known as *Kingsfelde*.
57. I.P.M., Arch.Cant.3 (1860), p. 255.
58. Muhlfeld, 1933, Introduction, p. xxiii.
59. I.P.M., Arch.Cant.3 (1860), p. 255.
60. Du Boulay, 1966, pp. 117–24.
61. E.g., CS 321 of A.D. 805 (S. 161), which speaks of one *geocled* of land, and CS 341 of A.D. 812 (S. 169), which speaks of an *ioclet*.
62. The term *inman*, as denoting the tenants of inland, was used in later manorial times, e.g., at Sundridge; *see* Knocker, 1932.
63. As at Wye; *see* Muhlfeld, 1933, Introduction, pp. xxxix–li.
64. Knocker, 1932.
65. Baker, 1964.
66. Muhlfeld, 1933.
67. B.BK.S.Aug., Part I, 1915, pp. 68–80.
68. Du Boulay, 1966, pp. 164–81, and B.Bk.S.Aug., *passim.*
69. Jolliffe, 1933, *passim.*
70. Kent Costumal of Edward I; *see* Slater, 1932, pp. 325–29.
71. Jolliffe, 1933, p. 37.
72. *Ibid.*, pp. 32–4; and Du Boulay, 1966, pp. 176–81.
73. K.Dom., *passim.*
74. K.Dom., sub. Newington Manor.
75. *Ibid.*, sub. Sandwich and Luddenham.
76. From Teynham; *see* Du Boulay, 1966, p. 178.
77. From Plumstead; *see* B.Bk.S.Aug., Part I, 1915, pp. 307–308.
78. Jolliffe, 1933, p. 32; Du Boulay, 1966, pp. 164–76; and Baker, 1964.
79. *See*, e.g., Muhlfeld, 1933, Introduction, p. xliv.
80. Knocker, 1932.
81. B.Bk.S.Aug., Part I, 1915, p. 101.
82. Du Boulay, 1966, pp. 166–68; but he does not distinguish between the services required from the outland and inland tenants, a distinction which appears very clearly in the manorial accounts, e.g., of St. Augustine's Abbey (B.Bk.S.Aug.).
83. Muhlfeld, 1933, Introduction, p. xxxix.
84. B.Bk.S.Aug., Part I, 1915, pp. 101–102.
85. Stenton, 1971, p. 279.
86. For Tribal Hidage, *see* Stenton, 1971, pp. 295–97 and Loyn, 1970, pp. 316–318.
87. Tait, 1902; and Stenton, 1971, p. 279.
88. For East Anglian *caracute, see* Homans, 1957.
89. CS 341 (S. 169).
90. Vinogradoff, 1904.
91. Bede, *Hist.Ecc.*, I, 25.
92. Æthelberht, Laws, cap. 16 and 25.

93. *See* Alcock, 1973, pp. 335-36.
94. Witney, 1976, pp. 69-74.
95. CS 426 (S. 287).
96. CS 45 (S. 8).
97. CS 341 (S. 169).
98. CS 370 (S. 186).
99. Æthelberht, Laws, cap. 26.
100. Muhlfeld, 1933, Introduction, pp. xliv and lxxvi.
101. CS 263 (S. 1614).
102. CS 507 (S. 332).
103. Attenborough, 1922, Notes, p. 176, n.13.2.
104. Æthelberht, Laws, cap. 6.
105. Hlothere and Eadric, Laws, cap. 1 and 3.
106. Du Boulay, 1966, pp. 169-70.
107. *Ibid.*, pp. 145, 170-71 and 180-81; and *see* Jolliffe, 1933, pp. 33-9.
108. E.g. Morris, John, 1973, pp. 318-20.
109. Jolliffe, 1933, p. 119.

Chapter Four

1. Blair, 1977, p. 26.
2. Bede, *Hist.Ecc.*, I, 15.
3. Nennius, c. 62-3; and *see* Stenton, 1971, p. 76.
4. Myres, 1937, pp. 418-22; and Alcock, 1973, pp. 119-20.
5. Stenton, 1971, pp. 48-9.
6. Cf. Myres, 1942, pp. 330-41, in particular p. 333.
7. It appears from Felix's *Life of St Guthlac*, written at the beginning of the 8th century, that the Mercian royal family were known as the Icelingas (Felix, pp. 72-5). Icel stands five generations back in the ancestry of Penda, who became king in 633 (Bede, *Hist.Ecc.*, II, 20). The genealogies of the Mercian and other royal lines are set out by Dumville (1976, pp. 25-30, in particular pp. 30-37).
8. Bede, *Hist.Ecc.*, II, 15.
9. Nennius, c. 59.
10. Stenton, 1971, p. 53.
11. *De Bello Gothico*, IV, 20.
12. The principal source used in this account of early kingship is *Early Mediaeval Kingship*, ed. P. H. Sawyer and I. N. Wood, 1977, and in particular contributions by Wood, pp. 6-29, and Dumville, pp. 72-104.
13. Tacitus, *Germania*, 7.
14. Dumville, 1977 (E.Med.King.), p. 77; and Stenton, 1971, p. 54.
15. Wood, 1977.
16. Cf. Stenton, 1971, pp. 66-73; and Wood, 1977, p. 19.
17. *See* comment by Dumville (1977, E.Med.King., pp. 90-1 with n. 103).
18. Eormenred in A.D. 640; *see* Chapter 7, pp. 166-67.
19. Cf. Eadric's consent to a grant by Hlothere in A.D.679; CS 45.
20. Morris, John, 1973, p. 320.
21. Cf. Grierson, 1959, pp. 123-40.
22. Procopius, *De Bello Gothico*, IV, 20, gives land shortage as the reason; but, as the passage as a whole shows, his ignorance of conditions in Britain was profound.
23. *Germania*, ch. 14.
24. *De Bello Gothico*, IV, 20.
25. Harrison, 1971, pp. 527-33, and 1976, pp. 127-30.
26. Hodgkin, 1952, I, p. 129.
27. *Ibid.*
28. Bede, Hist.Ecc., III, 7.

29. King List prefaced to Parker manuscript of A-SC.
30. Sisam, 1953.
31. Stenton, 1971, pp. 24-5.
32. Asser, ch. 2.
33. Myres, 1937, p. 366.
34. Bede, *Hist.Ecc.*, I, 15.
35. Jolliffe, 1933, pp. 82-90.
36. Myres, 1937, p. 364.
37. Stenton, 1940.
38. A-SC sub. A.D. 495.
39. Loyn, 1953.
40. Bede, *Hist.Ecc.*, IV, 16; and A-SC sub. A.D. 686.
41. Bede, *Ibid.*
42. Stenton, 1971, pp. 295-97; and Loyn, 1970, pp. 316-318.
43. *De Bello Gothico*, IV, 20.
44. Leeds, 1935, pp. 48-9.
45. Chadwick, S. E., 1958.
46. Leeds, 1935, pp. 56-7. But Leeds, believing the Jutes to have been Ripuarian Franks, considered the middle Rhine to have been the common source of the style exhibited in this cemetery, in Kent and on the Isle of Wight.
47. Pfister, 1967, pp. 113-114.
48. Bede, *Hist.Ecc.*, I, 32.
49. Hawkes, C. F. C., 1956.
50. Grierson, 1959.
51. Kent, 1961.
52. Lyon, 1976.
53. Loyn, 1970, pp. 79-89; and Hill, 1958.
54. Cf. Kent, 1961.
55. Æthelbert, Laws, cap. 30.
56. Harden, 1956.
57. Wihtred, Laws, cap. 26.
58. The evidence is assembled by Levison (1964, Introduction, pp. 1-14).
59. Bede, *Hist.Ecc.*, II, 1.
60. Letter of Pope Gregory to Candidus, Sept. 595; EHD I, p. 727.
61. Hlothere and Eadric. Laws, cap. 16. And *see* Chapter 8, pp. 192-93.
62. Witney, 1976, pp. 18-21.
63. CS 72 (S. 12).
64. CS 148, 214 and 341 (S. 23, 111 and 169).
65. *Uuiae*, A.D. 839; CS 426 (S. 287). *See* Wallenberg, 1931, p. 182 and Stenton, 1941, p. 13.
66. Witney, 1976, pp. 60-6, 86-7, 98 and App. D, pp. 201-205.
67. CS 91 (S. 22).
68. Collingwood, 1937, p. 239. Significantly, the chief discovery of a villa devoted to fulling cloth is at Darenth in Kent.
69. Tester, 1968.
70. Gaz.A-S.Bur., pp. 108, 123-4, 127-8, 137 and 141-2.
71. Evison, 1956.
72. Detsicas, 1973 and 1974.
73. Gelling, 1978, pp. 121-29.
74. Dodgson, 1966.
75. The rendering given by Margaret Gelling (1978, p. 112).
76. Æthelberht, Laws, cap. 77.
77. Gelling, 1978, p. 114.
78. Wallenberg, 1931 and 1934, *passim.*
79. Reaney, 1961.
80. Dodgson, 1973.

81. Cox, 1972-3.
82. The tendency of early burial sites to neglect the Roman roads and to be found in the proximity of navigable rivers was noted by E. T. Leeds nearly 70 years ago (Leeds, 1913, pp. 17-19).
83. Dodgson, 1973.
84. Æthelberht, Laws, cap. 13, 17 and 77.
85. *Westarham*, A.D. 871–89. *See* Wallenberg, 1931, p. 227.
86. Gregory of Tours, IX, 26.
87. Cf. Deansley, 1941.
88. Pfister, 1967, pp. 116–117.
89. William Thorne, II, 2.
90. Jessup, R. F., 1974, pp. 12–13.
91. Gaz.A-S.Bur., pp. 118-119.

Chapter Five

1. Bede, *Hist.Ecc.*, II, 5.
2. Garmonsway, 1972, Introduction, p. xii. *See also* Blair, 1977, p. 354.
3. A-SC sub. A.D. 626.
4. Bede, *Hist.Ecc.*, IV, 1 and V, 8.
5. For Ceawlin's accession, *see* A-SC sub. A.D. 560.
6. The earliest recorded forms of Wimbledon show little resemblance to *Wibbandun: see* Dic. Eng.Pl.N., p. 521.
7. Harrison, 1976, pp. 122–24.
8. *Ibid.*, pp. 132–36.
9. A-SC sub. A.D. 556.
10. Jolliffe, 1933, pp. 90–2.
11. The foundation of Chertsey Abbey by Egbert is referred to in a charter of A.D. 672–74 (CS 34: S. 1165).
12. Bishops, Kings and Nobles, pp. 330–31.
13. Stenton, 1971, p. 27; and Gelling, 1978, p. 14.
14. Stenton, 1971, p. 34.
15. *Ibid.*
16. Kirby, 1968.
17. Stenton, 1971, p. 29.
18. *Ibid.*, p. 30.
19. Bishops, Kings and Nobles, pp. 330–31.
20. Bede, *Hist.Ecc.*, II, 5. But he himself does not use the term *bretwalda* in referring to the supreme ruler. That appears in the Anglo-Saxon Chronicle, sub. A.D. 827.
21. Alcock, 1973, p. 20.
22. In the same passage which purports to record the year of Æthelberht's birth, sub. A.D. 552.
23. Stenton, 1971, pp. 63–9; and Wood, 1977.
24. Under Caedwalla; *see* A-SC sub. A.D. 686, and Chapter 8, pp. 200-202.
25. Bede, *Hist.Ecc.*, II, 3, and A-SC sub. A.D. 604.
26. Bede, *Hist.Ecc.*, I, 25 and II, 5.
27. This was the view of Liebermann (1916, p. 2).
28. Bede, *Hist.Ecc.*, II, 5.
29. Wallace-Hadrill, 1972, pp. 33–9.
30. Bede, *Hist.Ecc.*, II, 5.
31. Wallace-Hadrill, 1972, pp. 41–3; and Loyn, 1974.
32. Wallace-Hadrill, 1972, pp. 43–4.
33. This is evident from the Laws; in particular cap. 72 compared with cap. 54 and 55.
34. Chadwick, H. M., 1905, in particular pp. 2 and 51–62.
35. Lyon, 1976.

36. For blood-prices of eorls and freemen, *see* Hlothere and Eadric, Laws, cap. 1 and 3, and Æthelbert, Laws, cap. 26.
37. Æthelberht. Laws, cap. 30.
38. Loyn, 1974.
39. *Ibid.*
40. Æthelberht, Laws, cap. 22.
41. *Ibid.*, cap. 23.
42. cap. 64.
43. cap. 43 and 69.
44. cap. 38 and 39.
45. cap. 67.
46. cap. 54.
47. cap. 51.
48. cap. 72.
49. cap. 57.
50. cap. 33.
51. cap. 58 and 59.
52. cap. 8, 14 and 15.
53. cap. 5 and 13.
54. cap. 17.
55. cap. 18–20.
56. Ine, Laws, cap. 63.
57. Chadwick, H. M., 1905, pp. 113–14.
58. Æthelberht, Laws. cap. 2.
59. Gregory of Tours, Vol. I, 1927, ed., Introduction by O. M. Dalton, p. 386.
60. Æthelberht, Laws, cap. 2.
61. *Ibid.*, cap. 1.
62. cap. 9.
63. cap. 84.
64. Hlothere and Eadric, Laws, cap. 9 and 11–14.
65. Chadwick, H. M., 1905, pp. 130–31.
66. Æthelberht. Laws, cap. 6.
67. EHD I, p. 357; footnote to translation of Æthelberht, Laws, cap. 6.
68. Liebermann, 1916, pp. 5–6.
69. Hlothere and Eadric, Laws, cap. 3.
70. Finberg, 1972, p. 433.
71. Æthelberht. Laws, cap. 7.
72. Hlothere and Eadric, Laws, cap. 16.
73. Æthelberht, Laws, cap. 73 and 74.
74. Loyn, 1974; and extract from *Textus Roffensis*, EHD I, p. 431.
75. Æthelberht, Laws, cap. 77.
76. *Ibid.*, cap. 82–4.
77. cap. 31.
78. cap. 73.
79. cap. 78–80.
80. Cf. Hlothere and Eadric, Laws, cap. 6.
81. Æthelberht, Laws, cap. 75.
82. *Ibid.*, cap. 76.
83. cap. 14, 16 and 25.
84. cap. 10, 14 and 16.
85. cap. 11.
86. cap. 16.
87. cap. 12 and 25.
88. cap. 87.
89. cap. 89.

90. cap. 85.
91. cap. 90.
92. *Poenitentiale Theodori*, Book Two, section XIII.
93. Finberg, 1972, p. 431.
94. Æthelberht, Laws, cap. 90.
95. Wihtred, Laws, cap. 10, 13, 15 and 23; and Ine, Laws, cap. 3 and 48.
96. Lyon, 1976; and Chadwick, H. M., 1905, pp. 13-18.
97. Ine, Laws, cap. 70.
98. *Ibid.*
99. Chadwick, H. M., 1905, pp. 113-114.
100. Lyon, 1976.
101. Æthelberht, Laws, cap. 6; and Ine, Laws, cap. 70.
102. For levels of *mund* in Wessex, *see* Ine, Laws, cap. 6 and 45. For the two classes of noble they were 30 and 80 shillings, and for the ceorl six shillings; which in Kentish money would represent 12 shillings, seven shillings and two and a half shillings respectively.
103. Deansley, 1941.
104. Æthelberht, Laws, cap. 30.
105. *See*, in particular, charter of Eadberht of Kent, *c.* A.D. 761 (CS 189).
106. The material from this excavation is in the British Museum. *See also* Gaz.A-S.Bur., p. 117.
107. For swords, and ring swords in particular, *see* Davidson and Webster, 1967.
108. For Kentish polychrome jewellery, *see* Jessup, R. F., 1974, especially pp. 39-40 and 68-75.
109. Davidson and Webster, 1967.
110. Harden, 1956.
111. The finds from both burials are in the British Museum. *See also* Gaz.A-S.Bur., pp. 58-9 and 85.
112. Dic.Eng. Pl-N., p. 460.
113. Bede, *Hist.Ecc.*, II, 5.
114. Bruce-Mitford, 1979, pp. 93-7.
115. Bede, *Hist.Ecc.*, II, 5.
116. Bruce-Mitford, 1979, pp. 102-103.
117. *Ibid.*, pp. 107-115.
118. *Ibid.*, pp. 84-92 and 110-111.
119. *Ibid.*, pp. 40-43.
120. *Ibid.*, pp. 98-106.
121. Bede, *Hist.Ecc.*, I, 32.
122. Bruce-Mitford, 1979, pp. 27-31.
123. *Ibid.*, pp. 26-27.
124. Bede, *Hist.Ecc.*, II, 16.
125. *The Earliest English Poems*, ed. Michael Alexander, 1977, Introduction, p. 10.
126. Bruce-Mitford, 1979, p. 119.
127. Wallace-Hadrill, 1971, p. 38 with n. 69.
128. *The Earliest English Poems*, ed. Michael Alexander, 1977, pp. 32-42.

Chapter Six

1. Bede, *Hist.Ecc.*, II, 2.
2. William Thorne, pp. 2-3.
3. Bede, *Hist.Ecc.*, I, 25 and 26.
4. *Ibid.*, Preface.
5. *Ibid.*, II, 5.
6. Letter to priest Candidus; EHD I, p. 727.
7. EHD I, pp. 727-28.

8. Wallace-Hadrill, 1971, p. 29.
9. William Thorne, p. 5.
10. Bede, *Hist.Ecc.*, II, 5.
11. Harrison, 1976, p. 79.
12. EHD I, p. 728.
13. Bede, *Hist.Ecc.*, I, 26.
14. Stenton, 1941.
15. Gelling, 1978, pp. 154-61.
16. Jessup, R. F., 1974, pp. 84-6.
17. Wihtred, Laws, cap. 12 and 13.
18. *Germania*, c. 40.
19. *Poenitentiale Theodori*, Book I, section XV, 3.
20. For a general account of English heathenism, *see*, e.g. Whitelock, 1954, pp. 11-28.
21. Councils, pp. 17-18.
22. Wallace-Hadrill, 1971, p. 97.
23. Deansley, 1941.
24. Wallace-Hadrill, 1971, p. 46.
25. Bede, *Hist.Ecc.*, I, 27.
26. Letter from Gregory to Eulogius, bishop of Alexandria, July 598 A.D.; EHD I, p. 728.
27. Bede, *Hist.Ecc.*, I, 27 and 29-31.
28. *Ibid.*, I, 32.
29. *Ibid.*, I, 33.
30. *Ibid.*, II, 3.
31. A-SC sub. A.D. 604.
32. Fowler, 1926, map facing p. 112.
33. William Thorne, p. 10.
34. Bede, *Hist.Ecc.*, I, 29.
35. Thomas of Elmham, pp. 96-102.
36. E.g. record of council summoned by Wihtred at Bapchild *c.* A.D. 708; (CS 91; S. 22).
37. Bede, *Hist.Ecc.*, II, 5.
38. *Ibid.*, III, 22.
39. *Ibid.*, II, 3 and IV, 22.
40. Hlothere and Eadric, Laws, cap. 16.
41. As, for instance, it appears in Domesday Book.
42. CS 248 (S. 125).
43. Bede, *Hist.Ecc.*, I, 29.
44. *Ibid.*, II, 3.
45. *Ibid.*, I, 27.
46. Æthelberht, Laws, cap, 1 and 4.
47. Bede, *Hist.Ecc.*, I, 26.
48. *Ibid.*, I, 32.
49. *Ibid.*, II, 15.
50. Gildas, ch. 10.
51. Bede, *Hist.Ecc.*, I, 27.
52. Harrison, 1976, pp. 57-62.
53. Finberg, 1976, p. 47; and Lloyd, Vol. I, 1912, pp. 175-77.
54. Bede, *Hist.Ecc.*, II, 2.
55. Stenton, 1971, pp. 43-44.
56. Bede, *Hist.Ecc.*, II, 2.
57. Finberg, 1976, p. 40.
58. Bede, *Hist.Ecc.*, II, 2.
59. *Ibid.*
60. A well-balanced account of the considerations is given by Lloyd, Vol. I, 1912, pp. 171-78.
61. Gregory, in his letter to Æthelberht, said that Augustine had been trained under monastic rule and had a complete knowledge of Holy Scripture: *Hist.Ecc.*, I, 32.

62. Wallace-Hadrill, 1971, p. 31.
63. Bede, *Hist.Ecc.*, II, 1.
64. *Ibid.*, II, 3.
65. *Ibid.*, II, 5.
66. A-SC sub. A.D. 597.
67. Bede, *Hist.Ecc.*, II, 5.

Chapter Seven

1. Bede, *Hist.Ecc.*, II, 9.
2. *Ibid.*, III, 25.
3. *Ibid.*, II, 5.
4. *Ibid.*
5. *Ibid.*
6. *Ibid.*
7. *Ibid.*
8. *Ibid.*, I, 27.
9. *Ibid.*, II, 5 and 6..
10. Finberg, 1976, p. 41.
11. Bede, *Hist.Ecc.*, II, 6.
12. Fowler, 1926, p. 133.
13. CS 12 and 13 (S. 6 and 1609).
14. Du Boulay, 1966, p. 23.
15. Thomas of Elmham, p. 142. *See also* Bishops, Kings and Nobles, pp. 258–59.
16. Stenton, 1971, p. 61.
17. Bede, *Hist.Ecc.*, II, 9.
18. *Ibid.*
19. Dic.A-S., p. 170.
20. Bede, *Hist.Ecc.*, I, 34.
21. This is the date given by Stenton (1971, p. 78). The Anglo-Saxon Chronicle gives A.D. 605 or 607.
22. Bede, *Hist.Ecc.*, II, 2.
23. *Ibid.*, II, 12; and A-SC sub. A.D. 617.
24. Blair, 1977, p. 252.
25. Bede, *Hist.Ecc.*, II, 9 and 16.
26. *Ibid.*, II, 5.
27. *Ibid.*, II, 9–14.
28. *Ibid.*, II, 9.
29. A-SC sub. A.D. 626.
30. Bede, *Hist.Ecc.*, II, 13.
31. Stenton, 1941.
32. Bede, *Hist.Ecc.*, II, 16.
33. *Ibid.*, II, 15.
34. Stenton, 1971, p. 45.
35. Felix, pp. 72–5. *See also* Dumville, 1976, pp. 30–37.
36. Stenton, 1971, pp. 38–42.
37. *Ibid.*
38. Bede, *Hist.Ecc.*, II, 20.
39. Stenton, 1921, pp. 80–82; and Lloyd, Vol. I, 1912, pp. 185–86.
40. Bede, *Hist.Ecc.*, III, 1.
41. *Ibid.*, II, 20; and Thomas of Elmham, pp. 176–77.

42. Florence of Worcester, I, p. 259.
43. Livett, 1926, p. 12; and Jenkins, 1860, pp. 26–28.
44. Stenton, 1971, pp. 161–62.
45. *Ibid.*, p. 111.
46. Bede, *Hist.Ecc.*, III, 2.
47. *Ibid.*, III, 6.
48. *Ibid.*, III, 9–13.
49. *Ibid.*, III, 3–5.
50. *Ibid.*, III, 7.
51. *Ibid.*, III, 8.
52. Thomas of Elmham, p. 176.
53. Simeon of Durham, p. 4; and Roger of Wendover, pp. 136–37.
54. Dic.Eng.Chr.N., p. 95.
55. Bede, *Hist.Ecc.*, III, 9.
56. *Ibid.*, III, 12.
57. *Ibid.*, III, 9.
58. Lloyd, Vol. I, 1912, pp. 188–89.
59. *Ibid.*, pp. 189–90.
60. Bede, *Hist.Ecc.*, III, 21.
61. Stenton, 1971, pp. 46–47.
62. Bede, *Hist.Ecc.*, III, 7.
63. Stenton, 1971, p. 83.
64. Bede, *Hist.Ecc.*, III, 18; and A-SC.sub. A.D. 654.
65. Bede, *Hist.Ecc.*, III, 24; and Lloyd, Vol. I, 1912, p. 190.
66. Bede, *Hist.Ecc.*, III, 24.
67. Lloyd, Vol. I, 1912, pp. 190–91.
68. Bede, *Hist.Ecc.*, III, 24.
69. *Ibid.*
70. *Ibid.*, III, 21.
71. *Ibid.*, III, 22.
72. *Ibid.*, III, 21 and 24.
73. Eddius, ch. 14, pp. 30–31.
74. Blair, 1977, pp. 133–34.
75. Stenton, 1971, p. 113.
76. Bede, *Hist.Ecc.*, II, 5 and III, 18.
77. *Ibid.*, III, 7.
78. *Ibid.*, III, 8.
79. Wihtred, Laws, cap. 12 and 13.
80. Bede, *Hist.Ecc.*, III, 8.
81. Stenton, 1971, p. 61.
82. *Lives of the Kentish Royal Saints.*
83. The Anglo-Saxon Chronicle, sub. A.D. 617, names as the sons of Æthelfrid, of the Bernician royal house, Eanfrith, Oswald, Oswy, Oslac, Oswudu, *Oslaf* and Offa.
84. Eddius; Notes on ch. 2, p. 151.
85. Bede, *Hist.Ecc.*, III, 25.
86. *Ibid.*
87. *Ibid.*, II, 20 and III, 25.
88. Eddius, ch. 2 and 3, pp. 4–9.
89. Bede, *Hist.Ecc.*, III, 25.
90. Eddius, ch. 3, pp. 8–9.
91. Bede, *Hist.Ecc.*, III, 25.
92. *Ibid.*, III, 25 and 26.
93. Thomas of Elmham, pp. 188–89. Eddius refers to a certain Berhtwald, son of Wulfhere and Eormenhilda, who in A.D. 681 was acting as a Mercian reeve, or sub-king (ch. 40, pp. 80–81). It seems, therefore, that this marriage must have preceded Earconberht's death in A.D. 664.

94. Since Aebba (*aliter* Domneva) appears to have become Abbess of Minster *c.* A.D. 670, by which time she had had three daughters and one son by her husband Merwal, her marriage must, it seems, also have preceded Earconberht's death in A.D. 664.

95. Bede, *Hist.Ecc.*, IV, 1.

96. *Ibid.*, III, 8.

97. *Ibid.*, IV, 26.

98. *See*, in particular, Florence of Worcester, I, p. 259.

99. Leeds, 1935, pp. 96–108.

100. *Ibid.*

101. William Thorne, pp. 10–11.

102. *See* Evison, 1956; Detsicas, 1973 and 1974; and Charles and Stoyel, 1975, pp. 25–27.

103. CS 97 (S. 19).

104. Æthelberht, Laws, cap. 5, 13 and 17.

105. Hlothere and Eadric, Laws, cap. 5.

106. CS 1321 of A.D. 975.

107. CD 745 of A.D. 1032 (S. 1465).

108. For a useful distinction between *-inga-* and *-ing-* formations, *see* Reaney, 1960, pp. 114–116.

109. CS 408 (S. 323 and 1623).

110. Wallenberg, 1931, pp. 74–76.

111. Ekwall, 1923; and Stenton, 1933.

112. Dodgson, 1966.

113. *Ibid.*, in particular pp. 14–15.

114. Hastings was used by Stenton, 1933, as a prime example of an *-ingas* name.

115. Simeon of Durham, ch. 47.

116. With Birling, Halling and Malling; Wallenberg, 1931, pp. 71, 75 and 253, and 1934 pp. 116, 146 and 148.

117. Wallenberg, 1934, pp. 168, 395 and 411.

118. Jolliffe, 1933, pp. 74–82.

119. *Ibid.*, p. 74.

120. Searle, Eleanor, 1963.

121. Wallenberg, 1931, pp. 336–41, in particular 340–41.

122. *Ibid.*; and *see also* Dodgson, 1976, p. 2.

123. CS 160.

124. Bede, *Hist.Ecc.*, IV, 26.

125. Hasted, VIII, p. 480.

126. CS 141.

127. Bede, *Hist.Ecc.*, IV, 1.

128. *Ibid..* III, 30.

129. McNeill, 1979, in particular ch. 2, pp. 40–77.

130. *Ibid.*, ch. 3, pp. 78–140 and in particular 112–24.

131. Lloyd, Vol. I, 1912, p. 131.

132. Morris, C., 1971, pp. 205–24.

133. Bede, *Hist.Ecc.*, IV, 1.

134. *Ibid.*, III, 30.

Chapter Eight

1. Eddius, ch. 40, p. 81.

2. Fowler, 1926, p. 149.

3. Bede, *Hist.Ecc.* IV, 1.

4. *Ibid.*, IV, 2 and V, 1.

5. Arch.Cant. 91 (1975) pp. 15-27.

6. Simeon of Durham, chs. 2-9, pp. 4–13.

7. Simeon of Durham speaks of *Thunerhleaw*. The term *lope* appears e.g. in the 15th century (Thomas of Elmham, p. 207).
8. Stenton, 1941.
9. William Thorne, pp. 233–44.
10. *Ibid.*
11. Thomas of Elmham, p. 250.
12. William Thorne, p. 234.
13. A-SC sub. A.D. 694.
14. William Thorne, p. 23, n. 5.
15. CS 40 (S. 14).
16. Eddius, ch. 14, p. 31.
17. Bede, *Hist. Ecc.*, IV, 1.
18. CS 34 (S. 1165).
19. Stenton, 1918.
20. A-SC sub. A.D. 661.
21. CS 34 (S. 1165).
22. Bede, *Hist.Ecc.*, IV, 13.
23. *Ibid.*
24. *See,* e.g. A-SC sub. A.D. 652, 658 and 661; and Finberg, 1976, p. 312.
25. Bede, *Hist.Ecc.*, III, 29.
26. *Ibid.*, IV, 5.
27. Stenton, 1971, p. 141.
28. CS 45 (S. 8).
29. Harrison, 1976, pp. 38–39.
30. CS 36 (S. 7).
31. CS 34 (S. 1165).
32. CS 42 (S. 10).
33. Stenton, 1918.
34. Whitelock, 1976 (*see* Harrison, 1976, App. I, pp. 142–46).
35. Harrison, 1976, App. I, pp. 142–46.
36. On Wulfhere's *bretwaldaship, see* Stenton, 1918.
37. CS 36 (S. 7).
38. Bede, *Hist.Ecc.*, IV, 5 and 17.
39. Stenton, 1918.
40. Eddius, ch. 20, p. 43.
41. A-SC sub. A.D. 675.
42. *Ibid.*
43. William of Malmesbury, GP, IV, 183, p. 323.
44. Bede, *Hist.Ecc.*, IV, 12.
45. Hlothere and Eadric, Laws, cap. 16.
46. Bede, *Hist.Ecc.*, II, 3.
47. *Ibid.*, IV, 21 and 22.
48. *Ibid.*, IV, 22.
49. CS 45 (S. 8).
50. *Poenitentiale Theodori*, Book Two, XII, 36.
51. CS 44 (S. 1648).
52. Cf. Bishops, Kings and Nobles, p. 259.
53. Æthelberht, Laws, cap. 10–12, 14, 16 and 25.
54. Seebohm, 1911, p. 469.
55. Wihtred, Laws, cap. 21.
56. Morris, John, 1973, p. 320.
57. Stenton, 1955, 34–35.
58. Hlothere and Eadric, Laws, cap. 11–13.
59. *Ibid.*, cap. 14.
60. Chadwick, H. M., 1905, pp. 130–31.

61. *Poenitentiale Theodori*, Book Two, XII, 36.
62. Ward, 1954.
63. For a general description of the practice of vouching to warranty, *see* Pollock and Maitland, 1911, pp. 58–60.
64. *Wyke*, A.D. 1358; Wallenberg, 1934, p. 217. For a more general account of the use of the term *see* Ward, 1940, and Evans, 1953, pp. 144–45.
65. Sawyer, 1977.
66. *Ibid.*
67. Wihtred, Laws, cap. 28.
68. Lyon, 1976.
69. Eddius, ch. 13, pp. 28-29.
70. For the early existence of the Eastry estuary, *see* Chadwick, S. E., 1958.
71. Bede, *Hist.Ecc.*, IV, 26.
72. *Ibid.*, IV, 13.
73. *Ibid.*, IV, 15; and Eddius ch. 42.
74. Bede, *Hist.Ecc.*, IV, 26; and Thomas of Elmham, p. 250.
75. Henry of Huntingdon, pp. 105–106.
76. CS 67 (S. 9).
77. Cf. Ward, 1954.
78. Bede, *Hist.Ecc.*, IV, 26.
79. A-SC sub. A.D. 685.
80. Stenton, 1971, p. 69.
81. Eddius, ch. 42, p. 85.
82. Bede, *Hist.Ecc.*, IV, 15.
83. A-SC sub. A.D. 685.
84. Bede, *Hist.Ecc.*, IV, 16.
85. *Ibid.*, IV, 15.
86. A-SC.
87. CS 89 (S. 233).
88. A-SC.
89. William Thorne, p. 23.
90. A-SC sub. A.D. 687.
91. Bede, *Hist.Ecc.*, IV, 16.
92. *Ibid.*, V. 7.
93. CS 35 (S. 13).
94. Stenton, 1918, p. 32, n. 3.
95. CS 73 (S. 12).
96. CS 42 (S. 11).
97. Whitelock, 1976 (*see* Harrison, 1976, App. I, pp. 142–46).
98. CS 89 (S. 233).
99. Ward, 1938.
100. Gordon Ward opts for Æthelberht, but apparently in the mistaken belief that he was the elder of the two princes. The contrary appears from *The Lives of the Kentish Royal Saints*, the earliest account written *c*. A.D. 1000.
101. CS 40 (S. 14).
102. CS 73 (S. 12).
103. CS 35 (S. 13).
104. Appointed archbishop in A.D. 792. He was already Abbot of Reculver in A.D. 679; *see* CS 45.
105. CS 73 (S. 12).
106. CS 35 (S. 13).
107. CS 41 and 42 (S. 11 and S. 10).
108. CS 41 (S. 11).
109. CS 42 (S. 10).
110. Bede, *Hist.Ecc.*, V, 9.
111. *Ibid.*, V, 8.

112. Whitelock, 1976 (*see* Harrison, 1976, App. I, pp. 142–46).
113. CS 44 (S. 1648).
114. CS 45 (S. 8).
115. CS 97 and 98 of A.D. 697 (S. 19 and 21).
116. *See*, e.g. CS 99 (S. 20).
117. Bede, *Hist.Ecc.*, V, 9.
118. *Ibid.*, V, 20.
119. Councils, III, pp. 118–22.
120. Finberg, 1976, p. 50.
121. For a brief account of the salient facts, *see* Blair, 1977, pp. 136–38.
122. Bede, *Hist.Ecc.*, IV, 19.
123. Eddius, chs. 24 and 40, pp. 49 and 81.
124. *Ibid.*
125. *Ibid.*, ch. 14.
126. The original source is Wilfrid's contemporary biographer Eddius; but *see also* Finberg, 1976, pp. 48–55 and Stenton, 1971, p. 139.
127. *Praesulam sanctae Cantuariorum ecclesiae*; Councils III, p. 263, *anno*. 704.
128. Levison, 1946, pp. 18–22.
129. Bede, *Hist.Ecc.*, III, 7.
130. EHD I, pp. 729–30.
131. Cf. Bede, *Hist.Ecc.*, IV, 2 and 6.

Chapter Nine

1. Pfister, 1967.
2. Becker, 1967.
3. On the work of Pirenne, *see* Havighurst, 1958.
4. Kent, 1961.
5. Bede, *Hist.Ecc.*, IV, 26.
6. For the identification of *Cilling*, *see* Ward, 1934 and 1947.
7. Bede, *Hist.Ecc.*, IV, 26.
8. Cf. CS 96 of April A.D. 697 recording a grant made by Wihtred in what is stated to be the sixth year of his reign. (S. 18).
9. Bede, *Hist.Ecc.*, V, 8.
10. Eddius, ch. 45, pp. 90–93.
11. Cf. Stenton, 1971, p. 73; and Finberg, 1976, p. 94.
12. At 20 *sceattas* to the shilling.
13. Chadwick, H. M., 1905, p. 17f.
14. EHD I, p. 731.
15. Wihtred, Laws, cap. 5.
16. *Ibid.*, cap. 9–11 and 25; and Ine, Laws, cap. 3 and 12.
17. Wihtred, Laws, cap. 28; and Ine, Laws, cap. 20.
18. Witney, 1976, pp. 39–40.
19. *Ibid.*, and pp. 217–22.
20. Jolliffe, 1933, pp. 90–93.
21. CS 160 (S. 24).
22. CS 141 (S. 1180).
23. EHD I, p. 31, n. 1.
24. It appears as *Berghamstyde* in the Prologue to the Laws. For identification, *see* Wallenberg, 1931, p. 18 (note on CS 88) and Stenton, 1971, p. 62.
25. For the boundary between the two dioceses, *see* Fowler 1926, in particular map facing p. 112. The division follows the old lathe boundaries, except for the inclusion of Maidstone in the diocese of Canterbury; but this seems to have been an adjustment made when Maidstone became a manor of the archbishop.

26. cap. 5; and *see* EHD I, p. 362, n. 3.
27. cap. 20; and *see* Stenton, 1971, pp. 488-89.
28. cap. 28.
29. cap. 8.
30. cap. 25-27.
31. Attenborough, 1925, p. 182, note on cap. 26.1.
32. Ine, Laws, cap. 11.
33. Wihtred, Laws, cap. 1.
34. cap. 2.
35. cap. 16-24.
36. cap. 7.
37. cap. 6.
38. Bede, *Hist.Ecc.*, III, 8.
39. cap. 12.
40. Æthelberht, Laws, cap. 21 and 22.
41. Wihtred, Laws, cap. 13.
42. *Poenitentiale Theodori*, Book One, XV, 1-5.
43. cap. 11.
44. cap. 9, 10, 14 and 15.
45. *Poenitentiale Theodori*, Book Two, XIII, 3.
46. cap. 3-5.
47. Æthelberht, Laws, cap. 77-81.
48. EHD I, p. 431.
49. *Poenitentiale Theodori*, Book Two, XII, 33-36.
50. Bede, *Hist.Ecc.*, I, 27.
51. *Poenitentiale Theodori*, Book Two, XII, 25.
52. EHD I, p. 431.
53. *Poenitentiale Theodori*, Book Two, XII, 5-12 and 17-24; and XIII, 4-7.
54. Councils, III, p. 263, *anno.* 704.
55. Eddius, ch. 46-47, pp. 92-99.
56. *Ibid.*, ch. 50-4, pp. 102-121.
57. *Ibid.*, ch. 58-9, pp. 124-129.
58. *Ibid.*, ch. 60-61, pp. 128-133.
59. *Ibid.*, ch. 65, pp. 140-143.
60. *Ibid.*, ch. 41-2, pp. 80-85.
61. CS 97 and 98 (S. 19 and 21).
62. Fowler, 1926, p. 133.
63. CS 99 (S. 20).
64. William of Malmesbury, GP, IV, 183, p. 323.
65. The fullest version of the text is in CS 91 (S. 22).
66. Cf. *Poenitentiale Theodori*, Book Two, XIII, 36.
67. Ward, 1939.
68. CS 178 (S. 92).
69. CS 89 (S. 2331); and *see* Stenton, 1971, p. 160.
70. Stenton, 1971, pp. 158-61.
71. Eddius, ch. 46-47, pp. 92-99.
72. Stenton, 1971, pp. 159-61.
73. EHD I, pp. 735-45.
74. Stenton, 1971, pp. 306-310.
75. CS 148 (S. 23).
76. CS 173 and 189 (S. 29 and 1612).
77. Brooks, 1971.
78. CS 848 (S. 134).
79. CS 335 (S. 168).
80. Rollister, 1962, pp. 25-58.

81. For Tribal Hidage, *see* Stenton, 1971, pp. 295–97.
82. Finberg, 1972, pp. 442–43.
83. Rollister, 1962, pp. 52 and 54 with n. 4.
85. Jolliffe, 1933, pp. 42–43; and for the distribution by sulungs of the charges for the upkeep of Rochester Bridge, Lambarde, 1826 ed., pp. 344–46.
85. *Poenitentiale Theodori*, Book Two, I; and, for a general discussion, Stenton, 1971, pp. 148–51 and Whitelock, 1977, pp. 164–66.
86. Ine, Laws, cap. 4 and 61.
87. Page, 1915, pp. 61–102.
88. EHD I, pp. 735–45.
89. Ine, Laws, cap. 4 and 61.
90. Stenton, 1971, pp. 152–57; and Whitelock, 1977, pp. 166–68.
91. Æthelberht, Laws, cap. 7.
92. Bede, *Hist.Ecc.*, II, 5.
93. Hlothere and Eadric, Laws, cap. 8.
94. Wihtred, Laws, preamble.
95. CS 91 (S. 22).
96. Æthelberht, Laws, cap. 7.
97. Hlothere and Eadric, Laws, cap. 16.
98. CS 45 (S. 8).
99. CS 91 (S. 22).
100, CS 175 (S. 30).
101. CS 332 (S. 1264).
102. Chadwick, H. M., 1905, pp. 110–114.
103. Cf. Stenton, 1971, p. 73.
104. *Ibid.*, p. 73 and pp. 202–203.
105. Wallace-Hadrill, 1971, p. 29; and Bede, *Hist.Ecc.*, III, 18.
106. Stenton, 1971, pp. 184–87.
107. Bede, *Hist.Ecc.*, IV, 2.
108. *Ibid.*, V, 23.
109. Stenton, 1971, pp. 181–82.
110. Bede, *Hist.Ecc.*, Preface.
111. She attended the council at Bapchild, but Aebba that at *Cilling* in A.D. 699.
112. CS 149 (S. 87).
113. Simeon of Durham, chs. 9 and 10, pp. 12–13; and William Thorne, ch. 24, pp. 233–44.
114. Cf. William Thorne, ch. 24, pp. 242–44.
115. Thomas of Elmham, pp. 317–318 and 328–30; and William Thorne, ch. 7, pp. 26–28.
116. CS 869 (S. 535).
117. William Thorne, ch. 24, p. 241.
118. Corr.S.Bon., ed. Kylie, 1966, pp. 61–67.
119. CS 141 (S. 1180).

Chapter Ten

1. Bede, *Hist.Ecc.*, V, 23.
2. *Ibid.*, V, 7 and A-SC sub. A.D. 726.
3. EHD I, pp. 751–56.
4. Simeon of Durham, sub. A.D. 757, p. 41.
5. Stenton, 1971, pp. 203–204.
6. *Ibid.*
7. CS 162 (S. 90).

8. CS 178 (S. 92).
9. Bede, *Hist.Ecc.*, IV, 12.
10. Thomas of Elmham, p. 337.
11. William of Malmesbury, GR, I, 15, p. 24.
12. Ward, 1939.
13. CS 91 (S. 22).
14. *See* regnal lists in Dumville, 1976.
15. CS 159 (S. 27).
16. CS 191 (S. 25).
17. CS 192 (S. 1182).
18. CS 159 (S. 27).
19. CS 175; and for his relationship to Eadberht CS 199.
20. E.g. CS 177, 189 and 190 (S. 91, 28 and 29).
21. CS 193 (S. 32).
22. Garmonsway, 1972, p. 46, n. 1.
23. Ward, 1939.
24. CS 160 (S. 24).
25. Regnal lists in Dumville, 1976.
26. Stenton, 1971, p. 206.
27. CS 159 (S. 27).
28. *Ibid.*
29. Corr.S.Bon., ed. Kylie, 1966, pp. 154-57.
30. CS 141 (S. 1180).
31. 159 (S. 27).
32. Cf. Stenton, 1971, pp. 165-76.
33. *Ibid.*, pp. 145-46.
34. Bede, *Hist.Ecc.*, V, 23.
35. CS 45 (S. 8).
36. Bede, *Hist.Ecc.*, Preface; and (for Tatwine), Stenton, 1971, p. 183.
37. CS 160 (S. 24).
38. Correspondence in Councils, III, pp. 376-82 and 390-94.
39. CS 162 (S. 90).
40. EHD I, pp. 751-56.
41. Corr.S.Bon., ed. Kylie, 1966, pp. 138-40.
42. CS 291 (S. 1258).
43. Thomas of Elmham, pp. 317-318.
44. Corr.S.Bon., ed. Kylie, 1966, pp. 49-50, 57-60 and 61-67.
45. *Ibid.*, pp. 68-70.
46. *Ibid.*, pp. 154-57.
47. The last record of St. Mildred is in 732-3; *see* CS 149 (S. 87).
48. One of Boniface's correspondents; EHD I, pp. 745-46.
49. EHD I, pp. 734-35. For Leofgyth, *see* Stenton, 1971, p. 173.
50. EHD I, pp. 746-47.
51. Corr.S.Bon., ed. Kylie, 1966, pp. 130-31.
52. Thomas of Elmham, p. 217.
53. CS 177 (S. 91).
54. Corr.S.Bon., ed. Kylie, 1966, pp. 132-34.
55. CS 317 (S. 160).
56. Thomas of Elmham, p. 220.
57. Councils, III, pp. 398-99. And *see* Stubbs, 1877 (entry under *Bugga*, Dic.Chr.B., I, pp. 355-56).
58. Witney, 1976, 110-117.
59. Harris, 1719, p. 320.
60. Witney, 1976, p. 108; and Wallenberg, 1934, pp. 463, 464 and 469.
61. CS 880 (S. 546).
62. In A.D. 814; *see* CS 343 (S. 173).

63. Warrington near Paddock Wood (*Warblyngton*, A.D. 1314) and Winton in Rolvenden (*Wylmynton*, A.D. 1338); *see* Wallenberg, 1934, pp. 196 and 355.

64. Wallenberg, 1934, p. 368.

65. CS 316 (S. 159).

66. CS 418 (S. 280).

67. *Liber de Hyda*, A.D. 993; *see* Wallenberg, 1931, p. 337.

68. CS 194 (S. 33).

69. Witney, 1976, pp. 110-116, for a more detailed account of these early settlements.

70. For the final displacement of the herds in the 14th century, *see* Witney, 1976, pp. 154-86.

71. *Begingeden*, A.D. 993; *see* Wallenberg, 1931, p. 337. This is possibly Bevenden in Great Chart; Witney, 1976, p. 265.

72. Witney, 1976, pp; 66-67.

73. *Ibid.*

74. CS 141 (S. 1180).

75. CS 35 (S. 13).

76. Wallenberg, 1931, pp. 223-25.

77. B.Bk.S.Aug., Part I, pp. 210-25.

78. CS 98 (S. 21).

79. For the identification of these places, *see* Witney, 1976, p. 272.

80. *Ibid.*

81. CS 248 and 263 (S. 123 and 125).

82. For identification of these places, *see* Witney, 1976, p. 274.

83. CD 715 (S. 914), and Witney, 1976, p. 269.

84. Furley, Vol. II, Part 2 (1874), pp. 723 and 727; and Shaw, 1870, p. 55.

85. Witney, 1976, p. 274.

86. CS 175 (S. 30).

87. Witney, 1976, p. 83, and for *Holanspic*, p. 234 sub. *Frindsbury*.

88. *Ibid.*, p. 191, sub. *Sights Camp* (b).

89. CS 194, 253 and 260 (S. 33, 129 and 37).

90. CS 316 (S. 159). For identification of dens, *see* Witney, 1976, pp. 246-47.

91. For a detailed study of the break-up of the commons, and the character, size and spacing of the resulting dens, *see* Witney, 1976, pp. 78-103.

92. CS 343 (S. 173). For identification of pastures, *see* Witney, 1976, p. 248.

93. Witney, 1976, pp. 132-39.

94. CS 160 (S. 24).

95. Harris, 1719, p. 264.

96. Wallenberg, 1931, pp. 37-38.

97. CS 148 (S. 23).

98. *Snoad* means royal wood; *see* Witney, 1976, pp. 61-63. For identification of *Sibersnoth*, *see* Wallenberg, 1934, pp. 473-74; and for its continuing use as a source of fuel and timber Du Boulay, 1961, p. 87.

99. CS 341 (S. 169).

100. Cf. Loyn, 1970, pp. 85-86.

101. CS 149 and 150 (S. 86 and 87).

102. CS 152 (S. 88).

103. CS 177 (S. 91).

104. CS 189 (S. 29).

105. CS 173 (S. 1612).

106. CS 191 (S. 25).

107. Finberg, 1972, p. 499.

108. Hinton, 1977, pp. 112-113.

109. Æthelberht, Laws, cap. 11.

110. Councils, III, pp. 400-401.

111. CS 193 and 194 (S. 32 and 33).

112. Thomas of Elmham, p. 324.

113. CS 190 (S. 28).
114. Cf. Levison, 1946. App. I, pp. 174–225.

Chapter Eleven

1. Campbell, 1973, pp. xxii–xxiii.
2. Councils, III, pp. 400-401.
3. CS 193 (S. 32).
4. CS 189 (S. 29). She may have become Abbess in A.D. 751, the date given by Thomas of Elmham for Eadburga's death (pp. 219-20), but which was more probably that of her retirement.
5. Cf. Florence of Worcester, I, p. 250.
6. When he witnessed a charter under the title *sub-regulus*; CS 373.
7. CS 227 (S. 35).
8. A-SC sub. A.D. 754 and 755. (The chronology is two years adrift here).
9. CS 194 (S. 33).
10. CS 846 (S. 26).
11. CS 192 (S. 1182).
12. As appears from a later charter; CS 243.
13. CS 332 (S. 1264).
14. CS 194 (S. 33).
15. Stubbs, 1880 (entry under *Eahlmund* in Dic.Chr.B., Vol. II, p. 11).
16. A-SC sub. A.D. 855.
17. A-SC.
18. CS 194 and 195 (S. 33 and 105).
19. CS 196 (S. 34).
20. CS 193 (S. 32).
21. Stubbs, 1880 (entry under *Heaberht* in Dic.Chr.B., Vol. II, p. 4).
22. CS 196 (S. 34).
23. Thomas of Elmham, pp. 319 and 328–30; and William Thorne, pp. 26–30.
24. Blunt, 1961.
25. CS 196 (S. 34).
26. Stenton, 1971, p. 208.
27. Simeon of Durham, II, p. 44.
28. Stenton, 1971, p. 210 with n. 2.
29. CS 208 S. 108, and *see* Stenton, 1971, p. 208 with n. 5 and 6, and p. 209.
30. CS 213 and 214 (S. 110 and 111).
31. Compare Bishops, Kings and Nobles, pp. 130, 144 and 154.
32. CS 227 (S. 35).
33. Stenton, 1971, p. 209.
34. CS 319 (S. 1259).
35. CS 293 (S. 155).
36. CS 159 (S. 27).
37. Henry of Huntingdon, p. 126.
38. Stenton, 1971, p. 207.
39. CS 227 and 243 (S. 35 and 38).
40. Described in a letter later sent by his successor Ceolwulf to Pope Leo; CS 287.
41. CS 227 and 228 (S. 35 and 36). The first is an original.
42. Blunt, 1961.
43. CS 227 (S. 35).
44. A-SC sub. A.D. 837 (the chronology being two years adrift here).
45. A-SC sub. A.D. 777 (allowing for the two year error in date).

46. CS 243 (S.38); and *see* Stenton, 1971, pp. 207–210.

47. Thus Stenton, who comments on Eahlmund's rule in Kent as an independent king, omits to mention that Egbert had preceded him in that capacity and was ruling in the period immediately following the battle at Otford. The nearest he comes to acknowledging that Egbert was the leader of the resistance (in collaboration with Jaenberht) is in a footnote, and by inference (1971, p. 216, n. 1).

48. CS 293 (S. 155).

49. Stenton, 1971, p. 215.

50. For a summary of the mission and its proceedings, *see* Stenton, 1971, pp. 215–17, and for the report made by the legates to the Pope EHD I, pp. 770–74.

51. *Poenitentiale Theodori*, Councils III, pp. 173–203.

52. Sub. A.D. 785 (correctly 787). *See also* Stenton, 1971, p. 218.

53. As appears from a letter sent by Pope Le o to Offa's successor Cenwulf; CS 288.

54. The admission was made by Cenwulf in his correspondence with Pope Leo; CS 287.

55. EHD I, pp. 788–89.

56. Mathew Paris, p. 21.

57. Simeon of Durham, II, p. 53.

58. William Thorne, pp. 28–29.

59. The position he held at the time of the legantine mission; *see* EHD I, pp. 770–74.

60. And described as a 'province' in, e.g. CS 247, 248 and 254 (S. 123, 125 and 128).

61. E.g. CS 247 and 254 (S. 123 and 128).

62. Cf. CS 247, 254, 255 and 257 (S. 123, 128 and 131); and, for derivation of Chelsea, Dic.Eng. Pl-N., p. 99.

63. Cf. CS 223, 230, 231, 239, 240 and 241.

64. A-SC sub. A.D. 784 and 787 (dates that should be corrected by two years).

65. CS 247, 254 and 301 (S. 123, 138 and 1258).

66. CS 293 (S. 155).

67. Stenton, 1971, p. 207.

68. Thus the land at Ickham granted in 785 to the king's thegn Ealdbeorht and his sister Selethryth was expressed as being 'free of all tributes' and bequeathable at will; CS 247 (S. 123).

69. CS 496. As to this charter and the nature of *folkland* in general, *see* Stenton, 1971, pp. 309–312.

70. CS 192 (S. 1182).

71. CS 332 (S. 1264).

72. CS 247 (S. 123).

73. Calculating by the number of ploughs then kept on demesne as compared to the number owned by tenants; *see* Chapter 3, p. 78.

74. A-SC sub. A.D. 755 (correctly 757).

75. A-SC sub. A.D. 836 (correctly 839). There is some confusion about when the expulsion occurred. The Chronicle says that it was three years before Egbert won the throne of Wessex, which would make it in 799, when Offa was dead; for which reason a number of commentators have corrected the interval to 13 years. 789 would seem a likely date.

76. Blunt, 1961.

77. A-SC sub. A.D. 792 (correctly 794).

78. An insight into the circumstances of Northumbria at this time is given in a letter sent by Alcuin in 797 to the Mercian ealdorman Osbert, in which he describes how 'our kingdom, that of the North-umbrians, almost perished from intestine dissensions and false oaths' and says that he fears that 'the end of the evil is not yet'. See EHD I, pp. 786–88.

79. A-SC sub. A.D. 785 (correctly 787). See also Stenton, 1971, pp. 218–19.

80. Stenton, 1971, pp. 219–21; and EHD I, pp. 774–75.

81. Letter of Charlemagne to Offa, A.D. 796; EHD I, pp. 781–82.

82. EHD I, pp. 786–88.

83. Stenton, 1971, p. 215.

84. For a good short account of Eadberht Pren, *see* Stubbs, 1880 (entry in Dic.Chr.B., Vol. II, pp. 4–5).

85. Henry of Huntingdon, pp. 132–33.

86. Bartholomew Cotton, ch. 8, p. 13.
87. Stubbs, 1880 (Dic.Chr.B., Vol. II, p. 4–5).
88. Simeon of Durham, II, p. 52.
89. EHD I, pp. 781–82.
90. Councils, III, pp. 495–96.
91. EHD I, pp. 788–90.
92. CS 293 (S. 155).
93. Stenton, 1971, p. 227, n. 1.
94. Councils, III, pp. 509–11.
95. A-SC.
96. *See*, in particular, his letters on this subject to Ethelred, King of Northumbria, and Higbald, Bishop of Lindisfarne; EHD I, pp. 775–79.
97. EHD I, pp. 791–93; and CS 287.
98. EHD I, pp. 793–94; and CS 288.
99. Simeon of Durham, II, p. 59.
100. Henry of Huntingdon, pp. 130–31; and Simeon of Durham, II, p. 59.
101. William of Malmesbury, GP, p. 294.

Epilogue

1. He last appears as a witness to a charter in 806 (CS 325) (S. 182). The date of his death is given as 807 by Roger of Wendover (p. 270), and this is accepted by Haddan and Stubbs (Councils, III, pp. 556–57).
2. Thomas of Elmham, pp. 340–41, for the date of his appointment, and CS 316 (S. 159) for his relationship to the king.
3. CS 445.
4. CS 289 (S. 153).
5. Assuming he was identical to the Oswulf who witnessed a charter of Egbert II in 779 (CS 228, S. 36).
6. CS 247 (S. 123).
7. CS 378.
8. A-SC sub. A.D. 800 (correctly 802).
9. A-SC sub. A.D. 855.
10. For Eadburh, *see* Finberg, 1976, pp. 105–107.
11. A-SC sub. A.D. 800 (correctly 802).
12. A-SC sub. A.D. 813 (correctly 815).
13. Stenton, 1971, pp. 227–28.
14. CS 312.
15. Cf. CS 332 and 381 (S. 1264 and 1266).
16. Gervase of Canterbury, *Actus Pontificum*, 1880 ed., Vol. II, pp. 347–48.
17. Cf. William Thorne, p. 237. She is entered as St Sigeburga in the account of Minster given by Fowler (1926, p. 151).
18. Finberg, 1976, pp. 105–106.
19. CS 284.
20. CS 291 (S. 1258). And *see* Du Boulay, 1966, p. 26.
21. The Chronicle says this was in A.D. 796 (for 798); but the surviving record (CS 312) shows that it was in 803, as one would expect.
22. Ward, 1946.
23. A-SC sub. A.D. 829 and 830 (correctly 832 and 833).
24. CS 332 (S. 1264).
25. CS 303, 326 and 343 (S. 157, 163 and 173)   For identification of land near Cooling, *see* Wallenberg, 1931, pp. 57–58 and 88.

26. CS 316 (S. 159).
27. CS 293 (S. 155).
28. For the equation of one *mancus* with 30 silver pennies, *see* Lyon, 1976.
29. CS 319 (S. 1254).
30. Simeon of Durham, sub. A.D. 798, p. 59.
31. Lyon, 1976.
32. CS 341 (S. 169).
33. Councils, III, p. 557.
34. William of Malmesbury, GP, pp. 130–31; and Roger of Wendover, p. 264.
35. CS 337 and 338 (S. 167).
36. Councils, III, pp. 572–74.
37. CS 328 (S. 164).
38. Councils, III, pp. 562–64.
39. CS 378.
40. CS 317 (S. 160), and 378.
41. CS 445.
42. CS 330 and 445.
43. CS 321, 322, 323, 328, 329, 335 and 336 (S. 161, 163, 164 and 168). The transactions are summarized by Du Boulay, 1966, pp. 26–27.
44. Du Boulay, 1966, pp. 18–22.
45. CS 332 (S. 1264).
46. CS 381 (S. 1266).
47. Deanesley, 1925.
48. Stenton, 1955, pp. 39–42.
49. CS 340, 344 and 346 (S. 170, 176 and 175).
50. A-SC sub. A.D. 812 (correctly 814).
51. CS 353 (S. 178).
52. Councils, III, pp. 586–87.
53. *Ibid.*
54. CS 384.
55. Ward, 1946.
56. Cf. CS 335 of A.D. 811 (S. 168).
57. CS 317 (S. 160).
58. Stenton, 1971, pp. 229–30.
59. *Ibid.*, p. 229, n. 5.
60. CS 384.
61. Chadwick, H. M., 1905, pp. 17–18.
62. Du Boulay, 1966, p. 28, n. 5.
63. CS 247 (S. 123 and 125).
64. CS 380 (S. 1268).
65. CS 402; and *see* Du Boulay, 1966, pp. 30–31.
66. CS 381 (S. 1266).
67. Thomas of Elmham, p. 343; Roger of Wendover, pp. 273–74; and William of Malmesbury, GP. IV, ch. 156, pp. 294–95.
68. Stenton, 1971, p. 231 with n. 1.
69. Lyon, 1976.
70. CS 370 (S. 186).
71. CS 373 (S. 187).
72. CS 372 (S. 1620) and 378.
73. CS 384.
74. CS 318 (S. 41).
75. CS 412 (S. 1482).
76. Cf. Du Boulay, 1966, pp. 23–25.
77. The entry on Barham in Domesday Book reads 'This manor Archbishop Stigand held, but it was not part of' (the fief of) 'the archbishopric but belonged to the demesne ferm of King E'(dward).
78. Apart from Lenham the only estate it acquired outside east Kent was Plumstead.

79. For a map of the Canterbury lands, *see* Du Boulay, 1966, facing p. 56.
80. CS 380 (S. 1268).
81. A-SC sub. A.D. 823 (correctly 825).
82. *See* Stenton, 1971, p. 231 with n. 3.
83. Roger of Wendover, p. 270.
84. CS 373 (S. 187).
85. The grant is known to us through the recovery of the land by Archbishop Ceolnoth in 838 (CS 421, S. 1438). This says that it had been disputed whether it was a true grant because it had been made in the course of Baldred's flight.
86. A-SC sub., A.D. 823 (correctly 825).
87. Lyon, 1976.
88. A-SC sub. A.D. 823 (correctly 825).
89. *Ibid.*
90. A-SC sub. A.D. 828 (correctly 830).
91. The arrangements are summarized in Stenton, 1971, p. 233 with n. 1.

Appendix A

1. Gray, 1915, in particular p. 290.
2. Baker, 1964.
3. Ward, 1930.
4. Slater, 1932.
5. Nightingale and Stevens, 1952.
6. Richmond, 1963, p. 128.
7. Nightingale and Stevens, 1952 (Introductory Note).
8. Loyn, 1970, pp. 146-56.
9. Muhlfeld, 1933, pp. xxxii-iv.
10. For this process, *see* Du Boulay, 1966, pp. 117-25.
11. *Ibid.*
12. Baker, 1964, and Muhlfeld, 1933, pp. xxxiii-iv.
13. CS 332; and *see* Jolliffe, 1933, pp. 1-19.
14. Baker, 1964, and Muhlfeld, 1933, pp. xxxiii-iv.
15. Jones, 1961 (Ant. 35).
16. Alcock, 1962.
17. Jones, 1961 (WHR I), and 1964.
18. *Ibid.*
19. In particular those of Æthelberht, *c.* A.D. 603.

Appendix B

1. Gelling, 1967; and 1978, pp. 67-74.
2. Gelling, 1978, pp. 74-78.
3. CS 741 (S. 447).
4. Witney, 1976, p. 232.
5. Gelling, 1978, p. 74.
6. Kendrick, 1933.
7. Cf. Leeds, 1935, pp. 96-108.
8. Gelling, 1978, pp. 82-3 and 96-9.
9. Bede, *Hist.Ecc.*, I, 26.
10. Gelling, 1978, pp. 80-2.

Appendix C

1. Ward, 1933.
2. CS 1322.
3. CS 41 of A.D. 690; CS 97 of A.D. 697; and CS 254 of A.D. 788 (S. 11, 19 and 128).
4. CS 254 and 335 (S. 128 and 168).
5. CS 214, 191 and 159 (S. 111, 25 and 27).
6. CS 141 (S. 1180).
7. CS 214 (S. 111), and 1322.
8. Wallenberg, 1934, pp. 355-56.
9. Witney, 1976, p. 45.
10. Jolliffe, 1929.
11. Jolliffe, 1933, p. 44, n. 7.
12. At Margate; version of Domesday Book in Chartulary of St Augustine's Abbey.
13. CS 880 (S. 546).
14. Dom.Mon.
15. Bede, *Hist.Ecc.*, I, 25.
16. Witney, 1976, p. 46.
17. CS 189 (S. 29).
18. Leeds, 1935, in particular pp. 118-20.
19. CS 294.
20. CS 248 (S. 125). It was still a limb of Ickham at the time of Domesday Book.
21. CD 715 (S. 914).
22. At *Lambaham* (unidentified); *see* CS 402 of A.D. 832 (S. 1414).

Appendix D

1. Dodgson, 1973.
2. *Hwaetanstede*, A.D. 838; CS 418 (S. 280).
3. Wallenberg, 1931, pp. 288-89.
4. Wallenberg, 1934, p. 287.
5. *Ibid.*, p. 534.
6. *Fressyngeham*, A.D. 1327; *see* Wallenberg, 1934, p. 352.
7. *Fresynhurst*, A.D. 1270, and *Frisingehegh*, A.D. 1254; Wallenberg, 1931, p. 89.
8. Wallenberg, 1934, p. 365.
9. The manor of *Lambin*, otherwise Halden, acquired its name from Lambin de Langham in Henry III's reign; Hasted, VII, p. 185. It thus also became known as the manor of Langham. The original Langham, however, seems to have been near Forsham in Rolvenden parish; KBA., Arch.Cant.10 (1867), p. 140. It appears as Langeburnan in A.D. 833; *see* CS 408 (S. 1623).
10. CS 159 (S. 27). *De Stokes quae antiquitus vocabatur Andscohesham.*
11. *Mundelingeham*, A.D. 761; CS 190 (S. 28).
12. *Roegingaham*, A.D. 811; CS 335 (S. 168).
13. *Uuigincggham*, A.D. 824-34; CS 380 (S. 1268).
14. Stenton, 1941.
15. Gelling, 1978, pp. 158-61.
16. *Denglesham*, A.D. 832; CS 403. *See* Wallenberg, 1931, p. 169.
17. Chadwick, S. E., 1958.
18. CS 372 (S. 1620).
19. CS 1322.
20. E.g. *Beardingaleag*, A.D. 814 (CS 343, S. 173); *Peppingeberia* (Pembury), *c.* A.D. 1100 (Wallenberg, 1934, pp. 185-86); *Aegylbyrhtingahyrst*, A.D. 833 (CS 408).
21. Stenton, 1933, p. 51.

22. Cox, 1972-73.
23. Dodgson, 1973.
24. CS 291 (S. 1258).
25. CS 459; and *see* Wallenberg, 1934, p. 227.
26. *Liber de Hyda; see* Wallenberg, 1931, pp. 336-41.

Appendix E

1. Finberg, 1972, p, 434, and 1976, p. 59.
2. Æthelberht, Laws, cap. 21.
3. Hlothere and Eadric, Laws, cap. 3.
4. *Ibid.*, cap. 1.
5. Æthelberht, Laws, cap. 26.
6. Finberg, 1972, p. 433, and 1976, p. 58.
7. Æthelberht, Laws, cap. 6.
8. *Ibid.*, cap. 9 and 90.
9. *Ibid.*, cap. 73.
10. *Ibid.*, cap. 24.
11. Wihtred, Laws, cap. 8.
12. For the calculation of 20 *sceattas* to the shilling compare Æthelberht, Laws, cap. 54, 55 and 72.
13. For the calculation of four pennies to the shillings, *see* Ine, Laws, cap. 59.1; the note on this clause by Attenborough (1925 ed.), p. 191; and Chadwick, H. M., 1905, p. 12.
14. Lyon, 1976.
15. Wihtred, Laws, cap. 11; and Æthelberht, Laws, cap. 22.
16. Ine, Laws, cap. 3.2, 23.3, and 74.
17. Æthelberht, Laws, cap. 12 and 25. The figure for killing an eorl's slave is to be inferred from cap. 14 compared with cap. 16 and 25.
18. Chadwick, H. M., 1905, pp. 129-31.
19. Æthelberht, Laws, cap. 8.
20. Ine, Laws, cap. 6.3, 6.4, 45, 51 and 52.
21. Æthelberht, Laws, cap. 13 and 14.
22. Chadwick, H. M., 1905, p. 121.
23. Æthelberht, Laws, cap. 15; and Ine, Laws, cap. 6.3. *See also* Chadwick, H. M., 1905, p. 121.

Appendix F

1. Dodgson, 1966, in particular p. 22.
2. Witney, 1976, pp. 233 and 263.
3. *Ibid.*, p. 248; and Wallenberg, 1931, pp. 125-26.

Appendix G

1. Rollason, 1978, and Swanton, 1975.
2. Florence of Worcester, I, p. 259.
3. E.g. CS 35, 40, 41, 42 and 44 (S. 13, 14, 11 and 10).
4. As in the *Lives of the Kentish Royal Saints.*
5. CS 99 (S. 20).

6. Eddius, ch. 24, p. 49.
7. Bede, *Hist.Ecc.*, IV, 26.
8. Fowler, 1926, p. 149.
9. CS 73 (S. 12). And *see* Chapter 8, p. 202.
10. Eadburga, for instance, who was buried there; CS 317 (S. 160).
11. Florence of Worcester, I, p. 30 sub. A.D. 672; and *see also* Dic.Nat.B., Vol. 6, reprint 1921-22, pp. 885-86.
12. *Cilling* charter; CS 99 (S. 20).
13. CS 91 (S. 22).
14. Eddius, ch. 40, p. 81.
15. Thomas of Elmham, pp. 219-20; and William Thorne, p. 236.
16. Corr.S.Bon., ed. Kylie, 1966, pp. 61-67.
17. *Ibid.*, pp. 154-57.
18. Stubbs, 1887 (entry under *Eangitha*, Dic.Chr.B., Vol. II, p. 16).
19. Corr.S.Bon., ed. Kylie, 1966, pp. 61-67.
20. Councils, III, pp. 400-401.
21. CS 91 (S. 22).
22. She appears as Abbess at the Bapchild Council, a position still held by her mother when the *Cilling* charter was issued nine years or so earlier.
23. Florence of Worcester, I, sub. A.D. 675.
24. CS 91, (S. 22).
25. CS 784 (S. 489).
26. Bede, *Hist.Ecc.*, IV, 26.
27. Corr.S.Bon., ed. Kylie, 1966, pp. 57-60.
28. The various resting places are listed by Rollason, 1978, p. 73, n. 3.
29. A-SC.

INDEX OF PERSONS

INDEX OF PLACES

I. In Kent

(See also place-names entered in App. B, pp. 234-35; App. D, pp. 239-41; App. F, p. 244)

II. Elsewhere